Supreme Court
FOR
DUMMIES®

Supreme Court

FOR

DUMMIES®

by Lisa Paddock, Ph.D., Llb.

Wiley Publishing, Inc.

Supreme Court For Dummies®

Published by
Wiley Publishing, Inc.
909 Third Avenue
New York, NY 10022
www.wiley.com

About the Author

Lisa Paddock is a lawyer and freelance writer who has been writing about the law since graduating from the University of Michigan Law School in 1989. While practicing law in New York City, she acted as consulting legal editor for *Great American Trials* (Gale Research, 1994). In 1996, her book, *Facts About the Supreme Court of the United States of America* (H.W. Wilson, 1996), was voted one of the year's best reference books by the Reference and User Service Association of the American Library Association. Since then, she has continued to write about the Supreme Court — and other courts — for publications such as *The Encyclopedia of American Biography* (HarperCollins, 1996) and *Courtroom Drama* (UXL, 1998).

Before becoming a lawyer, Lisa taught literature and worked as a stock broker. Her PhD in English, when combined with a law degree, almost inevitably led to an interest in intellectual property, and she has frequently advised other writers, as well as writers' organizations, on copyright matters. One of her best clients is her husband, the biographer Carl Rollyson. Lisa and Carl — and their Scotties — live in Cape May County, New Jersey, where they frequently collaborate on literary projects and long walks on the beach.

Dedication

For Holmes & Watson, no legal beagles.

Author's Acknowledgments

Thanks go to my agent, Elizabeth Knappman, for thinking of me in connection with this project. I'd like to extend my gratitude, too, to her staff at New England Publishing Associates for their help along the way.

At Wiley Publishing, Inc., my first thanks go to Acquisitions Editor Greg Tubach, who did a supremely wonderful job formulating this project and shepherding it through the early stages. Editorial Supervisor Michele Hacker and Project Coordinator Nancee Reeves helped smooth out the transitions from conception to completion. And the always upbeat, ever encouraging, utterly professional Kelly Ewing — who served as both Project Editor and Copy Editor — has earned my everlasting gratitude and respect.

My technical editor (and hero), Pam Heatlie, saved me from some faux pax and helped keep me au courant.

I had help retrieving illustrations from several individuals and institutions. Thanks to Franz Jantzen and the staff of the United States Supreme Court Curator's Office; Kelly M. Jones and the staff of the Supreme Court Historical Society Gift Shop; and Margaret Harman and the staff of the AudioVisual Archives at the Lyndon B. Johnson Library & Museum.

And then there's my husband, Carl Rollyson, who carried far more than his share of the burden while I was working on this project. Without him — truly — this book would never have been finished.

Thank you, one and all.

Publisher's Acknowledgments

We're proud of this book; please send us your comments through our Dummies online registration form located at www.dummies.com/register/.

Some of the people who helped bring this book to market include the following:

Acquisitions, Editorial, and Media Development

Project Editor: Kelly Ewing

Senior Acquisitions Editor: Greg Tubach

General Reviewer: Pamela Heatlie

Senior Permissions Editor: Carmen Krikorian

Editorial Supervisor: Michelle Hacker

Cover Photos: ©Corbis

Cartoons: Rich Tennant www.the5thwave.com

Production

Project Coordinator: Nancee Reeves

Layout and Graphics: Amanda Carter, Joyce Haughey, LeAndra Johnson, Jackie Nicholas, Barry Offringa, Heather Pope, Jeremey Unger

Proofreaders: Laura Albert, TECHBOOKS Production Services

Indexer: TECHBOOKS Production Services

Publishing and Editorial for Consumer Dummies

Diane Graves Steele, Vice President and Publisher, Consumer Dummies

Joyce Pepple, Acquisitions Director, Consumer Dummies

Kristin A. Cocks, Product Development Director, Consumer Dummies

Michael Spring, Vice President and Publisher, Travel

Brice Gosnell, Publishing Director, Travel

Suzanne Jannetta, Editorial Director, Travel

Publishing for Technology Dummies

Andy Cummings, Vice President and Publisher, Dummies Technology/General User

Composition Services

Gerry Fahey, Vice President of Production Services

Debbie Stailey, Director of Composition Services

Contents at a Glance

Table of Contents

Introduction

∙ ∙

*T*he decisions of the United States Supreme Court have more impact on the lives of Americans than those of any other institution of government — as everyone who watched the resolution of the 2000 presidential election knows. As an individual, you have both an indirect and a direct relationship with this imposing body, once fondly known as the "nine old men." This book explains that relationship by demystifying the federal court system, describing how cases reach the Supreme Court, clarifying legal terms, relating Court decisions to government policies, and detailing how you can — both literally and figuratively — get inside the Court. It also introduces you to a number of black-robed men (and two women) who are mere mortals.

About This Book

This book helps you understand why we need a national supreme court, what kinds of cases the justices hear, how the court arrives at and delivers its opinions, and what consequences result from these decisions. It also provides you with methods of determining these things for yourself.

You need not read the entire book or read the chapters in any particular sequence in order to get information about the Court. The structure of the book assumes that not every reader will be interested in following a case through the hierarchy of the court system or in the details of certain landmark decisions. If, for example, you want to know how to find out about a recent decision and the issues it involved, you can use the chapter headings in the Table of Contents at the front of the book or the index to find out where in the book you should go. Afterward, however, you may want to go back and read more about how the case or issue that interests you fits into the larger scheme of American law as defined by our supreme judicial body.

Conventions Used in the Book

The United States has many courts, many of which are supreme courts (usually the highest state courts). However, only one Supreme Court of the United

States exists, and to differentiate it from its namesakes, it's referred to as the *U.S. Supreme Court,* the *High Court,* or simply the *Court,* with an uppercase "C."

Cases are named after the parties involved in the original lawsuit. In trial courts, the name of the person who brought the suit (the *plaintiff*) appears first, followed by the name of the person who is being sued (the *defendant*). For example, if Mary Smith filed a suit against Fred Jones, that case is named *Smith v. Jones* (2000), with the plaintiff's name coming before the "v" and the defendant's name following it. (The date in parentheses following the case name is the year in which the decision is handed down.)

But by the time the case reaches the Court, it may be known as *Jones v. Smith (2002).* The reason for the reversal is that most cases heard by the High Court are appeals from the decision of a lower court, where the defendant may not have been happy with the result. If the defendant then files an appeal, he or she or it becomes the "appellant" or *petitioner* and the first named party. The second party is now the *appellee* or *respondent*. The "v," by the way, stands for *versus*. However, you will sometimes see the "v" replaced by "and," as in "Jones and Smith."

Foolish Assumptions

In writing this book, I have made a number of assumptions about why you are reading it:

- ✔ You've heard or read journalists reports about U.S. Supreme Court cases and their ramifications, and you want to know more.
- ✔ You're interested in the way the law works.
- ✔ You've been involved with the law in some way in your own life (jury service, will drafting, small claims court, and so on) or know someone who has.
- ✔ You feel sure that what goes on at the Court cannot be all that mysterious.
- ✔ You may know a lot about history, but you don't know much about the Supreme Court.
- ✔ Even if you're an expert on the Supreme Court, you'll enjoy reading colorful anecdotes about notable and notorious cases and justices.

How This Book Is Organized

The contents of this book fall into eight parts, each of them divided into several chapters. The last part of the book contains three appendixes.

Part I: "We'll Take It All the Way to the Supreme Court!"

This part describes the Supreme Court's role in the federal government, as well as its relationship with other federal and state courts. It explains how a case reaches the Supreme Court and how, once it gets there, it's decided.

Part II: Judging the Justices

This part explains the nomination and confirmation process for Supreme Court justices and the role of the chief justice. It also provides thumbnail sketches of some of the most notable and some of the most notorious people who have sat on the high bench as well as descriptions of who is sitting there now.

Part III: Setting Precedents: Cases That Count

This part is devoted to some past Supreme Court decisions that affect the life of the nation, as well as your own life! As you see in this part, so much of what defines Americans — freedom of speech, for example — flows from the First Amendment. And as this part also shows, many of the rights you take for granted — due process and equal protection under the law — are grounded in the Fourteenth Amendment.

Part IV: High Drama on the High Court

This part explores the background of two of the most dramatic cases ever heard by the Supreme Court: *Dred Scott v. Sandford* (1856) and *Brown v. Board of Education of Topeka, Kansas* (1955). What the Court decided in these cases changed the course of history — twice, and in opposite directions.

Part V: Understanding Supreme Court Decisions

This part of the book shows you how to find Supreme Court decisions and decipher what they really mean, both to the parties involved and to the rest of the world.

Part VI: Becoming a Court Insider

This part explains who, besides the justices, works at the Court, how they got there, and what they do.

Part VII: The Part of Tens

In every Dummies book, you'll find the irreverent Part of Tens. This part is designed to give you interesting information quickly and easily. The Part of Tens provides you with some neat information you can store away for future reference or use to impress your friends.

Part VIII: Appendixes

The appendixes are devoted to a glossary that deciphers the legalese, the Constitution — and a very long list of everybody who has ever served on the Court.

Icons Used in This Book

Icons are a familiar part of the *For Dummies* series. If you've looked at other *For Dummies* books, you will recognize some or all of the icons used in this book as signposts for material that you might want to pay special attention to or skip altogether — depending upon your reasons for reading *The Supreme Court For Dummies*.

This icon highlights humorous or telling human interest stories about individual Supreme Court justices, Washington politicos, or historical events pertinent to the Court.

You've heard of legalese, where something is defined in such a way that it's hard to understand. This icon alerts you to an appearance and explanation of a term taken from this foreign language.

When you see this icon, you'll know that the accompanying text includes material that will be helpful to you elsewhere in the book.

Technical stuff might use some words from the dreaded legalese, but it might also be written in English. This icon helps you find translations.

This icon marks a tip that can save you time or effort. It may point out a shortcut to doing something, such as researching a case, or a great resource you'll want to peruse.

Where to Go From Here

This book begins with a detailed Table of Contents that gives you a quick overview of what's between the covers. The book ends with a detailed Index to help you quickly locate specific information. You can begin by looking up the particular topic that you're interested in either the Table of Contents or Index. But if the Supreme Court — or the law in general — seems a formidable, impenetrable institution, starting this book at the beginning is a good idea.

If you want to know why the Court is more than just a building or the repository of received wisdom, start with Part II, which is devoted to the justices, who together make up the Court. Part III provides you with information about crucial aspects of the law and the cases that shaped them. If you're a history buff, you might want to start with Part IV, where you can find background information about two watershed decisions — one bad and one good — that addressed similar issues. Part VII is for readers who are interested in the Court's minor players, the clerks, and other administrators who help ensure that the business of the Court runs smoothly. And last but not least, the Part of Tens is for those of you who like just the straight facts.

Part I

"We'll Take It All the Way to the Supreme Court!"

The 5th Wave   By Rich Tennant

In this part . . .

*E*verybody understands that the U.S. Supreme Court is
not just the court of last resort, but the one place to
go to get a final answer on what's *right*. You can't trust
those elected politicians in Congress or the Oval Office to
decide much of anything — even *they* go to the Supreme
Court for answers. In these chapters, you discover the
secret of the Court's power: a little thing of its own
devising called *judicial review*, which means the justices
always get to have the last word. Remember who decided
which candidate got to move into the White House after
the 2000 presidential election?

Even if you're not running for president, you'd probably
like to know how a case gets into the Supreme Court. It's a
long and winding road, but you can find a detailed map
inside. Like all good maps, it shows you forks in the road,
dead ends, and that the surest route from A to B is not
always a straight line. Enjoy the ride!

Chapter 1

Considering the Court of Last Resort

*I*n order to understand the significance of the Supreme Court and the way it functions, you need to know some basic facts about its makeup and its relationship to the other branches of the federal government, to the federal court system, and to state courts. Looking at how the Court decided the outcome of the 2000 presidential election helps explain how all these factors work together in the highest court in the land.

The Cast of Characters

The United States Supreme Court is both a building (see Figure 1-1) and a group of people. The Constitution does not specify how many people should make up this group. When the founding fathers organized the Court, they apparently did not consider that cases might end in a tie vote (in fact, they didn't think too much about the Court at all), and in 1789, the First Congress initially set the number of justices at six: five associate justices and one chief justice.

As the nation expanded, so did the number of justices — most of the time. There was a brief interval in 1801 when the size of the Court actually shrank to five. Political considerations forced the number back up to six the next year. Political considerations were also responsible for nudging the number up to a hefty ten during the Civil War and back down to seven during the reconstruction period that followed. (As you see in Chapter 4, for example, politics is every bit as important to the Court as it is to the rest of government.) Since 1869, however, the number of justices has remained fixed at nine, one of whom is still the chief justice.

Until 1967, when civil rights pioneer and prominent lawyer Thurgood Marshall joined the Court, all of the faces in the Court were white. Women came later still: Sandra Day O'Connor, appointed in 1981, was the first. The second — and only other female justice — is Ruth Bader Ginsburg, who took her place on the high bench in 1993. (See Chapter 4 for an explanation of how designated *seats* evolved on the Court.)

The Third Branch of Government

The judiciary is often called the third branch of government. Why, you might ask, if it's so important, does the Court come in last in our tri-partite system? In part, this designation is the result of the federal court system having been outlined in Article III of the Constitution. (Article I concerns the legislature, and Article II addresses the executive branch.) But Article III is also remarkably short and makes the judicial branch seem almost like an afterthought. One of the chief architects of the Constitution, Alexander Hamilton, believed that that the Supreme Court, lacking both money and a militia, would be the weakest of the three branches.

How many justices make a Supreme Court?

The Judiciary Act of 1789, the legislation that created the federal court system, tied the number of justices to the number of federal circuits. Initially, these circuits numbered three, and as part of the justices' job was to serve on the lower courts located in each of these circuits, the number of justices was set at six, two for each circuit. In 1801, the connection between the Supreme Court and the federal circuits was severed and the number of justices reduced to the sensibly odd number five. No sitting justice was fired, however, and no one retired before the Jeffersonian Republicans took control of the federal government and repealed the 1801 Judiciary Act. Six was the magic number until 1807, when the addition of another federal circuit necessitated the creation of another justiceship. In 1837, two more circuits and two more justices were added, and in 1863, the number grew to ten.

Ten justices proved to be too many (and once again, there was no tiebreaker). Besides, the Republicans who controlled Congress after the Civil War were at odds with President Andrew Johnson and his Reconstruction plans. So in 1866, Congress passed legislation slashing the Court to seven members, depriving Johnson of appointments and therefore, of justices he could count on. In 1869, yet another judiciary act fixed the number of circuits and the number of justices at nine, and there it has remained, despite some subsequent efforts to stack the deck.

Figure 1-1:
The present-
day U.S.
Supreme
Court.

Checks and balances

Alexander Hamilton predicted that the Supreme Court would be the weakest branch of the federal government. But Hamilton also knew that the government needed a police force to ensure that the two elected branches, the legislature and the executive, did not overstep their bounds in an effort to hang onto power. Someone had to make sure that the delicate dance being performed between the people's representatives and their leader would not interfere with the smooth running of the country or — more importantly, perhaps — violate the Constitution. The party ultimately responsible for maintaining the government's *checks and balances*, assuring that none of the branches abuses its authority, is the Supreme Court.

The three-part structure of federal government results in what is also confusingly called the *separation of powers.* The three branches are said to be both independent and interdependent. In reality, the separate branches are probably more blended than individual. Congress holds the quasi-judicial impeachment power that it can use to check both presidents and federal judges, for example. The glue that holds the parts together is the party system, which enables — and encourages — Republican presidents to work closely with Republican legislators and to nominate Republicans to sit on federal courts.

Once those Republicans take their seat on the high bench, however, presidents have no real control over them — as more than one chief executive has learned to his dismay. Federal judges, including Supreme Court justices, have what amounts to lifetime tenure and a guaranteed salary. Although justices can theoretically be removed from office by impeachment, none ever has been. The last time Congress attempted to pull this off was two centuries ago. The attempt failed, in the process proving the point that little short of criminal behavior could result in judicial removal. Political views — and especially personal judicial views — are plainly off limits to those who might wish to impeach a hostile jurist. Congress can overturn Supreme Court decisions only by means of the cumbersome process of constitutional amendment. Such efforts have succeeded exactly four times in the history of the republic. In each instance, it was the Supreme Court that determined the meaning and application of the amendment.

Judicial review

The federal judiciary is arguably the most independent of the three branches of federal government, the one least accountable to the others and the one that always has the last word. The reason for this unique status is *judicial review*, which is in essence the power to say what the law is. The federal bench, and the Supreme Court in particular, is the only branch of the federal government endowed with the ability to interpret the Constitution. In one fell swoop, for example, the Court declared in *Roe v. Wade* that abortion on demand is, under certain circumstances, a right guaranteed by the Constitution. Had abortion on demand been legislated, it would have taken coordination and agreement among the House of Representatives, the Senate, and the president — a cumbersome process, to be sure. And then, if someone had challenged a law granting a woman's right to choose (and surely someone would have), it would have been up to the federal courts to decide whether such a law passed constitutional muster.

"Unelected" senators

Until the ratification of the Seventeenth Amendment in 1913, U.S. senators were not elected directly by the citizens of their states, but by the legislatures of those states. This election mechanism is provided for in Article I, section 3 of the Constitution. Clearly, some of the founding fathers feared that the passions of the multitude might interfere with the engines of government. The founders' hope, apparently, was that senatorial representatives of the states' elected legislatures would represent a different constituency than that of the House of Representatives, whose members have always been popularly elected. In effect, however, the original method of electing senators served to enhance the power of local political bosses. Such concentration of muscle was eventually seen as undemocratic, and in the end, few elected officials dared oppose this constitutional amendment making senators directly accountable to their constituents.

Amending the Court

Four of the amendments to the Constitution were enacted specifically to reverse Supreme Court decisions:

✔ The Eleventh Amendment, adopted in 1795, overruled *Chisholm v. Georgia* (1793), which permitted a state to be sued in federal court by the citizens of another state.

✔ The Fourteenth Amendment, adopted in 1868, overruled *Scott v. Sandford* (1857), in which the Court declared African-Americans not to be citizens of the United States.

✔ The Sixteenth Amendment, adopted in 1913, overruled *Pollock v. Farmers' Loan and Trust Co.* (1895), which held that Congress did not have the power to collect income taxes.

✔ The Twenty-sixth Amendment, adopted in 1971, overruled that part of the Court's decision in *Oregon v. Mitchell* (1970) declaring that Congress could not force the states to set the voting age at eighteen in elections for state office.

The principle of judicial review was established by — what else? — a Supreme Court case. In what some commentators call the definitive Supreme Court decision, the 1803 *Marbury v. Madison* opinion, Chief Justice John Marshall wrote, "It is emphatically the province and duty of the judicial department to say what the law is." And judicial review permits the Supreme Court to rule both on actions of the other branches of federal government and on decisions of state courts concerning constitutional interpretation.

A home of its own

When the Supreme Court convened its first session on February 1, 1790, the justices did not even have a home of their own. They made do with a room in the Royal Exchange Building in New York City (see Figure 1-2), quarters which they shared with the lower house of the state legislature. What's more, only three of the five justices who had been confirmed made it to the session on time. Once convened, the Court found it had no real business to conduct and adjourned on February 10. The Court's second term in 1790 lasted just two days.

In 1790, the nation's capital moved from New York to Philadelphia, where the Court first occupied temporary quarters in the State House, and then shared space with the Mayor's Court in the newly constructed city hall (Figure 1-3). Even after the federal government moved to Washington, D.C., in 1800, the Court was shuffled around from an unfinished room in the Capitol, to the Library of Congress, and even to a local tavern. It was not until 1810 that the Court convened in a room of its own (Figure 1-4). Apparently, the justices were just about the last members of the federal government to do so.

Figure 1-2:
The Royal Exchange Building in New York City, the "first" Supreme Court.

Library of Congress, Prints and Photographs Division [LC-USZ262-99273]

Figure 1-3:
Old City Hall, Philadelphia, where the Court met 1791–1800.

Library of Congress, Prints and Photographs Division [LC-USZ262-114320]

Figure 1-4:
Old Supreme
Court
Chamber,
where the
Court met
1810–1814.

© Bettmann/CORBIS

The Federal Judicial System

With the 1789 Judiciary Act, Congress set up the three-tiered federal judicial system that exists to this day. The U.S. Supreme Court occupies the top tier. A system of federal district courts makes up the bottom tier. The middle layer consists of a lesser number of federal appeals courts.

Federal district courts

The job of *federal district courts* is to act as trial courts for cases involving federal law. The number of district courts has increased with the population and currently numbers 94.

Each state has at least one federal district court, which carries that state's name, plus — if there is more than one district court in the state — a geographical designation, such as the U.S. District Court for the Western District of Michigan. With one quirky exception, none of the district courts serves an area outside the state where it is situated. That exception is the U.S. District Court for the District of Wyoming, which includes those portions of Montana and Idaho that fall within the boundaries of Yellowstone National Park. In addition to the 90 district courts located in the states, there are four others in U.S. territories: Guam, the Northern Mariana Islands, Puerto Rico, and the U.S. Virgin Islands.

District courts are staffed by presidentially-appointed judges (now numbering more than 600), assisted by magistrates, minor officials who assist with matters such as pretrial proceedings and trials of lesser misdemeanor offenses. The district court judges themselves appoint their own magistrates and bankruptcy judges.

As in all federal courts, each district court is headed by a chief judge who not only hears cases but is in charge of court administration. But unlike the procedure followed in the Supreme Court and the courts of appeals, district court trials are heard by only a single judge. For much of the 20th century, Congress required certain cases tried by district courts to be heard by a three-judge panel, consisting of one district court judge and two circuit court judges. By 1990, however, Congress had all but done away with these panels. In 2001, U.S. district courts decided more than 300,000 cases.

Federal appellate courts

Each of the district courts feeds appeals from cases it has already decided into a *federal appellate court* — also called a *federal circuit court* — located in the same general geographical region.

Circuit riders

One of the justices' primary complaints during the early decades of the federal judiciary was the responsibility of *circuit riding,* which involved traveling from state to state to sit on all of the district courts within the circuits they were responsible for overseeing. The work was taxing, to say the least. Justices working the Southern Circuit, for example, were required to cover some 1,800 miles over poor or nonexistent roads in all kinds of weather.

Congressmen, who had to travel back and forth between Washington, D.C., and their sometimes distant districts, were not sympathetic. They believed that by making the federal judiciary travel to all manner of far-flung places, they could impress the American people with the importance — and omnipresence — of federal authority. The poor saddle-sore justices were not permanently relieved of the burden of circuit riding until 1891. By that time, the Civil War had settled the matter of federal government supremacy.

When the federal judicial system was first put into place, there were only three federal circuits, none of which had permanent staffs. Instead, each bench was occupied by a three-judge panel consisting of the district court judge from the state in which the circuit was in session, plus two Supreme Court justices.

Today, 13 federal circuit courts, now called courts of appeal, exist (see Figure 1-5). These courts are staffed by presidentially appointed judges who hear appeals from cases decided by the district courts in their respective circuits. They also hear cases referred by federal agencies such as the Immigration and Naturalization Service and from specialized trial courts such as military courts and the Tax Court. The 13 intermediate courts also include the Court of Appeals for the Federal District, which Congress created in 1982 by combining the United States Court of Claims, which cases involved claims against the U.S., and the Court of Customs and Patent Appeals. In 2001, U.S. courts of appeals decided more than 50,000 cases.

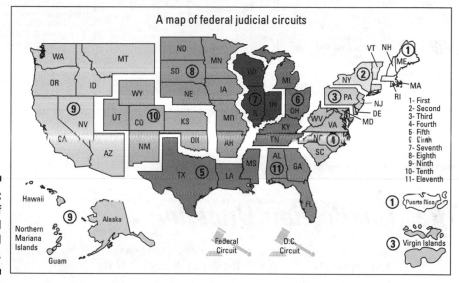

Figure 1-5:
A map of federal judicial circuits.

The Supreme Court

There are many federal courts, but there is only one Supreme Court. If you are unsatisfied with the results of your trial in federal district court, you can conceivably appeal your case to the appropriate federal court of appeals. If you don't like the outcome in this court, the only place to go from there is up. See the road map to the Supreme Court, Figure 1-6.

A Road Map to the Supreme Court

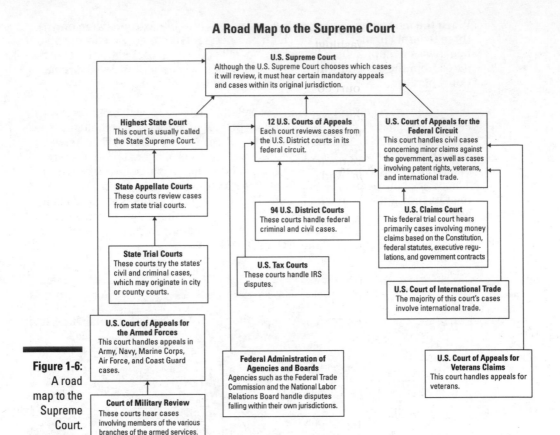

Figure 1-6:
A road
map to the
Supreme
Court.

The Jurisdiction Question

Before the Court agrees to hear a case, that case must meet a number of requirements. The first of these requirements is that the case falls within the Court's ability to hear and decide specified legal matters. If a case comes from the federal court system, it seems pretty clear that the U.S. Supreme Court should be able to hear it. But the Court also reviews appeals from cases originating in state courts — again, providing that they meet certain requirements.

More than geography

Jurisdiction is a deceptively simple concept that can be hard to wrap your mind around. Most people think of jurisdiction in geographic terms, and often this mindset is perfectly accurate. The United States Federal District

Court for the District of Columbia customarily hears cases that have some relationship with Washington, D.C. The United States Court of Appeals for the Eleventh Circuit usually hears cases that have a relationship with the Eleventh Circuit, an area that includes Alabama, Florida, and Georgia. And the U.S. Supreme Court covers the whole landscape.

But jurisdiction also refers to different types of cases. There are bankruptcy courts that hear only bankruptcy cases. U.S. district courts are trial courts or courts of *original jurisdiction,* while U.S. circuit courts of appeals hear appeals from cases that were decided at the district court level and are said to have *appellate jurisdiction*. And some courts — the U.S. Supreme Court is exhibit A here — have more than one type of jurisdiction. The Supreme Court as the court of last resort would seem on its face to have only appellate jurisdiction. Not so! The Supreme Court also enjoys original jurisdiction, even though this jurisdiction is limited to cases involving public officials, such as ambassadors, and cases in which a state is a named party.

Jurisdiction, then, is the power to hear and decide legal cases. The cases that come before any given court can be limited to those that arise in the geographic area served by that court, but they need not be. And jurisdiction applies to *every* type of legal action brought, whether civil, criminal, maritime, matrimonial — or simply a small claims court action.

Federalism v. states' rights

It's an old story. In the beginning, the founding fathers, unhappy with the loose structure of the Articles of Confederation, drafted the Constitution. The Constitution established a powerful three-part federal government that was to bind the new nation together. One of these parts was a federal judiciary, whose job was to enforce federal law. Not all of the founders were pleased with the notion of a federal judicial system — or with the notion of a strong central government, for that matter. Those founders, like Thomas Jefferson, who wanted states to retain a high degree of local autonomy, managed to attach the Bill of Rights to the Constitution as its first ten amendments. These amendments were intended to act as a bulwark to individual and states' rights and a brake on federal power.

The group of individuals who favored states' rights (they later became known as *Anti-Federalists*) also pointed out that the country already had a court system in place: the state court system. The price for these individuals' endorsement of Article III of the Constitution, which outlines the federal judiciary, was the continued existence of these state courts.

In the beginning, there was no federal law for the federal courts to enforce, and the relationship between state and federal courts was undefined either by practice or the Constitution. With the rise of a body of federal legislation, however, the concept of *judicial federalism* took hold. Under judicial federalism, when a conflict exists between state and federal law, the latter trumps the former. State courts can still decide matters arising under federal law, but in doing so they must apply federal, not state law, and they must look to U.S. Supreme Court precedents. And the U.S. Supreme Court reserves to itself the right to say whether a state's laws are in line with the federal Constitution, laws, and treaties.

So which court gets the case?

State courts still retain a large measure of authority. Even under so-called *federal question* jurisdiction, the U.S. Supreme Court will not entertain any case that involves a question of federal law until after the highest appellate court of that state has reached a final decision. And that decision usually stands, because the Supreme Court is not obligated to hear appeals from state court decisions. Fewer than ten percent of all state appeals ever reach the nation's highest court. In addition, criminal cases — most of which are governed by state law — almost never reach the U.S. Supreme Court. The Court has ruled that it will only consider petitions for *habeas corpus,* in which incarcerated individuals challenge the legality of their imprisonment, after prisoners have exhausted all possible state remedies.

So-called *diversity jurisdiction* applies to suits between individuals from different states. In such cases, the plaintiff gets to decide whether to go the state court route or make a federal case of his or her grievance. However, despite this concurrent jurisdiction, such a case only gets into federal court if it meets an amount-in-controversy requirement (now $75,000 or more).

Case Study: Bush v. Gore

Perhaps no event better illustrates the power of the Supreme Court than the resolution of the 2000 presidential election. Just when you thought the separation of powers issue had been settled once and for all, the Court, shown in Figure 1-7, stepped in to adjudicate who had won the biggest political contest of all. Legions of Court watchers, law professors, media commentators, and armchair legal analysts across the country thought the Court's willingness to step into the fray was a major misstep. Still, somebody had to decide who's in charge!

Background info

Election night 2000 was a cliff-hanger that went on for weeks. Many people went to bed that night thinking that Al Gore had won, only to discover the next morning that George W. Bush was being declared the winner. In fact, the election was simply too close to call. Several states were up for grabs, but in the end it came down to one: Florida, where Bush's younger brother, Jeb, was governor. Florida electors were unable to commit themselves to either Bush or Gore owing to the closeness of the vote. Brush fires erupted in several precincts where the candidates' surrogates traded allegations about various improprieties. Recounts were started, then stopped as Republicans and Democrats wrangled over what standards to apply. It was more than a little chaotic.

Figure 1-7:
The Rehnquist Court, the folks who brought the curtain down on the 2000 presidential election debacle.

Collection, The Supreme Court Historical Society, Photographed by Richard Strauss, National Geographic Society

The Court steps in

The Supreme Court actually interposed itself into the election contest three times. Only the last two are known as *Bush v. Gore*. In the first of these cases, *Bush v. Palm Beach County Canvassing Board*, the Court hoped to end the election crisis by putting a stop to the Florida Supreme Court's decision to extend the time for certifying the vote past the period set by state law. But by the time the Court began hearing arguments in the appeal on December 1, the certification had already occurred. The embarrassed justices sent the case back down to the Florida Supreme Court, instructing the lower court to rewrite its opinion so that it would not create a conflict between state and federal law.

A week later, the Florida Supreme Court ordered a statewide recount of ballots. Unlike its earlier decision, however, this one was not unanimous. With the Florida justices split 4-3, the U.S. Supreme Court once again exercised its discretionary appellate review jurisdiction and granted *certiorari*, or review (see Chapter 2), to *Bush v. Gore.* The day after the Florida Supreme Court had ordered a recount, the U.S. Supreme Court granted a temporary *stay,* or delay, in enforcing the Florida Supreme Court's order. The U.S. Supreme Court justices, too, were narrowly divided, 5-4. The five justices voting in favor of the stay were the same five conservatives who had been moving the Rehnquist Court to the right for more than a decade. The first hearing of *Bush v. Gore* telegraphed to the nation what would happen if the Court took further action in the case.

The Court's third and final intervention in the 2000 presidential election came just days later. In its unsigned opinion, the Court explained that it had voted 5-4 to put a stop to the Florida recount. To allow the recount to go forward, the Court said, would violate the Equal Protection Clause of the Fourteenth Amendment (see Chapter 10). The U.S. Supreme Court sent the case back down to the Florida Supreme Court, which had no alternative but to dismiss it. The presidential election of 2000 had been decided, in essence, by the vote of one Supreme Court justice.

Needless to say, the George W. Bush camp was jubilant. Al Gore supporters were incensed. Many people were simply happy to have things settled. But others worried that the Court had gone too far. In the past, in landmark cases like *Brown v. Board of Education* (1954), which put an end to legal segregation, and *United States v. Nixon* (1974), which led to the first presidential resignation under threat of impeachment, were unanimously decided. After *Bush v. Gore,* the concern was that the Court had not only overreached itself but undermined its authority by not speaking with one voice. That split decision, 5-4, suggested that *Bush v. Gore* was a political, not a judicial, decision.

Precedents

Bush v. Gore wasn't the Court's first foray into the realm of king making. The election of 1876 pitted Samuel J. Tilden, the Democratic governor of New York, against Rutherford B. Hayes, the Republican governor of Ohio. After the votes had been counted, it seemed that Tilden had won the popular vote and had 184 uncontested electoral votes to Hayes's 165. The magic number was 185 electoral votes. Twenty votes of the Electoral College were still up for grabs, however — all but one of them in the southern states of Florida, Louisiana, and South Carolina. (The exception was Oregon. They always have marched to a different drummer.)

The Twelfth Amendment stipulates that in a contested presidential election, "The President of the Senate shall, in the presence of the Senate and the House of Representatives, open all the certificates and the votes shall then be

The Electoral College: Time to graduate to other things?

The founding fathers did not entirely trust the American people to elect their own president and vice president. Article II, section 1 of the Constitution directs that, "Each State shall appoint, in such Manner as the Legislature thereof may direct, a Number of Electors, equal to the whole Number of Senators and Representatives to which the State may be entitled in the Congress." No senator, representative, or officer of the U.S. government can serve as an elector. To win, a candidate must have the endorsement of a majority of the electors, each of whom has one vote.

Before the Twelfth Amendment was ratified in 1804, a tie vote in the Electoral College threw the election into the House of Representatives, which the Constitution directs to choose from among the top five vote-getters. The vice president was the person who had received the most (or second-most) Electoral College votes. When this system was tested in 1800, however, it proved unwieldy: It took 36 ballots for the House to elect Thomas Jefferson president. The man who had tied with Jefferson in the Electoral

College, Aaron Burr, became vice president. This was a mess, not a marriage made in heaven. So in 1803, Congress proposed what became the Twelfth Amendment, which stipulated that there would be separate balloting for president and vice president in the Electoral College. This change did not, however, prevent the election of 1824 from being settled in the House, which chose John Quincy Adams.

After 1832, electors were chosen not by state legislators, but by popular vote (except in South Carolina, which held out until the Civil War). A political party, however, needs only a *plurality* to carry the whole state (that is, in a contest between more than two parties, the one getting the most votes wins, even though it may not have captured half of the votes). This equation means that a presidential candidate who wins the popular vote may not win in the Electoral College. This has happened ten — and counting Albert Gore, Jr., maybe 11 — times. For many, this is no way to run a railroad — or a democratic election.

counted." Because in 1876 Congress was equally divided between Democrats and Republicans, the Republican-controlled Senate and the Democrat-controlled House set up an electoral commission to decide who would become president. The Senate chose three Republicans and two Democrats to sit on the commission, and the House chose two Democrats and three Republicans. The remainder of the commission was to consist of five justices of the Supreme Court. The bill setting up the commission named two Republican justices and two Democratic justices, but let those four select their own nonpartisan tiebreaker.

The only truly neutral member of the Court at the time was David Davis. But Davis resigned from the Court almost immediately, leaving only Republican justices as alternatives. Joseph Bradley, seemingly the least partisan of those remaining, was selected as the final member of the commission. To no one's great surprise, the commission voted along party lines, selecting the Republican Hayes. Democrats, who were mostly Southerners, cried foul, claiming that Davis, and perhaps Bradley, had been subjected to political blackmail. When the uproar threatened to derail the orderly transfer of power, a deal was struck. The Republicans agreed to withdraw the federal troops still occupying the South in the wake of the Civil War, to appropriate funds for Southern improvement, and to appoint at least one Southerner to the cabinet. In return, the Democrats agreed not to delay Hayes's inauguration. It was a flat-out political deal, and ever since its implementation, the Court has been criticized for having played a part in what many saw as outright log rolling.

And the winner is . . .

Why, then, did the Supreme Court agree to get back into the fray after the election of 2000? In a sense, the justices had no choice. When the contest between George W. Bush and Al Gore proved too close to call, the contestants resorted to a series of lawsuits in an effort to settle the matter. These suits proceeded simultaneously in the state court system and in federal court. The cases largely concerned the matter and manner of vote counting (and recounting) in the pivotal state of Florida. There were charges of voter intimidation, ballot rigging — all manner of political shenanigans. Something had to be done.

Chapter 2

Getting to Cert

- -

- -

*O*ver the long history of the Court, appellants have used a variety of methods for getting their cases before the justices. Since 1988, however, only one procedure has been available to most seeking Supreme Court review: certiorari (Latin — Medieval Latin, no less — for "we wish to be certified").

Making an Appeal

Restrictions on the jurisdiction of the Supreme Court — and that of all federal courts — are set out in Article III, section 2 of the Constitution. The Constitution stipulates that federal courts can hear only "Cases" and "Controversies." As simple as that sounds, like most legal matters, these requirements have been elaborated to such an extent that they have come to mean a great deal more than you think they might.

Controversy: Between a rock and a hard place

Perhaps it goes without saying: In order to get to the Supreme Court, a case must involve a real controversy whose outcome has genuine consequences for all parties involved. The reasoning behind this requirement is that in order for a matter to be fully aired and for the parties to receive full and zealous representation, the two sides in a case cannot actually be on the same side. There is a general ban on *collusive suits,* in which the parties cook up an artificial dispute in order to get a definitive reading on the meaning of some law or other. Since 1850, the Court has treated this type of *test case* (not all test cases are collusive; see the discussion of *Brown v. Board of Education* in Chapter 12) harshly, sometimes citing the parties for contempt of court. The Court also takes a dim view of parties who go to great lengths to manufacture diversity jurisdiction (see Chapter 1) in order to take their case out of the state system and into federal court, where they hope to receive a more favorable judgment.

Just as not all test cases are dismissed, not all collusive suits are jettisoned. Some of the Court's most significant decisions began life as collusive law suits. Examples include *Pollack v. Farmers' Loan and Trust Co.* (1895), in which a bank shareholder sued his bank in order to prevent it from paying taxes it had no wish to pay. The Court, knowing full well that the case had been concocted, agreed not only to hear the case, but to expedite its hearing. At stake was the constitutionality of the income tax, an issue considered so important and pressing that the Court was willing to throw its case requirements out the window. This decision was a bad one. *Pollock* was the most controversial case of its era, and the emotional issue of income taxes inspired both the lawyers and the justices involved to behave badly, even irrationally. In the end, *Pollock* — which was heard twice! — settled nothing, and Congress had to introduce the Sixteenth Amendment to get what it wanted: income tax. Bad things happen when the Supreme Court does not follow its own rules.

States' rights live!

The Court jealously guards its privilege of having the last word. Even the prohibition against hearing federal questions has not prevented the justices from deciding cases concerning the issue of federalism. The Tenth Amendment, which specifies that "powers not delegated to the United States by the Constitution, nor prohibited by it to the States, are reserved to the States respectively, or to the people," has in recent times generated a flurry of Supreme Court decisions.

This insurance of reservation of powers was insisted upon by those founding fathers favoring states' rights (see Chapter 1). After the liberals on the Court headed by Chief Justice Harlan F. Stone gutted the Tenth Amendment in *United States v. Darby Lumber Co.* (1941), which upheld Congress's authority to regulate wages and hours, the amendment was revived by Associate Justice William Rehnquist's opinion in *National League of Cities v. Usery* (1976), in which the application of federal fair labor standards to the states was declared unconstitutional. *Usery* was reversed by the Court in 1985, but Rehnquist was not ready to declare defeat. The very next year, he became chief justice and began using his new position to fulfill his states' rights agenda. Rehnquist assigned himself the job of writing the Court's opinion in the 5-4 decision that endorsed state autonomy in the area of gun legislation in *United States v. Lopez* (1995).

Another aspect of the cases or controversies requirement concerns the Court's unwillingness to address political questions or offer *advisory opinions* about matters not being litigated. The first time the Court was asked to render such an opinion was in 1793, when George Washington asked the justices to review a treaty with France. After dragging their feet for a time, the justices reluctantly wrote to the father of our country, declining his request. Citing the separation of powers doctrine, Chief Justice John Jay told the president that as "the court of last resort," the Supreme Court should not be obligated to pass judgment on matters that did not involve active litigation. The logic of the argument is clear: If some member of the executive or legislative branch refused to follow a decision of the Supreme Court, the Court would lose its status, upsetting the balance of power.

Ripeness: A threat to your rights

It's true: In order to be picked by the Supreme Court, cases must be ripe. The *ripeness* doctrine is a variation of the cases and controversies doctrine and is one of the requirements that must be met before the Court can exercise its jurisdiction over a matter. All of these requirements are covered by the umbrella concept of *justiciability,* which the Court has defined as a state which makes cases "appropriate for judicial determination." If a case has not matured to a point where the controversy involved actively threatens property, liberty, or some other right, that case is not ripe for judicial consideration.

Ironically, the best illustration of the ripeness doctrine can be found in a Supreme Court case. In *United Public Workers v. Mitchell* (1947), a group of federal workers asked the Court to *enjoin,* or stop, the enforcement of the Hatch Act, which barred executive branch employees from participating in most political activities. The workers believed this legislation violated their right to freedom of expression guaranteed by the First Amendment. The only problem with this argument was that they had not yet engaged in any political activities. Instead of simply throwing the case out, the Court delivered an opinion spelling out the ripeness doctrine and refusing to enjoin the Hatch Act. The threat to the workers' right of free expression was, the Court said, merely "hypothetical," presenting no case or controversy.

Mootness: Still up for grabs

Mootness is another aspect of the Supreme Court's appellate jurisdiction. In order for a case to be heard by the Court, it must involve a controversy that is still alive and capable of being affected by the Court's decision. The mootness issue enters the picture when the issue being litigated will clearly be resolved in one way or the other before the Court renders its own decision about what should happen. The leading mootness case is *DeFunis v.*

Odegaard (1974), in which the appellant, a white male, challenged the admissions policies of the University of Washington Law School, claiming they denied him equal protection under the Fourteenth Amendment (see Chapter 10). While his case was still pending, the appellant was provisionally admitted to the law school. By the time his case actually made it onto the Court's schedule, he was about to graduate. The Court dismissed his case, declaring that by the time it was decided, the issue at stake would already be moot.

The mootness doctrine does have an important exception. When an issue is "capable of repetition, yet evading review," the Court can decide to decide it. The best illustration of this exception is probably *Roe v. Wade* (1973), in which the Court was asked to consider the legality of abortion on demand after the initially pregnant, unmarried "Jane Roe" had already given birth. The Court agreed to hear her case because of the obvious fact that any woman who met the ripeness requirement in this context would almost certainly have a moot case by the time the Court could decide her case. It may take only nine months for a baby to be born, but the gestation period for a Supreme Court case is far longer.

Standing: A stake in the case

Standing is that aspect of Supreme Court justiciability that addresses *who* may bring a case before a federal court, rather than *what* issues will be heard (no political or hypothetical questions) or *when* a case must be filed to have a hearing (ripeness and mootness doctrines apply). Standing is somewhat different from these other jurisdictional determinants because it chiefly concerns plaintiffs who challenge government actions.

In general, only those who have been directly injured by some government action have standing to sue in federal court, unless the case is brought to federal court under diversity jurisdiction (see Chapter 1). Such a plaintiff might be a criminal defendant who claims police conducted an illegal search that netted evidence later used against him or her. Sometimes, however, the injury is indirect, as when a taxpayer protests some government use of the revenues it collects from its citizens. In such a case, the taxpayer has standing as a stand-in for all taxpayers, if you see what I mean.

In cases concerning constitutional issues, two qualifications apply to a grant of standing to sue. A showing of *injury-in-fact* requires the plaintiff to demonstrate that the challenged government action caused the injury claimed. In addition, there must be some remedy which will eliminate the injury and which the court can order. Case in point: The plaintiffs in *Simon v. Eastern*

Kentucky Welfare Rights Organization (1976) challenged an Internal Revenue Service ruling that made it easier for hospitals to retain their tax-exempt status if they curtailed their services to poor people. The Supreme Court found that the plaintiff welfare rights organization had no standing to sue because the injury they allegedly suffered resulted from hospital administrative decisions, not the IRS decision. What's more, if the Court were to reverse this ruling, there was no guarantee that the poor people of eastern Kentucky would receive better medical care.

The second qualification that applies to a grant of standing in a constitutional case is the doctrine of *prudential limitations*. This vaguely defined limitation seems to be designed as a gloss on the separation of powers. Prudential limitations allow the Court to withhold standing when it deems the issue at stake can be better resolved by letting the political process take care of it, as when an appellant — often a taxpayer — challenges a law that may be unconstitutionally applied to others. Alternatively, the Court could cite prudential limitations if it fears that by inserting itself into a controversial matter, it will provoke a contradictory response from the legislative branch.

Both the injury-in-fact requirement and the prudential limitations doctrine have been criticized for their lack of definition and cited as double-edged swords that the Court uses to play politics. A denial of standing based on a finding that there is no injury-in-fact can be a convenient excuse for the Court's unwillingness to address the merits of an issue that is also a political football. In fact, such a denial can be seen as the equivalent of a decision on the merits, denying the plaintiffs their day in court. On the other hand, if the Court wants to avoid criticism for failing to deal with a tough constitutional question, no prudential limitation is going to prevent a case that raises this issue from going forward.

It needs to be said that despite the requirement of injury-in-fact and the qualification of prudential limitations, the Court does grant Congress the power to confer standing on almost any person if Congress wants to challenge government action through him or her. The Court views this grant of authority as an invitation for judicial review. As always, the justices want to have the last say — but they know how to be polite.

Thinking of the Supreme Court as a Trial Court

The U.S. Supreme Court is known as the court of last resort. It may come as a surprise, then, to learn that it can act both as an appellate court and as a trial court. Ordinarily, the Court only reviews questions of law, but on rare occasions, it acts as a fact finder — the Constitution requires it to do so. Article III, section 2, however, limits these instances to suits involving public officials and cases in which a state is a named party to the lawsuit. In such cases, the Court is said to exercise its *original jurisdiction*.

Public officials

The constitutional grant of original jurisdiction has been determined to be self-executing — that is, Congress cannot enlarge or restrict it. Congress has, however, granted concurrent jurisdiction to other federal courts in cases involving public officials such as ambassadors, consuls, and other such ministers. Concurrent jurisdiction in these instances means that the Supreme Court hears virtually no cases involving public officials.

State as plaintiff or defendant

In cases in which a state appears as a party, the Supreme Court's original jurisdiction is, by federal statute, exclusive. Most of these cases involve border disputes between states, and in recent times only one or two such cases per year will come before the Court. And in practice, even these cases are treated like appeals. The justices customarily appoint a special master (who is often a former federal judge) to hear the evidence, determine the facts, and make a recommendation as to how the case should be settled. The special master's report, much like the ruling of a lower court, is then accepted, modified, or rejected in a final opinion issued by the Court.

Courting the Court

A variety of methods exist for getting the Court's attention. In the early history of the Supreme Court, when the judges of lower federal appellate courts were divided on the outcome of a case, certification of the case for Supreme Court review was automatic. When state courts decisions involving federal questions were appealed to the U.S. Supreme Court, a writ of error was the vehicle of choice. When Congress passed the Habeas Corpus Act of 1867, permitting prisoners in state custody to inquire into the legal grounds for their imprisonment, lawyers could send appeal directly to the Court. (*Habeas corpus* is a delicate way of saying, in Latin: "You shall have the body." Another way of putting it is, "Get me out of here.")

Avenues of appeal

In more recent times, other avenues for appealing to the Court became available. A right of appeal, limited to issues involving federal law, could be used under two different scenarios:

- When a federal appellate court used federal law to invalidate state law
- When federal law was declared unconstitutional in the context of a civil case in which the United States itself was a party

Mandatory review

In rare instances, a U.S. court of appeals could certify that a particular question was of such importance and moment that the Court should immediately review the case raising that issue. Both the invocation of the Court's "appeal" jurisdiction and certification led to mandatory review by the Court.

Mandatory review did not, however, mean that the Court would actually hear the case. More often than not, the Court summarily dismissed certifications because of technical flaws. And appeals as of right were limited by the federal question requirement. If a case also involved state law issues, in order to have the entire case considered, the appellant had to revise his appeal, making it conform to the third — and only discretionary — form of requesting Supreme Court review: a petition for certiorari.

Direct appeals from lower courts

Direct appeals from federal district court decisions are still possible, but only just.

In order to go this route, an appellant must first have a decision rendered by a three-judge panel, but these panels have all but disappeared (see Chapter 1). An appellant can instead file a petition for certiorari before the appropriate court of appeals has reached a decision. Most appellants seeking Supreme Court review just go through the motions of filing an appeal with the circuit court before petitioning the Supreme Court. But the Court, no longer under any obligation to hear these appeals, usually denies these petitions, letting the circuit court determine the outcomes. The Court lightens its workload further by getting rid of *certified questions* (questions about the law to be applied to a case posed by federal circuit courts). Either the Court dismisses the lower court's certification of the importance of these questions as improper, or the justices issue an order requiring the appellate judges to rule on the question in a specified fashion.

Appeals from state court decisions are also strictly limited. Such appeals have customarily come from the states' highest courts. In every state but one, these courts are also, confusingly, called *supreme courts*. (In New York, where a supreme court is a trial court, the highest state court is known as the *court of appeals*. Go figure.) Occasionally, however, the Court has heard appeals from decisions made by lower state appellate courts, usually called courts of appeal or superior courts. (Still with me?) And sometimes even a state trial court's decision has made it to the Court for review. The Court is only obligated, however, to review state court decisions either declaring a federal law invalid or upholding a state law that apparently contradicts some federal statute. Every other state court decision reviewed by the Court gets there via certiorari, which is, again, discretionary. And since 1988, certiorari or appeal review of state court decisions has been limited to federal questions on which a state's highest court has already issued a final judgment. Also, if the Court decides that the state supreme court's decision is adequately supported by state law, there may not even be a review of any federal questions wrapped up in the case.

Petitioning for Certiorari

In 1988, Congress revised the laws concerning the Court's appellate jurisdiction to make virtually all appeals discretionary. By default, certiorari became just about the only method of getting to the Supreme Court.

Today, all but a handful of cases heard by the Court are there because the justices have issued a *writ,* or written order, requiring the last court that heard the case to forward the record of all earlier proceedings.

Lower court decision

To petition for certiorari, or review, you have to have a decision from a lower state or federal court. Without that verdict or judgment, there can be no appeal. In fact, by the time you are ready to petition the Court for certiorari, you may have already appealed your case more than once. If your case is coming from a state court system, you will have to have in hand a final decision from your state's highest court. Courts can issue all sorts of interim decisions, such as *temporary restraining orders,* which are issued to prevent the action you are suing about from continuing while your case is being heard. This type of provisional decision does not count.

On the other hand, the issue you are suing about may itself be a judgment about a procedural matter rather than a substantive issue. For example, in the case *Masson v. New Yorker Magazine, Inc.* (1991), the initial issue was whether or not the plaintiff had been libeled in a series of articles published in the defendant magazine. Dr. Jeffrey Masson, a prominent psychoanalyst, claimed that the author of these articles had deliberately misquoted him in such a manner as to damage him professionally. He was especially distressed that he was quoted as having referred to himself as an "intellectual gigolo," something he claimed not to have said.

While the author of the articles, Janet Malcolm, admitted that she may have misquoted Masson, the federal district court that tried the case did not find that her actions amounted to libel. The court granted the defendant's *motion for summary judgment,* a legal action that stops a case from being fully adjudicated because the judge finds that the plaintiff's claim has no legal basis. (Needless to say, it is almost always the defendant's counsel who makes such a trial motion.) On appeal, this judgment in favor of the defendant magazine was affirmed. The circuit court indicated that altered quotations are protected by the First Amendment (see Chapter 8) as long as they contain the "substantial truth" of what was said.

By the time the case reached the Supreme Court, the issue was that grant of summary judgment. *Masson* is what is known as a case of *first impression,* one concerning a legal question that had never been considered by a court. In this instance, the Court was asked to determine whether the disputed quotations demonstrated that Malcolm's articles were written with sufficient maliciousness to have met the legal standard for libel. If they were, then the district court judge had made a procedural error in granting summary judgment — he should have tried the case all the way to a final judgment. The Court decided that the trial court had erred, and so had the circuit court that affirmed the district court's decision. The Supreme Court sent the case back to the circuit court for reconsideration.

You see the point, I'm sure. But you probably still want to know what happened. The case was actually tried two more times. The first time, the jury ruled in Masson's favor but could not agree on how much money the *New Yorker* should pay in damages. A completely new trial resulted in a verdict in Malcolm and the *New Yorker*'s favor. Such are the quirks of the law.

Questions of law

Unless you're a public official able to invoke the Court's original jurisdiction (see Chapter 2), you're not going to be able to get the Supreme Court to consider the facts of your case. The vast majority of the cases the Court agrees to hear every year (somewhere in the neighborhood of 100-125) come before it on appeal from a judgment rendered by a lower court. You are only going to be able to get your foot in the door if you can show the Court that a question of law arose in the course of your trial or a prior appeal. Often — but not always — these are questions about the way the trial or appeal in the lower court was conducted (see "Lower court decision").

Gideon's Trumpet

Remember *Gideon's Trumpet*? This 1964 book by journalist Anthony Lewis (in 1980, it was made into a film starring Henry Fonda) tells the true story of a semi-literate drifter and petty thief, Clarence Earl Gideon. In 1961, Gideon was convicted of breaking and entering a Florida pool hall with the intention of robbing it. Under Florida law at the time, this combination of offenses amounted to a felony. And under Florida law at that time, the state was not required to provide counsel for indigent criminal defendants except in capital cases (that is, cases where conviction could lead to the death penalty). So Gideon was denied the legal representation he requested and convicted of a crime he said he did not commit.

Gideon was no genius, and he was no lawyer — but he did have an innate sense of justice. When the Florida Supreme Court denied his habeas corpus petition, he appealed directly to the U.S. Supreme Court from his prison cell. His petition, written by hand and in pencil, led to the landmark case *Gideon v. Wainwright* (1963). The Court appointed one of the most prominent attorneys of the day, Abe Fortas (who would later become a Supreme Court justice himself), to represent Gideon. Fortas did well by his client, and the Court found that the Sixth Amendment requirement that all criminal defendants be assisted by counsel applies to state as well as federal prosecutions. Gideon was granted a new state trial and, represented by a lawyer from the American Civil Liberties Union, he was acquitted in August 1963.

Gideon's petition was what is known as an appeal *in forma pauperis* (more Latin: "in the manner of a pauper"). I hope you never have to make use of this method of contacting the Court, because in order for the justices to accept such a petition, you would have to be broke and probably also a criminal defendant. Even if you met these requirements, your chance of getting a hearing before the Court is almost nil. Less than 1 percent of the *in forma pauperis* petitions filed with the Court are granted review.

The maxim is that questions of law are for the judge and questions of fact for the jury. Actually, trials are often heard before a judge or a panel of judges and without a jury. In this situation, the judge (or judges) acts as both the *trier of fact* and the *trier of law*. But what's the difference between questions of law and questions of fact? After all, you have gone to trial to have the law settle a dispute. Doesn't that imply that every question put to rest at trial is a legal question?

The short answer is that whether or not an event occurred is a question of fact. The significance of this occurrence or non-occurrence is a question of law. In practice, it can be hard to tell the difference between questions of law and questions of fact. And to make matters more complicated, there are also *mixed* questions of law and fact. In this situation — no surprise — the judge gets to answer the question.

So by the time you get into the courtroom of an appellate court, such as the Supreme Court, all of the facts of your case should — ideally — have been settled. The appellate court will focus instead upon the question or questions of law that are the basis for your appeal. Again, these questions can sometimes look like questions of fact. In the *Masson* case, for example, one of the questions the Court had to decide was whether, "[t]he evidence presents a jury question whether Malcolm acted with requisite knowledge of falsity or reckless disregard as to the truth or falsity of five of the [quoted] passages." At first glance, it might seem that the Court was considering whether or not the disputed passages were false, or if Janet Malcolm knew they were false. Actually, the Court is trying to figure out if there *was* a question of fact there that should have allowed the trial to proceed and the jury to answer it. As discussed in the earlier section "Lower court decision," the issue for the Supreme Court here was whether or not the district court had erred in granting the defendant summary judgment, which in effect granted *The New Yorker* victory before trial.

Paperwork

Before you can get to the Supreme Court, you need to do the paperwork. For this step, you will probably need a lawyer — specifically, a lawyer admitted to practice before the Court. But maybe not — the sidebar on Gideon's Trumpet outlines just such an exception.

The only realistic choice for getting the Court to hear your appeal is a petition for certiorari. The form and content of this petition are spelled out in Rule 14 of the "Rules of the Supreme Court of the United States." The specifics are as follows:

- ✔ You must begin by stating the legal questions you want the Court to consider.

- ✔ You must list all of the parties involved in the appeal.

- ✔ If your petition is more than five pages, you must include a table of contents and a list of the legal authorities you are relying on. (These authorities are usually earlier Supreme Court cases.)

- ✔ You need to include a list of all the opinions and court or administrative orders your case has generated.

- ✔ You need to convince the Court that it has jurisdiction over your case. In doing so, you must include the following:

  - The date the judgment or order you want the Court to review was filed.

  - If you have been granted a rehearing in a lower court, you need to indicate when the date of the court order granting it and of any order granting an extension of time to file this petition for certiorari.

  - If a cross petition has been filed by the respondent in your case, you need to give the Court specifics about that filing.

- You need to state what statute or statutes you believe give the Court the authority to hear your appeal.

- If your appeal questions the constitutionality of a federal or a state law, you will need to notify the appropriate authorities (the U.S. solicitor general or the state attorney general) of your petition. Then you have to tell the Court you have done so in the petition itself.

✔ You have to spell out chapter and verse of all the laws your appeal will be relying on.

✔ You have to include a brief statement of the facts of your case.

✔ If you're appealing a state court judgment, you have to give particulars about any questions of federal law your case raised there.

✔ If you're appealing a federal circuit court judgment, you need to state the basis for federal jurisdiction at the *court of first instance* (meaning the very first federal court that considered your case before any appeal).

✔ You have to convince the justices that your case is worthy of certiorari.

✔ You need to include an appendix, which covers the following items:

- All the opinions, orders, finding of fact, and conclusions of law related to the judgment you're appealing.

- All the same documentation concerning any *companion* case that was heard in conjunction with your own.

- Any order of rehearing issued by a lower court.

- Any other relevant documents.

Rule 14 goes on sternly to say that you're not allowed to file a legal brief in support of this petition. Your petition must be written using plain language and cannot exceed 30 pages. Failure to follow these directions to the letter, says Rule 14, "is sufficient reason for the Court to deny a petition."

Other rules go on to stipulate what type of paper must be used, what format must be followed, the color of the cover (white) — even what types of type are acceptable. Within 90 days after the time the judgment you're appealing was officially recorded in the court below, you must file 40 copies of your certiorari petition with the clerk of the Supreme Court. Oh, and you have to pay a $300 filing fee. All of this work — if you've been careful — merely gets you on the Court's *docket,* or list of cases the justices must consider.

You see why you will probably need a lawyer?

The Supreme Court bar

Not just every lawyer can waltz into the Supreme Court and state your case. You'll probably not be surprised to find out that the Court has rules about whom it will listen to. First, the applicant has to have been admitted to practice before the highest court of his or her state at least three years before applying to the Supreme Court. Second, the applicant cannot be the subject of any disciplinary action. Evidence of the applicant's professionalism and good character takes the form of a personal statement, a certificate from the state court where he or she is admitted, and the statements of two sponsors who are already members of the Supreme Court bar. If this application is accepted, the lawyer pays a fee and then swears an oath before a notary public or — more dramatically — in open court. Today 4,000 to 5,000 lawyers apply every year to be admitted to practice before the Supreme Court.

Becoming Certworthy

The most compelling reason to have a lawyer draft your petition for certiorari is not that it's a legal document. The real reason is that you need a pro to present your case in the best possible light — you need someone in your corner who knows how to make the justices *want* to hear your case.

Standing out in a crowd

The Court receives thousands of cert petitions every year. The justices are not obliged to give any of them their full attention. The Judiciary Act of 1925, the so-called *Judges' Bill,* put a stop to the exponential growth of the justices' workload by expanding the Court's certiorari jurisdiction. By the 1970s, 90 percent of the Court's docket consisted of petitions for certiorari. Legislation passed in 1988 did away with almost every other avenue to the Supreme Court. To make matters worse, the Court's calendar has only enough space on it to hear slightly more than 100 cases each year.

America, it is often said, is a litigious society. Many outraged litigants swear that they will take their case all the way to the Supreme Court, if that's what it takes to see justice done. The sad fact is that few of these people stand a chance of having their day in the U.S. Supreme Court. So how can one lonely petition be made to work its way to the top of the heap? What can be done to make this appeal *certworthy?*

Improving your odds

No one really knows what criteria the justices will use in making up their calendar. There really are no rules governing the selection process, as #10 of the "Rules of the Supreme Court" indicates.

Rule 10. Considerations Governing Review on Writ of Certiorari

> Review on a writ of certiorari is not a matter of right, but of judicial discretion. A petition for a writ of certiorari will be granted only for compelling reasons.

Rule 10 does not end there, however. While cautioning that what follows is neither complete nor controlling, the rule lists three scenarios that hint at what the justices might be looking for:

- ✔ Two federal circuit courts of appeal disagree about an important matter; or, a federal appellate court is in disagreement with a state's highest court about an important federal question; or, a federal appellate court is so far off the mark that it needs reining in.

- ✔ A state court of last resort has decided an important federal question in a way that conflicts with a decision of another state's highest court or that of a federal appeals court.

- ✔ A state court or a United States court of appeals has decided an important question of federal law that has not been, but should be, settled by the Supreme Court; or, a state court or federal appellate court has decided an important federal question in a way that conflicts with Supreme Court decisions.

Political scientists who have studied the cert winnowing process have been unable to pinpoint any real patterns, aside from the obvious. If the United States itself is listed as the appellant on a cert petition, clearly the justices are going to sit up and pay attention when this set of papers comes around. (The government's lawyer, the solicitor general, is — with good reason — often referred to as the *tenth justice*.) Sometimes a so-called *friend of the court* files an *amicus brief* in support of either the petitioner or the respondent, and this action seems to up the ante. The fact that nonparties to the case are interested enough in its outcome to go to so much trouble is impressive, you must admit.

Aside from following all of the Court's rules, you can control little else about this process. Certainly it helps to emphasize the policy ramifications of your case in your petition. If yours is a case of first impression concerning a question the Court has never faced before, your chances might improve. And if you can convincingly argue that your issue is one that will come back to haunt the justices if they don't hear your appeal, this tactic doesn't hurt either.

In the end, though, the factors that make a petition certworthy are hard to pin down. The justices want things that way. Some Court watchers have estimated that even when all of the obviously unworthwhile petitions have been discarded, something like 400 to 500 cases each year remain. Of these, only about a quarter gets the nod. Only the justices know why — and they're not saying.

Understanding the Cert Process

Once you get through the process of filling out the paperwork, you (or rather, your petition) have to go through the selection process. By this point, your appeal is out of your hands. But it's not yet in the justices' hands, either. It's in a limbo some call Clerkworld.

The initial screening

Because of the Court's increasing workload, justices have come to rely more and more on their clerks. The first individual with this title who handles your petition is an administrative person bearing the title clerk of the Court. He (and it always has been he) and his staff are the ones who receive petitions for cert, and they are responsible for performing an initial screening that separates out the in forma pauperis petitions (see "Paperwork") and determines whether or not the other petitions appear to be acceptable. If a petition passes muster, the office of the clerk of the Court records it, obtains the record of the case from the last court that considered it, and sets the case down on the Court's *docket,* a list of cases on the Court's calendar. The clerk of the Court then distributes copies of these cert petitions to the individual justices' chambers.

Before the justices actually sit down to take a look at the cert petitions that have been docketed, however, another group of clerks goes to work on the paperwork. Clerks of the justices are, after the justices themselves, the most significant people working in the Supreme Court building. You may be surprised to learn that these clerks are almost uniformly young, untested, and new to the job. Matter of fact, they just graduated from law school. But these clerks are not run-of-the-mill young lawyers; they are top graduates of top law schools. To have gotten to their positions of power and influence, they are doubtless also pretty good politicians.

The principal job of a law clerk is to help his or her justice select cases for Supreme Court review. Clerks are usually responsible for reading through a mountain of cert petitions, teasing out the *real* legal issues in each case, and then writing memoranda about these issues for his or her particular justice.

In short, much of what the justices did before they became overwhelmed with work has been shifted onto the shoulders of their law clerks. These clever young folks came up with a solution to their problem, however: In 1972, they instituted the *cert pool*. That year, for the first time, a number of justices allowed their clerks to work together, so that one clerk would be assigned to write a *pool memo* on each case for all of the participating justices to read. This method saved a great deal of duplication of work.

Most, but not all of the justices, have jumped into the cert pool. Justice John Paul Stevens jumped in, only to jump back out. For him, it was not a timesaver. For others, the cert pool has amounted to cutting corners by reducing the number of people who actually review each petition. For Justice William O. Douglas, the review process wasn't exactly a sacred duty, but rather "in many respects the most important and interesting of all our functions."

Completed pool memos are reviewed for technical errors by an administrator in the chief justice's chambers. If a memo passes inspection, it is then copied and distributed to the justices participating in the pool. But before a justice actually gets his hands on a memo, it's reviewed once again by one of his or her own law clerk or clerks. (Some justices have as many as four.) These clerks may agree with the pool memo's recommendation about whether or not the Court should grant cert (agree to hear the case). If they disagree, well, they write another memo.

The discuss list

The final decisions about which cases the Court will hear rest with the justices themselves. Some justices rely heavily on the recommendations of their clerks, while others — even in modern times — have insisted on doing their own thinking. Justice William J. Brennan, for example, is said to have read every cert petition that landed on his desk.

Before the justices meet to discuss what they have decided, the chief justice sends around a *discuss list* of the cases that have made it through the law clerks' screening process. (Until around the time of the Second World War, this was a *dead list*, which included cases the chief justice thought unworthy of further consideration.) The discuss list usually contains only 25 to 30 percent of the cert petitions filed with the clerk of the Court. And the list, which is one of the ways the chief justice helps control the Court's agenda, also reflects the chief's judgment. Any associate justice who wishes to do so may, however, add cases to the list.

Final decisions are made during a private convocation known as the judicial conference. The conference convenes twice weekly during the regular Court session, which opens the first Monday in October and usually ends in May.

Beginning in the 1970s, however, the Court added a series of judicial conferences in late September, prior to the official start of that year's term. The sole purpose of these additional meetings is to consider the cert petitions that have piled up over the summer while the Court was in recess. Also, if the Court calendar has been especially full, judicial conferences can continue until July, well after the Court had stopped hearing cases for that year's term.

The judicial conference, like much about the Court, is steeped in tradition. On Wednesday mornings and Friday afternoons, the current chief justice summons his brethren by ringing a buzzer. At least six justices have to be in attendance to constitute a quorum. The justices gather in a wood paneled conference room (Figure 2-1). It's always the same room, dominated by a portrait of *The Great Chief Justice,* John Marshall. The justices, who no doubt have seen each other fairly recently, go through a ceremony of shaking hands all around, a ritual started during the late 1800s by Chief Justice Melville W. Fuller. Then everyone takes his or her assigned seat around a long table, with the chief justice at one end and the most senior associate justice at the other. The most junior member of the Court sits near the door, which he or she is responsible for monitoring. No one — absolutely no one — other than the nine justices is allowed in this room during the judicial conference.

Figure 2-1:
The justices'
conference
room.

Franz Jantzen, Collection of the Supreme Court of the United States

The first item on the agenda after the chief justice officially opens the Friday conference is always the discuss list. Usually the list generates only a brief period of discussion, which is initiated by the chief justice. After the chief briefly outlines the facts of each case, each of the other justices, in order of seniority, comments on the case. Then they take a vote, in reverse order of seniority. By tradition (there is no governing rule), it takes four affirmative votes to accept a case for a hearing before the Court.

The orders list

Cert petitions approved for review are placed, together with appeals and in forma pauperis applications and miscellaneous orders such as those disbarring attorneys, on an *orders list* prepared by the clerk of the Court. The list indicates whether a cert petition has been accepted or denied. Rationales for these decisions are seldom given. The vote is not made public. The order list is released each Monday the Court is in session at the beginning of the session. Unlike opinions of the Court in cases that have had a full hearing, decisions on the orders list are not orally announced. Instead, the list is made available through the office of the clerk of the Court or the Court's public information officer. It is also posted the day of its release on the Court's official Web site at www.supremecourtus.gov/orders/orders.html. Orders lists are also routinely published near the end of the official record of the Court's activities, *United States Reports*. Don't hold your breath for this one, though — a volume of *U.S. Reports* can appear years after the events they chronicle.

Just because your petition for cert is granted does not, however, mean that your case will actually be argued before the high bench. In granting cert, the justices can also deal with a case summarily by *vacating* or setting aside the judgment below. Then the case is remanded or sent back to the lower court, such as in *Bush v. Gore* (see Chapter 1). Usually an order for remand is accompanied with the instruction that the case is to be reconsidered in light of a specific Supreme Court *precedent,* a related, previously decided case considered authoritative. This outcome may not be what you had in mind, but at least you have a second chance. When a case is remanded by the justices, it's pretty clear that the highest court in the land does not agree with that last opinion you didn't like either.

When Cert Is Denied

Although the Court receives its share of frivolous appeals — many of them generated by incarcerated individuals with too much time on their hands — preparing and filing a cert petition is an expensive and time-consuming business. For most petitioners, this application represents their last hope, the culmination of years of disappointment. Many of them know how slim their chances are of actually getting the Supreme Court to hear their appeal, but persevere nonetheless, believing wholeheartedly in the merits of their cases. Indeed, if they did not have so much faith and hope vested in their cases, they would never have gotten this far. What happens to these people when their petitions are denied?

The Court does not ordinarily give reasons for denial

The whole purpose of certiorari is to give the justices a free hand in deciding which cases are worthy of a full-blown hearing. The steady growth of their certiorari jurisdiction at the expense of mandatory appeals has been necessitated by the exponential increase in the number of appellants knocking on the Supreme Court door. Another way of cutting the judicial workload down to size is to decline to address the Court's reasons for denying cert.

Occasionally, a justice will feel so strongly about a petition that has been turned down that he or she will address cert denial in writing on the orders list. Justices William J. Brennan and Thurgood Marshall, for example, always used the list as a forum for airing their undying opposition to the death penalty when a majority of the Court had voted down an appeal for a stay of execution. And sometimes these written opinions about summary orders denying cert can be as lengthy as the written opinions recording the Court's judgment in a case it has actually heard. In the recent federal justices' salaries case of *Williams v. United States* (2002), for example, Justice Stephen Breyer wrote a 13-page opinion (with three additional pages of charts and graphs!) dissenting from the Court's denial of cert.

The lower court decision usually stands

Opinion is divided about the meaning of a denial of cert. As a matter of law, denying cert has no significance other than indicating that the case will not be reviewed. Technically, denial of cert cannot be viewed as an endorsement by the Court of the decision of the lower court. Neither is denial necessarily an indication of where the Court stands on the issues questioned in the petition for certiorari.

Still, a denial of cert means that the decision of the lower court stays on the books. The petitioner is generally left with no further legal recourse. His case — and the legal questions it raised — would seem to be dead. Many Court watchers are convinced that a denial of cert means that these questions are, if not dead, at least settled, as far as the Court is concerned. But the

Court is not monolithic. It is both an institution and a collection of individuals. When old justices retire and are replaced by new ones, almost invariably nominated by a new president, the political orientation of the Court can shift. Issues that have lain dormant for decades can come back to life. Judicial determinations, both those made by lower courts and those made by the Supreme Court, can be completely turned around. Racial segregation, which the Court made the law of land in 1896, was finally outlawed when the Court reversed itself nearly a half century later (see Chapter 12).

Chapter 3

Making a Decision

The inner workings of the inner sanctum of the Supreme Court *are* inscrutable. This chapter describes what you can see of typical Court proceedings and what the public knows about the Court's procedures for hearing, deciding, and letting the world know what the justices think about a case.

The Paper Chase: Briefs, Briefs, and More Briefs

Frequently, months elapse between the time the Court announces that it will hear a case and the actual appearance before the justices of the attorneys representing the parties to the case. Most of the interval is taken up with the paper chase. The Supreme Court rules are quite specific about the form and content of the parties' *briefs,* which are written statements outlining the facts of the cases and the legal arguments used to support their respective views.

In the early days of the Court, no rules governed briefs, and they weren't even required. Not every party submitted a brief (these were the sublimely confident parties, no doubt), but in 1821, the Court began requiring that every party to a case submit a brief. (A case can include multiple appellants and multiple respondents.) The 1821 rule outlined two basic requirements:

> ✔ The brief should *briefly* set out the facts of the case and the questions of law involved.
>
> ✔ The brief should set forth the party's legal analysis of its case, or *argument,* citing the statutory and case law supporting this view.

Parties took these instructions to heart, and many of them went on at great length about the issues involved with their cases and how the law supported these concepts. Justice John H. Clarke, who sat on the high bench from 1916 to 1922, was known to complain about briefs of a thousand pages or more. Fifty years later, Chief Justice Warren Burger suggested that briefs should be limited to 50 pages, and in 1980, the Court made this a rule. Number 24.6 of the Rules of the U.S. Supreme Court sternly warns, "A brief shall be concise, logically arranged with proper headings, and free of irrelevant, immaterial, or scandalous matter. The Court may disregard or strike a brief that does not comply with this paragraph."

If this rule seems harsh, recall that the justices have to wade through thousands of petitions — and briefs opposing these petitions — each term, only to have a whole other set of papers to read for the 100-plus cases they decide to review. Recall, too, that many of these petitions and briefs are not written by lawyers with a lot of Supreme Court time under their belts. A fair amount of paperwork is generated by jailhouse lawyers or people who otherwise have too much time on their hands. And the appellants' briefs are only the beginning. These briefs are almost always linked to briefs from the respondent parties, which share many characteristics with the appellants' briefs — including length. Appellants are given the chance to write another brief, called a *reply brief,* answering the arguments raised in the appellees' briefs. As if these briefs weren't enough, at any time before the case is actually heard, any of the parties may file a supplemental brief addressing new legislation or other matters that have changed since the initial briefs were filed.

Then there are friends of the Court who are not parties to the case but who file amicus briefs because they have a political or ideological (not personal or financial) interest in the outcome of the case. (An *amicus curiae* is almost always aligned with either the appellant or the appellee.). And, oh yes, there are all the *motions* filed with the Court while a case is still pending, requesting the Court to issue orders that favor the moving parties. In the Supreme Court, these motions are most often requesting that the case be dismissed for one reason or another — and they are invariably followed by countermotions.

Opposing parties to a case do usually cooperate on one set of papers: a *joint appendix* that includes the official record of the case thus far. The justices have to be familiar with this document, too.

I'm sure it won't surprise you to learn that the Court's rules also stipulate a briefing schedule for those cases they will review. Forty copies of the appellant's brief must be filed within 45 days after his or her case is granted certiorari. The appellee then files 40 copies of his or her brief within 30 days after receiving the appellant's brief. An appellant who chooses to file a reply brief has to turn 40 copies over to the Court within the next 30 days, but no later than one week before the date of oral argument. Forty copies of any supplemental brief can be filed right up to the time the case is called for oral argument. Finally, the Court can change any or all of these dates if it chooses to do so.

Each case generates so much paperwork that it is hard to know how much attention any of it receives. And yet it's hard to overstate the importance of good briefing. It is through your brief that the justices become familiar with your side of the story. The indefatigable Justice William J. Brennan wrote that, "[M]ost of the members of the Court follow the practice of reading the briefs before argument. Some of us, and I am one, often have a bench memorandum prepared before argument. This memorandum digests the facts and the arguments of both sides, highlighting the matters about which I may want to question counsel at the argument." And the celebrated Justice Oliver Wendell Holmes declared that oral argument seldom influenced his views about a case. Those views arose from his reading of the briefs and the record. Oral argument is over in a twinkling, but a brief is forever. Not only can it be referred to while the justices are deliberating after they have heard a case, but briefs become an official part of the record of a case, a historical document available to the public.

Oral Argument: Not Really a Back-and-Forth

The setting is intimidating. The justices, wearing black robes, enter from behind a curtain. They sit in high-backed chairs behind an imposing raised desk, also called the *bench,* which has a winged shape that makes the lawyer standing before it feel both small and encircled (see Figure 3-1). The justices are seated in a predetermined order: The chief justice always sits in the middle, with the most senior associate justice on his right, the second most senior associate justice on his left, and so on. Twenty quill pens — that's right, quill pens — rest on the tables where the attorneys sit. And some of those attorneys will be attired in so-called *morning dress,* the striped pants, wing-collared shirt, and long-tailed coat most people associate with bridegrooms. At an earlier time, all attorneys appearing before the Court wore morning dress, although today only government lawyers like the solicitor general make a habit of it.

Figure 3-1:
Interior of
the current
Supreme
Court
courtroom.

© Bob Rowan; Progressive Image/CORBIS

Most attorneys arguing a case before the Supreme Court play it safe and assume that the justices have forgotten what they read about the case by the time it reaches the courtroom. Counsel thus go to great lengths to prepare a full account of the facts of their cases and the important points of their arguments. And those who have not had much experience at the Supreme Court bar are shocked to discover that they will seldom be given a chance to deliver much of this material. Oral argument is strictly limited to a half hour per side, and almost as soon as the words, "May it please the Court . . ." are out of a lawyer's mouth, the justices begin firing questions at him or her. Sometimes, in fact, the justices even begin arguing among themselves. The following exchange in the case of *Boy Scouts of America v. Dale* (2000), concerning the Boy Scouts' disallowance of homosexual scout leaders, is typical:

> QUESTION: Is it — and I take it — we may have touched on this, but I take it that the position that you've just described is not stated anywhere in a Boy Scouts manual, or even a troop leader manual? This is in effect sort of Boy Scout common law. It's determined by the council, and the council makes individual decisions, and that's the way the policy is expressed, is that correct?
>
> MR. DAVIDSON [George A. Davidson, counsel for the Boy Scouts]: Well, the record shows, although the actual article is not in the record, that in

the magazine sent to all adult Scouters in 1992 there was an article about the policy, so it's not a stealth policy, but the general principle of morally straight is really very, very widely known in the Scouting movement. It's —

QUESTION: The general principle is, but this particular application of the Scouts' view of the principle I take it is not stated in any official manual, either the handbook for boys that the Scouts get, or a troop leader's manual, is that right?

MR. DAVIDSON: Well, in Mr. Dale's 1972 Scout master's handbook there is a reference in dealing with incidence of sexual activity that might occur in a troop that speaks disapprovingly of homosexual conduct, but there's not a —

QUESTION: But that's —

MR. DAVIDSON: — formal policy statement in the troop — in either of those, of the publications, nor is there anything about adultery or any other — or a number of other —

QUESTION: And I —

QUESTION: But —

QUESTION: — I take it you've just touched on something that I think — again, I think I understand your position, but I want to be clear. I understand that the Scouts' position on this does not in any way depend on a judgment that Mr. Dale is — presents or would present an undue risk of homosexual conduct with the Scouts in his troop, is that correct? It's not a fear of conduct?

At times, the lawyer presenting the case hardly has a chance to get a word in edgewise. And when the 30 minutes allotted to that side's argument are up, they're up: A red light on the lawyer's lecture turns on, and if that isn't enough to stop the argument, the chief justice will simply interrupt the lawyer — sometimes in midsentence. Chief Justice Charles Evans Hughes once put a stop to oral argument just as a lawyer was saying, "If . . . ."

Lawyers didn't always have to worry about time. In the early days of the Court, there were no times limits. Oral argument sometimes went on for days. In the late nineteenth century, the Court developed a novel way of coping with boredom. If what the lawyers had to say was not particularly pertinent to the case and interfered with the Court's lunchtime, the justices would simply retreat behind a curtain in back of the high bench and proceed with their meal. The oral argument went on without them. Others in the courtroom heard both the speaker and the sounds of the justices enjoying their meal.

Sometimes oral argument resembled nothing so much as the kinds of impassioned jury summations you see on television. The famous lawyer and orator Daniel Webster concluded his argument in *Dartmouth College v. Woodward*

(1819), a case about the state's ability to change the college's charter, with these words: "It is a small college . . . and yet there are those who love it." Not a dry eye was left in the house.

Modern rules and customs surrounding oral argument tend to cut through any such attempt at manipulation. Although rules prevent the lawyers from reading their speeches from a written text, abrupt and frequent interruptions of an intricate argument can unnerve even the most seasoned advocates. And many of the justices have been renowned for their impatience — even rudeness — to advocates who took their time getting to the point or who tried to evade a direct question from the bench.

Still, pointed questioning is a valuable part of the exercise, serving to point up those aspects of a party's case that need shoring up or further elaboration. An advocate who is quick on his or her feet sees the justices' questions as an opportunity to drive home important points. A lawyer who is less agile can entirely drop the ball under this pressure. It is a truism that while cases are seldom won in oral argument, they are frequently lost there. No matter how sound the case and how good the briefing, if the questions put to a party's lawyer in open court go unanswered, this failure can sabotage the whole effort.

It bears saying that not every case granted review gets its day in court. Sometimes the justices simply reverse the decision of a lower court without entertaining oral argument. Appellants in these cases are the lucky few. And sometimes, when events conspire against a particularly important issue being properly aired, the justices request a second, even a third, hearing. In the case *Brown v. Board of Education* (1954) (see Chapter 12), when the justices could not agree or disagree about how to implement school desegregation, they requested reargument, and they put it off for a year. The parties had to prepare new briefs in the meanwhile, but the main event of this interval was the death of Chief Justice Fred Vinson. He was succeeded by Earl Warren, a liberal chief justice who saw *Brown* as his first important test. Because of his assumption of Vinson's seat — and the persuasive power he brought to bear on the other justices — Warren was able to unite the entire Court. A unanimous opinion in favor of the appellants was their and their lawyer's reward for a year devoted to briefing, waiting, and making another long climb up the Supreme Court steps.

Decisions, Decisions: The Judicial Conference

Justices require the secrecy and security of the conference room to decide which cases they will decide (see Chapter 2). Retreating to the judicial conference to review a case after oral argument is even more essential. In the early years, the justices used to meet to discuss cases in one of the D.C.

boardinghouses where they lived during the Court term. And even after they had a proper conference room, they were only alerted to the need for secrecy by premature disclosure of the outcome of a case. Suspicion initially fell on a couple of gofers who attended the justices during their conferences, but the page boys were cleared after a lawyer confessed that he had merely made an educated guess about their impending decision. Nonetheless, ever since this false alarm was sounded, the justices have held their conferences in solitude.

Cases for which oral argument has been heard are discussed at both of the Court's weekly conferences. Four cases are usually heard during the Monday session of court and are then discussed at the Wednesday afternoon judicial conference. The eight cases heard on Tuesday and Wednesday are customarily discussed during the Friday conference.

Having a say

As with cert petitions, the chief justice takes the lead by introducing each case to be discussed and having his say before turning to the most senior associate. Discussion proceeds in descending order of seniority. Theoretically, there is no limit to how much time each justice can take up having his or her say. However, during the tenure of the autocratic Chief Justice Charles Evans Hughes (1930-1941), justices were encouraged to speed things up in light of the Court's increasing workload.

Similarly, justices are not supposed to interrupt each other during this formal discussion. No one really knows what goes on during the judicial conference, but occasional hints of discord are heard, indicating that the atmosphere of the conference is not always cordial. During the tenure of Chief Justice Melville W. Fuller (1888-1910), Justice Oliver Wendell Holmes is said to have interrupted Justice John Marshall Harlan by exclaiming, "That won't wash! That won't wash!" Fuller, ever the diplomat, smoothed things over with a little humor, saying, "But I just keep scrubbing away, scrubbing away."

In the past, after the most junior justice had finished what he had to say, the chief justice would call for a vote. The justices would then vote in reverse order of seniority, with the newest member voting first, owing to the theory that he or she might feel intimidated or pressured by more senior members. Now, appearances indicate that there usually is no need for a formal vote after the discussion, as the justices have already indicated which way they will vote. The chief justice then announces his tally and moves on to the next case.

Not every justice participates in every case. Sometimes, even justices get sick. They may also *recuse* themselves, not hearing a case or at least not participating in its decision because of some conflict of interest. In order for a case to be decided, however, a majority vote of those participating must be reached. (Supreme Court rules stipulate that six justices constitute a quorum, the minimum number to conduct business.) If a majority isn't reached, or if some of the justices remain undecided, the case can be ordered to be reargued. (See the section "Oral Argument: Not really a back-and-forth" earlier in this chapter.)

Writing the majority opinion

Once a decision is reached, responsibility for writing the all-important majority opinion is assigned. If the chief justice is in the majority, it is his responsibility to write the opinion or give the assignment to another member of the majority. If the chief is in the minority, the most senior member in the majority makes the assignment.

Needless to say, assignments in important cases are political decisions. The assignor's first responsibility is to make sure that the work of opinion writing is evenly distributed among the justices. That's not always the way it works, though. Warren Burger was criticized for taking advantage of his position as chief justice by assigning himself important decisions such as the Nixon tapes case *U.S. v. Nixon* (see Chapter 4) in an effort to inflate his reputation.

Sometimes it seems like opinions no one wants to touch are foisted off on the most junior justice. Harry Blackmun had served on the Court for only a year and half when he was assigned the job of writing the majority opinion for the most controversial Supreme Court case in recent times, the abortion rights case *Roe v. Wade* (1973). Nobody seemed to like his first draft, so the case was reargued ten months after the parties made their first appearance in Court. Blackmun's second opinion was endorsed by the majority, but three of the six who voted with him wrote separate concurring opinions (see "Concurring," later in this chapter).

The wait can be excruciating

Months can pass between the time a case is heard and a decision is rendered. During this period, when votes may be in flux, the secrecy surrounding Court deliberations is especially crucial. In 1979, the media publicized the gist of two opinions, together with the names of their authors, several days before the decisions were due to be announced. A typesetter attached to the Court was apparently the source of these leaks, as well as the dishy tidbit that the justices were overheard shouting at one another in the Court's conference room. If these disclosures had been inaccurate or had occurred earlier in the process — say, before the draft opinions were printed — they could have been devastatingly misleading to the parties and the nation. Following an investigation ordered by Chief Justice Warren Burger, the typesetter was fired. The Court, of course, declined to comment.

Votes can shift between the time of the conference's initial tally and the official announcement of the Court's opinion. A justice who voted with the majority but seems less than steadfast in his commitment may be given the job of writing the Court's opinion. Theoretically, the exercise of working through the logic of the decision strengthens the writer's commitment to it. Another way of strengthening a fragile coalition is to assign the majority opinion to an opinion maker capable of persuading others to see things from his or her perspective. This logic may help to explain why William J. Brennan, whom Earl Warren called his right-hand man, wrote so many of the Warren Court's majority opinions. Not only were the two men close personally, Brennan's ability to make his brethren see things his — and the chief's — way assumed the status of legend.

Majority opinions need to be especially persuasive when the initial vote is not unanimous. Any justice may write his or her own opinion, and when drafts of the various opinions circulate among all the justices, some who originally voted with the majority might find a dissenting opinion (see "Dissenting," later in this chapter) more convincing or choose to write their own concurrence. A multiplicity of opinions — even when some concur — can serve to weaken the authority of majority's analysis.

In recent years, there has been much speculation about who actually writes the Court's opinions. William O. Douglas apparently seldom sought his law clerks' input when writing opinions. He appears to have been an exception, however. There is general approval of the practice of using a law clerk to research the law and provide analyses useful to the opinion writer. But the suspected use of clerks as ghostwriters is highly controversial. While the justices are clearly responsible for approving final drafts of the opinions that bear their signature, some are rumored to have written those drafts with their hands in their pockets. Many Court critics are alarmed by the prospect of law being made by newly minted lawyers, no matter how smart they are.

It bears remembering that a ruling of the Court on a constitutional matter is final, for all intents and purposes. There are only two ways of effecting a reversal: Congress can undertake the rare and unwieldy process of amending the Constitution, or — almost as rare — the Supreme Court can reverse itself in a ruling on some subsequent case. (The justices *hate* doing that.)

Making the Decision Known

Once the justices have finalized their opinions, they need to let the parties and the public know what they've concluded. After the justices agree to a final draft of the Court's opinion — or to separate opinions, if individual justices choose to write them — the draft is proofread by the office of the reporter of decisions (see Chapter 16). At this stage, a *syllabuse* summarizing the case is added, as is a *lineup* showing how the individual justices voted. Great care is taken to see that no copies of the opinions are prematurely released. In addition — believe it or not — the opinions are not yet "official" ones sanctioned by the Court. It may be years before the public sees the true end product of a case heard in the Supreme Court of the United States.

Oral summaries

Opinions of cases that have been fully adjudicated and decided (approximately 100 every year) are first delivered orally in open court. Prior to 1965, they were usually announced on Mondays. Since then, they have typically been announced on Tuesdays and Wednesdays, as well as on the third Monday of each month when Court is in session. The bulk of the Court's decisions are handed down in May and June, when the justices take the high bench only to announce orders and opinions.

Until 1930, the justices typically read their opinions aloud in their entirety. This exercise was time-consuming. When the Court delivered its opinions in the critical *Dred Scott (Scott v. Sandford)* case (1857) declaring African-Americans noncitizens and overturning the Missouri Compromise (see Chapter 11), it took two whole days for the justices to read through seven separate opinions. After he became chief justice in 1930, the able administrator Charles Evans Hughes put a stop to this waste of time by pressuring the justices merely to summarize their opinions from the bench.

The Court follows this practice today, with the author of the majority opinion delivering a summary and the authors of any dissenting opinions summarizing their views. Discrepancies between these summaries and the written opinions can crop up. The famously irascible James C. McReynolds, who served from 1914 to 1941, once got so carried away while delivering his dissent in open court that he exclaimed, "The Constitution is gone.'" Of course, remarks like this one have no real authority and bear no relationship to the official written opinions.

Written reports

The Constitution doesn't require the justices to write out their decisions. In fact, before 1801, the announcement from the bench was ordinarily the only publication of a Court decision. Only the most significant decisions were also reduced to writing. *Chisholm v. Georgia* (1793), which granted the citizen of one state the right to sue another state, was the first decision — and one of the only ones delivered during the Court's first decade — to be written down. (*Chisholm* was so important that it prompted Congress to adopt the Eleventh Amendment to overturn this decision.)

Today, the Court issues initial *bench opinions* at the same time it delivers summaries from the bench. Only a couple hundred of these are made available to the lawyers and transcription service representatives in the courtroom and to journalists and other interested parties in the Court's public information office (see Chapter 16). Four thousand copies of the still unofficial opinions are distributed within the next three days to the media and the public. Called *slip opinions,* these publications were originally nothing more than page proofs once handed out to a select few by private printing services or individual justices. During the 1920s, slip opinions came to be distributed as a matter of course as aids to the media. Slip opinions include headnotes meant to help journalists interpret the decisions. They also include a disclaimer regarding the legal authority of the headnotes, as well as an invitation for corrections to the opinion.

Within a few months, edited but still preliminary versions of opinions still bearing a legend requesting corrections appear in the series *United States Reports. United States Reports* is also the official *reporter* of Supreme Court decisions. But the Court's written opinions total somewhere in the neighborhood of 5,000 pages each year. The sheer volume of the material means that it can take years for the official versions of opinions to find their way into print in chronologically organized bound volumes printed by the U.S. Government Printing Office.

In the meantime, the Court's opinions are published in a variety of other venues. Annotated texts are available from two commercial series, West Publishing Company's *Supreme Court Reporter* and the Lawyer's Co-Operative Publishing Company's *United States Supreme Court Reports, Lawyer's Edition. United States Law Week,* a periodical published by the Bureau of National Affairs publishes full texts of the Court's opinions within days of their announcement. Even faster access is available from online sources such as WESTLAW, LEXIS, and FindLaw (see Chapter 13).

Interpreting the Opinions

During the Court's first decade, the 1790s, multiple opinions were the norm. Each of the justices delivered his own *seriatim* opinion, in inverse order of seniority. But when John Marshall (see Chapter 5) took charge as chief justice in 1801, he determined that one of the best ways for the Court to shore up its authority was to speak with one voice. Under Marshall, a single opinion, called the *opinion of the Court,* came to be the norm — and Marshall wrote many of these himself. In the last decade of Marshall's 35-year tenure, however, the Court's united front was frequently broken by concurrences and dissents. Much of the time, they were written by one justice, William Johnson (see Chapter 6).

Still, the Court largely adhered to the tradition of a single opinion for the next century. Since then, opinions concurring with and dissenting from the majority opinion have proliferated. Unanimity is now rare. Frequently, even when the justices agree on a particular outcome, they cannot agree on an opinion. The result can be a plurality opinion, which is endorsed by less than a majority of the justices. As if it weren't hard enough already to interpret what the Court is saying, contemporary opinions are frequently further fractured by hybrid *concurring in part* and *dissenting in part* or, worse yet, *concurring in part and dissenting in part* opinions. Many commentators feel that such elaborate hair-splitting is the inevitable result of handing opinion writing responsibility to law clerks, fresh from the academic exercises of moot court and law review. Most commentators feel that a return to what amounts to *seriatim* opinions seriously undermines the Court's authority with the American people, few of whom can begin to comprehend those now rare unanimous, single Court decisions. Just what do all these opinions mean anyway?

Dissenting

Dissent in the Supreme Court has a long and honored history. Some dissenting opinions — those of "The Great Dissenter," Oliver Wendell Holmes, come to mind (see Chapter 6) — are so persuasive that over time they come to be more highly regarded than the majority opinions they criticized. In part, these dissents owe their memorable qualities to the simple fact that dissenters need not worry about appeasing other justices. They are writing to express their own view, which is often passionately felt, well reasoned, and untouched by compromise. And often dissenters write with an eye towards the future, calling upon universal values and eternal truths that the majority opinion has no time to dwell upon.

Perhaps no one has summed up the spirit of dissent more eloquently that Chief Justice Charles Evans Hughes, who wrote, "A dissent in a court of last resort is an appeal to the brooding spirit of the law, to the intelligence of a future day, when a later decision may possibly correct the error into which the dissenting judge believes the court to have been betrayed." John Marshall Harlan's lone dissent in *Plessy v. Ferguson* (see Chapter 6), the 1896 case that made racial segregation the law of the land, is one of the most vivid illustrations of the truth of Hughes's comment.

Towards the end of the twentieth century, dissent became more common than not. Chief Justice William Rehnquist attributes the rising tide of dissent to the increasing number of cases that come before the Court because they raise a constitutional issue. As the ultimate arbiters of constitutionality, justices are more or less obliged to see such issues from all sides. Justice William J. Brennan went so far to defend dissent as a judicial duty. For him, the motivation was conscience, not egotism.

Still, critics of the Court have come to see dissent as an exercise in pettiness. Issues once considered too minor to merit separate opinions were taken up with gusto for reasons often hard to fathom. Worse, they seemed at times to be the expression of knee-jerk ideological reactions. For many, they amounted to little other than public bickering. In the understated words of the gentlemanly Justice Lewis F. Powell, a dissenting opinion is not "a model of temperate discourse."

Concurring

Even more than dissents, concurring opinions can seem to be expressions of personal opinion. Concurring opinions are those written by justices who agree with the outcome of a case but disagree with the majority's reasons for reaching that decision. During the early days of the Court, dissents often masqueraded as concurrences. In recent times, justices feel free to dissent and equally free to point out what they see as the flaws in the reasoning employed to reach a result with which they agree. Justice Sandra Day O'Connor, for example, regularly writes concurring opinions to point out alternative legal grounds for reaching decisions.

As critics see it, a multiplicity of concurring opinions robs a decision of its value as legal *precedent* upon which future laws can be based. Justices who write these sorts of opinions are often seated astride hobbyhorses that get them and the Court nowhere. Such opinions are not opinions of the Court, so they rarely serve as any sort of precedent for subsequent cases.

Felix Frankfurter, who served on the Court from 1939 to 1962, wrote more concurring opinions than any other justice during that period. Frankfurter, a former Harvard Law School professor renowned for his brilliance, labored long and hard over his opinions, sometimes writing as many as 30 drafts before he was satisfied. All that work netted him little. John P. Frank studied the separate opinions Frankfurter wrote and found that few of them were ever cited by anyone in subsequent cases. In his 1958 book *Marble Palace: The Supreme Court in American Life* (Knopf), Frank arrived at this damning conclusion: Frankfurter "consumed a large portion of his energy and talent in essays which, for all practical purposes, might as well have been written on paper airplanes and thrown out a Supreme Court window."

Dissenting in part and concurring in part

This hybrid type of opinion has a mirror image: concurring in part and dissenting in part.

✔ When a justice dissents in part and concurs in part, he or she is typically saying that although the majority's decision is wrong, at least part of its reasoning is dead on and should have led to the opposite result.

✔ When a justice concurs in part and dissents in part, he or she endorses the outcome of the case, but can only support some part of the logic that led to that outcome.

Sometimes the impulse to express an individual opinion results in the complete absence of a majority opinion. Sometimes it makes for a maddening cacophony of voices. Exhibit A: *United States v. United Mine* Workers (1947). In 1946, President Harry S. Truman stopped a union strike and seized control of the nation's coal mines, citing the necessity of continued coal production in the aftermath of World War II. When the United Mine Workers took their case all the way to the Supreme Court, the justices rejected the union's case by a vote of 7-2.

The decision proved popular with the American public — but not because they could understand what the justices had to say about it. Chief Justice Fred Vinson voted with Justices Stanley F. Reed and Harold H. Burton against the union for two cited reasons. Justices Wiley B. Rutledge and Frank Murphy both dissented on the same grounds. Justices Felix Frankfurter and Robert H. Jackson agreed with one of Vinson, Reed, and Burton's reasons, but not the other. Justices Hugo L. Black and William O. Douglas concurred with Vinson & Co. for the same reason Frankfurter and Jackson dissented, but Black and Douglas did not agree with reasoning Frankfurter accepted.

In case you couldn't follow that summary of *U.S. v. United Mine Workers*, let me put it this way: Five of the justices voted with the majority for one reason, five voted with the majority for another reason, and four didn't really support either reason. Can't do the math? They say the vote was 7-2 in favor of the government. I think we'll just have to take their word for it.

Per curiam opinions that nobody wants to sign

Per curiam is Latin for "by the court." Per curiam opinions reflect the view of the whole Court or at least a majority of the justices. This type of opinion is anonymous. Originally, this type of opinion was used only in cases that were disposed of summarily — that is, given short shrift. Usually, such cases involve uncomplicated matters.

The Court has also, however, used per curiam decisions when they have been deeply divided over hot button issues. In *New York Times Co. v. United*

States (1971), the Court rejected the government's request to ban publication of the "Pentagon papers," confidential documents concerning the Vietnam War. The case was heard by the Court on an expedited basis, and what some justices saw as a rush to judgment made them balky. Others balked at the notion of the government violating the First Amendment prohibition on *prior restraint,* government press censorship. (see Chapter 8.) In *Furman v. Georgia* (1972), the issue was the death penalty, which some justices felt to be unconstitutional cruel and inhuman punishment and others thought was states' business. *Buckley v. Valeo* (1976) concerned rules governing campaign contributions. The politicians are still trying to figure out that opinion.

It's Not Over 'til It's Over: Sending the Case Back

Sometimes the Court gives a case the full treatment — briefing, oral argument, written opinion — only to remand it, or send it back to the lower court from whence it came. Remanding happens most often when the lower court's judgment is reversed, and the justices send the case back for a new trial to be carried out in a manner consistent with the principles announced in the Court's opinion.

McKennon v. Nashville Banner Publishing Co. (1995), for example, was remanded to the court of appeals for further consideration after the Court ruled that the appellee newspaper had tried to find a loophole in the Age Discrimination in Employment Act. The paper claimed that a 62-year-old employee's misconduct, discovered after her termination, would have resulted in her termination if they had not already fired her. The federal appellate court agreed with the employer that there was therefore no violation of federal law and granted summary judgment in the newspaper's favor. The justices plainly thought there was still a legal issue to be settled there. And as you see, the Supreme Court is not a trial court — in some cases, it isn't even the court of last resort.

Part II
Judging the Justices

From the very beginning, Wilbur Prescott's nomination to the Supreme Court was suspect due to Prescott's liberal use of the double-finger quotation mark while taking various oaths of office.

In this part . . .

Who *are* those people sitting up on that high bench deciding the destinies of millions? One wag — using a bit of gallows humor — referred to them as the "Nine Old Men." While this description may have been true in that moment, every part of it has been wrong at some point in the history of the Supreme Court. There haven't always been nine justices, they haven't always been old, and they haven't always been men. But there is one thing they have *all* had in common, always: All the justices have been politicians.

In these chapters, you see just how these people get to the top of the heap. But just because they get there doesn't mean they stay there. Much can go wrong during the confirmation process . . . and after. As you can see in this part, even chief justices have been responsible for major mistakes. But for the most part, the winnowing process works pretty well. Many of the people who have occupied that bench have performed nobly and well, leaving their mark on history and leaving the Court — and the country — a better place for their service. This part is your chance to meet some of the good, the bad, and the mediocre.

Chapter 4

Make No Mistake, These Justices Are Politicians: The Confirmation Contest

● ●

In This Chapter

▶ Understanding how Supreme Court justices are chosen

▶ Demystifying the job requirements

▶ Looking at the confirmation process

▶ Examining some problem candidates

▶ Comparing confirmations of associate and chief justices

● ●

Supreme Court justiceships are lifetime appointments. Is it any wonder that the process of nominating and confirming these powerful people can be hard-fought, even theatrical? In this chapter, I walk you through the process of selecting and confirming Supreme Court justices and examine the political and professional considerations involved. Then I look closely at some candidates who survived and some who didn't.

The Selection Process: A Mixed Bag

The Constitution offers precious little guidance about selecting a Supreme Court nominee. Like so many other aspects of the law, High Court appointments are largely a matter of precedent and tradition. Still, the consequences of putting someone on the bench of an institution that is free to *make* laws without having to answer to an electorate — or even to the president responsible for putting that person on the Court — are enormous. It's the politics of the appointment process that make it the most intricate, most closely watched chess game around.

Justices without a legal education?

Theoretically, it is possible for nonlawyers to become Supreme Court justices, although this possibility has never happened. The Founding Fathers may simply not have thought to mention legal education as a prerequisite for the job. When they drafted the Constitution, there were — not surprisingly — no law schools in the new nation. The first American law school was established by Tapping Reeve in Litchfield, Connecticut, in 1784. However, for decades after the foundation of the republic, lawyers became lawyers by "reading law" — that is, apprenticing themselves to practicing lawyers. It is still possible to be admitted to some state bars without having graduated from law school.

Constitutional requirements

Article II of the Constitution — a notably terse document — has this to say about how Supreme Court nominees are chosen:

> [The President] shall nominate, and by and with the Advice and Consent of the Senate, shall appoint . . . Judges of the Supreme Court.

That's it for the nomination process. Article III, which governs the judicial branch of the federal government, is mum about who might qualify to sit on the court that has the final say about the parameters of the nation's life.

Presidential prerogatives

You might think that the president has a relatively free hand in choosing the individuals he wishes to chart the country's course into the future — and to a certain extent, you would be right. However, this premise has a fundamental problem. Although the president retains his appointment power, the Senate has the offsetting power of "advice and consent." The drafters of the Constitution hotly debated the judicial selection issue. As a compromise between the Federalists' desire for a strong executive branch and the Anti-Federalists' concern that the president not become an autocrat, they gave the final word on such appointments to the people's representatives in the Senate. And, as always, the drafters of the provision wrote with remarkable economy. As a result, the Constitution has had both elasticity and longevity, insuring that the process of appointing a Supreme Court justice would not be a cake walk.

Before the president can even bring his (or, someday, her) nominee before the Senate, however, he has other obstacles to overcome. Although presidents can, and often do, simply pick their friends or name individuals to whom they owe political favors, they are also obliged to consider factors such as geographical balance. In the twentieth century, considerations of religion, race, and gender all add to the mix of conflicting interests that have to be served.

The Politics of Interest Groups

In choosing a Supreme Court nominee, the president receives suggestions, both solicited and unsolicited, from a number of parties, each with a vested interest in the outcome. In addition to the list of potential candidates kept by the White House staff, the Justice Department often feels free to put in an oar. Sometimes these two factions within the Administration do not pull in the same direction: When Ronald Reagan's nomination of Robert Bork went badly awry (as you see later in this chapter), his White House staff wanted to smooth the waters by replacing Bork with a more politically moderate candidate, while Justice continued to hew to a hard conservative line.

Countless interest groups outside the Administration also bring pressure to bear on the selection process. These groups can, like film studios vying for Oscar nominations, promote their own candidates and lobby hard for them. Or they can, as in the case of the ill-fated Robert Bork, work just as hard to derail a candidate. For example, the American Civil Liberties Union (ACLU), the National Association for the Advancement of Colored People (NAACP), the National Organization for Women (NOW), the AFL-CIO labor organization, the public advocacy group Common Cause, and the conservation organization Sierra Club all actively opposed the Bork nomination. Presidents are obliged to pay some of these groups considerable attention, as evidenced by so-called *assigned seats* on the high bench, discussed in the following sections. Although these seats are not simply a matter of quid-pro-quo ("I'll give you something, if you give me something else in return"), the fact that they exist demonstrates that presidents are concerned about at least appearing to maintain balance on the Court. These seats are a reminder that the Supreme Court is a significant part of any given president's legacy to the nation — that is, for those presidents lucky enough to be able to make an appointment or two.

The Roman Catholic seat

With the exception of the brief interval from 1949 to 1956 (caused by the death of sitting Catholic justice Frank Murphy, who was replaced by the Protestant Tom Clark),at least one Roman Catholic has occupied a seat on the Court since 1894.

Edward Douglass White was the first Catholic to sit on the Court, but the circumstances of his appointment were so fraught with other conflicts that his religion was little discussed at the time. What mattered most about White's appointment was not his Catholicism, but his status as a southerner and a U.S. senator. He was Grover Cleveland's third nominee for a seat left vacant by the death of Samuel Blatchford in 1893. Cleveland's two earlier attempts to appoint fellow New Yorkers ran afoul of New York Senator David Hill's eternal hatred of the president. White was just the ticket: A former Confederate and a sitting senator, he was irresistible to the Senate (as Cleveland rightly calculated), which could hardly refuse to confirm one of its own. White's presence on the Supreme Court was thought to promote cohesion of the still divided nation. White's Catholicism didn't even enter the picture — not in 1894 or in 1910, when he was tapped as chief justice.

Because of White's successful career on the Court, Catholicism became more or less a non-issue. The same cannot be said of the Court's Jewish seat.

The Jewish seat

The first Jew to occupy a seat on the Court was Louis Brandeis. Woodrow Wilson nominated Brandeis in 1916 in return for his crafting of the campaign platform that helped Wilson win the 1912 election.

Brandeis as a legal force in the country was hard to ignore. He was not only one of the most successful lawyers of his day, he was also one of the most innovative, helping to "invent" the right of privacy (see Chapter 8) as well as the *Brandeis brief* (see Chapter 6), which uses more social policy than law to argue its case. Still, his appointment proved highly controversial, and the battle to confirm him lasted four months. Brandeis was a progressive, and for many who opposed him, his liberal politics could not be separated from his religion. The forces arrayed against him were legion: The American Bar Association took the unprecedented step of opposing a Court candidate. Former president William Howard Taft, who had his own axe to grind against Brandeis, went so far as to put his feelings in writing, stating categorically that "Mr. Louis D. Brandeis . . . is not a fit person to be a member of the Supreme Court." Brandeis proved them all wrong, going on to be one of the most heralded justices in Supreme Court History.

Benjamin Cardozo was the next Jew nominated to the Court. When his name was first raised in 1932 as a possible candidate, one of the arguments against him was that Cardozo would be the third New Yorker on the Court, and his presence there would unbalance the bench. And while it was true that both Chief Justice Charles Evans Hughes and Associate Justice (and future Chief Justice) Harlan F. Stone hailed from the Empire State, many Court watchers suspected that Cardozo might be unwelcome because Brandeis already occupied the *Jewish seat.* In the end, after Stone made the gesture of offering to resign so that one of country's most accomplished jurists could assume his rightful place on the high bench, President Herbert Hoover — finally grasping Cardozo's legal stature — surrendered to the inevitable. As one Court scholar has wryly observed, "One of the few positive things for which President Hoover is remembered is his appointment of Cardozo . . . ."

Cardozo had large shoes to fill, since he was replacing the eminent Oliver Wendell Holmes, who had retired after nearly 30 years on the High Court. Cardozo proved himself a worthy successor, and after he died in 1938, his seat was filled by a succession of Jewish justices: Felix Frankfurter, Arthur Goldberg, and Abe Fortas. All three had their share of problems, but none seemed to encounter the anti-Semitism that was an initial impediment to their Jewish predecessors. After Fortas was forced to resign under a cloud of scandal in 1969, however, it would be nearly a quarter century before another Jew sat on the Supreme Court — and she was a woman. (See the upcoming section "Women justices.")

The African-American seat

An *African-American seat* was effectively created in 1967. President Lyndon Johnson, declaring that it was "the right thing to do, the right time to do it, the right man and the right place," nominated Thurgood Marshall to serve on the Supreme Court. Marshall, for 20 years the head of the NAACP and the lead counsel in the 1954 landmark *Brown v. Board of Education* school desegregation case, had gone on to serve as a federal judge. At the time of his nomination to the High Court, he was serving as the first African-American solicitor general. Marshall's initial appointment to the federal bench in 1961 had been hard won; by the time he was confirmed, he had already served 11 months while a hostile group of southern senators fought his appointment. Confirmation as solicitor general took half that time. But despite his sterling credentials, Marshall as jurist was once again opposed by a southern contingent, who subjected him to prolonged grilling. In the end, the confirmation vote was 69-11.

Marshall joined the Court in the waning days of the liberal reign of Chief Justice Earl Warren. When Warren was replaced in 1969 by the more conservative Warren Burger, the change signified a turn to the right that grew more pronounced over the years. Marshall increasingly found himself a dissenter on the Court. He had hoped to serve long enough to see his successor appointed by a Democratic president, but in 1991, weighed down by ill health and exhaustion, Marshall retired. His replacement, the heir to the African-American seat, was the very conservative, highly controversial Clarence Thomas.

Women justices

When Ronald Reagan nominated Sandra Day O'Connor to the High Court in 1981, he was fulfilling a campaign promise to appoint the first female

Supreme Court justice. He was also appointing the only member of the Burger Court to have served in all three branches of government. When O'Connor graduated third in her class from Stanford University Law School in 1952, the only job she was offered in private practice was as a legal secretary. Consequently, she began her career as a deputy county prosecutor in her native Arizona. After taking time off to raise two children, she went back to work for the state of Arizona, first as an assistant state attorney general and then as a state senator. And in 1974, when she was elected to the bench of the Maricopa County Superior Court, she began her work in the third branch — work that culminated in her precedent-setting appointment to the highest court in the land.

The introduction of a woman's perspective to what used to be known as the Court of Nine Old Men has changed more than the standard signature line on a written opinion from "Mr. Justice _____" to simply "Justice _____." (Actually, this custom was changed in 1980 with the knowledge that it was only a matter of time before women would arrive.) O'Connor, who is politically conservative with regard to most issues, is less so when it comes to matters of gender discrimination. On the hot button issue of abortion, she has often served as a swing vote whose opinion helps to determine the outcome of the case. Although she has certainly helped to restrict access to abortion, it can equally be said that she has helped to keep *Roe v. Wade* alive. After a bout with breast cancer in 1988 (during which she did not miss a day in court), many believed she would retire. Instead, she has stayed on, and as speculation grows about the retirement of the ailing William Rehnquist, many Court watchers consider O'Connor a strong candidate to replace him as chief justice.

Ruth Bader Ginsburg, who joined O'Connor on the high bench in 1993, made her name as a crusader against gender discrimination and was referred to as "the Thurgood Marshall of gender-equality law." On the Court, Ginsburg has maintained a fairly low profile, exchanging her activism for a more restrained approach to the law. Criticized for her tepid support of *Roe v. Wade*, she has also received high marks for her efforts to promote collegiality among the group sometimes still referred to as "the Brethren."

Political Affiliation and Policy Considerations

Well over 90 percent of Supreme Court nominees have the same party affiliation as the presidents who appoint them. Sometimes, the nominees are close personal friends of the president. Harry Truman appointed four of his pals to the Court: Harold Burton, Sherman Minton, Fred Vinson, and Tom Clark.

Sometimes presidents repay political debts with Court appointments, as John F. Kennedy did in naming his campaign aide Byron White as a candidate for associate justice. Sometimes presidents name their top advisors to the High Court and continue to call on them for counsel after these advisors have moved on — as Franklin D. Roosevelt did with Felix Frankfurter and Lyndon Johnson did with Abe Fortas. Such relationships are at best questionable and at worst unconstitutional, given the necessity of keeping the executive and judicial branches of government separate.

It is a truism, however, that once justices are confirmed and do not have to answer to any master, they cannot be controlled. Often they disappoint their presidents, as the staunch Republican-turned-liberal Earl Warren disappointed Dwight Eisenhower. Richard Nixon, a president with a decided control problem, tried to reinforce his law-and-order domestic agenda by appointing *strict constructionists,* those fundamentalists of the Constitution. Warren Burger appeared to fit the bill, but the Court he oversaw continued and even enlarged on the liberal reforms written into the law by the Warren Court. And Harry Blackmun was a real disappointment to Nixon and other conservatives. The man they thought of as a low-profile "stealth candidate" who quietly shared their agenda was transformed on the high bench into the author of *Roe v. Wade*.

To prevent such embarrassments, presidents have increasingly politicized the appointment process. During the hotly contested presidential campaign of 2000, George W. Bush declared that if he were elected, he intended to nominate candidates like Antonin Scalia and Clarence Thomas, arguably the most conservative members of the highly conservative Rehnquist Court. This declaration was also a covert way of assuring his supporters that Bush as president intended to do away with two of the knottiest legal problems that haunted the administrations of conservative predecessors: legal abortion and affirmative action.

A coded construction

Strict construction is coded language for a conservative — and in particular law-and-order — approach to the Constitution. The term, which implies a back-to-basics interpretation of the law, became part of the political lexicon during the era of the Warren Court (1953-1969) as American society underwent a civil and personal rights sea change many blamed on rulings handed down by the liberal Warren Court. Earl Warren, as well as other justices serving on the Court at the time, were repeatedly threatened with impeachment. None of these threats materialized, but beginning with Richard Nixon in 1969, Republican presidents have sought to undo liberal reforms set in place by the Warren Court. Their primary tactic is been to appoint strict constructionists to the Court, and they have largely succeeded in their efforts. Nixon's appointment of Warren Burger was only marginally helpful, but the results of his selection of William Rehnquist in 1972 have probably exceeded Nixon's wildest expectations.

The abortion litmus test

For nearly three decades, much of America (or at least most of America's elected representatives) has been caught up in a debate about the legality of abortion on demand. In reaction to the 1973 *Roe v. Wade* decision, activists on the right formed a *Right to Life* movement, while those on the left responded with a *Right to Choose* movement. Politicians have felt obliged to declare their allegiance to one side or the other, and these declarations have been known to make or break a candidate's bid for office.

As the Supreme Court selection and confirmation process has become more politicized, potential justices, too, have been subjected to a kind of litmus test concerning their stance on *Roe*. Good lawyers that they are, most nominees manage to formulate a response that alienates neither left nor right, neither liberals nor conservatives. Some, however, are less effective. Even when pressed repeatedly by members of the Senate Judiciary Committee, Clarence Thomas declared that he had no opinion about abortion. Many observers found this declaration hard to believe — but most of them were not voting members of the U.S. Senate.

The affirmative action litmus test

Affirmative action refers to government policies that, directly or indirectly, seek to provide employment, educational and business opportunities to historically disadvantaged groups such as racial minorities and women. The directness with which these opportunities are provided has decreased in recent years.

Like legal abortion, affirmative action is a legacy of the Warren Court and the social upheaval of the 1960s. Unlike abortion, which can clearly be linked with a single Supreme Court case, affirmative action has no one legal flashpoint. That said, it is clear that much of the confusion surrounding the issue stems from the 1978 *Regents of the University of California v. Bakke* case, in which the Court refused to speak with one voice. The 5 to 4 decision, delivered in six separate opinions, was effectively two decisions: While it was, on the one hand, illegal for the state to discriminate on the basis of race, on the other hand, it was also legally permissible for the state to develop policies intended to create "diversity" (including racially diversity). *Bakke* settled nothing, and affirmative action, like abortion, divided the country. And like abortion, affirmative action has been steadily undercut as the Court, like the country, has moved to the right. With the decidedly conservative orientation of the Rehnquist Court, the change of a single vote could undo a policy already seriously under siege.

Professional Qualifications

The job of Supreme Court justice has no written requirements. Although all Supreme Court justices have been lawyers, not all have had judicial experience. Some of the most illustrious names in Court history fall into the latter category, including Louis Brandeis, Felix Frankfurter, William O. Douglas and the chief justices John Marshall and Earl Warren. Clearly, time spent warming a bench on another court is not a prerequisite — sometimes it is actually a hindrance to being confirmed. In 1970, when Nixon nominated G. Harrold Carswell, then a federal appellate judge, Carswell was attacked by members of the Senate Judiciary Committee. The Republican senator acting as floor manager for the nomination stuck his foot in his mouth by complaining, "Even if [Carswell] is mediocre, there are a lot of mediocre judges and people and lawyers. They are entitled to a little representation, aren't they, and a little chance? We can't have all Brandeises, Cardozos, and Frankfurters, and stuff like that there." Needless to say, the mediocre Carswell never made it to the Supreme Court.

In 1946, the American Bar Association formed a Standing Committee on the Federal Judiciary that acted as another mechanism for screening the credentials of Supreme Court nominees. The committee normally evaluates the candidates after they are formally nominated. It then presents its findings (ratings include "well qualified," "not opposed," and "not recommended") to the Senate Judiciary Committee prior to confirmation hearings. Some presidents, however, have asked the influential ABA committee for advice prior to actually nominating a candidate. This practice was discontinued in the spring of 2001, when the Bush Administration, displeased by some of the committee's previous rulings and desiring to diminish its power, publicly announced its decision to stop asking this independent, nongovernmental body for its opinion.

The Confirmation Process: Advice and Consent

The president is constitutionally required to seek the Senate's "advice and consent" on nominations to the federal judiciary. At times, the president has needed to make a *recess appointment* when a justice dies or retires while the Senate is not in session, but every appointment must be approved by the Senate before it becomes official. In one notable case, that of the second chief justice, John Rutledge, a recess appointment was rejected: Rutledge was forced out of office after serving only fours months and three days.

A whole new deal

When Franklin Roosevelt was elected to his first term in 1932, the country was mired in the Great Depression. Roosevelt began with a whirlwind of reforms, which he called the *New Deal*. Many of the economic recovery measures initiated during his first *Hundred Days* did not withstand legal challenges and were quickly declared unconstitutional by the Supreme Court. In 1935, Roosevelt introduced a second New Deal, and after winning reelection by a landslide in 1936, he helped ensure acceptance of his new legislation by threatening to change the composition of the Court. Although he did not succeed in *packing* the Court, his reforms succeeded. The rest, of course, is history.

Step One: Senate Judiciary Committee hearings

Before the full Senate votes on a nomination, the candidate is reviewed by the Senate Judiciary Committee, a practice that began in 1868. Although this committee is responsible for evaluating all federal judicial appointments, as a rule only Supreme Court nominees receive the attention of the full committee, which conducts these reviews as hearings.

Prior to 1925, candidates never appeared before the committee. In fact, before 1955, after which such appearances became de rigueur, only three candidates had testified before the committee, either voluntarily or at the committee's request. Since John M. Harlan's testimony in 1955, however, virtually every Supreme Court nominee has made at least a brief statement at some point during the committee's hearings.

The advent of regular — and expected — candidate appearances before the committee brought increased scrutiny of these men's and women's politics and personalities. Even when the committee's questions apparently concern ethical soundness and professional qualifications, such inquiries can be smoke screens for ideological attacks. In recent times — particularly when the Senate and the White House have been in different hands — an attack on a Supreme Court nominee is an attack on a presidential surrogate.

The downfall of Abe Fortas

Abe Fortas, once an important member of Franklin D. Roosevelt's New Deal administration, went on to become a name partner at the powerhouse law firm of Porter, Arnold & Fortas. The firm represented primarily large corporate clients; like other lawyers there, however, Fortas, shown in Figure 4-1, also did extracurricular legal work. In 1948, he rescued Lyndon Johnson's contested victory in the Texas Democratic senatorial primary. As Johnson continued on his path to the White House, he continued to rely heavily on Fortas for legal advice. Johnson, a man who understood that politics consists of a certain amount of asking for and returning favors, tried to make Fortas attorney general. Fortas declined that job. In 1965, after forcing Arthur Goldberg to resign from the Supreme Court, Johnson nominated Fortas as Goldberg's replacement — without first informing Fortas. Fortas, of course, could hardly say no. See Figure 4-2, for an example of the *Johnson treatment*.

Figure 4-1:
Justice
Abc Fortas
(left), talking
with Ted
Kennedy.

© Wally McNamee/CORBIS

Fortas encountered little resistance during his initial confirmation hearings. Over the next three years, he did a credible job as an associate justice on the Warren Court, consistently voting with the liberal bloc of justices that dominated the Court during Earl Warren's tenure as chief justice. He also continued to do extracurricular work for Johnson, still serving as one of the president's most trusted advisors. Then, in 1968, when Warren advised the president of his intention to retire, Johnson nominated Fortas as Warren's replacement.

By this time, Johnson was a lame duck president, having announced his decision not to seek reelection for a second term. Republicans seized this opportunity to humiliate both Johnson and the man whom they looked on as Johnson's crony. Fortas's nomination as chief justice required that he once again go through the Senate Judiciary Committee vetting process. While serving as Senate majority leader, Lyndon Johnson had become an adept vote counter. He now accurately saw that although Republicans did not

control the Senate, they had the ability to recruit enough conservative southern Democrats to filibuster the Fortas nomination. He also thought that by
nominating federal judge and native Texan Homer Thornberry to replace
Fortas as associate justice, he could mollify the southern senators.

Figure 4-2:
President
Lyndon
Johnson
using his
powers of
persuasion
on Abe
Fortas.

Thornberry didn't get the job — he never even had a hearing. In pushing the
Fortas promotion through, Johnson had been counting on the support of his
former Senate mentor, Richard Russell. But Johnson lost Russell when the
administration delayed the nomination of the senator's own candidate for a
Georgia federal judgeship. Johnson had also been counting on Republican
Minority Leader Everett Dirksen's admiration for Fortas's legal brilliance.
This hope also failed to materialize. Fortas made history by becoming the
first sitting Supreme Court justice to testify at his own confirmation hearing,
and the hearings were brutal. Hostile Republicans, joined by equally hostile
(and anti-Semitic) southern Democrats, attacked Fortas's record on the Court
and his confidential relationship with the administration, which they said
threatened to undermine the separation of powers. The hearings unearthed
other improper relationships, as well as evidence of Fortas's greed: He had
accepted a stipend equal to 40 percent of his judicial salary — funded by
Fortas's friends and former clients — in exchange for teaching a summer
course at American University.

The committee ultimately recommended confirmation, but once Fortas's nomination reached the Senate floor, it sparked the first filibuster in history over a Supreme Court appointment. In the end, there were not enough votes to end the filibuster. The Senate never voted on Fortas's nomination, and he made history again by asking the president to withdraw his name from consideration. Fortas was the first candidate for the chief justiceship to be denied Senate approval since 1795, when the mentally unstable John Rutledge was rejected.

Fortas's return to his role as associate justice was also unprecedented, but he did not last much longer on the Court. A year after his first humiliation, *Life* magazine published an article revealing that Fortas had accepted $200,000 to serve as a consultant for a charitable foundation. The foundation had been set up by a former client who was under investigation for stock manipulation. Although Fortas later rejected the offer, this fine point didn't matter. With the likelihood of impeachment hanging over his head and the new Nixon administration actively working against him, Fortas resigned from the Court. When he returned to private practice, his old firm refused to take him back.

The Bork controversy and its aftermath

By 1987, when Ronald Reagan nominated Robert Bork (seen in Figure 4-3) to replace the retiring Justice Lewis Powell, Bork had a sterling record of achievement. After enjoying years of success in private practice, he distinguished himself as a legal scholar at Yale Law School before serving as acting attorney general and as a judge on the esteemed U.S. Court of Appeals for the District of Columbia.

Bork's record, in fact, was his problem. Everywhere his legal career had taken him, he had left a paper trail documenting his legal philosophy. It detailed a conservative, strict constructionist interpretation of the Constitution and a complementary disapproval of such doctrines as the right of privacy, affirmative action, and First Amendment protection for nonpolitical speech. And then there was the little matter of the Saturday Night Massacre of 1974, during which Bork, stepping in as acting attorney general, did Richard Nixon's bidding and fired special prosecutor Archibald Cox, who had ordered Nixon to turn over those incriminating Watergate tape recordings

The Senate, then controlled by Democrats, was clearly opposed to the Bork nomination. The Republican Reagan Administration should have known it faced more than an uphill battle over its nominee, but weakened and distracted by the recent Iran-Contra scandal, the Administration forged ahead. Opposition was fierce. Liberals feared that replacing Powell, who had frequently served as a swing vote in civil rights and liberties cases, with Bork would result in the abolition of abortion on demand and the repeal of affirmative action. The battle lines were drawn along party lines. Even southern Democrats, newly mindful of the sensitivities of their anti-Bork African-American constituents, declined to change sides.

Figure 4-3:
Robert Bork.

Because the Supreme Court consists of nine justices, one of them often serves as a tie-breaker or *swing vote*. The swing vote usually emerges when the Court is deeply divided between liberals and conservatives or over a particular issue. Needless to say, a swing vote wields enormous influence at these times; when a replacement must be found for a swing justice, confirmation hearings can become a pressure cooker.

The Senate Judiciary Committee hearings on the Bork nomination were like none that had come before. Stretching to 87 hours over the course of 12 days, they were longer than any others. Bork's own detailed testimony about his political and legal philosophy lasted more than 30 hours. It was followed by a parade of witnesses longer than any seen before or since at a Supreme Court confirmation hearing. Many of these witnesses belonged to pressure groups that also worked behind the scenes to influence senators as well as the media. Many of them used the occasion to raise money for war chests that would fund future political battles.

Although only six Republican senators voted against Bork, his nomination was defeated by a substantial margin, 58 to 42. The fallout from the confirmation battle has been even more substantial, further polarizing the parties. Evidence of the Bork effect includes expressly political competitions such as the Republican-controlled Senate's foot dragging on federal judicial appointments during the Clinton Administration, as well as the culture wars that helped define American society at the end of the twentieth century.

The Watergate watershed

The political scandal known as *Watergate* resulted in Richard Nixon's fall from grace and eventual resignation in 1974. The events leading up to his resignation started two years earlier, when the Committee to Reelect the President (CRP, pronounced "CREEP" — the Watergate story is full of wonderful lingo!) hired a group of burglars to break into the Democratic National Party headquarters in the Watergate apartment complex. When the burglars were caught, the White House denied any involvement and began covering its tracks. In the end, it came down to a set of tapes that recorded Oval Office conversations. When Archibald Cox, the special prosecutor appointed by the Administration to investigate the burglary, began investigating the coverup and demanded that the tapes be handed over, Nixon stalled. After Nixon fired Cox, his replacement sued. The Supreme Court, in *United States v. Nixon,* ordered the president to turn the tapes over. One tape contained undeniable proof of Nixon's connection with a conspiracy to block investigation of the initial Watergate burglary. Faced with imminent impeachment, Nixon resigned.

The personal is political

Although inquiries about a Supreme Court nominee's policy judgments and professionalism — ethics as well as legal smarts — have always been considered part of the mix, it was only in the twentieth century that personal matters came under close scrutiny during confirmation. In part, the justification for this practice can be found in most judicial codes, which stipulate that a judge is a judge 24 hours a day. So the Senate really does have a right to know what potential justices do under their sheets.

Hugo L. Black and the Ku Klux Klan

Many business leaders in Birmingham, Alabama, during the early years of the twentieth century regarded Hugo Lafayette Black (see Figure 4-4) as a Bolshevik, owing to his populist politics and his legal representation of labor unions. But at the same time Black was demonstrating his liberality, he was also pandering to religious and racial prejudice in order to win cases. And in 1923, he made a big mistake: He joined the Ku Klux Klan. Later he would say that he had taken this step precisely because many Alabama jurors were also members of the Invisible Empire. These Klansmen were in part responsible for Black's election to the U.S. Senate in 1926. Although Black resigned from the Klan shortly afterward, he continued to be indebted to them politically.

Once in the Senate, however, Black exhibited pronounced liberal tendencies, ardently embracing the New Deal and vigorously investigating questionable business lobbying tactics. When Franklin Roosevelt's first opportunity to name a new justice came up, the president turned to Black.

Black's confirmation process was not entirely smooth. (He won Senate approval by a vote of 63 to 16.) However, the opposition he encountered had more to do with Congressional concern about Roosevelt's attempts to reshape the Court than concern about Black's qualifications for the job (although a number of Senators openly speculated about rumors of Black's Klan involvement). Black's previous KKK membership did not become public knowledge until shortly after he took his seat on the high bench. After a newspaper reported that Black had once belonged to the Klan, public opinion turned against him. Black confronted the issue head on. In a radio address, he confessed his past membership but indicated that it had been a minor chapter in his life. This direct approach, coupled with the public's distraction over the looming threat of global warfare, soon made Black's KKK involvement truly a thing of the past.

Figure 4-4:
Justice
Hugo L.
Black.

© Bettman/CORBIS

The Clarence Thomas soap opera

In 1991, when George Bush nominated Clarence Thomas (see Figure 4-5) to replace Thurgood Marshall in the Court's African-American seat, Thomas at first seemed like a dream candidate. A prominent black conservative, Thomas was also a self-made man who had, through determination and hard work, risen from a childhood of dire poverty to a seat on the District of Columbia Circuit Court of Appeals. He had only been a judge for one year before his Supreme Court nomination, however, and he came to his confirmation hearings with less experience in the law than any other justice appointed in the twentieth century. Initially, the Judiciary Committee's concerns focused on the adequacy of Thomas's professional qualifications. These doubts intensified when Thomas proved unwilling to answer questions about controversial issues he would surely confront on the Court. A Roman Catholic, he professed to have no opinion about abortion. A beneficiary of affirmative action who had spent the bulk of his career as a public official involved with enforcement of civil rights and equal employment opportunity, he dodged questions about his own views regarding affirmative action.

Despite Thomas's unwillingness to be forthcoming about policy matters, the committee voted to recommend his confirmation. It was only after his nomination had reached the full Senate that the media broke a story about allegations of sexual harassment being made by Anita Hill, one of Thomas's former employees at the Department of Justice and the Equal Employment Opportunity Commission. Key senators insisted that the charges be fully investigated, and the Judiciary Committee reconvened under the glare of television lights. As the nation watched, riveted to their TV screens, a stream of witnesses testified to Hill's veracity or to Thomas's good character. Toward the end of the three-day ordeal, Thomas categorically denied the charges, dramatically denouncing the proceedings as "a high-tech lynching for uppity blacks." The strategy seemed to work. The Senate voted to confirm Clarence Thomas by a vote of 52 to 48 — the slimmest margin of victory of any Supreme Court justice confirmed in the preceding 100 years.

Figure 4-5:
Justice Clarence Thomas (second from left), being sworn in by Justice Byron White, with President George Bush and Mrs. Thomas looking on.

© Reuters NewMedia Inc./CORBIS

Some can't take the heat — some can

Some Supreme Court nominations never reach the Senate for a vote. Some never even reach the Senate Judiciary Committee. In the entire history of the Court, however, only eight nominations have been formally withdrawn. The earliest of these, William Paterson's 1793 nomination, was withdrawn owing to a technicality: Because the Constitution prohibits such a nomination while the appointee is serving in the Senate (as Paterson was), George Washington had to resubmit the nomination four days later, after Paterson's Senate term had expired.

No more withdrawals occurred until the nineteenth century. Political problems forced the Whig John Tyler, who had managed to alienate both his own party and the Democrats, to withdraw two nominations (the Senate rejected a third and refused to act on a fourth). Ulysses S. Grant, too, had problems getting along with the Senate, which rejected one of Grant's Court appointments and forced the withdrawal of two others, both accused of cronyism. The intertwined fates of Lyndon Johnson's nominees Abe Fortas and Homer Thornberry are discussed in the section "The downfall of Abe Fortas," earlier in this chapter. In 1987, Douglas Ginsburg's candidacy became the final one withdrawn in the twentieth century.

Douglas Ginsburg withdraws his nomination

Douglas Ginsburg (see Figure 4-6) had the misfortune to be the follow-up act to Robert Bork. A legal scholar and former Reagan Administration Justice Department official, Ginsburg at the time of his nomination had less than a year's judicial experience. A Reagan appointee to the U.S. Court of Appeals for the District of Columbia, Ginsburg was one of Robert Bork's former colleagues and also an ideological soul mate. Unlike Bork's crash, however, Ginsburg's undoing was not his politics so much as his personal life. Owing to the Bork fiasco, Ginsburg was nominated before the customary background checks had been completed. Almost immediately after his name was called, he was assailed for alleged conflicts of interest during his time at Justice and accused of overstating his actual courtroom experience. What did him in, though, was the revelation — later admitted — that Ginsburg had smoked marijuana during the 1970s while serving on the Harvard Law School faculty. His nomination, which had lasted all of nine days, was quickly withdrawn.

William Rehnquist (twice) withstands close scrutiny

Not all controversial candidates melt under the heat. William Rehnquist, who would rise to the position of chief justice in 1986, not only survived the hearings but thrived in their combative atmosphere.

William Rehnquist was a conservative, and a politician, from the start. An official of the Republican Party in his native Arizona, his championship of Barry Goldwater's doomed 1964 presidential bid eventually brought Rehnquist to Washington. As an assistant attorney general in the Nixon Administration, he was an eloquent spokesman for such conservative causes as warrantless searches, preventive detention of criminal suspects, and the abolition of the so-called exclusionary rule.

The exclusionary rule prevents the use at trial of any evidence obtained through an illegal search or seizure. It is an outgrowth of the Fourth Amendment, which prohibits unreasonable searches and seizures of material that might later be used by the government in a criminal prosecution. The Warren Court extended the rule so that it applied not just in federal courts, but also in state courts — which is precisely where most criminal cases are tried.

Figure 4-6: Douglas Ginsburg, one of President Ronald Reagan's (on left) doomed Supreme Court nominees.

© Bettman/CORBIS

In 1971, a grateful Richard Nixon named Rehnquist as the replacement for the retiring Justice John M. Harlan. This would not be Rehnquist's first Supreme Court service. In 1952, after graduating first in his class at Stanford Law School, Rehnquist began a two-year clerkship for Justice Robert H. Jackson. During that period, the landmark civil rights case *Brown v. Board of Education* first came before the Court. As Jackson's clerk, it was Rehnquist's job to write legal memoranda to help the justice prepare to consider the case. One of these memos surfaced during Rehnquist's confirmation hearing some 17 years after Jackson's death. The memo, which categorically stated, "I think *Plessy v. Ferguson* was right and should be re-affirmed," was a bombshell. *Plessy*, the case that made racial segregation the law of the land for nearly half a century, had been overturned by *Brown*. By this time, the earlier case had been thoroughly discredited. In his testimony before the Judiciary Committee, Rehnquist claimed that the memo was intended to reflect Jackson's thinking, not his own.

Many did not believe Rehnquist. During his early days of Republican activism in Arizona, Rehnquist had opposed local school busing measures, and he had participated in a program intended to challenge the legitimacy of minority voters at the polls. The Judiciary Committee hearings were brutal. In his book about the confirmation, *The Rehnquist Choice*, former Nixon counsel John Dean quotes Nixon telling Rehnquist to "be as mean and rough as they said you were." Rehnquist was not only rough, he was smarter than his inquisitors, and he won. Five weeks after his nomination had been announced, Rehnquist was confirmed by a vote of 68 to 26.

ANECDOTE

Politics as usual

For those who bemoan the contemporary politicization of the Supreme Court confirmation process, looking at how the Senate treated Court nominees historically can be instructive. In 1811, for example, Federalist senators helped defeat Republican James Madison's nomination of Alexander Wolcott, citing Wolcott's too vigorous enforcement of a federal trade law when he had served as a customs official. In 1866, the Radical Republicans who controlled Congress and despised Andrew Johnson to the point of impeaching him refused to vote on Johnson's nomination of his gifted attorney general, Henry Stanbery, simply because Stanbery *was* his attorney general. And in 1870, the Senate rejected Ulysses S. Grant's nomination of attorney general Ebenezer Hoar because Hoar refused to permit political patronage!

Yet the memo would come back to haunt Rehnquist again 15 years later, when Ronald Reagan tapped him to succeed the retiring Warren Burger as chief justice. But as *Time* magazine declared, by this time Rehnquist was "The Court's Mr. Right," having steered his brethren in that direction by becoming their undisputed intellectual leader. Rehnquist was again confirmed, if by a smaller margin (65 to 33). Some senators clearly still believed, like John Dean, that the candidate had lied, not once but twice — and both times under oath.

Step Two: Senate voting or stonewalling

After the Senate Judiciary Committee makes its recommendation on a candidate, the full Senate is obliged to offer its "advice and consent." Of the 145 candidates put forward since the inception of the Supreme Court in 1789, 28 have been formally rejected and 11 have been effectively turned down by the Senate's refusal to act on their nominations. The bulk of these rejections occurred in the first half of the Court's existence, with only seven nominees rejected since 1900.

In part, the reduction in Supreme Court rejections in more recent times stems from the executive branch's increasing power and influence owing to the proliferation of administrative agencies that answer to the president. The 1913 ratification of the Seventeenth Amendment, making the selection of senators a matter of public choice rather than state legislature selection, also increased the president's authority as head of his political party. When Supreme Court nominations have gone badly in recent times, they have tended to do so because of some inherent fault with the candidate, not because the Senate was merely playing politics with the president.

Probably the most extreme examples of twentieth-century Court nominees who have failed owing to their own weaknesses are two Nixon candidates, Clement Haynsworth and Harold Carswell. The two men, both southerners, were nominated back-to-back, with the first nomination succumbing to allegations of ethical improprieties and anti-union bias, and the second to proof of a poor judicial record and suspected racial bigotry. In both cases, Nixon had selected candidates as part of his overall "southern strategy" to satisfy elements of the coalition that had elected him and he hoped would re-elect him. Both nominations were demonstrably cases in which the president was playing politics.

Chief Justice Appointments

Candidates for the Court's top job undergo the same screening process applied to nominees for associate justiceships. There can be little doubt, however, that the Senate examines potential chief justices with an extra degree of care. Although the chief justice, like his associates, has only one vote to cast, he does control the Court's agenda and in some measure shapes both its docket and its decisions.

With the exception of John Rutledge, who resigned as an associate justice in 1791 and returned four years later to serve an aborted four-month tenure as chief justice, all the early chief justices were recruited from outside the Court. In 1910, Edward D. White became the first to be elevated from associate to chief justice. Of the seven men who succeeded White as chief justice, four — William Howard Taft, Fred Vinson, Earl Warren, and Warren Burger — were outsiders. A fifth, Charles Evans Hughes, was a lapsed justice who returned to the Court after a failed presidential bid.

Hiring from outside the firm is thus the dominant practice when choosing a chief justice, so it cannot be said that individuals who have not already had a chance to show their stuff are subjected to extra scrutiny. Indeed, some of these men — Roger Brooke Taney, Salmon P. Chase, Morrison R. Waite, and Earl Warren — had no judicial experience before taking on the job. Perhaps nothing acts as a better illustration of the president's prerogatives and appointment power than the fact that he can name career politicians like these five to head the nation's court of last resort. In the end, it is *always* a political decision.

On the other hand, just because a candidate for chief justice has been recruited from among the ranks does not mean that he or she will have an easy time of it. An associate justice tapped for the top job is obliged to go through the whole confirmation process again. And the second time around can be rougher than the first: Charles Evans Hughes was taken to task for the political ambition that lured him away from the Court; William Rehnquist was forced to revisit that unfortunate memo he had written about the preferability of Jim Crow to desegregation. These individuals' willingness to put their feet to the fire not once but twice proves something about their toughness — and their ambition.

Chapter 5

First Among Equals:
The Chief Justice

- -

In This Chapter

▶ Outlining the chief justice's role

▶ Understanding Court management

▶ Defining "Court guardianship"

▶ Considering chief justices as statesmen

▶ Looking at some admirable and less than admirable chiefs

- -

*T*he chief justice has some extra responsibilities and some extra perks — but, like the other justices, only one vote. Among the judicial brethren, the chief justice's extra measure of power lies chiefly in the administrative realm, leading case deliberations and, at times, assigning opinion writing duties. Still, a chief justice inevitably leaves his mark on history. Only 16 men have sat in the chief justice's chair since the Supreme Court's inception in 1789, and the Courts they led will always be known by these men's names. Some chief justices have chosen to make something of their special role, while others have preferred to rest on their laurels.

A Leader or Just a Presiding Officer?

The Constitution established the position of chief justice, but it gave the nation's chief judicial officer only one job: presiding over presidential impeachment proceedings. To this day, a large part of the chief justice's responsibilities are administrative or ceremonial. These men take the lead on public occasions — administering the oath of office to a newly inaugurated president and officiating while the Supreme Court sits in public session — and in closed door proceedings, chairing the judicial conference where the justices consider the cases before them.

The chief justiceship carries enormous prestige today. It was not always so. George Washington actually had a hard time finding candidates for the job.

Not only was the position poorly paid, it got no respect. The judicial branch was at the time a toothless tiger, and without the power of judicial review (see Chapter 1), the chief justice headed up a rather insignificant institution. What's more, the chief justice, like all of the associate justices, was obliged to spend the bulk of his time traveling long distances over rough or nonexistent roads performing circuit duty. It is still true that all nine justices serve as federal appellate judges in the circuits they are assigned, but in the early days of the republic, getting to and from this job was literally dangerous to one's health. The first chief justice, John Jay, complained long and bitterly about this onerous chore, in 1795 resigning to become governor of New York, where he could stay put.

Washington turned next to John Rutledge, who in 1791 had resigned his position as associate justice to become chief justice of South Carolina. Rutledge himself offered to replace Jay, a gesture some might have regarded as crazy. And in fact, just months after he was sworn in — while Congress was still in recess — Rutledge's rumored mental instability was one of the reasons for his rejection by the Senate. Washington's offer of the chief justiceship was turned down by both presidential aspirant Henry Clay and associate justice William Cushing before founding father Oliver Ellsworth agreed to take on the position in 1796.

After poor health forced Ellsworth to resign in 1800, John Adams was at first unable to come up with a better potential replacement than John Jay. Jay, who had found the post "intolerable," turned down his president. Then Adams made a selection that would utterly transform the Supreme Court: He nominated his secretary of state, John Marshall, as the Court's fourth chief justice.

John Marshall: Thomas Jefferson's antagonist and the Great Chief Justice"

John Marshall's beginning was not auspicious. Marshall (see Figure 5-1) assumed his seat as chief justice under something of a cloud. He began by serving two roles, straddling the executive and judicial branches by acting simultaneously as John Adams's secretary of state and as chief justice of the Supreme Court during the final days of the Adams administration. Then, one month later, Marshall found himself setting another unhappy precedent when Adams's term ended and Marshall became the first justice to serve with a president from the opposing political party.

Marshall, like all of the justices who preceded him, was a Federalist. The bedrock principle of members of the Federalist Party was belief in a strong central government. Those who favored states' rights belonged to the Republican Party, and in 1800, they elected their first president. That president, Thomas Jefferson, was also a distant cousin of John Marshall. Soon Jefferson would also be Marshall's arch enemy.

Figure 5-1:
Chief
Justice
John
Marshall.

Library of Congress, Prints and Photographs Division [LC-USZ62-54940]

Just days before Jefferson's inauguration, the Federalist-controlled Congress passed legislation governing the federal judiciary. Among other things, the Judiciary Act of 1801 reduced the number of Supreme Court justices and created six new circuit courts, which were immediately staffed with judges appointed by the outgoing John Adams. One of the first acts of the Jefferson administration was to make sure that Congress repealed this legislation, clearly intended to pack the federal judiciary with Federalist loyalists.

Another law pushed through in the final days of the Adams administration created a number of new justice of the peace positions in the District of Columbia. Adams forwarded his nominees for these positions to the Senate on March 2, 1801, and the appointments were confirmed the next day. However, some of the commissions were not delivered to the new judicial officials until after midnight on March 3, the day Jefferson took office. Jefferson subsequently ordered his secretary of state, James Madison, to hold on to the "Midnight Judges" commissions still in his possession. One of these was intended for an individual named William Marbury, who later that year petitioned the Supreme Court for an order requiring Madison to hand over his commission. This case became known as *Marbury v. Madison* (1803), arguably one of the most significant cases ever heard by the Court.

Marbury established the Court's power of judicial review once and for all. It also established Marshall's own authority. The case appeared to present the Court with a dilemma: If it ordered Madison to deliver the commission and he refused, the Court would be weakened; if the Court ruled against Marbury, it would be accused of caving in to the Republicans. Marshall's solution to this problem was worthy of Solomon. In his opinion for the Court, the Chief Justice found that although Marbury deserved his commission, it could not be delivered because the legislation authorizing it was an unconstitutional enlargement of the Court's original jurisdiction (see Chapter 2). While preventing a head-on collision between the executive and judicial branches, Marshall managed at the same time to transform into law the Court's own status as the final arbiter of the constitutionality of legislation. As Marshall wrote, "It is emphatically the province and duty of the judicial department to say what the law is." Take *that*, Mr. President.

By most accounts, Marshall had a forceful but engaging personality, which he used to unite his brethren. He reinforced the power of the Court by writing most of its opinions himself, and at a time when the Court was dominated by Republican appointees, he managed to make most of its decisions unanimous. In *McCulloch v. Maryland* (1819), the case that best illustrates the power of judicial review, the Court upheld Congress's right to charter a national bank by a vote of 6-0 in the face of Republican opposition. Jeffersonian supporters of states' right argued that the Constitution did not give Congress this power. What's more, the Tenth Amendment stipulates that those powers not spelled out in the Constitution are reserved to the states. Marshall stood firm in his support of federalism, famously countering, "We must never forget that it is a *constitution* we are expounding . . . intended to endure for ages to come, and consequently, to be adapted to the various *crises* of human affairs."

Marshall has been called the "Great Chief Justice" because he dominated the Court as no other chief justice has. He withstood Jefferson's numerous attempts to undermine his control by appointing Republican loyalists to the high bench. Only William Johnson (see Chapter 6) succeeded in introducing a dissenting voice to the Marshall Court. Marshall's own dissents were few, although towards the end of his 35-year tenure he was surrounded by states' rights supporters. His experienced his first significant defeat in the wake of *Worcester v. Georgia* (1832), in which his opinion for the Court upheld the independence of the Cherokee Nation. Andrew Jackson refused to implement the Court's ruling, which obligated Georgia to respect both Cherokee sovereignty and federal treaties with the Indian nation. The President is reported to have said, "Well, John Marshall has made his decision, now let him enforce it." Marshall hoped to outlast Jackson, so that the next president could return balance to the Court. He did not succeed. In 1835, he succumbed to a combination of illness and grief over his wife's death, becoming the first chief justice to die while still on the bench.

Salmon P. Chase and the lust for power

There's no doubt about it: Salmon Portland Chase (see Figure 5-2) benefited enormously from Abraham's Lincoln's generosity of spirit and from the some of the seamier aspects of Civil War-era politics. Chase was driven by two things, religious fervor and political ambition. The early years of his legal career were shaped by the values imparted to him in boyhood by his uncle Philander Chase, an Episcopal bishop of Ohio. When Salmon Chase practiced law in Cincinnati in the 1830s to 1850s, he became known as the "attorney general for runaway slaves," owing to the amount of time he devoted to defending fugitive slaves at risk of being returned to their masters because of court rulings.

Figure 5-2:
Chief
Justice
Salmon P.
Chase.

Library of Congress, Prints and Photographs Division
[LC-USZ62-11378]

Soon, however, Chase turned this identity to political advantage. Initially a member of the Whig Party, Chase switched to the Liberals in the late 1840s, when they dominated Ohio politics. The Liberal Party was aligned with the Free-Soil Party, which advocated the admission of only nonslaveholding states to the union. The Free-Soilers struck a deal with the Democrats whereby the Free-Soil Party agreed to allow the Democrats to organize the Ohio legislature if the Democrats agreed to send a Free-Soiler to the Senate. (See Chapter 1 for an explanation of "unelected" senators.) Chase was their man.

In the Senate, Chase devoted himself to the antislavery movement. When the controversy over the Kansas-Nebraska Bill (which was intended to maintain the status quo between slaveholding and nonslaveholding states) gave birth to a new Republican Party, Chase was one of the first on board the new bandwagon. At the 1860 Republican convention, he was also one of the top contenders for the party's presidential nomination.

Lincoln ultimately won both the nomination and the election. He showed his gratitude for Chase's support by naming him treasury secretary. Chase showed his gratitude by lobbying against Lincoln behind the scenes to challenge him in the 1864 presidential nomination contest. Lincoln accepted Chase's resignation from his cabinet, but never one to hold a grudge, the president granted Chase's subsequent request to succeed Roger Brooke Taney as chief justice.

Lincoln was assassinated shortly after Chase's appointment, and both Chase and Lincoln's successor, Andrew Johnson, did battle with the Radical Republicans who controlled Congress. When Johnson insisted upon carrying out Lincoln's plans for reconstructing the post-war South, Congress impeached him. As chief justice, Chase presided over Johnson's trial before the Senate. He managed the proceedings well, and his insistence upon proper courtroom procedures saved Johnson, who escaped removal from office by one vote.

Johnson's impeachment nevertheless served to undermine his power. Chase, on the other hand, seized the moment, capitalizing on his new visibility by once again seeking the presidential nomination. Seeing that his own party had already settled on Ulysses S. Grant, Chase looked to the Democrats, turning a blind eye to the racism with which they were associated at the time. In the end, he lost more than that nomination. The transparency of his political opportunism served to undermine the Court. The associate justices, as well as the country as a whole, read political expediency into his subsequent opinions. As the power of the Court waned, the balance of power shifted to Congress. Chase, for his own part, found himself cast most often in the role of dissenter. His hope of escaping to the higher ground of the presidency never left him until he died of a massive stroke in 1873, still only the chief justice of the Supreme Court of the United States.

Earl Warren: Eisenhower's " . . . biggest . . . mistake"

What Dwight D. Eisenhower actually said was that appointing Earl Warren (see Figure 5-3) as chief justice was "the biggest damn-fool mistake I ever made." In naming Warren, Eisenhower was actually returning a political favor. In his third term as a popular Republican governor of California, Warren was a serious contender for the 1952 presidential nomination. In the end, he threw his support to Eisenhower, who went on to win the presidency. A grateful Eisenhower promised Warren the first vacancy on the Supreme Court.

The first vacancy turned out to be a plum. Chief Justice Fred Vinson died unexpectedly on June 8, 1953, but Eisenhower, who had already offered the post of solicitor general to Warren, was slow to honor his promise. Warren was not slow to remind him of it. Appointed on October 2, 1953, while Congress was in session, Warren was officially sworn in as the Court's 14th chief justice on March 2, 1954.

As a politician, Warren had possessed solid Republican credentials — he had even been a favorite of party conservatives. In announcing his appointment as chief justice, Eisenhower stressed Warren's "integrity, honesty [and] middle-of-the-road philosophy." How mistaken Eisenhower was — the Warren Court was one of the most liberal on record. Warren's tenure is a vivid illustration possible of the truism that presidents lose control over these people as soon as they assume the high bench. A lifetime appointment coupled with a salary constitutionally guaranteed not to diminish has stiffened the resolve of many justices.

Warren immediately faced an enormous problem. The school desegregation case *Brown v. Board of Education* (see Chapter 12) had been held over for rehearing by the Vinson Court. The problem lay in the fact that the justices were ideologically divided between those eager to end official segregation and those opposed to overturning *Plessy v. Ferguson* (1896), the Supreme Court precedent that made racial separation the law of the land (see Chapter 12). Warren immediately made his opinion known to his fellow justices: Racial segregation could only be upheld if the premise of racial inequality was acceptable — for him, it was not. Still, mindful of the strong undercurrents of emotion surrounding the case, Warren did not insist that the others adopt his view. He knew how important it was for the Court to speak with one voice on this important issue, and he wanted a unanimous opinion.

Warren's patience paid off. He got his unanimous decision, and he himself wrote the opinion of the Court in what history records as one of its watershed cases. The opinion displayed the traits that characterized Warren's nearly 16 years as chief justice: straightforwardness and a casual attitude toward legal scholarship. Though trained as a lawyer, Warren had spent little of his professional life practicing law. His experiences in the realm of public affairs, however, had given him something more valuable than legal acumen — an unerring concern for justice. Faced with a detailed legal argument in the courtroom, Warren was known to lean over the bench to interrupt and inquire, "Yes, but is it *fair?*"

It was almost inevitable that Warren would lock horns with the Court's resident scholar, Felix Frankfurter (see Chapter 6), and he did. Twice during the 1962 Court session, Warren publicly chastised Frankfurter, once for enlarging on his written opinion as he announced it in court, and another time for lecturing the other justices while delivering a dissent. Frankfurter looked on Warren as a mere politician, considering Hugo Black (see Chapter 6) to be his only intellectual equal on the Court. But as Justice Potter Stewart remarked, "If Black was the intellectual leader, Warren was the *leader* leader." As with John Marshall, Warren's personal affability contributed mightily to his effectiveness as chief justice. He rarely had to employ the kind of discipline he used on Frankfurter to persuade the other justices see things his way.

Warren's even-handedness resulted in greater efficiency within the Court, which handed down one groundbreaking case after another. The Warren Court is remembered for the social upheaval it abetted, starting with *Brown v. Board of Education*. When Warren joined the Court, a *due process* (see Chapter 9) revolution emphasizing individual rights and led by Justice Black, was already underway. During Warren's tenure, this revolution was extended by such watershed cases as *Reynolds v. Sims* (1964), upholding the "one person, one vote" principle; *Griswold v. Connecticut* (1965), proclaiming a constitutional right to privacy; and *Miranda v. Arizona* (1966), mandating that individuals accused of crimes be read their rights. Warren did not write the opinion of the Court in all of these cases, but in each of them, he was an active participant, urging his fellow justices to exercise the Court's powers to uphold social justice.

Warren's activism came with a price. More than once, he was the object of impeachment drives. In the Senate, the Jenner-Butler Bill proposed to limit the Court's jurisdiction in matters of national security was a slap in Warren's face. None of these attacks succeeded, but in the decades following Warren's retirement in 1969, the balance of the Court shifted sharply to the right, largely in reaction to the sweeping social changes forever linked with his name.

Court Management: All Are Called, Some Answer

Some chief justices distinguish themselves not so much by their opinion writing as by their administrative abilities. Internally, these chiefs are noted for their interpersonal skills with their fellow justices and with the Court bureaucracy. Great chief justices manage to achieve unanimity among the brethren so that the Court speaks with one voice concerning issues of great national importance. But they also manage to finesse delicate matters: More than one chief justice has been able to convince a mentally or physically disabled associate justice that his time is up.

Melville Fuller — a man who set great store by the dignity of his office — had the title of his office changed from Chief Justice of the Supreme Court of the United States to Chief Justice of the United States. Several of the men who have sat in his seat since 1910 took that title to heart, looking not only to the interests of the Supreme Court, but to those of the entire federal judiciary — even the entire nation.

William Howard Taft "massing the Court"

William Howard Taft (see Figure 5-4) was the nation's 27th president. He did not, however, enjoy being the America's chief executive — he wanted to be an administrator. In running for the presidency, Taft bowed to his wife's ambitions as well as those of his predecessor, Theodore Roosevelt. Roosevelt did not want to run again himself, but he wanted to keep a hand in, anointing Taft as his successor. Taft's four years in the White House were generally lackluster, and in 1914, he ran an unenthusiastic — and unsuccessful — reelection campaign.

While he was still serving in the Roosevelt administration, Taft had let his president know that the post he most coveted was that of chief justice. And when Taft was himself president, he made a strategic move designed to help him gain the highest seat on the high bench. When Melville Fuller died in 1910, Taft chose as Fuller's successor the 65-year-old Associate Justice Edward Douglass White, rather than the man considered to be the front-runner for the job, Associate Justice Charles Evans Hughes, who was then only 48. In doing so, Taft (who was then 52) hoped to preserve his own chances. Almost immediately after losing his bid for a second term as president, Taft began campaigning to become chief justice. President Warren G. Harding, who never seemed to turn down a request for a political favor, could not say no to a former president. In 1921, Taft got his wish.

Figure 5-4:
Chief
Justice
William
Howard
Taft.

Taft set to work with a vengeance. He had a passion for what he called "massing the Court" behind issues he considered important. In his eight and a half years on the high Court, he himself wrote 249 opinions of the Court and a mere four dissents. He had a lifetime of political experience and capital to draw upon, and he used some of it to ensure that like-minded men were appointed to the Court. As president, in fact, Taft had prepared the way for his chief justiceship not only by elevating an older associate justice to that role, but by essentially reshaping the entire Court through five other appointments.

As chief justice of the United States, Taft used his clout to help those he considered worthy of secure positions with lower federal courts. He was a political conservative who had served in the executive branch during an era of marked social progressivism. While he remained ideologically conservative as chief justice, he ardently pursued reform within the court system. Immediately after assuming his new office, he began a speechmaking and article writing campaign aimed at rooting out administrative defects in the federal judiciary. The fruit of these labors was the establishment in 1922 of the Judicial Conference of the United States and passage of the Judiciary Act of 1925. The Judicial Conference, consisting of senior federal judges and chaired by the chief justice, streamlined what had been a largely decentralized system and bolstered the judicial branch's autonomy. The Judiciary Act, by giving the Court almost complete discretion about which cases it heard (see Chapter 2), increased the justices' control over the course of law while cutting down on their workload.

Taft did not live to see two other favorite projects — procedural changes and a new Supreme Court building — realized. During his last years on the Court — a place he once said was his idea of heaven — Taft saw the unanimity he had so carefully fostered begin to slip away. He came to regard Justices Harlan F. Stone, Oliver Wendell Holmes, and Louis D. Brandeis — none of whom he had appointed — as dangerously liberal. Determined to maintain the Court's conservative majority, the gravely ill Taft stayed on the bench almost until the last. He died only one month after tendering his resignation, probably content with the knowledge that Herbert Hoover chose as his successor a man Taft himself had put on the Court, Charles Evans Hughes.

Two contrasting styles of marshaling the brethren

Warren Burger (see Figure 5-5) never was known for his legal mind, and William Rehnquist (see Figure 5-6) is renowned for his legal acumen. Yet both men, in very different ways, made a success of their Court leadership. And both men in a sense owe their elevation to the role of chief justice to Earl Warren, whose stewardship of the Court created not just a revolution in individual rights, but a backlash against it.

Figure 5-5: Chief Justice Warren E. Burger.

© Owen Franken/CORBIS

Figure 5-6:
Chief
Justice
William H.
Rehnquist.

© Bettman/CORBIS

Warren Burger

As a judge on the prestigious District of Columbia Circuit Court of Appeals, Burger made a name for himself in the 1950s and '60s as a "law and order" man, opposed to what he saw as the Warren Court's leniency toward criminal defendants. He made these views known not only in his legal opinions, but in what amounted to a public relations campaign. In May 1961, for example, he used a speech at Duke University as an occasion for criticizing the modern insanity defense as the last refuge of scoundrels. He also used the public forum to advocate for judicial reforms. For Burger, the two causes were linked: Because the modern American judicial system coddled criminals, court dockets were clogged with what were essentially frivolous lawsuits. Court dockets were so backlogged that it could take as long as five years for a case to come to trial. Still, criminal defendants could file endless habeas corpus petitions and other appeals that permitted them multiple court appearances. In a widely publicized speech delivered at Rippon College in 1967, Burger declared that the court system was "not working" for "decent people," who feel "a suppressed rage, frustration and bitterness" toward criminal defendants who "feel they can 'get by' with anything."

Burger's campaign hit its mark the next year when Richard Nixon, who had coincidentally run on a "law and order" platform, won the presidential election. One of his first orders of business was to fulfill a campaign promise to find a strict constructionist (see Chapter 4) — preferably a sitting federal judge — to take over from Earl Warren. Burger, a favorite of Republican conservatives, fit the bill. What's more, as journalist David Savage wrote, Burger, with his broad shoulders and shock of snowy hair, "looked as though he had been cast by Hollywood for the part of chief justice."

Contrary to expectations, Burger for the most part failed to roll back what many viewed as the excesses of the Warren Court. In fact, the Court led by Burger can be said to have consolidated the expansion of individual rights that characterized his predecessor's tenure. Under Burger, the Supreme Court added to the "new" constitutional right to privacy by voting in favor of a woman's right to abortion on demand in *Roe v. Wade* (1973). And Burger himself wrote the opinion of the Court in *United States v. Nixon* (1974), the decision that caused Nixon to resign under threat of impeachment! One reason for the continued flow of liberal decisions clearly was the make up of the Burger Court. William J. Brennan, once Earl Warren's right hand man, continued to be highly influential with the other associate justices, the balance of them holdovers from the Warren era.

Burger was not without allies on the Court he headed, but his abrasive personality meant that he was unable to unite the justices in the fashion of Chief Justice Taft. Although he was straightforward about his own views of what the law was, he was not above changing his vote in order, some said, to be in a position to assign himself authorship of the majority's opinion. Some of his brethren disliked what they saw as Burger's posturing; others felt he was a lightweight. Leaks to the press concerning his poor leadership were not uncommon. As a result, dissents and concurrences (see Chapter 3) proliferated, confusing the public and detracting from the Court's prestige.

Burger was, nonetheless, an able administrator. Under his leadership, the Court saw the introduction of word processors and copying machines. The time allotted to oral argument before the Court was slashed in half, and justices were encouraged to summarize their opinions, rather than reading them from the bench. Burger also spearheaded reforms in the lower federal courts. He didn't manage to convince Congress of the need to establish a national court of appeals to lighten the Supreme Court's burden, but in 1970, he did push through the Institute for Court Management, charged with training non-judicial personnel to perform more of the tedious work involved in hearing and deciding cases. Many federal jurisdictions adopted Burger's proposal that civil juries be limited to 6, rather than 12 members, speeding the jury selection process. The chief justice convinced the Federal Bureau of Prisons to rein in all those habeas corpus petitions. As a result, by 1980, the federal judiciary was able to process 30 percent more cases than it had a decade earlier.

Burger did not stop there. He turned his hand to improving state courts, too, setting up cooperative councils that eliminated the need for parallel state and federal trials in certain *tort* or civil injury cases involving masses of plaintiffs. He urged membership in the newly formed National Center for State Courts, so that state judicial systems could pool their experiences and resources. Bent on streamlining the legal process wherever he saw fit, Burger even trained his eye on the Supreme Court bench itself. What was once a straight bench became a "winged" half-hexagon, allowing all of the justices to view one another.

For all Burger's energetic reforms, many felt he had failed at his primary task of holding the Court together. To be sure, he failed in his mission to roll back the Warren Court's "constitutional revolution." That task was left to his successor. And by the time Burger retired in 1986, the identity of the next chief justice was obvious to all. William Rehnquist, who had sat on the Burger Court for more than a decade, had slowly but surely become its intellectual leader.

William Rehnquist

The key to William Rehnquist's success as chief justice has been consistency. It seems that nearly all of the justices who have served with him on the high Court have admired his intellect, eloquence, and ability to parse the law, but what has mattered most is his unswerving commitment to a conservative agenda. During his 14 years as an associate justice on the still liberal Burger Court, Rehnquist acted as a lone dissenter 54 times. This ability to stick to his guns earned him a record and a nickname: the "lone dissenter." (His clerks even gave him a Lone Ranger doll to decorate his office.) By the time he was elevated to the chief justice's chair, however, he had become, in the words of *Newsweek* magazine, "The Court's Mr. Right."

While still an associate justice, Rehnquist had not been shy about publicly criticizing the Court. On May 3, 1985, he said in the *New York Times*, "I don't think that the Burger Court has as wide a sense of mission [as the Warren Court had]. Perhaps it doesn't have any sense of mission at all." *His* mission, as he had always made clear, was to undo much of what the Warren Court had done and to shift the balance of power away from the federal government and back to the states. Needless to say, not everyone agreed with him. But even those who were his ideological opposites respected — even liked — Rehnquist. Justice Marshall declared, "He has no problems, wishy-washy, back and forth. He knows exactly what he wants to do, and that's very important as a chief justice." And Justice Brennan commented more than once on his cordial relations with the new chief.

Rehnquist's good sense of humor has certainly helped him achieve popularity among his fellow justices. His ability to hold together a Court that is more often divided than united is also helped by the country's shift to the right in the later decades of the last century. Republican control of the White House for much of that time has meant that many recent Court appointees share many of Rehnquist's beliefs. From the current perspective, however, it's hard to say whether the American people have moved to the right of their own accord or whether Rehnquist has pushed them. Rehnquist has said that he has modeled his leadership on that of Chief Justice Charles Evans Hughes, but under Hughes, the Court was transformed from one favoring *judicial activism,* in which the Court makes law, to one noted for its *judicial restraint*

and deference to the legislative branch. Surely Rehnquist differs from Hughes in one important respect: Rehnquist has managed, even with a slim majority of the Court, to bring about the long-delayed counterrevolution that was to have taken place under Warren Burger. If that isn't judicial activism, I don't know what is.

Court Guardianship: Watching over the Marble Palace

In the early days of the republic when no one really knew what the Supreme Court's job should be and being a member of the Court involved low pay and saddle sores from circuit riding (see Chapter 1), most of the men recruited as justices accepted the job out of sheer patriotism. Most recognized the need for an institution that would enforce the laws, but few had any idea how to make it work. The Federalists in charge of the executive and legislative branches insisted that the justices spend much of their time riding around the countryside spreading the gospel of a strong central government. Not only was this job arduous, it literally distanced the Supreme Court from the nation's seat of power. It took the farsighted John Marshall, the Court's fourth leader, to hold the line on just how far the justices would go to do the states', Congress's, and the president's bidding. An end to circuit riding would not come for some time, but in the meanwhile, Marshall established the Supreme Court's right to have the last word about the law. It was a right that would not go unchallenged.

Judicial review revisited

The importance of judicial review (see Chapter 1) cannot be overstated. Without it, the Court is reduced to nine old people sitting around on Olympus swapping legal theories. Empowered with judicial review, the justices arguably become the most influential persons in the country. The Marshall Court laid the groundwork for the Supreme Court's power to review laws propagated by federal authorities in *Marbury v. Madison* (1803). (See the section "John Marshall: Thomas Jefferson's antagonist and the Great Chief Justice") and expanded it with regard to state laws in subsequent decisions such as *Martin v. Hunter's Lessee* (1816), in which the Supreme Court asserted its power over not just over state legislation, but over a state supreme court.

State governments were, needless to say, outraged by what they saw as an unwarranted expansion of federal authority. The Republican Jefferson bitterly fought against what he saw as the Marshall Court's encroachments on both state independence and the autonomy of the other branches of the federal government. Another great Republican president, Abraham Lincoln, likewise resisted the dominance of the Supreme Court. Although the infamous 1857 *Dred Scott* (see Chapter 11) decision certainly paid homage to states' rights by upholding slavery, it did so by declaring unconstitutional the Missouri Compromise, which limited the admission of slaveholding states to the union. In his first inaugural address, delivered in 1861, Lincoln declared that "if the policy of the government, upon vital questions, affecting the whole people, is to be irrevocably fixed by decisions of the Supreme Court, the instant they are made . . . the people will have ceased, to be their own rulers, having . . . practically resigned their government into the hands of that eminent tribunal." But Lincoln could no more overrule the Court than Jefferson could. It would take a civil war to undo *Dred Scott.*

There are other mechanisms for reining in the Supreme Court, of course. Chief among these methods is the constitutional amendment. (*Dred Scott* was actually overturned not by war itself, but by the Fourteenth Amendment, adopted in the wake of the Civil War.) But the process of amending the Constitution is cumbersome, requiring approval by two-thirds of both houses of Congress and ratification by three-fourths of the states. In the more than 200-year history of the Constitution, only 27 amendments have made it to ratification, and 10 of these make up the Bill of Rights, without which there would have been no Constitution. On numerous occasions, Congress has proposed various plans for restricting the Court's jurisdiction to certain areas of the law or certain types of cases, such as an attempt to prohibit the Court from considering the legitimacy of presidential pardons. The Court rejected that effort in *United States v. Klein* (1872), and it has withstood legislative challenges to its decisions concerning such controversial matters as school prayer and flag burning.

The Constitution does leave one window for curbing the Court slightly cracked: It does not specify the Court's size. And over time, fluctuations in the number of justices have reflected political considerations. Fortunately, the most outrageous attempts to exert control over the Court by adding or subtracting justices have been foiled by that ingenious invention of the founding fathers, the separation of powers.

Charles Evans Hughes and Franklin D. Roosevelt's "Court-packing" plan

When Franklin D. Roosevelt was elected president in 1932, the nation was mired deep in the Great Depression. Immediately after his inauguration, Roosevelt called for a special session of Congress, which lasted from March 9 to June 16, 1933. During this session, which came to be known as the *Hundred Days,* Roosevelt introduced and Congress passed a series of sweeping laws designed to reform the American economy from top to bottom. Most of these measures, collectively called the *First New Deal,* were meant to be short term. Many of them lasted for an even shorter time than Roosevelt intended when the Court found them to be unconstitutional.

How many justices make a court?

Initially, the number of justices on the Supreme Court was tied to the number of federal judicial districts or circuits. In 1789, those districts numbered three, and the judiciary act passed that year assigned two justices to serve each district, in addition to three resident district judges. So, when the Court first met in New York City on February 1, 1790, it consisted of six justices, one of them the chief justice.

Before the Republican Jefferson took office as president in 1802, the Federalist Congress passed the Judiciary Act of 1801 severing the relationship between Supreme Court justices and decreased the number of justices by one. This contraction had the effect of increasing the power of the central government, and, because the number of justices was only set to decrease after the next vacancy, it robbed Jefferson of at least one opportunity to appoint a new justice of his own political persuasion. The Jefferson administration and the Republicans in Congress rightly saw the legislation — which had also given the outgoing John Adams the right to appoint 16 circuit judges — as an attempt to pack the federal judiciary with Federalists. At Jefferson's insistence, the 1801 act was repealed, and new legislation was passed. The Judiciary Act of 1802 restored the federal judiciary to its earlier state, with this exception: Six federal circuits, each staffed by one of the six Supreme Court justices, now existed. Just to make sure that the Court would not immediately exercise its power of judicial review over the new legislation, the 1802 act also moved the start date of the Court's next term from June 1802 to February 1803.

Over the next 65 years, the size of the Court grew by increments, with new justices added as westward expansion of the country required the creation of new federal circuits. By the time of the Civil War, the Court consisted of nine justices. In March 1863, in order to assure implementation of Abraham Lincoln's war measures, Congress upped the number of justices to ten. Lincoln was then able to appoint another justice to increase the slim majority that had upheld his orders and proclamations up to that time.

Lincoln's successor, Andrew Johnson, proved to be unpopular with the Radical Republicans who controlled Congress after the Civil War. In order to defeat his Reconstruction program, Congress passed legislation in 1866 that reduced the number of justices by attrition to seven, thus depriving Johnson of the opportunity to fill any vacancies. The Judiciary Act of 1869 established the number of justices as nine, and there it has remained ever since, despite at least one highly concerted effort to pack the Court with presidential yes-men in 1937. (See the section "Charles Evans Hughes and Franklin D. Roosevelt's 'Court-packing' plan'," later in this chapter.)

Despite the First New Deal, the depression dragged on. Roosevelt responded by developing a program for long-term economic reform, a comprehensive plan that amounted to a whole new, second New Deal. The Supreme Court, then controlled by a highly conservative majority voting bloc, thought Roosevelt's new plan was more of the same. Even after he was reelected in 1936 by a landslide, the Court continued to reject many of Roosevelt's reforms — particularly those that interfered with private business — as unconstitutional. In an effort to counteract these rejections of what he saw as vital legislation, in February 1937 Roosevelt submitted a proposal to reorganize the federal judiciary to Congress. Roosevelt's scheme, immediately dubbed his "Court-packing" plan, proposed to increase the size of the federal judiciary, thus permitting Roosevelt to appoint judges who shared his political views. Included in the plan was a proposal to add one new Supreme Court justice for every sitting justice over the age of 70 for a total of 15 justices. Roosevelt next took his case to the public, using one of his "fireside chat" radio broadcasts to pitch his "plan to save our national Constitution from hardening of the judicial arteries."

Congress did not buy Roosevelt's rather lame excuse that the older justices simply weren't up to the job of handling all the litigation spawned by his new legislation. And Chief Justice Charles Evans Hughes (see Figure 5-7) plainly saw the plan as an assault on the Court's independence. Roosevelt had misjudged the mind of both the public and the Senate, and Hughes saw an opportunity to take advantage of the president's miscalculation. Hughes drafted a letter to Senator Burton K. Wheeler, a New Dealer who had taken the lead in the campaign against Roosevelt's proposal. The letter categorically denied every one of the president's assertions, adding that an increase in the number of justices would actually slow down the Court's work by dragging out its deliberations. Hughes's letter was also signed by Justice Louis D. Brandeis, who opposed the Court-packing plan on separation of powers grounds. Hughes told Wheeler that the other justices had not signed on simply because he had not had enough time to circulate his letter. This statement was not, however, entirely true: Later research revealed that Justice Harlan F. Stone would have declined to sign Hughes's letter. When Wheeler made the letter public during Senate Judiciary Committee hearings, this publication doomed the Court-packing plan.

As 20-20 hindsight makes clear, Hughes need not have resorted to guile in sidetracking Roosevelt's attempt to undermine the Court's integrity; Roosevelt's plan was defeated. But even though he lost the battle, Roosevelt won the war — and he did so with the help of the Supreme Court. The Supreme Court Retirement Act, which went into effect on March 1, 1937, allowed justices to retire at 70 with full pensions. Passage of this legislation — and who knows what other pressure from within the Court — prompted one of the New Deal's arch enemies, Justice Willis Van Devanter, to announce his retirement shortly thereafter. His was one of seven vacancies Roosevelt would fill over the next four years, assuring a friendly reception for New Deal measures in the Court. In addition, starting in the spring of 1937, the Hughes Court started handing down decisions upholding New Deal legislation — some of it almost identical to legislation the Court had struck down previously. This change in the Court's posture had begun to evolve before Roosevelt announced his plan to reorganize the Court, as Hughes and swing vote Owen J. Roberts began a constitutional revolution with *West Coast Hotel v. Parrish* (1937), a 5-4 decision that upheld a state minimum wage law. Although the decision was not announced until March 29, the votes had been cast weeks earlier. Such subtleties of timing were not obvious to the public, however, and the change in Roberts's voting pattern was dubbed "the switch in time that saved nine."

Figure 5-7:
Chief
Justice
Charles
Evans
Hughes.

Library of Congress, Prints and Photographs Division
[LC-USZ62-102280]

After April 1937, the Court upheld virtually every piece of New Deal legislation that came before it. It was not just self-preservation that caused this about-face. As Justice Roberts later declared, "Looking back, it is difficult to see how the court could have resisted the popular urge for uniform standards throughout the country — for what in effect was a unified economy." In the end, the Court was no more immune to social change than the other branches of government. The Great Depression gave rise to Franklin D. Roosevelt, the New Deal, and a constitutional revolution. Chief Justice Hughes had the flexibility that allowed him to stay the course during this abrupt transition. He also had the nerve — when pressed — to turn Roosevelt's own tactics against him. FDR may have won the war, but he paid dearly for his victory. His Court-packing plan cost him the confidence of a substantial portion of the American public, which had been reminded of the importance of keeping the Court above the rough-and-tumble of the political fray.

Statesmanship: When a Chief Justice Is More than a Chief Justice

Justices of the Supreme Court are by definition both politicians and public servants. Chief justices share these characteristics but are also imbued with a special aura of authority. Their special position in the Court itself often seems like more than it is, but most of the men who have sat in the chief's chair have gotten there because they have a special relationship with the president who appointed them, and therein lies the source of much of their prestige. This exalted position often comes with a price, as presidents are known to call in favors, requiring chief justices to serve two roles — and two masters — simultaneously. The results of such divided loyalties have seldom improved the standing of the chief justice or of the Court he heads.

John Jay as chief justice and diplomat

Before John Jay became the Court's first chief justice, he had had a brilliant career as a diplomat. His first foray into mediation occurred in 1773, when at the age of 28 he served as secretary to the Royal Boundary Commission, assigned to mediating a boundary dispute between New York and New Jersey. The following year, he was a member of the New York Committee of Correspondence, whose job it was to maintain good relations with Mother England. In 1779, Congress appointed him minister to Spain, and in 1782, he was sent to assist John Adams and Benjamin Franklin in formulating the Treaty of Paris, which ended the Revolutionary War. Jay's insistence that England recognize his country as the "United States," rather than as its former colonies, trading off America's insistence that England surrender control of Canada, helped bring all the signatories to the table. When he returned in triumph to American shores in 1784, Jay was named secretary of foreign affairs for the Confederation, a post he held until 1789.

Jay, who had grown increasingly skeptical about the viability of a confederation of states, authored three of the *Federalist Papers*, which were essentially public relations pieces promoting federalism. When the newly elected George Washington offered Jay the position of chief justice, Jay eagerly accepted. His expectations that he would be able to use his new position to ensure the supremacy of federal law were disappointed, however. Little business actually came before the Court, and the burden of circuit riding (see Chapter 1) only added to the Court's poor morale.

Jay grew bored and impatient. Convinced of the Court's ineffectiveness, he jumped at Washington's offer, in 1794, to serve as *envoy extraordinaire*, sailing to England to negotiate a variety of monetary disputes that lingered in the wake of the Treaty of Paris. The *Jay Treaty*, which exchanged American trading rights in the West Indies for England's withdrawal from their remaining North American military outposts, probably prevented another war. The agreement was also highly controversial, managing to alienate both Southern Republicans, who bore the brunt of Jay's financial settlement, and Federalists like Washington himself. The Senate, which finally ratified the Jay Treaty after months of debate, had cause to remember the heated debate about Jay's appointment as Washington's envoy. One proposal circulated at the time maintained that "to permit Judges of the Supreme Court to hold at the same time any other office of employment emanating from and holden at the pleasure of the Executive is contrary to the spirit of the Constitution and as tending to expose them to the influence of the Executive, is mischievous and impolitic."

Fortunately, while Jay was away in England doing the president's business, he had been elected governor of New York. Everyone was relieved when he handed in his resignation as chief justice before becoming his state's chief executive.

Earl Warren and the Warren Commission Report

After the assassination of John F. Kennedy in Dallas in 1963 prompted national debate about who actually killed the president, Lyndon B. Johnson set up a commission to investigate the circumstances surrounding the murder. Chief Justice Earl Warren was asked to head the commission, and to his everlasting unhappiness, he agreed to do so. Warren's instincts told him not to breach the separation of powers, but like so many others, he found himself no match for Johnson's powers of persuasion.

Inevitably, the commission became known as the Warren Commission and its final report as the Warren Report. The investigation, which lasted almost a year, took testimony from 552 witnesses and 10 federal agencies and took place almost entirely behind closed doors. Warren was not an active participant in these proceedings, but he did help shape the commission's final report. Chief among its findings was that there was no conspiracy — either foreign or domestic — to kill the president. Lee Harvey Oswald was declared the lone gunman, and *his* assassin, Jack Ruby, was found to have no connection to either Kennedy or Oswald.

When it was published in1964, the Warren Report not only failed to settle the controversy surrounding the Kennedy assassination, it raised even more questions. The Commission, which had not had complete access to the relevant FBI and CIA files, was itself accused of conspiring in a whitewash. Warren himself was unhappy not just with the inconclusiveness of the commission's findings, but also with the dissension among its members. As nominal head of the group of politicians and public figures who constituted the investigating committee, Warren was blamed for its shortcomings. Allegations of Communist sympathies that had led to previous impeachment efforts aimed at the Chief Justice came back to haunt him. Public dissatisfaction with the Warren Report led, in 1979, to a congressional investigation of the investigation. By that time, Warren was in his grave, remembered for the revolution in individual rights that occurred under his watch at the Supreme Court — and by the nagging suspicion of government collusion still connected with his mistaken venture outside the judicial realm.

Chapter 6

A Touch of Class: Some Notable Justices

*T*he Court — perhaps because we refer to it as the Court, the Supreme Court, the high bench, and so on — can seem to be a monolithic institution. It *is* an institution, no doubt about that, but it's also a collection of individual personalities. Because appointments to the Supreme Court are made by the president and confirmed by the Senate, they are by their very nature political and inevitably produce some mediocre justices. Others, however, have been extraordinary people who have added immeasurably to American jurisprudence and American life. This chapter introduces you to some of the more noteworthy people who have graced the high bench and their legacies to the law.

The Scholars

When you consider the law, and in particular the nation's highest court, you probably assume that it takes considerable smarts to wrestle with the kinds of complex legal issues that make up a justice's job. And indeed it is a rare justice who leaves the impression of being a dim bulb. Some of the justices have, however, been remarkable for their brilliance. A fair number have been recruited from among the ranks of law professors, and some of them have even begun their associations with law schools while serving on the Court. Here are two of the Court's most conspicuously learned individuals, both scholars of the first order. In one case, the justice's scholarship was an attribute. In the other, it often got in the way.

Joseph Story and the art of legal commentary

After Chief Justice John Marshall (see Chapter 5), Joseph Story (see Figure 6-1) was the most influential member of the Marshall Court. He is generally considered to have been the most learned justice ever to sit on the high bench, and he was the youngest person (he was 32 years old when appointed in 1811) ever to take a seat there. By that time, Story had already served as a state legislator and a U.S. Representative. He had also demonstrated his scholarship by writing several legal texts. And he was a published poet to boot.

Figure 6-1: Justice Joseph Story.

© Bettman/CORBIS

Story was born in 1779 in Marblehead, Massachusetts, where his father worked as a physician. The elder Story had also served under George Washington during the War of Independence, and he passed a strong sense of patriotism and a dedication to public service down to his son. Because of a fight with a classmate, Story was forced to leave Marblehead Academy before graduation, but he didn't let a small thing like expulsion stand in the way of his career goals. In six months and entirely on his own, he completed not only the remainder of his preparatory studies, but also the first semester of college course work. In 1798, he graduated second in his class from Harvard.

It must have been while reading law in the office of a Congressman that Story was bitten by the political bug. He was admitted to the bar in 1801, but almost immediately became active in state politics. Massachusetts was Federalist territory, and Story was a Jeffersonian Republican, but he still managed to get elected to the state legislature in 1805. In 1808, he was elected to the U.S. House of Representatives, but he resigned after one term after he was accused of party disloyalty for voting against President Jefferson's embargo on importation of foreign goods.

Story returned to Massachusetts to practice law in earnest, distinguishing himself both at home and before the U.S. Supreme Court. It was during this period that he also published a series of legal tracts that brought him national attention. But when a place on the Supreme Court opened up in 1810, James Madison turned to Story only after his first three choices turned down the offer. Story's party loyalty was in question, and Madison nominated him over Jefferson's objections that the nominee was a "pseudo-Republican."

Jefferson was right. In no time, Story became the Federalist John Marshall's alter-ego. It was Story's opinion in *Martin v. Hunter's Lessee* (1816), which grew out of Virginia's refusal to enforce a Supreme Court ruling, that established the supremacy of federal over state courts in cases involving federal law. Early in his tenure, Story also began to pressure the Court to accept the idea of federal jurisdiction over criminal law, then solely the province of the states. When he found his colleagues uncooperative, Story formed an alliance with the statesman Daniel Webster, who helped get Story's criminal code through Congress in 1825. Story continued to write for Webster, both legislation and some of the speeches that helped make Webster's reputation as a great orator.

Story was also responsible for drafting a number of highly influential Supreme Court opinions, particularly in the area of commercial and maritime law. Using his in-depth knowledge of English legal history, Story almost single-handedly carved out an area in American jurisprudence for *private law,* the rules governing the conduct of business and other nonpublic affairs. His nationalism was economic as well as political, and he regarded private property as central to republicanism. John Marshall wrote the opinion of the Court in *Dartmouth College v. Woodward* (1819), in which Story's friend Daniel Webster — perhaps employing some of Story's legal advice — eloquently and successfully argued the case against state regulation of a private corporation. But it was Story's concurring opinion that linked the fate of private corporations to educational organizations, assuring both constitutional protection.

Story pursued his goal of creating a system of legal principles governing commerce by writing a series of legal treatises, which he used while teaching law at Harvard. He had been elected to the governing board of his alma mater in 1819. A decade later, he moved from Salem to Cambridge, Massachusetts, in order to help set up a law school at Harvard. Story not only succeeded in making Harvard Law School the first true institution for legal studies, he devised a national approach to the study of law that is still followed. If you are a law student at, say, the University of Michigan in the year 2002, you won't learn much about the laws of the State of Michigan. Thanks to Joseph Story, the educational focus is on national law.

In addition to the 286 opinions he wrote for the Court and his nine commentaries on the law, Story also published essays in popular magazines and contributed unsigned articles to the *Encyclopedia Americana*. His visibility and outspoken support for strong central government probably robbed him of any chance to succeed John Marshall as chief justice. After Marshall's death in 1835, the Southern Democrat Andrew Jackson surveyed the landscape and declared Story "the most dangerous man in America." Story stayed on after the Southern slaveholder Roger Brooke Taney was named chief justice, but increasingly found himself dissenting from a Court majority that favored states' rights. He was also profoundly disturbed by the upsurge in cases concerning the constitutionality of slavery. While he opposed it personally and politically, his understanding of the laws of commerce and private property convinced him that the Constitution sanctioned slavery. Attacked by abolitionists for his legal opinions on the subject, Story was planning to resign from the Court when he died unexpectedly in 1845.

Felix Frankfurter and "process jurisprudence"

Felix Frankfurter's (see Figure 6-2) origins speak volumes about his behavior on the Supreme Court. Born in Vienna, Austria, into a Jewish family, Frankfurter immigrated to the U.S. with his family when he was 12. The Frankfurters, like many Jewish immigrants early in the late 19th century, settled amid the tenement squalor of the lower east side of Manhattan. Frankfurter never lost the vision of himself as a 12-year-old immigrant who spoke no English, a boy who by dint of his own brilliance and tenacity raised himself by his bootstraps to a seat on the highest Court in the land.

Frankfurter's career before he became a justice provides ample evidence of his intelligence and drive. A standout at City College, he also graduated first in his class from Harvard Law School. From there, he briefly went into private practice before being tapped by Henry L. Stimson to work as an assistant U.S. attorney in the Southern District of New York. When Stimson was recruited as secretary of war in 1910, Frankfurter accompanied his mentor to Washington, where he served as a legal officer in the war department for the next four years.

In 1914, Frankfurter accepted a job on the faculty of Harvard Law School, where he was truly in his element. As more than one commentator has noted, Frankfurter had a rabbinical sense of the law (his father had, in fact, trained as a rabbi), and he reveled in the role of law professor, which allowed him to probe legal complexities and prod his students to do likewise. These traits never left him, contributing to his reputation as a demanding and respected teacher — and later, to his fellow justices' impatience when he lectured them in open court.

Figure 6-2:
Justice Felix
Frankfurter.

© Oscar White/CORBIS

Frankfurter kept his job at Harvard for the next 26 years, even while he was deeply involved in public affairs. In addition to serving as legal advisor to the American Zionist Movement, the National Association for the Advancement of Colored People, and the anarchists Nicola Sacco and Bartolomeo Vanzetti — who were convicted of murder after a much publicized and probably flawed trial — Frankfurter helped found the American Civil Liberties Union and the left-wing periodical, *The Nation*.

All these activities made Frankfurter one of the most visible liberal activists in the country and brought him into contact with Franklin D. Roosevelt, who became his fast friend. After Roosevelt moved into the White House in 1933, he offered Frankfurter the post of U.S. solicitor general. Frankfurter turned him down, apparently preferring to serve as a more informal advisor. Over the next six years, Frankfurter would become the principle architect of Roosevelt's New Deal (see Chapter 4), in addition to supplying the administration with bright young Harvard Law grads — "Happy Hot Dogs," as they were known — to staff the numerous agencies spawned by the national recovery effort. Frankfurter was, in the words of one administration insider, "the most influential individual in the United States."

Frankfurter v. Black

The leadership role that might have been Frankfurter's went instead to Hugo L. Black, an Alabama storekeeper's son and former Ku Klux Klan member (see Chapter 4) who was Roosevelt's first Supreme Court appointee. Black, unlike Frankfurter, did not pay a great deal of attention to the law's finer points. He was, instead, dedicated to the letter of the law — in particular to the First Amendment. Unlike Frankfurter, Black was concerned with political outcomes and provoking a revolution in individual rights — not with educating the public about the need for judicial restraint. Overtly cordial to Black on the bench, Frankfurter worked behind Black's back to undermine his rival's authority. Frankfurter went so far as to feed his allies on the Court, Justices John M. Harlan and Robert L. Jackson, unflattering gossip about Black, whom some of Frankfurter's correspondents referred to as a "skunk." The whole contest did smell to high heavens.

Because of his work at Harvard Law School, Frankfurter had also become a nationally recognized expert on the Constitution and the Supreme Court. His appointment to the Court by Roosevelt in 1939 seemed inevitable. He was widely expected to become the Court's intellectual leader. Things did not, however, turn out that way. While the other Roosevelt appointees helped move what had been an ultra-conservative Court leftward, Frankfurter developed into the Court's leading conservative. This attitude more often than not put him in the minority in important cases.

Frankfurter's lengthy, highly analytical opinions — many of them dissents — emphasized what came to be known as *process jurisprudence,* an approach to constitutional interpretation that emphasized history and produced evolution, not revolution. Many on the Court found them to be just another tedious example of Frankfurter's urge to lecture. Much of what he had to say went unheard in the din created by an explosion of individual rights that simply passed him by.

The Stylists

Nowhere does the Constitution require the Court to put its opinions in writing. In the 1790s, the justices simply delivered most of their decisions orally from the bench, committing only their most important ones to paper. Starting with the great chief justice, John Marshall, however, the justices realized that the most powerful tool at their disposal — the one guaranteed to increase their power and prestige — was the written opinion. All the public knows about the justices and how they are charting a future course for America comes from the words of their opinions. Furthermore, as Chief Justice Charles Evans Hughes observed, "[T]here is no better precaution against judicial mistakes than the setting out accurately and adequately the material facts as well as the points to be decided." As anyone who has ever written an essay knows, putting your thoughts down on paper helps you figure out what you really think.

There's no doubt that styles in opinion writing — as in everything else — have changed over time. What was known as the *grand style* of the early Court — as seen in the opinions of Chief Justice John Marshall, for example — conveyed an image of the Court as all-knowing, almost divine. That style, however, faded as the Court's place in the federal scheme of governance became clearer, its authority plain to all. After the middle of the 19th century, this style was replaced by a *formal style,* known for its obscurity, repetitiveness, and sheer dullness. After all, the justices' case load had greatly increased, leaving them little time to work on their prose. During the early to mid-20th century — inspired by the efforts of justices like Oliver Wendell Holmes and Benjamin Cardozo — many on the high bench took pains to make their words clear, even memorable. In recent times, as more and more opinions are apparently drafted by law clerks rather than the justices they work for, legal opinions have exhibited a *law review style* incomprehensible to most. Most Americans are now forced to rely upon the media to interpret what the Court says.

Oliver Wendell Holmes, Jr. and the art of legal epigram

Oliver Wendell Holmes, Jr. (see Figure 6-3) was born into a literary family. His father, a Boston physician, was also a well-known man of letters whose most famous work is the collection of essays and poems titled *The Autocrat of the Breakfast Table* (1858). While he was still living at home, the younger Holmes often sat in on conversations between his father and literary giants like Ralph Waldo Emerson, who encouraged the young man's independent thinking.

When Holmes graduated from Harvard College in 1861, the nation was immersed in civil war. True to the powerful sense of duty that was part of his mother's legacy (during the 25 years he sat on the Supreme Court, Holmes never missed a session), Holmes immediately enlisted in the Union army. He served with distinction and was wounded three times before his service ended in 1864. When Holmes told his father that his next step was to enroll in law school, the older man replied incredulously, "What's the use of that? A lawyer can't be a great man." His son would prove him wrong. After graduating from Harvard Law School in 1866, Holmes began a dual career that combined law and letters. While practicing law, he turned out a steady stream of essays devoted largely to legal topics. In 1880, when he was invited to deliver a series of public lectures, these essays provided him with subject matter. The next year, they were collected and published as *The Common Law,* a book that would change both Holmes's life and the course of American jurisprudence.

Figure 6-3:
Justice
Oliver
Wendell
Holmes, Jr.

Library of Congress, Prints and Photographs
Division [LC-USZ62-58677]

The Common Law was eye-opening. Holmes rejected the idea that law is rigid
and predictable like mathematics, instead seeing it as a reflection of the
human condition: "The life of the law has not been logic: it has been experience. The felt necessities of public policy, avowed or unconscious, even the
prejudices which judges share with their fellow-men, have had a good deal
more to do with the syllogism in determining the rules by which men should
be governed." It's impossible to overstate how revolutionary statements like
this seemed at the time. "Felt necessities" was just the first of many evocative
phrases that Holmes would contributed to legal discourse.

Holmes was appointed to the faculty of Harvard Law School in 1882. He
stayed there only one semester before his appointment to the Massachusetts
Supreme Court. He served on that court for 20 years, the last three as chief
justice. In that time, he wrote more than a thousand legal opinions, many
of them expressing the kinds of progressive attitudes that were shaping
American society at the time. Holmes's philosophy and his eloquence
attracted the attention of President Theodore Roosevelt, who was himself
an ardent progressive reformer as well as a writer. In 1902, Holmes became
Roosevelt's first Supreme Court nominee.

Holmes was already 61 years old when he took his seat on the high bench,
but over the next 29 years, he would become one of the most outspoken, pro-
ductive, and influential justices the Court has ever known. In that time, he
wrote 873 opinions, more than any justice who came before him. He wrote

proportionately fewer dissents than his fellow justices, but being in the minority seemed to bring out the best in him. In *Lochner v. New York* (1905), Holmes penned one of his most-quoted epigrams: "The Fourteenth Amendment does not enact Mr. Herbert Spencer's Social Statics." Holmes's point, made with trademark efficiency of language, was that economic principles like those spelled out by Spencer's treatise, are not legal ones. But his majority opinions also had their moments: The "clear and present danger" standard for determining whether speech is protected by the First Amendment (see Chapter 8) comes from a throw-away line in *Schenck v. United States* (1919), in which the Court upheld the conviction of Socialist Party leader Eugene V. Debs for speaking out against the military draft during World War I.

Holmes was a deeply committed man who stayed on the Court longer than he should have. After his health had begun to fail in his 91st year, he had to be coaxed to submit his resignation by Chief Justice Charles Evans Hughes. But Holmes's announcement of his retirement still exhibited his trademark understatement. After the Court had heard oral argument on January 3, 1932, Holmes casually announced, "I won't be here tomorrow."

Benjamin Cardozo and the common law

Justice Oliver Wendell Holmes first made a name for himself by writing a book called *The Common Law*. The legacy of Benjamin N. Cardozo (see Figure 6-4), Holmes's successor on the high bench, was to reshape the *common law* — the body of judge-made laws America inherited from England — to fit the modern age.

Cardozo was born into a community of Sephardic Jews that settled in what is now Manhattan in 1654. Emma Lazarus, author of the poem inscribed on the base of the Statue of Liberty, is only one of his distinguished relatives. Cardozo's own father, however, was forced to resign as a state supreme court judge when he was implicated in the political scandals associated with New York City's ruling elite, known collectively as Tammany Hall. Benjamin Cardozo followed his father into the law, motivated perhaps by a desire to redeem his father's memory. Cardozo' would become the most celebrated common law judge of his day — perhaps of any day — using traditional legal principles and clear language to adapt the law to meet society's changing needs.

One of Cardozo's early tutors was Horatio Alger, who went on write countless popular works of fiction based on a rags-to-riches formula. Otherwise, little about Cardozo's personal life is noteworthy. He never married and lived with his older sister until she died in 1929. He practiced law with his older brother in New York City for 20 years. In 1914, Cardozo was appointed to the New York Supreme Court and was elevated almost immediately to the Court of Appeals, the state's highest court. He stayed there until 1932, and between 1926 and 1932 served as the court's chief judge.

Figure 6-4:
Justice
Benjamin N.
Cardozo.

Library of Congress, Prints and Photographs
Division [LC-USZ62-75144]

It's no exaggeration to say that Cardozo's whole life was the law. He single-handedly transformed the New York Court of Appeals into the most respected state court in the nation, expanding and updating laws governing fraud and torts, or civil wrongs, and essentially inventing the concept of product liability. He published several books, including *The Nature of the Judicial Process* (1921), which lawyers used as handbooks on how to practice law. He became so widely read and respected that when Holmes's retirement opened a place on the Supreme Court, Cardozo was nearly everyone's choice to take his place.

Cardozo served only six years on the Court before his death in 1938. During that time, however, he succeeded in redefining constitutional law in a series of cases culminating in his opinion for the Court in *Palko v. Connecticut* (1937), a case concerning a criminal defendant tried twice in state court for the same offense. The Court found that the constitutional prohibition against *double jeopardy* could not be enforced against states. Cardozo's opinion, however, described an "essence of a scheme of ordered liberty," later became the basis for making virtually all of the guarantees of the Bill Rights applicable at the state level.

After Cardozo's death, he was remembered by his brethren for "the strangely compelling power of that reticent, sensitive and almost mystical personality." By subsequent generations, he is remembered as the justice who forged the law into a tool for the improvement of social welfare.

The Rebels

Today, very few opinions issued by the Supreme Court are unanimous. In the early days of the Court, however, differences of opinion rising to the level of dissent were nonexistent. When a justice writes a dissenting opinion, he or she doesn't simply disagree with the majority's legal reasoning — if that were all, the opinion would be a concurring one. A dissenter is one who also disagrees with the majority's treatment of the parties. For a justice to go to the trouble of writing a dissent (and justices don't always put their disagreement in writing), that justice has to have a powerful, out-and-out disagreement with entire outcome of the case. Some dissents even ridicule the majority, as Thurgood Marshall did in his dissenting opinion in *Holland v. Illinois* (1990). The majority's decision to uphold a state court's ruling against a criminal defendant who appealed his conviction on the basis of the racial makeup of the jury that tried his case demonstrated a "selective amnesia with respect to our cases in this area."

Dissents are often written for some future audience, in the hope that one day these opinions will become the law. And sometimes they do. Imagine how gratifying it was for Hugo Black, who dissented against the Court's ruling in *Betts v. Brady* (1942) that indigent defendants in state criminal actions are not always entitled to court-appointed lawyers, to be able to write the opinion of the Court in the case that reversed *Betts* nearly 20 years later, *Gideon v. Wainwright* (1963). Some complain that dissent undermines the Court's authority, diluting the force of its rulings and providing fuel to Court critics. But others, like Justice Ruth Bader Ginsburg, feel that that most Americans understand dissent to be an honest expression of disagreement. Certainly, it has a long and honorable heritage.

William Johnson and the invention of dissent

Before William Johnson (see Figure 6-5) joined the Court in 1804, there had been virtually no dissent. Under the first three chief justices, the Court had followed the habit of issuing *seriatim* opinions, with each justice delivering his own view of the case. Under John Marshall, the Court began to speak with one voice as the strong — some said dictatorial — chief justice sought to enhance the Court's power and prestige. But Marshall's consensus began to unravel with the appointment of Johnson, Thomas Jefferson's first nominee to the high court.

Johnson was a native of South Carolina who joined the party of Thomas Jefferson during his three terms in the state assembly. By the time he joined South Carolina's Constitutional Court, he was one of the state's leading Republicans. In appointing Johnson to the Supreme Court in 1804, Jefferson

believed that he was placing a loyal Republican in among his federalist enemies, chief among them the Chief Justice (see Chapter 5). Initially, Johnson
behaved that way, delivering his first dissenting opinion in his third term on
the Court. He went on to deliver many more, nearly half those written during
his 30 years on the Court. This record earned him the title "First Dissenter,"
although strictly speaking, the first Supreme Court dissent was filed by
Justice Thomas Johnson in the Court's very first reported opinion in 1792. As
the Court followed the practice of seriatim opinions at that time, though,
Thomas Johnson's difference of opinion with his brother justices did not
carry quite the wallop of William Johnson's willingness to defy Marshall's
insistence on unanimous opinions.

In truth, though, William Johnson was an independent. Three years after his
appointment to the Court, he enraged Republicans by relying on John
Marshall's opinion in *Marbury v. Madison* (1803), the hated case which had
established the Court's right of judicial review (see Chapter 5). When, a year
later in circuit court, Johnson denied the president the right to remove a tax
collector from office, the attorney general complained to Jefferson that
Johnson had been infected with "leprosy of the Bench." And for a time,
Johnson did seem to fall under Marshall's sway, signing silently on to opinions upholding Federalist principles.

Figure 6-5:
Justice
William
Johnson.

Library of Congress, Prints and Photographs
Division [LC-USZ62-118146]

Throughout much of his time on the Court, Johnson and Jefferson kept up a highly improper correspondence in which the president repeatedly urged his appointee to disrupt Marshall's control of the Court. Jefferson was Johnson's hero, and the justice had no particular fondness — or even respect — for his fellow justices, at one point writing to Jefferson, "[William] Cushing was incompetent. [Samuel] Chase could not be got to think or write — [William] Paterson was a slow man and willingly declined the trouble, and the other two judges [Bushrod Washington and John Marshall] you know are commonly estimated as one judge." But Johnson was unwilling simply to be the president's stooge. Had he dissented more often than he did, he might have undermined his own authority on the Court. Indeed, one of the keys to his staying power was his unpredictability. He was restless and readily admitted to being easily distracted by outside activities, such as his two-volume biography of the Revolutionary War General Nathanael Greene. And yet Johnson clearly was, as Justice Felix Frankfurter said more than a century later, one of the strongest minds in the Court's history.

John Marshall Harlan and the empowerment of dissent

John Marshall Harlan (see Figure 6-6) was born in Boyle County, Kentucky, in 1833, the son of James Harlan, a lawyer and politician. James Harlan, a committed member of the Whig Party, named his fifth son after the Whigs' patron saint, "the great chief justice" and great Federalist John Marshall.

The younger Harlan followed his father, first into law and then into politics. The beginning of Harlan's political career coincided with the death of the Whig Party. Searching for an alternative, he shifted his allegiance to the Know-Nothings, known for the opposition to immigration and named for their refusal to publicly discuss their party. Stumping in Kentucky for Know-Nothing candidates, Harlan made a number of anti-immigrant speeches that would later return to haunt him. In 1860, Harlan again changed parties. As a slave-holding member of the Southern aristocracy, he was attracted to the Constitutional Unionist platform, which pledged support for the Union but hostility to abolition. With the onset of civil war, however, Harlan dedicated himself to the Union cause, writing anti-secessionist editorials for the Louisville *Journal* and engaging in other activities that helped prevent Kentucky from joining the Confederacy. In September 1861, Harlan formed the Tenth Kentucky Volunteers, serving as the unit's colonel and seeing action in both his home state and Tennessee.

Just three weeks after he resigned from the Union army in 1863, Harlan was nominated by the Union Party as a candidate for attorney general of Kentucky. He won easily and used his position to maintain his home state's allegiance to the North, although he opposed the Emancipation Proclamation. Although it became law in 1863, the Emancipation Proclamation only applied in rebel states, and Harlan continued to support his family's slaves until the Thirteenth Amendment abolished slavery two years later.

When the Thirteenth Amendment was proposed, Harlan opposed it, too, on grounds that it violated state sovereignty. If he wanted to stay in office in Kentucky, he could hardly do otherwise. And in the election of 1864, Harlan and other Kentucky Unionists demonstrated their dislike of the policies of the Lincoln administration by supporting Democratic candidate George McClellan for president. Harlan soon became disenchanted with the Democrats, too, when they introduced former Confederates into state politics. In 1868, running on what was then the Conservative Unionist ticket, Harlan was defeated in his attempt to be reelected as attorney general. It would be his last race as a Unionist.

Figure 6-6:
Justice
John
Marshall
Harlan.

Library of Congress, Prints and Photographs Division
[LC-USZ62-107687]

Harlan was not finished with politics, however. In 1868, he supported Republican candidate Ulysses S. Grant for president. After Grant's election, Harlan threw himself into the campaign to establish the newly reformed Republican Party in Kentucky. Saying he would rather be right than be consistent, Harlan now embraced the very ideas he had formerly scorned. He now publicly endorsed not only the Thirteenth Amendment, but also the Fourteenth, which granted African-Americans full citizenship, including the right to vote. He also renounced his former Know-Nothing rejection of Roman Catholics and immigrants.

In the run up to the presidential election of 1876, Harlan swung the Kentucky delegation behind Rutherford B. Hayes. Hayes became the Republican nominee, and once he became president, he did not forget Harlan's crucial support. In 1877, Hayes, who had already made up his mind to appoint a Southerner to the Court, made Harlan his first Supreme Court appointment. The battle in the Senate over Harlan's confirmation lasted six weeks, during which Republican stalwarts, suspicious of Harlan's conversion to the party, raised issues such as his early Know-Nothing allegiance and his later opposition to the Civil War amendments. In the end, however, the Senate unanimously confirmed his appointment.

Harlan made a quick start on the high bench, dissenting in one of the first cases he heard after taking his seat. Harlan was on his way to becoming one of the Court's great dissenters. And his style was unique. Until 1930, the justices customarily read their opinions from the bench, but Harlan, a seasoned orator accustomed to speaking on the stump, often delivered his opinions extemporaneously. One of his most famous dissents occurred in *Pollock v. Farmers' Loan & Trust Co.* (1895), in which he objected to the slim majority's overruling a federal law that imposed the nation's first peacetime income tax. Reactions to the case were emotional across the board, but Harlan's dissent made an especially vivid impression. According to the New York *Tribune,* Harlan

> pounded the desk, shook his finger under the noses of the Chief Justice [Melville W. Fuller] and Mr. Justice Field, turned more than once almost eagerly upon his colleagues of the majority, and expressed his dissent from their conclusions in a tone and language more appropriate to a stump speech at a Populace barbecue than to an opinion on a question of law before the Supreme Court of the United States.

Harlan quickly developed a reputation for idiosyncrasy among his fellow justices. Oliver Wendell Holmes referred to him as "the last of the tobacco-spitting judges." (It is worth noting here that tobacco chewing is a time honored tradition of the Court, which until recently included multiple spittoons among its furnishings.) David J. Brewer remarked that, "Mr. Justice Harlan . . . believes implicitly in the Constitution. He goes to bed every night with one hand on the Constitution and the other on the Bible, and so sleeps the sweet sleep of justice and righteousness." And long after Harlan's death, Felix Frankfurter denigrated Harlan's contributions to American jurisprudence when he remarked that Harlan had been no more than "an eccentric exception" on the Court.

Who was underneath those Whigs?

The Whigs, a major political party in mid-19th-century America, was formed by a coalition of National Republicans, southerners whose support for the populist Republican president Andrew Jackson, and the Anti-Masons, a group opposing the Freemasons, an elitist secret organization with roots in Europe. In 1834, a New York newspaper named the group *Whigs*, after Britain's traditional anti-royalists, because of its hatred for *King* Andrew Jackson, who had, for some, become a dictator.

The Whig leader was the Kentuckian and perennial presidential candidate Henry Clay. Clay never made it to the White House, but in 1840, another Whig candidate, William Henry Harrison, did. When Harrison died of pneumonia after only a month in office, he was succeeded by John Tyler, whose term was marred by antagonism with the Whig-dominated Congress led by — who else? — Henry Clay. Clay succeeded in having Tyler ousted from the party, but even this maneuver failed to win Clay the presidency. In 1844, he lost to Democrat James K. Polk. Another Whig, the Mexican War hero Zachary Taylor, was elected president in 1848. Taylor died in office two years later and was succeeded by his vice president, Millard Fillmore, who represented the Whigs last gasp. As the debate over slavery heated up, most of the party was absorbed by yet another new political party, the Free-Soilers, whose platform consisted of opposition to admission of new slaveholding states.

His personal habits aside, Harlan tended to be a libertarian on the Court, a justice whose instinctual approach to constitutional interpretation frequently put him at odds with what he saw as the majority's employment of good logic to make bad law. For his part, Harlan would always rather be right than consistent. And he was often proven right. When later Court majorities endorsed many of his dissenting views, Harlan was labeled a "premature New Dealer" (see Chapter 5). Harlan served on the Court during a time when most of his fellow justices exercised a *laissez faire* approach in dispensing justice, deferring to business and ignoring the public welfare. Harlan was predisposed by his early Whig orientation to endorse the priorities of the national government over states' rights. In 1895, he registered the only dissenting vote in *United States v. E.C. Knight Co.,* which limited Congress's attempt to control interstate commerce by means of the Sherman Anti-Trust Act. And in one of his last written opinions, in *Standard Oil v. United States* (1911), Harlan sided with the majority's approval of the dissolution of one of the nation's largest monopolies.

Harlan's dissenting opinions in *Hurtado v. California* (1884) and *Twining v. New Jersey* (1908), in both of which he insisted the due process guarantees of the Fifth Amendment (see Chapter 9) were applicable to state criminal procedures, have also proved to be farsighted. The due process revolution fostered by Justice Hugo L. Black's championship of the *incorporation doctrine,* making the individual protections afforded by the Bill of Rights applicable at the state as well as the federal level, was still almost a half century away.

But it was in the field of civil rights that Harlan has left his most enduring mark. In his dissenting opinion in the 1883 *Civil Rights Cases,* he crafted a rationale for government control of public accommodations such as hotels and trains that Congress employed in drafting the Civil Rights Act of 1964. As he memorably argued, the constitutional amendments passed in the wake of the Civil War were intended to outlaw not only human bondage, but also "badges of slavery." The watershed case of *Brown v. Board of Education* (1954) (see Chapter 12) overturned the notorious "separate but equal" doctrine of *Plessy v. Ferguson* (1896), in which Harlan, the lone dissenter, memorably stated that the "Constitution is color-blind, and neither knows nor tolerates classes among citizens."

Harlan stayed on the Court almost until the day he died. He was one of the longest serving justices, and during his tenure, he participated in over 14,000 cases and wrote 1,161 opinions. Yet by the time of his death, his influence had waned. At his memorial service, one speaker recalled, "[Harlan] could lead but he could not follow. . . . His was not the temper of a negotiator." And for the next quarter century — during which a conservative, even reactionary philosophy held sway on the Court — Harlan's views were largely regarded as having been the product of an irascible and erratic temperament. It would take the due process revolution in the 1940s and of the civil right movement in the 1950s to rehabilitate Harlan's reputation. In hindsight, his opinions — particularly his dissents — came to seem prophetic.

The Progressives

The progressive movement of social reform is most obviously associated with former president Theodore Roosevelt's short-lived Progressive Party — also called the Bull Moose Party, after Roosevelt's jubilant assertion that he "felt like a bull moose," when he accepted the Progressive nomination in 1912. But the Progressive Party was itself a reflection of the times, which were characterized by optimism, uplift, and government efforts aimed at improving social welfare. Progressivism touched many political parties, ranging from Socialist liberals to Prohibitionist reactionaries. And progressivism produced three presidents, Theodore Roosevelt, William Howard Taft, and Woodrow Wilson. Roosevelt, the trust buster, hand-picked his successor, William Howard Taft, who also inherited Roosevelt's agenda.

Roosevelt, unhappy out of the limelight and unhappy with Taft's first term performance, decided to challenge him for the Republican nomination in 1912. Roosevelt's platform, called The New Nationalism, proposed making the president steward of the public welfare and would require more government bureaucracy to do so. Many progressives disapproved of the plan, and Taft and Roosevelt effectively split the Republican ticket, assuring Woodrow

Wilson, a nominal Democrat, of election. Wilson's platform, which he called the New Freedom, was almost indistinguishable from Roosevelt's.

Progressivism formally ended with World War I. But when Theodore Roosevelt's distant kinsman Franklin Roosevelt won the White House in 1932, his New Deal (see Chapter 4), with its proliferating *alphabet agencies,* was more than a distant echo of the New Nationalism. With FDR, progressivism — or more properly its offspring, liberalism — took root in the federal government, and it has never really gone away.

Louis Brandeis and the invention of new rights

The man who helped Woodrow Wilson draft the progressive program that won him the presidency in 1912 was a lawyer named Louis D. Brandeis (see Figure 6-7). Brandeis wasn't just any lawyer; he was one of the most successful and highly sought after attorneys of his day. Born to Jewish parents who had immigrated to America from Bohemia, Brandeis was raised amid affluence in Louisville, Kentucky. During the economic panic of 1873, Brandeis's father shut down his grain business to take his family on an extended European tour to escape the dire effects of the depression. Brandeis attended preparatory school in Germany during this period, but he did not obtain a degree. Still, when he returned to the United States, he was able to enter Harvard Law School at age 18. He graduated in 1877 with the highest grade point average that the school had ever seen.

Brandeis went into private practice in Boston with a former classmate, Samuel D. Warren Jr. Their firm was phenomenally successful, and by the age of 35, Brandeis was making in excess of $50,000 at a time when most lawyers in the country had annual incomes of around $5,000. But Brandeis had a social conscience. In addition to serving clients with deep pockets, he began to seek out progressive causes to support. His was an age of business monopolies that gave the country, as Brandeis said, "the curse of bigness." Brandeis countered it by helping Boston's municipal transportation authority fend off a corporate grab, by sidestepping the big insurance companies to set up savings bank insurance policies for ordinary folk, and by defending state maximum hour and minimum wage labor laws. And he did much of this work *pro bono,* for free. For such reasons as these, he became known as the *People's Attorney.*

Brandeis often represented clients before the Supreme Court, and on one such occasion, he introduced a radically new type of legal argument that has ever since been known as the *Brandeis brief.* He used it in *Muller v. Oregon* (1908), a case concerning limitations on the working hours of female laundry workers. In order to convince the Court to uphold a law restricting the work day to ten hours, Brandeis relied not just on legal precedents, but on statistical data, medical reports, psychological treatises, and so on. The Brandeis brief was long on facts and short on law: Only two of its 112 pages were devoted to a discussion of legal issues. By focusing on this type of *sociological jurisprudence,* Brandeis forced the Court to grapple with the same issues the Oregon legislature had considered in drafting its labor law — he forced the justices to consider the people affected by the law, not just the law's impact on other laws. It was a revolutionary approach, and it worked. Use of the Brandeis brief quickly became the norm in cases argued before the Supreme Court.

Figure 6-7:
Justice
Louis D.
Brandeis.

Library of Congress, Prints and Photographs
Division [LC-USZ62-92924]

Woodrow Wilson, too, saw the usefulness of Brandeis's approach to changing social policy and put him to work on his winning New Freedom election platform. After Wilson was elected president in 1912, he repaid Brandeis with a Supreme Court nomination. It almost goes without saying that this appointment was controversial. The battle over Brandeis's confirmation lasted four months, bringing out the worst in many. Bigots railed against Brandeis's religion, while conservatives assailed what they saw as the nominee's dangerous radical politics. Former President William Howard Taft, who bore a grudge against Brandeis over an investigation he had led against Taft's Secretary of the Interior, took his revenge by declaring the nomination "one of the deepest wounds I have had as an American and a lover of the Constitution." In the end, a vote of 47-22 made Brandeis the first Jew to sit on the U.S. Supreme Court (see Chapter 4).

During Brandeis's nearly 23 years on the Court, he was often at odds with the conservative majority. His well-honed, well-argued dissents became, like the Brandeis brief, instruments of instruction intended to educate his fellow justices about the evils of *laissez faire* justice, which opposed government regulation of commerce at the expense of individual liberties. His very first dissenting opinion, in the free speech case *Schaefer v. U.S.* (1920), described how Justice Holmes's "clear and present danger" test could be transformed from a measure of restriction to a measure of protection. In his dissent in *Gilbert v. Minnesota* (1920), Brandeis defended the appellant's right to speak out against military service. In writing his opinion, Brandeis became the first justice to suggest that the guarantees of the Bill of Rights extended to state law through the Fourteenth Amendment. This Court would accept this view five years later with regard to freedom of speech, and nearly three decades later, it would form the basis for a due process revolution in the law (see Chapter 9). Brandeis's concurring opinion in *Whitney v. California* (1927), a case concerning the anarchist International Workers of the World, includes one of the most eloquent defenses of free speech ever written:

> [The founders] believed that freedom to think as you will and to speak as you think are means indispensable to the discovery and spread of political truth. . . . To courageous, self reliant men . . . no danger flowing from speech can be deemed clear and present, unless the incidence of the evil apprehended is so imminent that it may befall before there is opportunity for full discussion.

Brandeis's most radical legal introduction concerned the right to privacy, a right not spelled out in the Constitution. As early as 1890, Brandeis and his law partner Samuel Warren had argued that privacy was a guiding principle behind our nation's foundation documents. And in his dissent in the 1928 government wiretapping case *Olmstead v. U.S.*, Brandeis argued this theory once again: "The makers of our Constitution . . . conferred, as against the government, the right to be let alone — the most comprehensive of rights and the right most valued by civilized men." More than a quarter century later, the Supreme Court finally accepted Brandeis's argument in, *Griswold v. Connecticut* (1965), a decision upholding the legality of contraception.

Brandeis remained politically engaged throughout his time on the Court. And during the era of Franklin Roosevelt's New Deal (see Chapter 4), he seemed to have revisited the role he played in creating Woodrow Wilson's New Freedom agenda. Although he may have overstepped his bounds by getting too cozy with the executive branch, Brandeis could not resist the urge to help government do the right thing by the people.

Earl Warren and the empowerment of a race

Many people think that Earl Warren's finest moment was his leadership of the Court in *Brown v. Board of Education* (1954) (see Chapter 12), the decision that ended school segregation and sparked the civil rights movement. For his part, Warren himself thought the reapportionment cases *Baker v. Carr* (1962) and *Reynolds v. Sims* (1964) were the most significant cases decided under his watch. Actually, all these decisions were of a piece. *Baker* and *Reynolds* simply expanded upon the conception of equal protection (see Chapter 10) used in *Brown* to overturn segregation. By concentrating on electoral reform in the later cases, the Warren Court literally recreated the political landscape of America, guaranteeing the concept of "one person, one vote."

America's legislative districts had originally been drawn up in a time when its population was largely rural. Over time, the population shifted toward cities, but the legislative districts had not been redrawn to reflect this shift. The districts in question in the *Baker* case had been drawn up in 1901. By 1962, a vote cast in the most densely populated district carried only a fraction of the weight of one cast in the least populated district. As a result, voters living in the heavily populated district were in essence disenfranchised; they had almost no say about who represented them in the state legislature. And the majority of those living in the underrepresented cities were black.

Before the Warren era, legislative apportionment had been considered a political question, outside the Court's jurisdiction. With *Baker,* the Supreme Court ruled that federal courts could indeed resolve apportionment disputes because such cases involved issues of equal protection of the laws. Warren himself wrote the opinion of the Court in *Reynolds v. Sims* calling for substantially equal political representation for all citizens. As usual, Warren's language was simple, straightforward: "Legislators represent people, not trees or acres. Legislators are elected by voters, not farms or cities or economic interests." The consequences of his opinion were not simple, however: As a result of *Reynolds,* at least one house in nearly every state legislature was invalidated — in most states, both houses had to be reconstructed.

The reapportionment cases represented another instance of the Warren Court's application of the Fourteenth Amendment — with its due process and equal protection provisions — to the states. And as happened so many times in American history, a diminution in states' rights led to an extension of civil rights — particularly to African-Americans. As Warren put it: "Many of our problems would have been solved a long time ago if everyone had the right to vote, and his vote counted the same as everybody else's. Most of these problems could have been solved through the political process rather than through the courts. But as it was, the Court had to decide." Sometimes, politicians simply can't be trusted to resolve political questions — and that's why we all need judicial review (see Chapter 1).

Two Vivid 20th-Century Personalities

Strong personalities have been a constant feature of the Supreme Court throughout its history. Here are two men who left an indelible impression on the Court and on American history in the 20th century.

Hugo L. Black: The First Amendment absolutist

Hugo Lafayette Black (see Figure 5-3), a one-time Ku Klux Klan member (see Chapter 4), may seem an unlikely defender of the First Amendment. But Black's elevation to the Supreme Court and — perhaps more importantly — his education were hard won, and the process of raising himself up from unpromising origins doubtless contributed to his fidelity to the word and letter of the law. Black was what is known as a *black-letter judge,* one who believed absolutely that the words of the Constitution meant what they said. He carried a dog-eared copy of it around in his right coat pocket and referred to it often. "The Constitution is my legal bible," he declared. "I cherish every word of it from the first to the last." And no part of the Constitution was more sacred to Black than the First Amendment, which, as he frequently noted, begins, "Congress shall make no law . . . ." He thought the framers of the Constitution meant what they said and demanded unqualified proof that any law being scrutinized by the Court did not violate any of the prohibitions that follow these words (see Chapter 8).

As the son of a poor Alabama farmer who improved his lot somewhat when he moved from the hill country near Harlan to the town of Ashland, where he improved his lot by setting up a store. Black attended public school in Clay County and then tried to study medicine at Birmingham Medical College, where he dropped out after a year. This beginning was not promising. Two years at the University of Alabama law school went better, and he returned to Ashland to set himself up in private practice. The next year, Black had another setback when his law office burned to the ground. He moved to Birmingham, where in 1911 he managed to get elected as a part-time police court judge.

Politics provided Black with the lever he needed to raise himself in the world. In 1914, he was elected county solicitor, and after a stint in the military during World War I, he returned briefly to private practice before declaring his intention to run for the U.S. Senate. Some might have called him an opportunist. He aligned himself with organized labor to line his wallet and increase his political base; this association earned him a reputation as a *Bolshevik.* But when acting as defense counsel in a notorious murder trial, he used racial and religious bias to win his client's acquittal. And in 1923, he joined the Klan because, he later said, most Alabama jurors were Klansmen. Klan support helped him win cases; it also helped him win his seat in the Senate in 1926.

Jackson v. Black

In leading the so-called *due process revolution*, Black stepped on a number of judicial egos. One of his rivals for Court leadership, Robert H. Jackson, became so incensed at Black's methods that he took their rivalry public in 1946. The controversy had its origins in the 1945 case *Jewell Ridge Coal Corp. v. Local No. 6167, United Mine Workers of America.* At issue was the federal Fair Labors Standards Act of 1938, regulating wages and hours. Initially, a majority of the justices sided with the employer, and Jackson was assigned to write the opinion of the Court. But when Stanley Reed changed his vote before the opinion was actually drafted, Black held the deciding vote. Jackson tried to get Black, whose former law partner represented the union, to recuse himself from the case because of a possible conflict of interest. Black refused, and Frank Murphy was given the job of writing the Court's opinion for the new majority.

That was not the end of the story. Jackson retaliated by writing a stinging dissent pointing out remarks Black had made while serving in the Senate that were at odds with the outcome in *Jewell Ridge.* Still, his enmity simmered. In 1945, Jackson took a leave of absence from the Court to serve as chief prosecutor at the Nuremberg trials of Nazi war criminals. While he was in Germany, Chief Justice Harlan F. Stone died, and Black, as the senior associate justice, temporarily took on the leadership role. Jackson, convinced that Black was trying to outmaneuver him in a power grab for the chief justice's seat, wrote an angry letter to Congress reiterating his view of the controversy surrounding *Jewell Ridge.* He even held a press conference to lambaste his rival.

This public display of enmity between justices was unprecedented. When Jackson returned to the Court, he and Black resumed an outwardly cordial relationship, but their battle robbed the Court of its aura of impartiality. Both men threatened to resign if the president nominated the other as chief justice. Their feud also undermined Jackson's effectiveness for the remainder of his time on the Court, where he continued to serve as an associate justice for another eight years. In an effort to calm the waters, Harry Truman appointed Fred Vinson as chief justice in 1946. Although this appointment settled the issue of who would succeed Stone, Vinson's tenure was marked by ongoing warfare among the justices (see Chapter 7).

Black was elected to Congress as the poor man's candidate, and once there, he applied his energies to investigating improper ties between big government and big business and pushing for a 30-hour work week. He also spent his nights in the Library of Congress making up for his lack of formal education by reading history, economics, and the classics, a practice he kept up for the rest of his life. His support for Franklin D. Roosevelt's 1937 Court-packing plan (see Chapter 5) helped make Black the president's choice to fill the first vacancy on the Court brought about by the plan.

Black's KKK affiliation came back to haunt him shortly after his confirmation to the Court. He tackled the controversy head on, making a public confession over the air waves. He explained that he regretted having joined the Klan and resigned his membership after three years. He did not, he said, share their values. His record during his 34 years on the Court proved his sincerity. His was one of the most liberal voting records on the Court, where he fought tenaciously for free speech and due process, leading a shift toward individual rights and liberties that Justice Abe Fortas would accurately label "the most profound and pervasive revolution ever achieved by substantially peaceful means." And Black, who referred to himself as a "backward country fellow," won the revolution using deceptively simple methods: He insisted on a literal interpretation of the First Amendment and a construction of the Fourteenth Amendment that relied heavily on what he called the framers' original intent. This strategy was hard to counter, especially since no one knows what the drafters of the Constitution had in mind when they drew up this notably terse and remarkably flexible document.

Black's reorientation of the Court perhaps succeeded better than he intended. Toward the end of his career there, he became increasingly conservative in his voting. He refused to endorse a right of privacy in the contraception case *Griswold v. Connecticut* (1965) because the Constitution does not spell out such a right. He also rejected the extension of the Fourth Amendment's prohibition against unreasonable searches and seizures to cover government wiretapping. Any stretching of the Constitutional fabric — particularly of the Bill of Rights — became unacceptable to him. To critics, Black seemed to be changing gears. In his own mind, however, Black's devotion to the letter of the law had remained consistent throughout.

William J. Brennan: The arm-twister

William J. Brennan (see Figure 6-8) was Chief Justice Earl Warren's right hand man in the drive to turn the Supreme Court into an instrument of social change. Warren, although trained as a lawyer, was a career politician before taking charge of the Court in 1953. His easy-going temperament and his poor grasp of legal subtleties have often been noted by commentators. To make up for whatever rigor he lacked, Warren turned to Brennan.

Brennan was the son of Irish immigrant parents who settled in Newark, New Jersey. His father, a brewery worker, later became a union leader and then a municipal reformer. Brennan, a gifted student, worked his way through business school at the Wharton School at the University of Pennsylvania and then through Harvard Law School. Afterward, he practiced law, joined the Army during World War II, and then returned to New Jersey, where he began a campaign to reform the state court system. This activism brought him to the attention of Governor Alfred Driscoll, who appointed Brennan to the state superior court. Brennan advanced to the court's appellate division and then the New Jersey Supreme Court, where he eventually became Chief Justice Arthur Vanderbilt's closest associate.

Figure 6-8:
Justice
William J.
Brennan, Jr,
bottom row,
second from
left.

© Bettman/CORBIS

So far, so good. Brennan had done well, but there seemed little about his career that made him an ideal candidate for the U.S. Supreme Court, other than Vanderbilt's recommendation. When Brennan took his seat on the Court in 1956, expectations for his future performance there were not particularly high. He was, after all, a state court judge — the *only* state court judge on the Warren Court. But Brennan very quickly showed his stuff, and he did so by forming a partnership with Warren. The Chief Justice was his power base; Brennan was — in every sense of the word — Warren's advocate. Brennan had been Justice Felix Frankfurter's student at Harvard Law School, but he did not adopt his former professor's philosophy of judicial restraint. As Frankfurter was to say of him, "I always encourage my students to think for themselves, but Brennan goes too far!"

Brennan became the chief architect of the Warren Court's activist program of social reform. The two would meet privately each week before the judicial conference to plot their strategy for winning a majority of the justices over to their assessment of how the cases on the docket should be decided. And while Warren achieved his aims by a demonstration of patience and under-standing, Brennan worked overtime behind the scenes to promote the Chief's views through a combination of astute legal analysis and old-fashioned politicking. He situated himself squarely in the middle of the Warren Court's political spectrum, positioned so as to balance the liberals and the conservatives if need be. It was an ideal vantage point from which to exercise power. In a piece published in 1966 in the *Harvard Law Review*, Warren had this to say about Brennan: "Friendly and buoyant in spirit, a prodigious worker and a master craftsman, he is a unifying influence on the bench and in the conference room." Others said less publicly that Brennan was a manipulator.

Brennan *was* a workhorse. Warren assigned him the job of writing up many of the Court's most important decisions, and Brennan always rose to the occasion. Furthermore, he was willing to craft his opinions to accommodate others' views — and hang on to their votes. These attributes helped him maintain his leadership role even when the chief justiceship changed hands. Warren Burger (see Chapter 5) was no match for either Brennan's mental keenness or his political agility, and Brennan's staying power may be one reason why the Burger Court consolidated many of the Warren Court's advances in civil liberties rather than rolling them back, as had been intended. Consider this "Dear Harry" letter that Brennan sent after *Roe v. Wade* was reargued in 1972, when the Court was split down the middle and Justice Blackmun was struggling with a second draft of a majority opinion:

> I read your proposed opinions as saying, and I agree, that a woman's right of personal privacy includes the abortion decision, subject only to limited regulation. . . . [R]ather than using a somewhat arbitrary point such as the end of the first trimester or a somewhat imprecise and technically inconsistent point such as "viability," could we not simply say that at that point in time where abortions become medically more complex, state regulation . . . becomes permissible?

Blackmun did not buy Brennan's argument, but this letter shows you just how persuasive the senior associate justice could be. Perhaps if he had prevailed, abortion would not have continued to be a legal and political lightning rod. And, in fact, many of the Court's subsequent decisions curtailing a woman's right to choose have followed Brennan's line of thought.

But Brennan's liberalism robbed him of his pivotal role as the Court moved to the right. By the time William Rehnquist took over as chief justice in 1986, Brennan was heard most often issuing caustic dissents. He and Thurgood Marshall became isolated in their consistent opposition to the death penalty. As early as the 1970s, Brennan saw which way the wind was blowing, and he began urging state courts to "thrust themselves into a position of prominence in the struggle to protect the people of our nation from governmental intrusions on their freedoms." In the end, he arrived back where he began, pushing for reform at the state level.

Chapter 7

Rogues Gallery:
Some Notorious Justices

The Supreme Court has not been without its embarrassments. Some of these missteps can be put down to misjudgments, political intrigue, or past prejudice. But others are clearly linked to personal problems or predispositions that make for a poor fit between certain individuals and the demanding job of being a justice. You would think that all the screening involved in selecting people to staff the highest court in the land would separate the wheat from the chaff. Plainly, the selection process is not flawless.

The Unstable: John Rutledge

John Rutledge (see Figure 7-1) was a blueblood, a founding father of the Republic, and a failed chief justice. Born in 1739 into an old aristocratic family in what is now Charleston, South Carolina, his father was a physician who died young, leaving his mother one of the wealthiest widows in the land. Rutledge was educated first in the law offices of his uncle, who was speaker of the South Carolina Commons House of Assembly, and then in those of James Parsons, who would go on to become speaker of the U.S. House of Representatives. When it came time for some *real* legal education, however, Rutledge left for Mother England, where he studied law at Middle Temple and was called to the bar in 1760.

When he returned home the next year, he was 21 years old. He set himself up in a law practice — which, with his connections, was immediately successful — and he was elected to the South Carolina Assembly. His career continued smoothly along this dual track for quite some time. In 1764, Rutledge was appointed as his state's attorney general. In 1765, at age 25, he was the youngest delegate to the Stamp Act Congress, called by colonial leaders to combat Britain's new stamp tax. In 1776, Rutledge led the South Carolina delegation to the First Continental Congress, where he tenaciously defended his state's interests. The price of Rutledge's vote for a colonial boycott of trade with Britain was an exemption for rice, South Carolina's largest export commodity.

Rutledge's loyalty to South Carolina was legendary, and his state responded by electing him as its first president of the state assembly after he drafted the state constitution. And although he is credited with America's first real victory in the War of Independence, Rutledge defended Fort Moultrie primarily because it was located in South Carolina. In 1779, Rutledge was elected as the first governor of the state.

Figure 7-1:
Chief
Justice
John
Rutledge.

Library of Congress, Prints and Photographs
Division [LC-USZ62-91143]

Rutledge returned to federal politics in 1782, when he served one term as a member of Congress. In 1787, he represented South Carolina at the Constitutional Convention, where he was instrumental in drafting the Great Compromise, giving all states equal representation in federal government through creation of the Senate. As chairman of the Committee on Detail, he also helped create the first draft of the Constitution, introducing the *supremacy clause,* which states that the Constitution and laws of the United States "shall be the supreme law of the land."

It seemed that Rutledge had settled on a career in national politics. When he lost the vice presidency to John Adams in 1788, Rutledge trained his eyes on the chief justiceship of the new U.S. Supreme Court. He was disappointed when President George Washington offered that post to John Jay, but he did accept the post of senior associate justice in 1789. Rutledge, however, never saw the inside of the Court as an associate justice. After two years of circuit riding (see Chapter 1), he decided to stay home, resigning from the federal court to take South Carolina's offer of a position he regarded as more prestigious: chief justice of the state's highest court.

But in June 1795, Rutledge learned that John Jay had resigned as chief justice of the U.S. Supreme Court. Rutledge immediately wrote to Washington, offering his services. Washington wrote back by return post and gratefully, in a letter dated July 1, accepted Rutledge's offer, asking him to preside at the Court's August term. Before he left for Washington, though, Rutledge presided over a public meeting in Charleston called to protest the newly signed Jay Treaty. John Jay had negotiated this agreement with England just before resigning as chief justice. It was a treaty meant to settle financial differences between the U.S. and the mother country, and although it was ratified by the Senate, it was not universally popular. Protest against the treaty was especially loud in the South, whose citizens carried the largest part of the burden for repaying outstanding debts to England.

At the meeting, Rutledge delivered a lengthy harangue against the Jay Treaty and the president that showed signs not merely of ingratitude, but of possible mental instability. He then proceeded to Washington, D.C. to take up his new role as chief justice, but he did not last long in the job. When the Senate reconvened that autumn and took up the matter of confirming Rutledge's appointment, its members were outraged by his behavior in Charleston. And there were rumors, as John Adams reported, of Rutledge's "accelerated and increased . . . Disorder of the Mind." Rutledge's appointment was defeated by a vote of 14-10.

Rutledge, who had been physically disabled by circuit riding and was still mentally unstrung by his wife's death in 1792, returned home in November 1795. After learning on December 26, 1795, of his rejection by the Senate, he attempted to commit suicide by jumping off of a wharf into Charleston Bay. He was saved from drowning, but not from his demons. He lived another five and a half years as an eccentric recluse.

The Unfit: Fred Vinson

One thing's for sure: Fred Vinson (see Figure 7-2) wasn't kicked upstairs because of his intellect. His predecessor in the job of chief justice had been Harlan F. Stone, who *was* an intellectual but, unfortunately, also an inept leader. When Stone died suddenly and dramatically in 1946 while reading his dissenting opinion from the Supreme Court bench, he left the Court ideologically and personally at odds. President Harry Truman turned to his friend and Treasury secretary Fred Vinson, whose ability to get along with people, Truman hoped, might heal the deep divisions hampering the Court's effectiveness.

Figure 7-2:
Chief
Justice
Frederick M.
Vinson.

© Oscar White/CORBIS

It was clear from the beginning that Vinson wasn't up to the job. The son of a small town Kentucky jail keeper, Vinson was educated at Centre College of Kentucky, where he received both his undergraduate and law degrees, and where he achieved the highest academic record in the history of the school. Still, Centre College was not Harvard, and Vinson inherited a Court dominated by intellectual giants and prima donnas like Hugo L. Black, Felix Frankfurter, and Robert Jackson (see Chapter 6). Even Stanley Reed, the least intellectual of the justices, commented to Frankfurter that Vinson was "just like me, except that he is less well-educated." And the brainy Frankfurter confided to his diary that Vinson was "confident and easy-going and sure and shallow . . . he seems to me to have the confident and easy going air of a man who does not see the complexities of problems and blithely hits the obvious points."

Frankfurter, who encouraged gossip, received this assessment of Vinson from one of his former clerks: "What a mean little despot he is. Has there ever been a member of the Court who is deficient in so many respects as a man and as a judge. . . . this man is a pygmy, morally and mentally. And so uncouth." Vinson may not have been a despot, but he clearly was unable to control the judicial conference where cases are discussed and decided. Frankfurter characterized Vinson's performance on such occasions as "float[ing] merely on the surface of the problems raised by the cases." The other justices responded by discussing in Vinson's presence the possibility of rotating Court leadership among themselves.

To make matter worse, Vinson was lazy. He was said to write his opinions "with his hands in his pockets," letting his clerks do the work. Even so, he signed his name to few opinions. Vinson was of the opinion that overwork had contributed to the early deaths of some of the justices. (Look at what happened to the previous chief, for heavens sake!) Accordingly, he cut the Court's docket virtually in half: Whereas the Hughes Court (1930–1941) had decided an average of 200 cases annually, the Vinson Court only managed to decide half that many. Of those, Vinson assigned relatively few important opinions to himself. Vinson was also ideologically at odds with the Court majority, deferring to presidential authority in cases such as the 1952 *Steel Seizure Case,* in which the majority voted against President Truman's attempt to seize control of the nation's steel mills as part of his prosecution of the Korean War.

As a consequence of such positions, Vinson frequently found himself on the wrong side of the issues. He wrote more than his share of dissents, averaging 13 per Court term, versus Chief Justice Hughes's 2. This record is another clear indication of Vinson's inability to lead the Court. Truman appointed him in hopes that he would heal the rifts that were undermining the Court's authority. Vinson only managed to deepen the division. During his first term, 36 percent of the Court's decisions were unanimous; by 1952, that percentage had dropped to 19.

Vinson's time as chief justice was shorter than most. He died suddenly of a heart attack in 1953. A 1970 poll of Court analysts rated him as one of the Court's "failures," one of only eight — and the only chief justice — to be judged so.

The Venal: James Wilson

James Wilson's career (see Figure 7-3) had a brilliant beginning but ended
sordidly. Born in Scotland to a family of poor farmers, Wilson set out to be a
clergyman. When his father died in 1760, however, Wilson was forced by
financial pressures to leave divinity school before graduating. This financial
setback was the first of a series that would ultimately prove his undoing.

Figure 7-3:
Justice
James
Wilson.

In 1765, Wilson emigrated to America, seeking a better life. After studying law
in Philadelphia, he was admitted to the bar in 1767 and very soon became the
leading attorney in central Pennsylvania. He used his status to seek public
office and his money for land speculation. In 1768, he wrote an important pre-
Revolutionary War pamphlet titled *Considerations on the Nature and Extent of
the Legislative Authority of the British Parliament,* which was published in
1774. In his writings and his public pronouncements, Wilson identified himself with those who believed that the British should have no say in the governance of America. His outspokenness won him election as a Pennsylvania
delegate to the Second Continental Congress, where he became one of the
signers of the Declaration of Independence, despite his personal opposition
to separation from England.

Wilson had in the meanwhile developed a reputation as a conservative aristocrat. His opposition to the adoption of a state constitution in 1776 drew criticism from populists who wanted local autonomy. After Wilson developed an active law practice in Philadelphia representing wealthy Tories and rich businessmen, public sentiment against him grew so strong that he was forced to go into hiding to escape an angry mob protesting rising inflation and food shortages which they blamed on Wilson and his ilk. Still, Pennsylvanians once again elected him to represent their interests at the 1787 Constitutional Convention. He signed that, too, becoming one of only six Americans to add his name to the bottom of the nation's two most important foundational documents.

Wilson not only signed the Constitution, he helped write it. He is credited with having developed the theory of the *separation of powers,* which divides federal government into three distinct branches, and advocating *popular sovereignty,* the democratic notion that government should be an expression of the will of the people. (In the period before the Civil War, popular sovereignty would come be associated with a policy of permitting citizens of newly admitted states to determine their own slaveholding status.) After making such important contributions to the formation of the federal government, Wilson had every reason to hope he would play an important role in administering it.

What Wilson hoped for — even asked for — was to be named chief justice of the new Supreme Court. He knew that his many investments, which were tainted by conflicts of interest, probably made him unelectable. But in 1789, Washington chose John Jay to be the Court's first leader. And when Washington had to fill this position again in 1775 and 1776, he again passed up Wilson, who had taken a seat on the Court as an associate justice in 1789. Wilson had, in fact, begun to falter not long after joining the Court. His written opinions were few in number, and with one notable exception, notably brief. This exception occurred in *Chisholm v. Georgia* (1793), in which the Court allowed a federal suit brought against Georgia by citizens of South Carolina to go forward. It was Wilson's declaration that "[a]s to the purposes of the Union, therefore, Georgia is not a sovereign state," as much as anything, that prompted Georgia to lead the movement for passage of the Eleventh Amendment. Ratified in 1795, the amendment was adopted explicitly to overrule *Chisholm* and marked the first time that a constitutional amendment undid a Supreme Court decision.

Wilson had other problems. Financially overextended by investments that had gone bad, he was hounded by his creditors. While riding circuit (see Chapter 1), he was chased by debt collectors and jailed. Followed by rumors of impeachment, in 1798 he fled to Edenton, North Carolina, where he hoped to hide from his pursuers. He failed. He was found and imprisoned again. Upon his release, he remained in Edenton where, ill and alone, he died in a sorry little inn next to the court house. At the time, he was still a member of the U.S. Supreme Court.

Three Who Outstayed Their Welcome

Many of the justices have stayed on the Court well after they lost their effectiveness because of old age, physical ailments, or mental infirmity. The three main reasons for this refusal to get off the high bench have been ideology, egotism, and lack of financial incentives.

Nathan Clifford

Nathan Clifford (see Figure 7-4) did his utmost not to abandon his post on the Supreme Court until a Democrat was in the White House. It was the only way he knew of to ensure that his replacement on the Court would be a Democrat.

Figure 7-4:
Justice
Nathan
Clifford.

Library of Congress, Prints and Photographs Division
[LC-USZ62-104077]

Clifford's politics were formed in childhood. He was one of seven children of a subsistence farmer who worked the rocky land of New Hampshire. Poverty prevented Clifford from getting a good elementary or secondary education. When his father died young, he took with him Clifford's dream of attending Dartmouth College. Denied opportunity because of the accident of his birth, Clifford early on swore allegiance to Andrew Jackson and the Democratic Party.

The Democratic king

Andrew Jackson, seventh president of the United States, was first elected to that office in 1828. Jackson was a populist, and when he took over the White House, he brought with him a whole new political outlook. Jacksonian democracy did not represent business as it was usually conducted by *either* Republicans or Democrats. Jackson's belief that the common man was the foundation of the republic lent an air of egalitarianism and equal opportunity to the workings of government, encouraging political reforms that made more public offices elective and gave more people the opportunity — and the incentive — to vote. Still, not everyone approved of Jackson's methods or ideology. A whole political party, the Whigs (see Chapter 6), was formed with the express purpose of defeating Jackson and his followers. For the Whigs — and increasingly, for nonwhites and Northerners — Jackson was a tyrant whose system of rotating appointments amounted to nothing more than a corrupt spoils system, and whose disregard for slavery and Native American sovereignty promoted white supremacy.

Instead, Clifford studied law in the offices of a local attorney, was admitted to the state bar in 1827, and moved to Newfield, Maine, to improve his chances of getting ahead. In Newfield, he was the only attorney, and when he married into a prominent local family, his fortunes seemed to be on the rise. In 1830, he was elected to the Maine legislature, where he served three terms before his election to the U.S. House of Representatives. Clifford's reputation as a hard worker and his staunch support for the Democratic Party brought him to the attention of President James K. Polk, who appointed Clifford U.S. attorney general. And Clifford's ability to mediate disputes between Polk and his secretary of state, James Buchanan, over prosecution of the Mexican War made a lasting impression on Buchanan.

In 1848, Clifford was sent to Mexico with a peace treaty, and he stayed on there as Polk's minister. After the Whigs won the White House in 1848, however, Clifford was forced to return to his law practice in Maine. But the political winds shifted again in 1856, when the Democrat Buchanan was elected president. When Buchanan needed to fill a Supreme Court vacancy the next year, he tapped his old stalwart, Clifford.

Clifford's nomination sparked a storm of controversy. He was seen as an unqualified political hack whose party loyalty made him a *doughface,* a northerner with southern sympathies. The Senate dragged its feet on Clifford's nomination for 34 days, finally approving it by the slimmest of margins, 26-23. Once on the Court, Clifford did seem to live up to his reputation. Out of his depth, he wrote a great many dissents and never drafted an opinion for the majority in a major constitutional case. Morrison Waite, chief justice during Clifford's final terms on the Court, only assigned the associate justice one majority opinion in six years.

Clifford's Democratic credentials led to his appointment as head of the electoral commission set up to decide the contested 1876 presidential election (see Chapter 1). He naturally supported the Democratic contender Samuel J. Tilden. When the Republican Rutherford B. Hayes was ultimately declared the winner, Clifford refused to attend his inauguration or even enter the White House during Hayes's residency.

Hayes's successor in 1880 was another Republican, James A. Garfield. That year, Clifford suffered a debilitating stroke, but despite frequent absences and disturbing memory lapses, he refused to resign, hoping to serve long enough to see a Democratic president name his replacement on the Court. Nathan Clifford died in 1881, his wish unfulfilled.

Stephen J. Field

After William O. Douglas, who served on the Court nearly a century later, Stephen J. Field (see Figure 7-5) occupied a seat on the high bench longer than any other justice. In the end, Field's only remaining ambition was to set a new record by outlasting any of his predecessors. It was a foolish, selfish goal that served neither him nor the Court well.

Field lived a colorful life before coming to the Court. One of eight children born to a Congregational clergyman in Connecticut, he had to compete with some distinguished siblings, among them Cyrus W. Field, who laid the first Atlantic cable in 1866, and David D. Field, a prominent law reformer. Stephen J. Field practiced law in New York with his older brother Dudley for a number of years before heading west to make a name for himself.

Field became a colorful figure in the colorful world of the old West. He had followed the Gold Rush to California, where he became a frontier lawyer, entrepreneur, and politician before beginning a 40-year judicial career when he was elected to the California Supreme Court in 1857. While still a lawyer and local official in Maryville, California, Field became embroiled in a fight with a judge that resulted in Field's disbarment, imprisonment, and involvement in a duel.

He seemed to have a talent for making enemies. A longstanding feud with another judge, David Terry, who was chief justice of the California Supreme Court when Field served there, followed Field all the way to the U.S. Supreme Court. While Field was serving as circuit court judge in California, he had issued an opinion declaring Terry's wife's previous marriage to have been invalid. When Field went back to California in 1889 to perform circuit duty as a U.S. Supreme Court justice, Terry assaulted him and was killed by David Naegle, a U.S. marshal assigned to protect Field. The upshot was *In re Naegle* (1890), which ended up in the U.S. Supreme Court. Field, at the center of the controversy, recused himself, and Naegle was cleared of a murder charge.

Library of Congress, Prints and Photographs Division
[LC-USZ62-104541]

On the high Court, Field was, not surprisingly, a combative figure. He also continued to be highly competitive, campaigning openly but unsuccessfully for the presidency in 1868, 1880, and 1884. When Chief Justice Morrison Waite died in 1888, Field felt that as the only Democrat on the Court, he was Waite's natural successor at a time when the White House was occupied by a Democrat. When President Grover Cleveland chose Court outsider Melville Fuller as chief justice, Field's ambitions were stuck another heavy blow.

For much of the 34 ½ years Field was on the high bench, however, he was one of the Court's intellectual leaders. Unafraid to be the lone dissenter, he lasted long enough to see many of his minority opinions become adopted by his brethren as law. Toward the end of his tenure, however, he did almost no work, and his mind began to wander. He became an embarrassment to his colleagues, one of whom was assigned the unhappy job of asking him to step down. When he refused, he was reminded that years earlier he had suggested that another justice tender his resignation. "Yes!" said Field, "And a dirtier day's work I never did in my life!" Field wanted to best the previous record for service on the Court, 34 years, 5 months, and 4 days, set by Chief Justice John Marshall. Field also despised Cleveland and did not want to give *that* Democrat the opportunity to appoint his successor on the Court. Finally, in 1897, having surpassed Marshall's record by two months, Field retired, to everyone's relief.

Ward Hunt

Before 1869, justices had no financial incentive to retire from the Supreme Court. Legislation passed that year, however, permitted them to retire at full salary if they had served at least 10 years and had not yet reached the age of 70. The legislation, however, did not benefit Ward Hunt (see Figure 7-6), who was determined to get more than his due.

Figure 7-6:
Justice
Ward Hunt.

Matthew Brady, Collection of the Supreme Court of the United States

Hunt began his professional career as a Democrat, but he broke with the party in the 1850s over slavery, which the Democrats assisted, if not supported, and Ward opposed. In 1855–1856, he helped establish a beachhead for the newly reformed Republican Party in New York. Thanks to the blessing of Roscoe Conkling, Republican state boss, Hunt's activism won him a series of choice appointments in the state court system. And Conkling was probably also responsible for bringing Hunt to the attention of President Ulysses S. Grant when a spot opened up on the U.S. Supreme Court in 1872.

Hunt's career on the court was short and undistinguished by anything other than his method of leaving it. He remained loyal to the Republican cause, voting to uphold the enabling legislation that allowed the three constitutional amendments — the Thirteenth, Fourteenth, and Fifteenth — ratified in the wake of the Civil War to be implemented. Otherwise, his impact on the Court was negligible, and he wrote not a single outstanding opinion before illness stopped him from working altogether. In 1877, he missed a number of Court sessions, and the next year, he suffered a debilitating stroke. He never returned to the bench, although he continued to be a member of the Court for four more years. His role as a justice was unquestionably over, but Ward refused to retire until he was vested. He was such a drag on the Court that in 1881, Senator David Davis, a former associate justice, introduced a special bill in Congress granting Hunt early retirement benefits conditioned on his resigning within 30 days of the bill's passage. The bill passed on January 27, 1882, and Hunt tendered his resignation that very day. He lived out the remainder of his days as an invalid.

Part III

Setting Precedents: Cases That Count

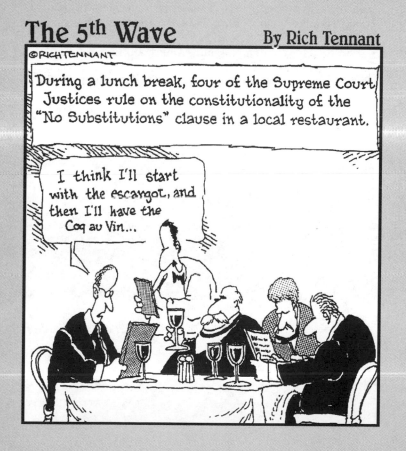

The 5th Wave   By Rich Tennant

During a lunch break, four of the Supreme Court Justices rule on the constitutionality of the "No Substitutions" clause in a local restaurant.

I think I'll start with the escargot, and then I'll have the Coq au Vin...

In this part . . .

Not all areas of the law are created equal. In law school, students can devote the better part of a year to studying just those cases generated by two small sections of the Constitution: The First Amendment and the Fourteenth Amendment. But these two amendments pack a punch. What can be more American than *free speech*, *freedom of religion*, *due process*, *equal protection of the laws*, and — for heaven's sake — *privacy*? But just when you thought there could be no confusion about what these words mean (they're our birthright, right?), here come the Supreme Court justices to tell you that lots of people have been plenty confused about them — including some of their predecessors. Take heart. In these chapters, I do my best to show you why these basic concepts *are* our birthright. That's the very reason people have fought over them so often.

Chapter 8

The First Amendment Is the First Amendment

· ·

In This Chapter

▶ Deconstructing the First Amendment

▶ Connecting freedom of religion with freedom of expression

▶ Tracing the evolution of the right to privacy

▶ Understanding how freedom of speech and press ensures democracy

▶ Exploring two lesser known First Amendment rights

· ·

*T*he founding fathers based the nation on a document that includes not only seven articles, but ten amendments. The first of these amendments addresses some of the considerations that were uppermost in their minds. It continues to be one of the most distinctive symbols of American culture and — not coincidentally — one of the most fertile areas for litigation in society.

Understanding Freedom of Religion

The First Amendment opens with these words: "Congress shall make no law respecting an establishment of religion, or prohibiting the free exercise thereof." Freedom of religion in America has always consisted of these two strands: the prohibition against government establishment or endorsement of religion, and the prohibition against government interference with religious practices. That said, it must be noted that until well into the twentieth century, freedom of religion was simply not an issue for most Americans, and litigation on the subject was almost nil.

Many Americans' forebears — starting with those who came over on the *Mayflower* — came to these shores seeking freedom from religious persecution. When the framers of the Constitution failed to address ongoing concerns about this and other individual rights in the body of that document, some of the states declined to sign up immediately. The framers believed that the three articles of the Constitution contained sufficient safeguards to prevent the federal government from interfering in peoples' lives. In addition, the individual states had their own bills of rights. Some of the states, however, were concerned about overreaching on the part of the new central government, and they wanted their rights to be spelled out before they would agree to ratify the Constitution. They got their wish, and the Bill of Rights was born, stipulating in unqualified language — first and foremost — that "Congress shall make no law . . ." infringing on freedom of religion.

Still, the vast majority of Americans were until recent times Protestant, and most of them took it for granted that religion — and in particular, their brand of religion — had a role to play in public life. Christmas and Easter, right along with Thanksgiving, were declared national holidays. Public school students frequently began their day with a flag salute and a recitation of the Lord's Prayer and/or a scripture reading. Many state legislative sessions began the same way. Most people gave little thought to these rituals. But for all intents and purposes, America had what amounted to a state religion. This state of affairs may — or may not — have been what the Founding Fathers had in mind.

The Establishment Clause

Thomas Jefferson and James Madison, the two men most responsible for the *Establishment Clause,* which requires only that church and state remain separate institutions, took an unconditional view of the ban on government "establishment of religion." For them, it meant that a government declaration making Thanksgiving a holiday was just as unlawful as a tax exemption for a church. You *know* their interpretation didn't prevail. For most Americans in the early days of the republic, a ban on government establishment of religion meant there was to be no national church in the sense that the Church of England was the Church of England, endowed with some of the same political and governmental privileges as the monarchy.

This rather relaxed attitude toward the Establishment Clause predominated for the first century and a half of U.S. history. The federal government, for the most part, had little impact on the day-to-day lives of Americans. And prior to the *due process revolution* of the 1940s that made the Bill of Rights applicable at the state level (see Chapter 9), the ban on government establishment of religion, like other aspects of the Bill of Rights, had not been applied at the local level, where most religious activity took place. Ironically, perhaps, it was only after the nation became secularized — when religion became an almost purely private matter — that the Supreme Court was asked to decide questions arising out of the Establishment Clause.

The "wall of separation" between church and state

The metaphor of a wall separating church and state originated with Thomas Jefferson, one of the primary backers of the Bill of Rights. Jefferson opposed any form of government support for religion, direct or indirect, and his strict view is reflected in the unqualified language that precedes the Establishment Clause. The first test of this language came in 1947 in the case *Everson v. Board of Education,* in which the Court was asked to consider the constitutionality of a New Jersey law permitting local school boards to reimburse parents for the cost of transporting their children to schools, including parochial schools. Although the Court upheld the law by a 5-4 vote, the real significance of *Everson* is that it was the first case to use the Fourteenth Amendment to apply the constitutional ban against government support for religion to the states.

Not surprisingly, the author of the opinion for the Court was Justice Hugo L. Black (see Chapter 6), the First Amendment absolutist who was also the author of the due process revolution (see Chapter 9). Surprisingly, though, Black and four other justices found that although the New Jersey statute had come right up to the verge of the wall separating the state from religion, no breach had occurred. The primary purpose of the law in question was to benefit parents, not church-affiliated schools — the law's intention and effect were *secular.* It was a very fine line that many found hard to see.

Schools — public schools, in particular — continued to be the scene of church-state standoffs. Two decisions concerning public school sponsorship of religious activities, *Illinois ex rel. McCollum v. Board of Education* (1948) and *Zorach v. Clauson* (1952), muddied the waters some more. In the first, Justice Black, writing for the Court, indicated that the barrier between church and state was well nigh impenetrable. But just four years later in *Zorach,* Justice William O. Douglas, writing for the Court, declared, "We are a religious people whose institutions presuppose a Supreme Being." In both cases, the issue was *released time* plans that permitted public school students to receive religious instruction during the school week. The three justices who had written in support of the outcome in *McCollum* dissented in *Zorach.* What's going on here? The deciding factor in these cases, as in real estate, was location: In *McCollum,* the religious instruction had taken place inside public school buildings, whereas in *Zorach,* these studies took place elsewhere. Was this a distinction without a difference? To many Court observers, these two decisions looked like hair-splitting.

It did not help that Justice Douglas did a complete about-face just a few years down the road, disavowing his own logic and language in a concurring opinion in *Engel v. Vitale* (1962), in which the Court voted 6-1 to strike down a New York State sanctioned, voluntary nondenominational school prayer. In dissent, Justice Potter Stewart wrote: "I cannot see how an 'official religion' is established by letting those who want to say a prayer say it." Things had, in a sense, come full circle, arriving back where the framers of the Constitution had begun.

The schoolyard as battleground

Education has provided the battlefield where many of the most significant battles over freedom of religion have been waged. This turn of events can be traced to the transfer, early in the twentieth century, of teaching duties from the clergy to professionally trained teachers. But Charles Darwin's theory of evolution was an even more important factor in making education the focus of this constitutional debate. The publication in 1859 of Darwin's *On the Origin of Species* shook most foundations: Not only did the book cast serious doubt on the *Book of Genesis,* it once and for all made science, not religion, the basis for public life in most western societies.

Darwin's influence on education is most dramatically illustrated by *Scopes v. State,* a 1927 Tennessee case that pitted man against monkey in a circus sideshow of a trial featuring two of the most colorful personalities of the time, the famed trial lawyer Clarence Darrow and the fabled orator and politician William Jennings Bryan. At issue was a state law making it a criminal offense to teach anything other than the biblical story of creation. John Scopes, a high school science teacher in Dayton, Tennessee, was recruited as a guinea pig to test

the validity of the law by teaching evolutionary theory to his students. The American Civil Liberties Union hired Darrow to defend Scopes at the "Monkey trial," which is remembered primarily for the lawyer's harsh grilling of Bryan. Bryan, who served as one of the chief prosecutors at the trial, was a fundamentalist Christian. Toward the end of the trial, he made the fatal mistake of agreeing to testify as an expert on the Bible. By pointing out the inconsistencies in Bryan's statements about his beliefs, Darrow reduced the expert witness to a sweating, quivering mass of contradictions.

Scopes was found guilty at trial, but his conviction was later overturned on a technicality. The U.S. Supreme Court did not have the opportunity to consider a case involving a "monkey law" until 1968, when, in *Epperson v. Arkansas,* the justices unanimously struck down a state statute forbidding the use of textbooks teaching "the theory or doctrine that mankind ascended or descended from a lower order of animals." Such laws, the Court declared, are unconstitutional precisely because they ban a body of knowledge because it conflicts with a particular religious doctrine. Nonetheless, the public debate over *creation science* continued.

At the time, Stewart's was a lone voice crying in the wilderness, but 23 years later, Justice William Rehnquist would echo Stewart in his influential dissent in *Wallace v. Jaffree* (1985), in which even the Court majority seemed to leave an opening for an undefined, uncommitted moment of silence in the classroom. The American public, for its part, had never endorsed the Supreme Court's ban on school prayer, and with conservatism gaining momentum, the winds had clearly shifted. So far, however, they have not blown so hard as to push a constitutional amendment endorsing school prayer through Congress.

The original "Lemon law"

After *Everson* (see "the preceding section'"), Establishment Clause decisions were based on a determination of whether a particular government action was or was not *secular* in its intention and primary impact. In 1971, however, the Court refined this test in *Lemon v. Kurtzman,* a case concerning state payments to teachers of secular subjects in parochial schools. A unanimous Court found that the payments violated the First Amendment, and in the process of describing the reasons behind this decision, announced a third prong to the test applied to legislation suspected of getting too cozy with religion: Laws must not foster excessive government entanglement with religion. In *Lemon v. Kurtzman,* the laws at issue were struck down because they required prolonged government surveillance to ensure that the secular subjects taught in church-sponsored schools remained wholly secular.

The new *Lemon test* satisfied no one. Conservatives like Chief Justice Rehnquist argued that the test is both unconstitutional and ahistorical, violating the framers' original intent. Dissenting in *Wallace v. Jaffree* (1985), a case concerning a public-school-authorized *moment of silence,* Rehnquist declared that while the First Amendment clearly prohibits endorsement of a national church, the framers never intended to require government to be neutral about religion itself. Liberals, on the other hand, were unhappy with what they saw as the arbitrariness of the *Lemon law,* which allowed majority religions to prevail over those with fewer adherents. In *Lynch v. Donnelly* (1984), for example, the Court used the three-pronged test to allow a crèche to be part of an otherwise secular publicly-funded Christmas display. It is hardly surprising that different justices have employed the test to the same set of facts only to arrive at contradictory results. The public, looking to the Court for guidance, often finds no clear directives.

The Reagan revolution

In the presidential election of 1980, Republican candidate Ronald Reagan garnered 489 electoral votes to Democrat Jimmy Carter's 49. Reagan was reelected in 1984, winning 58.4 percent of the vote and carrying 49 states. Armed with this mandate, he set about changing the American political landscape. Once a supporter of Franklin D. Roosevelt, Reagan left in place many of the social and economic programs — such as Social Security — instituted under FDR's New Deal (see Chapter 4), but he gutted Lyndon Johnson's Great Society antipoverty initiatives. In order to win the Cold War, Reagan oversaw the biggest peacetime military buildup the nation had ever seen. He withstood a sharp economic recession in order to curb inflation, and he slashed income tax rates in the higher brackets.

His enormous popularity with the electorate gave Reagan long coattails, and he was able to hold together a coalition of Republican stalwarts, disaffected Democrats, and politicized evangelical Protestants that helped him shift the focus of public policy from individual rights to a conservative — some said reactionary — agenda that included such goals as promotion of school prayer and abolition of abortion. Never a hands-on chief executive, Reagan left the mechanics of governance to others. He was not always fortunate in his lieutenants, but in elevating the brilliant and right-leaning William Rehnquist to the chief justice's chair, Reagan ensured that his conservative bequest would outlast his time in office.

The Free Exercise Clause

Whereas the focus of the Establishment Clause of the First Amendment (see "The Establishment Clause") is on government, that of the Free Exercise Clause is on "we the people." The presumption here, as with freedom of speech and freedom of assembly — without which religion arguably could not exist — is that people have a fundamental right to be themselves, free of government interference.

Most of the litigation concerning the Free Exercise Clause has involved questions of whether individuals are obliged to obey laws they say conflict with their religious beliefs. As American society has grown more secular, the Court has grown more expansive in its interpretation of the Free Exercise Clause. In 1890, the Court's definition of religion had changed little from what it had been a century earlier. "The term 'religion,'" wrote Justice Stephen J. Field in the Mormon polygamy case *Davis v. Beason* (1890), "has reference to one's views of his relations to his Creator, and to the obligations they impose of reverence for his being and character, and of obedience to his will."

But a half century later — spurred, no doubt, by the expansion of individual rights caused by the due process revolution (see Chapter 9) — the Court had all but done away with orthodox notions of what constitutes religious belief. And in 1953, Justice William O. Douglas, writing for the Court in the Jehovah's Witnesses public assembly case *Fowler v. Rhode Island,* declared with finality, "[I]t is no business of courts to say that what is religious practice or activity for one group is not religion under the protection of the First Amendment." Since that time, the Court has tried to erect a wall between *itself* and religion.

Mormon polygamy

Nineteenth-century America was considerably less diverse and considerably less tolerant than it is today. Followers of Joseph Smith, the Mormons, had experienced persecution almost from the time the Church of Jesus Christ of Latter Day Saints was founded in 1830. Driven steadily westward from New York to Illinois and finally to Utah, they were considered suspect by the larger society because of their unorthodox take on Christianity and their practice of plural marriage. In the 1870s, the administration of President Ulysses S. Grant began a campaign to end Mormon polygamy, which resulted in a series of Supreme Court cases. *Reynolds v. United States* (1879) was the first and most significant of these cases, developing the so-called *belief-action doctrine,* which holds that although government cannot punish a person for his or her beliefs, acts that violate criminal laws — even acts motivated by religious principles — are punishable. The government need show only that a rational basis exists for punishing these acts — a relatively easy matter. As Justice Field's opinion for the Court in *Davis v. Beason* (1890) demonstrates, the real issue was social norms: "It was never intended or supposed that the [First] Amendment could be invoked as a protection against legislation for the punishment of acts inimical to the peace, good order, and morals of society."

Amish children

By the time *Wisconsin v. Yoder* was decided in 1972, the Court — and the country — had changed dramatically from the period in which Mormon plural marriage was considered a threat to society. At issue in *Yoder* was an Amish challenge to a state compulsory education law. Jonas Yoder, a member of the Conservative Amish Mennonite Church, claimed that requiring his children to attend public school beyond the eighth grade violated his faith's belief that high school fostered values destructive to the Amish community.

Not only was the shoe on the other foot, it was an uncomfortable fit: In order to accommodate Amish distaste for mainstream American life, the Court had to raise the bar. Instead of only having to show that there was a rational basis for enforcing a law contrary to religious beliefs, government was now required to demonstrate that it had a compelling interest that outweighed infringement of the free exercise of religion guaranteed by the First Amendment. In his opinion for the Court, Chief Justice Burger indicated that it was the *Amish* who held the high ground in this fight for family values:

> [A] state's interest in universal education . . . is not totally free from a balancing process when it impinges on fundamental rights and interests, such as those specifically protected by the Free Exercise Clause of the First Amendment, and the traditional interest of parents with respect to the religious upbringing of their children. . . .

Jehovah's Witnesses

The Free Exercise Clause has received its most severe tests at the hands of the Jehovah's Witnesses. Virulently Anti-Roman Catholic and aggressively committed to public proselytizing, the sect has been much reviled — and often defended by the U.S. Supreme Court. In the first of a string of First Amendment cases brought by the Witnesses, *Lovell v. Griffin* (1938), the Court upheld the sect's practice of distributing religious handbills, citing press freedom. In *Cantwell v. Connecticut* (1940), the Court upheld a Witness's right to play a recording attacking Roman Catholicism, loudly and publicly, as — among other things — a constitutionally protected free exercise of religion. In *Martin v. City of Struthers* (1943), the Court found the sect's practice of door-to-door solicitation of converts to be protected by the First Amendment.

On at least two famous occasions, the Supreme Court did rule against the Witnesses — but then later reversed itself. In *Jones v. Opelika* (1942), by a 5-4 vote the Court upheld a city ordinance requiring all peddlers — including the Jehovah's Witnesses, who sell their literature door-to-door — to pay a license fee. The next year, the conservative Justice James F. Byrnes was replaced by the liberal Justice Wiley B. Rutledge. When the issue of licensing the Witnesses came before the Court again, clothed in somewhat different garments in *Murdock v. Pennsylvania* (1943), the Court overturned *Jones* by a vote of 5-4. Reasoning that because the Witnesses believe that each member is a minister whose mission is to preach the Gospel, the Court now found a licensing fee to be an unconstitutional tax on free exercise of religion. For Justice William O. Douglas, who wrote the opinion of the Court, peddling pamphlets was an activity that "occupies the same high estate under the First Amendment as do worship in the churches and preaching from the pulpits." Even the disdain heaped on the Witnesses by the mainstream lent the sect an air of sanctity:

> [T]he mere fact that the religious literature is "sold" by itinerant preachers rather than "donated" does not transform evangelism into a commercial enterprise. If it did, then the passing of the collection plate in church would make the church service a commercial project. . . . Freedom of speech, freedom of the press, freedom of religion are available to all, not merely to those who can pay their own way.

In the period leading up to World War II, the Supreme Court heard a case that involved three of the most potent elements involved in the debate over religious freedom: schoolchildren, the Jehovah's Witnesses, and the flag salute. In *Minersville School District v. Gobitis* (1940), two children, ages 10 and 12, refused to participate in the daily school salute to the flag because their faith taught them not to worship graven images. When they were expelled from school, the Gobitises took their case all the way to the Supreme Court. Writing for the Court, Justice Felix Frankfurter upheld the school's expulsion. It was clear, however, that the eight-justice majority was not immune to war fever. In Frankfurter's words,

> So pervasive is the acceptance of this precious right [to free exercise of religion] that its scope is brought into question, as here, only when the conscience of individuals collides with the felt necessities of society.

And clearly, he and seven other justices felt that this occasion was one of those times when society's "felt necessities" must prevail:

> The mere possession of religious convictions which contradict the relevant concerns of a political society does not relieve the citizen from the discharge of political responsibilities.

The *Gobitis* decision proved to be enormously unpopular with the legal community, with the media, and even with the American Legion. Two years later, in another, unrelated case involving the Witnesses, three of the justices who had voted with the majority in *Gobitis* took the opportunity to announce in a dissent that they had changed their minds about the flag salute. When the issue came before the Court again in *West Virginia State Board of Education v. Barnette* (1943), the lone dissenter in *Gobitis*, Harlan F. Stone, was now the chief justice. Stone had the pleasure of seeing his earlier view of the matter validated in an eloquent opinion written by Justice Robert H. Jackson:

If there is any fixed star in our constitutional constellation, it is that no official, high or petty, can prescribe what shall be orthodox in politics, nationalism, religion, or other matters of opinion or force citizens to confess by word or act their faith therein. If there are any circumstances which permit an exception, they do not now occur to us.

After 1943, the high Court began narrowing its free exercise exemptions, tailoring them to fit specific religious beliefs and practices. But the Jehovah's Witnesses, with their pamphleteering and proselytizing, had clearly made their point. It was a point brought home again as recently as June 2002, when the Court handed down its decision in *Watchtower Bible & Tract Society v. Village of Stratton*. By a vote of 8 to 1 (Chief Justice Rehnquist was the lone dissenter), the Court once again cited First Amendment guarantees of freedom of religion and speech in striking down an ordinance requiring canvassers to register with city hall.

Using Freedom of Expression

Freedom of expression, as Justice Felix Frankfurter said, "is the well-spring of our civilization." Like other rights guaranteed by the First Amendment, free expression has two branches — freedom of speech and freedom of the press — which are both given blanket protection by the framers of the Constitution: "Congress shall make no law . . . abridging freedom of speech, or of the press." Today, these freedoms, by ensuring that the government does not interfere with public debate about public affairs, form the basis for policy making in the United States. And yet, virtually all of the case law drawing out the meaning behind the framers' plain words has been decided since the Second World War.

It seems clear enough that the Founding Fathers wanted to do away with the sometimes arbitrary punishment for *seditious libel,* or criticism of government they had seen handed out in England and by the English in the American colonies. And yet, political rivalries between those who believed in a strong federal government, the Federalists, and their opponents, the Antifederalists, led both parties to commit abuses. In 1798, fearing the Antifederalists' rhetorical support for the radical ideas being bandied about during the French Revolution, the Federalist-controlled Congress passed the Sedition Act, making it a crime to "write, print, utter, or publish . . . any false, scandalous and malicious" sentiments aimed at the government. Several newspapers and their publishers were convicted under the act before it expired upon the election of Thomas Jefferson in 1800. But in 1803, the Antifederalist (soon to be known as Republican) Jefferson himself was responsible for bringing libel charges against the Federalist editor Harry Croswell. Over time, however, libel became a civil, rather than a criminal matter, and political speech was granted the highest level of protection available under the First Amendment.

John Peter Zenger's zingers

Arguably the most important political trial in American history took place long before America was actually a country, and it concerned not a politician, but a printer. In 1733, John Peter Zenger was a newspaper publisher in New York. Zenger's *New-York Weekly Journal* published editorials and political satire aimed at the colony's royal governor, William Cosby. Cosby responded by having Zenger arrested and charged with libel and *sedition,* which meant to encourage the locals to hold their government in contempt.

At Zenger's trial, the only question put to the jury was whether or not the publisher had actually published the articles in question. Since Zenger's attorney, Andrew Hamilton, never denied that his client had printed the pieces, the verdict seemed a foregone conclusion. But Hamilton, the most celebrated trial attorney of his day, delivered a summation that changed his client's fate, and perhaps also the fate of America. "Gentlemen of the jury," Hamilton declared, "it is not the cause of a poor printer, nor of New York alone, which you are now trying. No! It may in its consequences affect every freeman that lives under British government on the main of America. It is the best cause. It is the cause of liberty."

The jury acquitted Zenger, who immediately published a transcript of the trial. News of the trial and its dramatic conclusion spread quickly, gaining public approval and later inspiring the Founding Fathers to make freedom of expression a cornerstone of the Bill of Rights. The Zenger trial did not, however, change the law.

Free speech

Neither the First Amendment nor the Supreme Court has specifically distinguished *speech* from *press* when it comes to freedom of expression. The Court is fond of saying that a journalist has no more rights under the Constitution than an ordinary citizen. This memorable maxim is misleading, however: Case law indicates that press defendants are granted more leeway when it comes to libel, and ordinary citizens are not permitted to express just any thought that comes into their heads.

Crying fire in a crowded theater

The first significant free speech case to come before the high Court, *Schenck v. United States* (1919), presented the justices with a familiar scenario. While the First Amendment was apparently inspired — at least in part — by a backlash against laws prohibiting seditious libel, or treasonous statements, the law surrounding this subject remained muddy. Although *Schenck* did not arrive at the Supreme Court until after World War I had ended, it grew out of a violation of the 1917 Espionage Act, which prohibited interference with military recruiting.

Charles T. Schenck, who had served as general secretary of the Socialist Party, was accused with another man of printing and mailing 15,000 antidraft pamphlets to Philadelphia conscripts. The pamphlets urged recipients to resist the draft and refuse to participate in the war in Europe. Schenck defended himself by arguing that he had only been exercising his right of free speech. The Court, however, did not buy his argument, ruling 9-0 that the First Amendment did not trump the Espionage Act. In his opinion for the Court, Oliver Wendell Holmes considered the context of the speech as well as its content: "The question in every case is whether the words used are used in such circumstances and are of such a nature as to create a clear and present danger that they will bring about substantive evils that Congress has a right to prevent."

In time of war, Holmes reasoned, government had a right to limit conspiracies meant to undermine the war effort — even if they weren't successful: "[T]he character of every act depends upon the circumstances in which it is done. The most stringent protection of free speech would not protect a man in falsely shouting fire in a theater and causing a panic."

Later the same year, Holmes refined his *clear and present danger* test in his dissent in *Abrams v. United States* (1919), a case involving five Russian immigrant anarchists who were convicted of violating the Espionage Act of 1917 by printing and distributing leaflets calling for a general strike to protest the presence of U.S. troops in Russia. Holmes disputed the majority's use of his test in upholding the anarchists' convictions: here, the danger was not imminent, and the intent was not to cripple the war effort, merely to protest U.S. intervention in Russia. More importantly, Holmes used the occasion to set forth a major theory of free speech:

> [W]hen men have realized that time has upset many fighting faiths, they may come to believe even more than they believe the very foundations of their own conduct that the ultimate good desired is better reached by free trade in ideas — that the best test of truth is the power of the thought to get itself accepted in the competition of the market, and that truth is the only ground upon which their wishes can safely be carried out. That at any rate is the theory of our Constitution.

The clear and present danger test survived, but the Court adopted the interpretation of it that Holmes supplied in *Abrams* and refined — often in company with Louis D. Brandeis — in numerous subsequent dissents in free speech cases. Eventually the test would spin off a doctrine known as the *time, place, and manner rule,* which permits government to control the time, place, and matter of speech. Any restriction must be neutral concerning the content of the speech and must not — even incidentally — interfere with the free flow of ideas. Customarily such restrictions take the form of requiring licenses to control use of *public forums,* public places traditionally associated with demonstrations or speech making, such as streets, parks, and so on.

Perhaps the most memorable example of how the *time, place, and manner rule* functions is two cases that never reached the Supreme Court. The cases arose out of a proposed 1977 Nazi demonstration in the largely Jewish settlement of Skokie, Illinois. The citizens of Skokie attempted to stop the Nazis by developing an elaborate licensing scheme that would have prevented a march through their village. Both the Illinois Supreme Court and the U.S. Circuit Court of Appeals found that the scheme was impermissible because it interfered with the Nazis' free speech rights. The content of this *speech* may be hateful, but the method of expressing it — a slow march through the center of town — was not unduly disruptive, at least from the marchers' point of view. Any disruption that occurred would be caused by objections on the part of the citizens of Skokie to the *content* of the Nazis' expression, and government restrictions of content are impermissible violations of the First Amendment.

Despite what seems an improbable outcome here, the decision makes sense if you look on the First Amendment as a tool for shaping social policy. The courts that decided these cases may have been attempting, among other things, to encourage tolerance and self-restraint. And then there is the legacy of Holmes's *Abrams* dissent: "[T]he ultimate good desired is better reached by free trade in ideas."

Setting fire to Old Glory

Under the First Amendment, speech is more than mere words. Speech includes so-called *speech acts,* actions meant to convey a message. The 1977 Nazi Party march through the predominantly Jewish village of Skokie, Illinois, is an example of such a speech act. More often, the speech acts that result in First Amendment cases are symbolic. And more often than not, they involve what is, from a certain point of view, nothing more than a scrap of fabric or a piece of paper.

It's not too surprising that symbolic speech act cases often arise during periods of social upheaval or in time of war, when bits of cloth take on extra meaning. In *Stromberg v. California* (1931), a teacher at a summer camp was convicted of violating California's Red Flag Law, designed to prevent the spread of the revolutionary *Red Menace* of Communism. The Court overturned Yetta Stromberg's conviction, citing her raising of the red flag as symbolic speech.

In *Tinker v. Des Moines School District* (1969), high school and junior high school students were suspended for wearing black armbands to protest U.S. involvement in the war in Vietnam. The Supreme Court overruled these suspensions, declaring that since the wearing of armbands did not disrupt the school environment, this act could hardly be banned. What's more, as Justice Abe Fortas's opinion for the Court pointed out, the school district *had* allowed students to wear campaign buttons, which are only another form of political attire. Quoting a phrase made famous in an earlier case concerning alleged political subversion in an educational environment, Fortas pointed out that *especially* in what is supposed to be a "marketplace of ideas," students should not be forced to take in only what officials see fit for them to learn: "It can hardly be argued that either students or teachers shed their constitutional rights to freedom of speech or expression at the schoolhouse gate."

It is possible to push war protest too far, of course. In *United States v. O'Brien* (1968), the Supreme Court upheld a federal law prohibiting the mutilation of draft cards. Such actions interfere with the legitimate government interest in having conscription run smoothly during time of war. It is worth noting, too, that the draft protester in *O'Brien* had *burned* his draft card. As Oliver Wendell Holmes noted in the first important free speech case to come before the Court, *Schenck v. United States* (1919), fire can be mighty disruptive to public order (see the preceding section).

Burning things — in particular, burning the Stars and Stripes — continues to be a burning issue. In the flag-burning cases *Texas v. Johnson* (1989) and *United States v. Eichman* (1990), the Supreme Court found this particular speech act to be "expressive conduct" the government could not outlaw. Writing for the Court in *Johnson,* Justice William J. Brennan reasoned that, "If there is a bedrock principle underlying the First Amendment, it is that the government may not prohibit the expression of an idea simply because society finds the idea itself offensive or disagreeable." Johnson's act — he had burned the flag during the 1984 Republican convention to protest President Ronald Reagan's policies — was plainly meant to carry a political message. The Texas flag desecration statute he was accused of violating therefore came dangerously close to the kinds of suppression the Founding Fathers had attempted to preclude with the First Amendment. The Texas law was unconstitutional, and Johnson's flag burning was declared to be just about the *purest,* most unalloyed form of speech imaginable.

Needless to say, not everyone agreed with Justice Brennan. *Johnson* came down on the side of flag burning by the slimmest of margins — the vote was 5-4 — and Justice William Rehnquist wrote an eloquent dissent in defense of Old Glory that went right to the heart of the matter. The public reacted with anger to *Johnson,* and within months, their representatives in Congress passed the Flag Protection Act of 1989. When protesters challenged this law by burning several flags on the very steps of the U.S. Capitol, the Court declared the act unconstitutional in *United States v. Eichman* (1990). Once again, Justice Brennan wrote the opinion of the Court, in which he made it clear that the majority of the Court considered flag desecration laws inherently constitutionally suspect. Well, maybe. Once again the vote was 5-4, and the flag-burning issue refuses to go away. Every election cycle, at least one politician — figuratively, and sometimes literally — wraps himself or herself in the flag. And the specter of a constitutional amendment outlawing flag burning lingers.

People, of course, use other ways to demonstrate disrespect for or disapproval of government. In *Smith v. Goguen* (1974), for example, the defendant sewed a flag to the seat of his trousers. In *Cohen v. California* (1971), Paul Robert Cohen wore a jacket emblazoned with "F*** the Draft" in a Los Angeles courtroom. In *Wooley v. Maynard* (1977), a New Hampshire motorist taped over the portion of his license plate that read "Live Free or Die."

Not all these cases were decided on free speech or even First Amendment grounds, but in each of them, the Supreme Court upheld the conduct. All of them, however, have implications for the law governing freedom of speech. Clearly, these symbolic acts, however offensive, indecent, or irreverent, are meant as political expressions. Because they do not threaten immediate social disruption, they cannot be barred. To quote the sometimes mischievous Justice William O. Douglas, "The Constitution is not neutral. It was designed to take the government off the backs of the people."

Not-so-free speech

Despite the sweeping language of the First Amendment, some categories of speech receive second-class protection, and some are not protected at all by the First Amendment.

Speaking of business

For most of its history, the Supreme Court did not extend First Amendment protections to so-called *commercial speech* connected with advertising and business. This type of speech wasn't even on the docket until 1942 when, in *Valentine v. Chrestensen,* the Court held that advertising is not protected by free speech guarantees. In the landmark case of *Virginia State Board of Pharmacy v. Virginia Citizens Consumer Counsel* (1970), the high Court began to revise its view of business communications to the public. Because American society depends upon the free flow of commercial information, advertising that conveys something more than a mere come-on serves the public interest and deserves some protection. In *Bates v. State Bar of Arizona* (1977), the justices went so far as to extend First Amendment protections to their own kind, granting lawyers the right to advertise and freeing them of the professional ethical rules that had prevented such advertising up to that time. Ambulance-chasing lawyers still had to be careful, however: In *Ohralik v. Ohio State Bar Association* (1978), the Court upheld a ban on in-person solicitation.

Even as it eased restrictions on commercial speech, however, the Court made it clear that false, misleading, or deceptive advertising is not protected. In *Central Hudson Gas v. Public Service Commission of New York* (1980), the high Court announced a test to determine when commercial speech might be regulated:

- The government interest served by the regulation is substantial.
- The regulation directly advances the government interest.
- There is no less restrictive method of advancing the government interest in question.

This test is considerably more lax that those applied to regulation of ordinary speech. But there is a bottom line: When you're doing business, pay close attention not only to the medium, but also to the message. When it comes to the First Amendment and commercial speech, content matters.

Publishing libel

Definitions first. *Slander* consists of derogatory words spoken out loud. *Libel* is slander that appears in print. Both slander and libel are defamation, and both are published in the sense that they are broadcast to the world.

Prior to 1964, defamation actions were largely confined to state courts, where they were decided along common law lines, drawing upon earlier case law rather than the First Amendment. The definition of *common law libel* used prior to 1964 included any communications that "tend to expose one to public hatred, shame, obloquy, contumely, odium, contempt, ridicule, aversion, ostracism, degradation, or disgrace, or to induce an evil opinion of one in the minds of right-thinking persons, and to deprive one of their confidence and friendly intercourse in society." (This definition is from a 1933 New York case, *Kimmerle v. New York*.) Those words pretty much covered the landscape, making it all but impossible for people to know what they could and could not say about others — especially since some libel actions resulted in criminal convictions. This lack of clarity about what constituted libel had what is known as a *chilling effect* on free speech, meaning that people sometimes declined to say negative things that may well not have been libelous simply because they couldn't tell what libel *was*.

In 1964, however, the U.S. Supreme Court finally took up a defamation case that begged for First Amendment analysis. *New York Times v. Sullivan* concerned a civil libel suit brought by a Montgomery, Alabama, city commissioner against four African-American clergymen and *The New York Times*. The clergymen were associated with an organization calling itself the Committee to Defend Martin Luther King and the Struggle for the South, which had placed an advertisement in the newspaper. The commissioner, L.B. Sullivan, claimed that the ad, which called for support for the civil rights movement, criticized Montgomery and included false and libelous statements about him in particular. The Supreme Court found that although some parts of the ad may have been untrue, they were not libelous. A new definition of libel emerged from this watershed case: Public officials cannot recover damages for statements — even false statements — critical of their official actions unless they can prove *actual malice,* "knowledge that [the statement] was false or [was made] with reckless disregard of whether it was false or not."

The Court's reasons for granting certiorari (see Chapter 2) in *New York Times v. Sullivan* were plainly policy reasons. Without it, people like southern segregationists were able to suppress what amounted to political expression, the most hallowed category of speech protected by the First Amendment. Subsequent Supreme Court cases tinkered with the actual malice standard, extending it to *public figures* such as sports heroes and film stars and then shrinking it so that it does not apply to private persons even when they're associated with matters of public concern. The upshot has been that although some previously libelous speech is now protected as free speech, precisely what separates permissible public criticism from impermissible defamation is still unclear.

Fighting words

Fighting words, like libelous statements, are not protected by the First Amendment. And, in fact, distinguishing between the two is sometimes hard: Both involve disparaging, even insulting remarks leveled at one person or group of persons by another. To the law, though, there is a difference. It seems to boil down to this: In cases involving fighting words, the context in which they are delivered matters, whereas libel is libel whenever it is published. And because fighting words are intended to provoke an immediate reaction, they also come awfully close to the constitutionally unprotected act of crying fire in a crowded theater. (See the section "Crying fire in a crowded theater," earlier in this chapter.)

The definitive definition of fighting words can be found in the seminal Supreme Court case *Chaplinsky v. New Hampshire* (1942). Chaplinsky, a Jehovah's Witness, was distributing religious pamphlets surrounded by a hostile crowd when he was interrupted by a city marshal. Chaplinsky responded by calling the officer a "racketeer" and a "Fascist." The Supreme Court responded by denying First Amendment protection to fighting words, "those which by their very utterance inflict injury or tend to incite an immediate breach of the peace."

Chaplinsky was actually the last case in which the Supreme Court upheld a conviction for using fighting words against a public official. In *Brandenburg v. Ohio* (1969), the broadcast of a Ku Klux Klan rally in which the leader advocated racial strife led to his conviction under a *criminal syndicalism* law banning violent organization. Even though Brandenburg's speech advocated (as opposed to incited) lawlessness, the Court found that it did not constitute fighting words, largely because of its political content. And in another free speech classic, the Court found that wearing a jacket emblazoned with "F*** the Draft" into court did not constitute the use of fighting words, despite their provocativeness.

Chaplinsky more or less did away with the whole notion of fighting words. Its lasting significance, however, comes from some *obiter dicta,* or passing comments, in Justice Frank Murphy's opinion for the unanimous Court:

> There are certain well-defined and narrowly limited classes of speech, the prevention and punishment of which has never been thought to raise any Constitutional problem. These include the lewd and obscene, the profane, the libelous, and the insulting or "fighting" words. . . . It has been well observed that such utterances are no essential part of any exposition of ideas, and are of such slight social value as a step to truth that any benefit that may be derived from them is clearly outweighed by the social interest in order and morality.

There you have it, a complete guide to all the types of speech that receive no First Amendment protection. Ever since *Chaplinsky*, the Court — whether predominantly liberal or overwhelmingly conservative — has been busy carving out exceptions to these categories. The growth of free speech is a testament to the vitality and adaptability of the nation.

Just what is obscenity?

All that can really be said about obscenity is that it's in the eye of the beholder. The task of coming up with a workable definition of obscenity fell to Justice William J. Brennan in a series of cases decided in the 1950s and 1960s. He was *never* happy with any of the lines he drew between protected speech and the kind of lewd expression unworthy of the First Amendment. The only thing the justices have agreed on is that in order to be considered obscene, an expression must have something to do with sex. Talk about stating the obvious — defining obscenity seems to be harder than rocket science.

Okay, obscenity is not just sex related, it has to be erotic. Wearing a jacket bearing the phrase "F*** the Draft" may be offensive because it has something to do with sex, but it's certainly not erotic. The words have sex written all over them, but the act of wearing them carries another type of meaning, a purely symbolic one. If there's anything that *Cohen v. California* proves, it's that it's difficult to be allegorical and erotic at the same time — but not impossible. In fact, some very great works of art have achieved this feat, despite which they have been declared obscene. At one time, it was illegal to possess a copy of James Joyce's *Ulysses* or D.H. Lawrence's *Lady Chatterley's Lover* in the United States because both books were banned.

The first Supreme Court case to attempt a definition of obscenity was *Roth v. United States* (1957), when the justices ventured to say that pornography was not necessarily obscene, although both categories of speech are sexy *and* erotic. The difference, Justice Brennan wrote, is that obscenity is "utterly without redeeming social importance," the same quality that deprives fighting words of First Amendment protection. But then Brennan went on to say that "Obscene material is material which deals with sex in a manner appealing to the prurient interest." Following this logic, he proposed a test: "whether to the average person, applying contemporary community standards, the dominant theme of the material taken as a whole appeals to the prurient interest." As for *prurient interest,* well that could be either "[h]aving a tendency to excite lustful thoughts" *or* "a shameful and morbid interest in . . . sex." Take your pick.

This language was all pretty subjective, and it resulted in a flurry of contradictory attempts to refine Brennan's initial attempt to put into words something that is by its very nature pretty subjective. In *Manual Enterprises v. Day* (1962), Justice John M. Harlan wrote that obscene materials are "so offensive on their face as to affront current community standards of decency." In *Jacobellis v. Ohio* (1964), Brennan tried again: Obscene speech is "utterly without redeeming social value." In 1966, things got really messy when, in the course of one day, the justices issued 14 separate opinions in the course of deciding three obscenity cases. One of these cases, *A Book Named "John Cleland's Memoirs of a Woman of Pleasure" v. Attorney General of Massachusetts* concerned the 18th-century English novel known as *Fanny Hill* (you see why it's called the *Fanny Hill* case). The Court decided that because this particular book has "some minimal literary value," it is not obscene. The book also prompted Justice Brennan to announce a new three-part obscenity test: To be judged obscene, a work must appeal to the prurient interest, be patently offensive because it offends contemporary community standards, and be utterly without redeeming social value.

This new test — and in particular, its last requirement of minimal social value — was liberal indeed. For a time, the Court overturned every obscenity conviction that came before it, except in those cases where questionable material was sold to minors or advertised outrageously. The pornography business boomed, adding to the bad odor surrounding the Warren Court in conservative circles.

Fanny Hill and what followed it inevitable inspired a backlash. After Warren Burger took over the reins of the Court, determined to roll back the excesses of the Warren Court, he took the opportunity to present a revised obscenity test in *Miller v. California* (1973). Material could be declared obscene if

> (a) the average person, applying contemporary community standards, would find that the work, taken as a whole, appeals to the prurient interest; [and] (b) the work depicts or describes, in a patently offensive way, sexual conduct specifically defined by the applicable state law' [and] (c) the work, taken as a whole, lacks serious literary, artistic, political, or scientific value.

Burger then went on to stress that only *hard-core* pornography could be excluded from First Amendment protection.

Now, at least hard-core porn with some obviously tacked on social commentary would not pass muster. Now, at least the people of Maine or Mississippi were not obligated to accept all of the same questionable material that might be everyday fare in New York and Las Vegas. Nonetheless, *Miller* is viewed in some circles as still too liberal. Perhaps surprisingly, it's not just conservatives who have lodged this complaint. Feminist legal activists like the First Amendment expert Catherine McKinnon have proposed that pornography be removed from First Amendment protection because it exploits women and children. Attempts to pass laws to this effect have been blocked by lower federal courts.

Although *Miller* remains the test for obscenity, it has been modified in some respects. States have been permitted to ban non-obscene pornography featuring underage actors or characters. Zoning ordinances restricting sales of non-obscene pornography to certain areas have passed constitutional muster, as has a Federal Communications Commission rule limiting broadcasts of "indecent" material to certain times of the day.

Is there really a right to privacy?

The word *privacy* appears nowhere in the Constitution. For this reason, that fundamentalist of the First Amendment, Justice Hugo L. Black, refused to endorse a right to privacy. The word *private* does appear in the Fifth Amendment, which states that "private property [shall not] be taken for public use, without just compensation." Accordingly, the Supreme Court's initial approach to the right to privacy occurred in the context of the debate about due process (see Chapter 9) that occurred towards the end of the 19th century. *Substantive due process,* as developed by the Supreme Court, is a Fourteenth Amendment concept meant to protect private property and free enterprise.

And yet, the notion of a fundamental, constitutionally-guaranteed right to be free of *all* government interference has been a feature of the legal landscape ever since future Justice Louis D. Brandeis and his law partner Samuel D. Warren proposed in an 1890 law review article that such a right was implicit in our foundation document. In 1928, Brandeis introduced this idea into Supreme Court history in *Olmstead v. U.S.* Dissenting from the majority's assertion that government wiretapping did not constitute a violation of the Fourth Amendment ban on illegal search and seizure, Brandeis wrote, "The makers of our Constitution . . . conferred, as against the government, the right to be let alone — the most comprehensive of rights and the right most valued by civilized men."

The right to privacy was not, however, formally recognized by the Court until 1965, when the justices decided a case concerning the use of contraceptives by married couples. Privacy came up again in a 1969 pornography case. And it took center stage in the public consciousness in 1973, when the Court upheld a woman's right to abortion in *Roe v. Wade.* The right to privacy continues to evolve in Supreme Court jurisprudence, and it has certainly been discussed in widely varying contexts. Nonetheless, privacy clearly has a link with sexual expression and therefore to the First Amendment. This connection seems obvious, but things are never simple when it comes to the law.

Griswold v. Connecticut and contraception

The modern concept of the right to privacy, growing out of "penumbras and emanations" of the Bill of Rights and emphasizing civil rights, developed from Justice William O. Douglas's majority opinion in *Griswold v. Connecticut* (1965). In *Griswold,* the Court declared unconstitutional a state law prohibiting the use of contraceptives and the distribution to married couples of information about family planning. It had only been 35 years since feminist Margaret Sanger had been arrested for giving a public lecture on birth control. By 1965, however, the Supreme Court had undergone a revolution of sorts, deferring to legislation for protection of private property and discarding its prior allegiance to substantive due process, which had been used to protect the rights of private corporations. Instead, the modern Court had come to see its role as the defender of individual liberties from state interference. Privacy — particularly as it related to sexuality — was counted as one of the rights guaranteed by the first ten amendments to the Constitution, the Bill of Rights.

But *which* amendment? For Justice Douglas, the First, Third, Fourth, Fifth, and Ninth Amendments imply "zones of privacy," which are "formed by emanations from those guarantees [in the Bill of Rights] that help give them life and substance." At issue in *Griswold* was not just invasion of the privacy of the marital bed, but also an attempt to silence public exchanges of information about what goes on there. For John M. Harlan, who wrote a concurring opinion, the Connecticut statute defied the Fourteen Amendment's guarantee of due process. Justice Arthur Goldberg, in a separate concurrence, placed the emphasis on the Ninth Amendment's reservation of additional, *unenumerated* rights not spelled out elsewhere in the Bill of Rights. For the dissenting Hugo Black, there was no constitutionally protected right to privacy, and all this discussion about "natural justice" and "implied rights" was evidence of judicial overreaching.

Griswold soon gave rise to other cases about contraception. *Eisenstadt v. Baird* (1972) cleared the way for birth control to be sold to unmarried adults. *Carey v. Population Services International* (1977) permitted sales of contraceptives to minors under the age of 16 and allowed condoms to come out from behind the pharmacist's counter to be advertised in the open. Clearly, the right to privacy had outgrown the bedroom.

Stanley v. Georgia and porn

In the superheated atmosphere of the late 1960s, when the sexual revolution was at its peak and the Warren Court was cleaning up the odds and ends of personal liberties it had not yet liberated, the justices pondered a case about the personal possession of obscene pornography. In *Stanley v. Georgia* (1969), purely personal possession — at home — of even obscene pornography received the blessing of a unanimous Court. Thurgood Marshall's opinion for the Court provided a number of rationales for this conclusion:

- It was based on restrictions on search and seizure.
- It was based on freedom of expression.
- It was based on a broad right to privacy.

"If the First Amendment means anything," declared Marshall, "it means that a State has no business telling a man, sitting alone in his own house, what books he may read or what films he may watch. Our whole constitutional heritage rebels at the thought of giving government the power to control men's minds."

In *Stanley,* Marshall combined the First Amendment right "to receive information and ideas, regardless of their social worth," with the "right to be free, except in very limited circumstances, from unwanted governmental intrusions into one's privacy." While it seemed plain to him — and may seem as plain to you as it does to me — that there is a relationship between these two rights, the justices did not entirely agree. While all agreed with the outcome in *Stanley,* the *holding* of the case — its significance as legal precedent — was subsequently undermined. In *Bowers v. Hardwick* (1986), a case about private, consensual homosexual sexual relations, the Court voted 5-4 that the state could regulate private sexual conduct. And in *Osborne v. Ohio* (1990), *Stanley* was found not to apply to private possession of child pornography. "*Stanley,*" wrote Byron White for the Court, "should not be read too broadly."

While the majorities in *Bowers* and *Osborne* may have felt that Thurgood Marshall played fast and loose with the concept of privacy in *Stanley,* the fact is that the right to privacy remains relatively undefined. At the same time, it is plain enough that *Bowers* and *Osborne* were decided on policy, rather than legal grounds. The Court simply did not want to sanction either homosexuality or child pornography.

Roe v. Wade and abortion

In 1973, the right to privacy took on a whole new significance when it was used to uphold a woman's right to abortion in *Roe v. Wade.* Like *Griswold* (see "*Griswold v. Connecticut* and contraception") and *Stanley* (see "*Stanley v. Georgia* and pornography") before it, *Roe* concerned what might be called *sexual autonomy,* but *Roe* upped the ante by adding the element of terminating human life. Policy considerations and potential harm to society were certainly major considerations in the first two decisions, but in *Roe* the stakes became extraordinarily high.

At the time the unemployed, unmarried pregnant Texas woman calling herself *Jane Roe* filed suit against Texas District Attorney Henry B. Wade, nearly every state in the union outlawed abortion. Illegal abortions were both common and life-threatening. Feminists like the attorneys who represented Roe, Linda Coffee and Sarah Weddington, had made legalized abortion one of their priorities.

Roe v. Wade was argued twice before the U.S. Supreme Court. After the first hearing, in December 1971, a majority of the justices favored overturning the state laws against abortion. Justice Harry Blackmun, who had once served as counsel to the famed Mayo Clinic and who was now the Court's most junior member, was assigned to write the majority opinion. Blackmun's first draft, which argued for overturning antiabortion laws on grounds that they were unconstitutionally vague, was considered unpersuasive. The case was then put down for reargument and reheard in January 1973. Blackmun's second draft opinion for the Court based its opposition to antiabortion laws on a constitutional right to privacy, which Blackmun located, alternatively, in the Due Process Clause of the Fourteen Amendment (see Chapter 9) or in the *unenumerated rights* — those not specifically granted in the Constitution to any branch of the federal government — reserved to the people in the Ninth Amendment.

A private right to die?

In part because the constitutional basis of the right to privacy remain unsettled, courts have been asked to consider a number of new issues as versions of privacy. The most explosive issue to come along since abortion is the hotly-debated *right to die.* To date, the Supreme Court has not taken the question up, but lower courts have been asked to decide cases involving the right to forego life-saving medical treatment. In *In re Quinlin* (1976), for example, the New Jersey Supreme Court granted the request of the parents of 21-year-old Karen Ann Quinlin to remove their daughter's life support systems. By then, Quinlin had been on a respirator for a year and had virtually no chance of coming out of her coma and resuming a meaningful existence.

The state supreme court ruled that Quinlin's right to privacy gave her the prerogative to refuse life-saving medical treatment, and that since she was incompetent to do this herself, her father could assume this right in her stead.

Quinlin's parents presented precious little evidence that their daughter would have rejected treatment, and the New Jersey Supreme Court declined to consider what many contend was the real issue in this case: legal euthanasia. After her respirator was removed, Quinlin began breathing on her own and lived for another ten years. The U.S. Supreme Court denied a petition for certiorari (see Chapter 2) in the case.

Blackmun's opinion had many critics, including Justices Byron White and William Rehnquist, both of whom wrote dissenting opinions objecting to Blackmun's resort to a right either connected with a discredited interpretation of due process that invented a non-existent right, or something not found in the Constitution at all. But Justice William O. Douglas, in concurrence, noted that the right to privacy "includes customary, traditional, and time-honored rights, amenities, privileges, and immunities that come within the sweep of 'the Blessings of Liberty' mentioned in the preamble to the Constitution." What's more, he added, the right to privacy is one of a group of three rights that "come within the meaning of the term 'liberty' as used in the Fourteenth Amendment." Justice William J. Brennan, who did not write a separate concurring opinion, did write a letter to Douglas commenting on Douglas's draft opinion. That letter lays out, as no Supreme Court opinion ever has, a common sense explanation of the right to privacy:

> [T]he right [of privacy] is a species of "liberty" . . . but I would identify three groups of fundamental freedoms that "liberty" encompasses: first, freedom from bodily restraint or inspection, freedom to do with one's body as one likes, and freedom to care for one's health and person; second, freedom of choice in the basic decisions of life, such as marriage, divorce, procreation, contraception and the education and upbringing of children; and, third, autonomous control over the development and expression of one's intellect and personality.

Some Court watchers have interpreted the *Roe* decision as the justices' attempt to address not privacy issues, but societal change. But instead of treating abortion forthrightly as a gender discrimination issue brought to the fore by the women's movement, Blackmun's opinion muddied the waters by emphasizing the wrong aspect of the Fourteenth Amendment. Rather than offering a due process rationale for legalizing abortion, critics feel he should have made an equal protection argument (see Chapter 10), pointing out that women bear the burden of unwanted pregnancies.

The *Roe* decision had a polarizing effect. Adherents of *Roe v. Wade,* emphasizing the civil liberties aspect of the decision, called themselves *pro-choice,* while opponents adopted the label *pro-life.* A Committee of Ten Million, with backing from the Roman Catholic Church, began an unsuccessful petition drive for a "human rights amendment." But reaction to *Roe* arguably led to the defeat not only of the Equal Rights Amendment but of numerous pro-choice Democratic legislators. During the administrations of the Republican presidents Ronald Reagan and George Bush, commitment to overturning *Roe* also became a litmus test for potential Supreme Court appointees.

Free press

It's an obvious truth that bears repeating: Without a free press, without the ability to publish and distribute opinion, freedom of speech would be meaningless. And, in fact, journalists are granted more leeway than ordinary citizens in certain situations. They are, for example, sometimes granted the privilege of keeping their sources confidential in order to ensure that government does not have a chilling effect on public communication. And for the same reason, extra protection may be afforded media defendants in libel cases. As with free speech, however, restraints exist both on government regulation and on press freedom.

Prior restraint: A clear no-no

There has never been a Supreme Court case that resulted in a decision in favor of government restraint on publication. Heading off *prior restraint,* or government censorship, was in fact the primary impulse behind the Free Press Clause of the First Amendment. During the Constitutional Convention of 1787, Thomas Jefferson lobbied hard — from afar, he was in France — for inclusion of a guarantee of press freedom in the Bill of Rights:

> The people are the only censors of their governors. . . . The basis of our government being the opinion of the people, the very first object should be to keep that right; and were it left to me to decide whether we should have a government without newspapers or newspapers without a government, I should not hesitate for a moment to prefer the latter.

Despite the high-flown language, neither the Republican Jefferson nor his Federalist political rivals were always true to this ideal in their day. Their successors, too, have periodically trod on press freedom. Although the Court has on occasion hinted that in some extraordinary circumstance — involving, say, a threat to national security in time of war — prior restraint may be permissible, there has never yet been such a case. The balance of power in federal government does work.

Near v. Minnesota

The first time the Court declared prior restraint unconstitutional occurred in *Near v. Minnesota,* a 1931 case involving a state gag law that permitted judges, acting alone, to prohibit publication of periodicals they deemed "obscene, lewd, and lascivious" or "malicious, scandalous, and defamatory." Although the statute seemed like a good idea in theory, in practice it lived up to all the predictions of dire consequences usually associated with the notion of prior restraint. The first publication to be closed down was a muckraking newspaper that specialized in uncovering corruption in Minneapolis. After the *Saturday Press* trained its focus on the mayor and the police chief, further publication of the newspaper was *enjoined,* or stopped by court order.

The newspaper's publisher, J.M. Near, was himself a disagreeable character, known for his bias against Catholics, Jews, African-Americans, and labor unions. His appeal to the Supreme Court was funded by another questionable character, the ultra-conservative Chicago publisher, Col. Robert R. McCormack. Now, these two personalities certainly put the First Amendment to the test! It was a test the Court met — just barely. By a vote of 5-4, the Court struck the Minnesota gag law down, reasoning that the most widely accepted understanding of the First Amendment guarantee of press freedom was that it barred prior restraint. Writing for the Court, Chief Justice Charles Evans Hughes declared, "The fact that the liberty of the press may be abused by miscreant purveyors of scandal does not make any less necessary the immunity of the press from previous restraint in dealing with official conduct."

If the politicians wanted to put a stop to what was being said about them, they could sue for libel, but they could not be allowed to stop publication of newspaper reports about their conduct. Even if what was being reported was, as the officials claimed, disturbing the peace of their fair city, letting government pick and choose what news would reach their citizens was "a more serious public evil."

In *Nebraska Press Association v. Stuart* (1976), criminal defendants tried to stop negative pretrial publicity about a horrendous mass murder, claiming that news stories about the crime would prejudice potential jurors. While acknowledging that possibility, the Court said that setting aside a conviction was preferable to the alternative in this case. Prior restraint is, wrote Chief Justice Warren Burger, the "most serious and least tolerable infringement on First Amendment rights." Amen.

The Pentagon Papers case

New York Times v. United States (1971) is perhaps the best illustration of the rule that government cannot stop publication of information it dislikes. The facts in the so-called *Pentagon Papers* case are as follows. Daniel Ellsberg, a former State Department employee and antiwar activist, pilfered a copy of a classified 7,000-page document that had been commissioned by the administration of President Lyndon Johnson in 1967. The document revealed that many embarrassing facts about Johnson's prosecution of the war in Vietnam had been kept from the American people. Ellsberg leaked the document to the *New York Times* and the *Washington Post,* and on June 13, 1971, the *Times* published the first installment in a series of excerpts from the *Pentagon Papers.*

Then-President Richard Nixon's Republican administration, which was still involved in Vietnam, initially thought this publication would only blacken the reputation of its Democratic predecessor. But then National Security Advisor Henry Kissinger became concerned that the *Pentagon Papers* would call his own policies into question, and Nixon himself grew worried about some future president letting classified documents dating from the Nixon era slip through his hands. On June 15, the administration obtained a court order temporarily restraining publication of the excerpts. After some more procedural wrangling in the lower courts, on June 25 the Supreme Court agreed to hear the case on an expedited basis. The justices heard oral arguments the following day, and on June 30 issued a brief unsigned opinion denying the government's request for a permanent injunction.

The vote in the *Pentagon Papers* case was split 6-3, with Justices Hugo Black, William J. Brennan, and William O. Douglas indicating that any injunction granted the government would amount to impermissible prior restraint. The three justices making up the balance of the majority — Byron White, Thurgood Marshall, and Potter Stewart — stopped short of making a blanket statement. The dissenters — Warren Burger, Harry Blackmun, and John M. Harlan — objected to what they considered the majority's rush to judgment. In addition, Chief Justice Burger indicated that he thought publishers could be prosecuted for endangering national security — but only after the fact. Not long afterward, in fact, the Burger Court did rule in two separate cases that former CIA employees were obliged to submit book proposals to government review before they could publish their writings.

And Daniel Ellsberg? He was indicted and tried on charges of espionage and theft. But the government's illegal methods of gathering evidence against him — his confidential discussions with his therapist had been secretly taped — led to a mistrial.

Miami Herald v. Tornillo

If the First Amendment prohibits the government from preventing publication of speech it objects to, the reverse is also true: Government cannot force publication of information it likes. In *Miami Herald v. Tornillo* (1974), the Court struck down a Florida statute requiring newspapers to grant political candidates a *right of reply,* — that is, space in which to respond to the paper's editorial comments on the candidates' records. While acknowledging that consolidation in the newspaper business means that readers often hear only one side of a story, Chief Justice Burger's opinion for a unanimous Court stated that any "compulsion to publish that which 'reason tells [publishers] should not be published' is unconstitutional. A responsible press is an undoubtedly desirable goal, but press responsibility is not mandated by the Constitution and like many other virtues it cannot be legislated."

But just as different types of speech receive different levels of protection, different types of media are subject to different levels of government oversight. In *Red Lion Broadcasting Co. v. Federal Communications Commission* (1969), for example, the Court upheld an FCC regulation requiring broadcasters to grant *right of reply* time to individuals subjected to personal or political attacks. The so-called *fairness doctrine,* said the Court, required that air time be set aside for this purpose, as access to airwaves is restricted in ways that access to print is not.

One explanation for the apparent inconsistency between *Red Lion Broadcasting* and *Tornillo* is that when the Founding Fathers drew up the Constitution, they had not envisioned things like radio and television — or movies, for that matter. As the Court said when upholding motion picture censorship in *Burstyn v. Wilson* (1952), while the basic principles enshrined in the First Amendment do not vary, "[e]ach method [of publishing] tends to present its own peculiar problems."

The Supreme Court gets nasty

The Supreme Court, always uncomfortable with subject of obscenity (see "Just what *is* obscenity?" earlier in this chapter), has been forced to confront the American media's obsession with sex. Cases touching on this little matter have come in a surprising array of forms.

The case of the "Seven Dirty Words"

The Court's wary attitude toward the First Amendment rights of nonprint media and the unsettled state of the law governing obscenity (see "Just what *is* obscenity?") collided in *FCC v. Pacifica Foundation* (1978). At 2 p.m. on Tuesday, October 30, 1973, in the middle of a serious program about language and censorship, a New York radio station owned by Pacifica Foundation broadcast comedian George Carlin's routine about the seven dirty words "you definitely couldn't say on the air, ever." A few weeks later, the Federal Communications Commission received a letter from a man complaining that he had heard the routine while driving in his car with his young son. The man complained that he did not understand why he and — in particular, his child — should have been subjected to this offensive language, which was broadcast over "the air that, supposedly, you control."

The FCC responded by issuing an order forbidding broadcast of such language as Carlin's "seven dirty words," which it characterized as "patently offensive," although not necessarily obscene. After first noting that "of all forms of communication, it is broadcasting that has received the most limited First Amendment protection," Justice John Paul Stevens declared for the Court that although the First Amendment prohibits banning indecent speech altogether, the FCC could certainly regulate the airwaves. In the case of the "seven dirty words," regulation meant limiting the hours during which such language could be aired. As rationale for this restriction, Stevens offered the following:

> First, the broadcast media have established a uniquely pervasive presence in the lives of all Americans. Patently offensive, indecent material presented over the airwaves confronts the citizen, not only in public, but also in the privacy of the home, where the individual's right to be left alone plainly outweighs the First Amendment rights of an intruder. . . . Second, broadcasting is uniquely accessible to children, even those too young to read.

The restrictions imposed on broadcasts of the "seven dirty words" resemble nothing so much as the time, place, and manner limitations that can be constitutionally imposed on speech. And broadcasting, come to think of it, sounds more like speech than it looks like print. First Amendment purists continue to get their hackles up about this case, though, contending that it paved the way for a new age of Puritanism and the hated Communications Decency Act of 1996. This act, which attempted to keep minors from accessing pornography on the Internet, was struck down by the Court in *Reno v. ACLU* (1997) for being overly broad. The jury's still out on the issue of porn and the Net, though. Stay tuned.

New York Times v. Sullivan and its progeny

Before the Supreme Court agreed to hear *New York Times v. Sullivan* in 1964, it had reviewed only one action for libel, *Beauharnais v. Illinois* (1952), a so-called *group libel* case involving a state law making it illegal to publish any defamatory or derogatory lithograph, moving picture, play, drama, or sketch about "a class of citizens, of any race, color, creed or religion." The statute was challenged by the leader of a white supremacy group on First Amendment grounds. The Court upheld the law, based on language in a 1942 case indicating that libel, like obscenity and fighting words, are unprotected by the First Amendment. In *Sullivan*, the Court did a rare thing: It changed its mind.

L.B. Sullivan, an elected commissioner of Montgomery, Alabama, took offense at an advertisement taken out in *The New York Times* in 1960 by a group of civil rights leaders. He based his libel suit on two paragraphs in the ad, which was designed to raise funds for the legal defense of Dr. Martin Luther King, Jr., who had been indicted on perjury charges. These paragraphs read in part:

> In Montgomery, Alabama, after students sang "My Country, 'Tis of Thee" on the State Capitol steps, their leaders were expelled from school, and truckloads of police armed with shotguns and tear-gas ringed the Alabama State College Campus. When the entire student body protested to state authorities by refusing to re-register, their dining hall was pad-locked in an attempt to starve them into submission. . . .

> Again and again the Southern violators have answered Dr. King's peaceful protests with intimidation and violence. They have bombed his home almost killing his wife and child. They have assaulted his person. They have arrested him seven times — for "speeding," "loitering" and similar "offenses." And now they have charged him with "perjury" . . . .

Commissioner Sullivan, whose responsibilities included oversight of the Montgomery police department, claimed that although the ad did not refer to him personally, its accusations about police actions defamed him. He also pointed to a number of false statements in the ad — such as that the students had sung the "Star Spangled Banner," not "My Country, 'Tis of Thee." Because repeating a libel is no defense to libel and because the newspaper had a big name and deep pockets, Sullivan sued *The New York Times*.

The Supreme Court took on *Sullivan* both because the country was in the midst of a civil rights revolution and because, as William J. Brennan said in his opinion for the Court, "[L]ibel can claim no talismanic immunity from constitutional limitations. It must be measured by standards that satisfy the First Amendment."

The earlier libel claims the Court had declined to entertain did not, like *Sullivan*, use the laws "to impose sanctions upon expression critical of the official conduct of public officials." This case raised genuine First Amendment issues, and even though it concerned an advertisement, *Sullivan* wasn't about commercial speech, which has only second class First Amendment protection.

Brennan next dispensed with Sullivan's claims that some of the statements in the ad were false — an important issue, as truth had traditionally been a defense to accusations of libel. The admitted falsehoods in the ad were really immaterial here — and besides, they were beside the point:

> "[E]rroneous statement is inevitable in free debate, [which] must be pro-tected if the freedoms of expression are to have the 'breathing space' that they 'need . . . to survive.'"

What was needed here was a new standard: Libel defendants now enjoyed a new constitutional privilege when sued by politicians and could only be held liable by a showing that they had acted with *actual malice* and with *knowing falsity* or *reckless disregard* for the truth of their statements. Under this new standard, the *Times* was not guilty of libel.

The result in *Sullivan* came out the way it did in part because it shares common elements with that Holy Grail of First Amendment protection, political speech. Another important element was that the defendant was a broadsheet, and not just any broadsheet. *The New York Times* is the most national of all American newspapers, and — as the clergymen who placed the ad there knew — the *Times* is one of the very best places to stage a national debate about a matter of public concern.

A decade later, in *Gertz v. Robert I. Welch* (1974), the Court found that the *knowing falsity* or *reckless disregard* standard applied to libel cases involving *public figures,* individuals who are famous in their own right or who gain fame by injecting themselves into a matter of public controversy with the intention of influencing the outcome. Elmer Gertz was an attorney who represented plaintiffs who had sued a police officer for damages connected with the officer's conviction for murder. The right-wing John Birch Society, which accused Gertz of framing the policemen, also called the lawyer a criminal and a "Leninist," or communist. Gertz, the Court said, was not a public figure, but had he been, he would have had to meet the same standard of proof as L.B. Sullivan to win his libel case.

And just what do *Sullivan* and *Gertz* have to do with obscenity? Consider the colorful case of *Hustler Magazine v. Falwell* (1988), which pitted the televangelist minister Jerry Falwell against the porn king Larry Flynt. Flynt, an unlikely champion of the First Amendment, won his case against Falwell, who cried libel in the face of a *Hustler Magazine* satire indicating he had had sexual relations with his mother. While admitting that the speech involved here was "outrageous," the Court found for Flynt. Falwell was, after all, a celebrity of sorts, and Flynt's use of his name in a parody of a popular advertisement was intended to promote public discussion about what individuals like Falwell represent, not to libel a man who had parlayed his ultraconservative views and clerical status into a media empire. There was no *actual malice* here. Later, Falwell would embrace Flynt as a warm-hearted, generous person with much to offer society.

But surely, you say, some things must be sacred. In the Court's first libel case, *Near v. Minnesota* (1931), Chief Justice Charles Evans Hughes wrote that freedom of the press could be curtailed in order to prevent invasion of private thoughts. Since then, though, it's all been downhill for plaintiffs claiming invasion of privacy. In the 1967 case *Time Inc. v. Hill,* a family that had been held hostage by a group of escaped convicts sought damages for invasion of privacy. Although the convicts had treated the Hill family well, *The Desperate Hours* (1953), a fictionalized version of the family's story, later made into a play and a movie, presented a violent picture of what had happened to the unfortunate Hills. When Time, Inc., which owned *Look* magazine, did an article about the play that characterized it as a reenactment of the Hills' ordeal, the family had had enough — they sued. The Supreme Court felt badly for the family, but nevertheless ruled that the *actual malice* standard of *Sullivan* applied to even "false reports of matters of public interest." The Hills never asked for publicity; they were private individuals who had been drawn into the spotlight against their will, and they were out of luck.

If private citizens like the Hill family could not escape the media, certainly politicians like Gary Hart could not. In 1987, while running for president, the married Hart was trailed by the *Miami Herald,* which published a series of articles about Hart's (admittedly rather flagrant) infidelities. And consider the fate of President Bill Clinton, whose sexual peccadilloes led not just to a media feeding frenzy, but to impeachment. As Chief Justice William Rehnquist sternly wrote in *Hustler Magazine v. Falwell,* quoting an earlier decision of the Court, "[T]he candidate who vaunts his spotless record and sterling integrity cannot convincingly cry 'Foul!' when an opponent or an industrious reporter attempts to demonstrate the contrary."

Exercising Freedom of Assembly and Petition

The free expression and religious freedom clauses of the First Amendment have received far more attention than their poor stepsisters, freedom of assembly and the right of petition. But right up there with free speech, in the prime spot in the Bill of Rights, is the rule that "Congress shall make no law . . . abridging . . . the right of the people peaceably to assemble, and to petition the Government for a redress of grievances."

Freedom of association

Although the Constitution does not say it in so many words, the right to assemble and the freedom to associate with whomever or whatever a person wants to link up with are pretty much one and the same. Neither of these rights is absolute, however, in the sense that freedom of speech is absolute. Associating with others and/or assembling with them almost invariably involves something other than *pure speech*. Instead, public demonstrations like marching and picketing are *speech acts,* subject to time, place, and manner restrictions. You've no doubt noted that the Constitution says that the people have a right "*peacefully* to assemble" (emphasis added).

Yates v. United States

The first Supreme Court decision to address the right of assembly as a right on par with others guaranteed by the First Amendment was *De Jonge v. Oregon* (1937), concerning a labor demonstration called by the Communist

Party. For the first time, the Court also recognized that the Due Process Clause of the Fourteenth Amendment (see Chapter 9) guaranteed the right of assembly at the state, as well as the federal, level. First Amendment protection meant that the Oregon law prohibiting such gatherings was struck down, because "peaceable assembly for lawful discussion cannot be made a crime."

A flurry of Assembly Clause cases reached the Court during the Cold War decades of the 1950s and 1960s, when both the threat of nuclear holocaust and McCarthyism had officials looking back over their shoulders. (See the sidebar "McCarthy and the Red Menace.") Many of these cases involved assertions of the freedom to associate by members of communist or other left-wing organizations. In cases like *Dennis v. United States* (1951), the Supreme Court upheld the convictions of individuals who were found guilty of espousing subversive ideas or of associating with those who did. First Amendment rights were trampled on left and right after Chief Justice Fred Vinson's opinion in *Dennis* revised the *clear and present danger* test for free speech that had been in place since the beginning of the century. (See the earlier section "Crying fire in a crowded theater.") Over the next six years, the Justice Department used this new standard to round up scores of suspected communists, nearly 150 of whom were indicted.

Finally, in 1957, *Yates v. United States* put an end to guilt by association. In Yates, 14 members of the Communist Party had been convicted under the Smith Act, also known as the Alien Registration Act, of conspiring to overthrow the U.S. government. By a vote of 6-1, the Warren Court ruled that the law could not reach merely hypothetical subversion, distinguishing between advocacy of doctrine and advocacy of action. People were, once again, free to think their own thoughts and to meet with others who held similar convictions.

NAACP v. Alabama

During the early years of the civil rights movement, Alabama attempted to protect the status quo through a strategy of divide and conquer. Specifically, in order to expel the National Association for the Advancement of Colored People (the NAACP) from inside its borders, the state tried to order the organization to turn over its membership roster. The NAACP refused, claiming that compliance with this request would interfere with its organizational integrity. In *National Association for the Advancement of Colored People v. Alabama ex rel. Patterson* (1958), a unanimous Supreme Court agreed, asserting the members of the NAACP not only had a First Amendment right to associate freely with one another, but also to do so privately.

The conjunction of freedom of association with the right to privacy came under fire in the 1980s. In *New York State Club Association v. City of New York* (1988), the Court held that private associations that had public characteristics like letting dues be paid by nonmembers (such as employers) were actually a front for discrimination against groups such as women and gays.

McCarthy and the Red Menace

During the Cold War, there clearly were spies among us — but not as many as the American public was led to believe. The person most responsible for making a bad situation worse, and for whipping up public hysteria was a publicity-hungry senator from Wisconsin named Joseph McCarthy. From the start of his political career, McCarthy demonstrated a thorough lack of respect for truth. During his first campaign, he adopted the nickname *Tailgunner Joe*, but although he was a World War II veteran, he had spent the bulk of his time in the service behind a desk. Elected to the U.S. Senate in 1946, McCarthy spent four years on the back benches without capturing any more headlines. But then, in 1950, he *did* drop a bombshell, making a public announcement that he had a list of names of 205 communists then employed by the State Department. No one actually saw the list, and the number of names on his list fluctuated from speech to speech. Still, in the paranoid climate of the Cold War, McCarthy had grabbed hold of the brass ring.

Encouraged by his growing notoriety and his fellow Republicans, McCarthy's charges grew increasingly outrageous, as he took on Secretaries of State George Marshall and Dean Acheson and even the Democratic Party. McCarthy's antics soon overshadowed those of the now infamous House Un-American Activities Committee, which had been pursuing its own anticommunist course since 1938. In 1952, the Republicans won the White House, and McCarthy, as chair of the Subcommittee on Investigations of the Senate Committee on Governmental Operations, launched a high-profile investigation of the Voice of America broadcasting program and the Army Signal Corps. Seemingly unaware that he was attacking his own party, McCarthy was becoming an embarrassment. Finally, in 1954, during the televised hearings resulting from McCarthy's investigation of the Army itself, he was unmasked as a posturing, blustering fool — while the nation looked on. McCarthy disappeared from the headlines and was dead within three years, but his name lives on, used as shorthand to refer to a dark time when government stepped way over its boundary line.

The right of petition

The origins of the First Amendment right of petition reach back even farther than King John's grant of the Magna Carta to the English people in 1215. While the Magna Carta is usually considered the wellspring of English common law and, by extension, American constitutional law, 250 years earlier a benevolent English ruler known as Edgar the Peaceful suggested that his people had a right of *redress,* a right to ask its rulers directly to remedy wrongs. Before Thomas Jefferson pushed for adoption of the Bill of Rights, he enshrined his grievance against King George III's refusal to acknowledge *petitions for redress* in the document that many consider his masterwork, the Declaration of Independence. The right of petition is so deeply rooted in American law that it has come to seem a natural right. It has generated less litigation and less attention than any of the other rights guaranteed under the First Amendment.

Often, the right of petition has been treated by the Court as if it were a subset of freedom of association, as in *Hague v. Congress for Industrial Organization,* a 1939 case concerning denial of permits for union meetings. In fact, the right of petition is more closely related to political speech, the most protected form of the most protected right guaranteed by the First Amendment. The only significant right of petition cases to come before the Court have concerned lobbying. And even those cases, like *United States v. Hariss* (1954), which upheld the requirement that certain lobbyists register with Congress, have been limited in scope. Only once has government made a serious attempt to rein in what has seemed to the American people a God-given right. In 1836, inundated by petitions from abolitionists seeking to end slavery in Washington, D.C., the House of Representatives passed a *gag rule* preventing receipt of such petitions. The rule was immediately attacked by the antislavery Whig party (see Chapter 7), led by future president John Quincy Adams. Eight years later, the gag rule was finally repealed.

Chapter 9

Due Process: What Is It, and Who Gets It?

*N*ot to put too fine a point on it, due process is a double-edged sword. What *sounds* like a simple concept has, for much of American history, carried two distinct meanings. This duality derives, in part, from the appearance of the phrase "due process of law" in both the Fifth and the Fourteenth Amendments. Even within the two branches of due process, however, meanings vary. As Justice Frankfurter declared in 1951: "'[D]ue process,' unlike some legal rules, is not a technical conception with a fixed content unrelated to time, place and circumstances. . . . Representing a profound attitude of fairness between man and man, and more particularly between the individual and government, 'due process' is compounded of history, reason, the past course of decisions, and stout confidence in the strength of the democratic faith which we profess." Let me explain.

Procedural Due Process: Protecting Your "Life, Liberty, or Property"

Due process, like so much else in American law, originated with the English Magna Carta of 1215, the document that marks the start of the democratic process. *Due process of law* was originally *law of the land,* the doctrine that permitted English noblemen to limit the king's power over them. In our own Constitution, the phrase first appears in the Fifth Amendment, which states,

"No person shall be . . . deprived of life, liberty, or property, without due process of law." The Fifth Amendment, which was ratified in 1791, makes this constraint applicable to the federal government. The Fourteenth Amendment, which includes virtually identical language and which was ratified in 1868, makes due process protections applicable at the state level.

The *law of the land* was essentially equivalent to accepted legal procedures guaranteeing individuals fair treatment at the hands of government. When the government imposes a burden of some sort (taxes, draft registration, and so on) on all of its citizens, due process does not come into play. But when an individual, or a group of individuals, is subject to some sort of burdensome government action, procedural due process ensures that the individual or group will not be treated arbitrarily.

Bear in mind that this brand of due process, which is called *procedural due process,* only applies to the *way* government acts toward its citizens; limitations on government power do exist, but they come under the heading *substantive due process.* (See the section "Substantive due process," later in this chapter.) For example, if the federal government wants to run an interstate through your living room, you have a right, guaranteed by the Fifth Amendment, to "just compensation" for your property — but the government can still take it away from you. (This little maneuver goes by the quaint name *eminent domain.*) Or, if the government wants to deprive you of your life or liberty because you're accused of a crime, the Sixth Amendment guarantees that you'll have a "speedy and public" trial, but you have no guarantee that the outcome will be just.

In modern times, procedural due process has expanded to include different types of property or liberty that can be protected from government deprivation. The first category now includes, in addition to real estate and personal property, entitlements such as welfare, driver's licenses, and civil service status. Liberty now encompasses not only freedom from physical restraint, but freedom from corporal punishment in public schools, an individual's status as a parent, and even privacy itself (see Chapter 8). Given the evolving nature of life, liberty, and property, the number of cases involving procedural due process continues to expand. And as it does, government must constantly readjust notions of just what procedural protections are required for varying liberty and property interests (that is, how much "process" is "due" from the government to the citizen).

Remember, all claims are not created equal. Being deprived of property you expect to receive — such as continued employment as a tenured professor at a state university — is not the same thing as being deprived of property you already possess. Not every due process claim merits a full-blown — and expensive — trial. Few cases involving *new* property rights stand a chance of making it to the U.S. Supreme Court.

Substantive Due Process

The concept of substantive due process holds that the Constitution confers on individuals certain unalienable rights — above all, the right to be free of government intrusion — that are ensured by procedural due process (see the preceding section). Substantive due process, like procedural due process, has a long history, dating back to English common law and the notion of an unwritten constitution. Substantive due process did not, however, come into its own until the Fourteenth Amendment was ratified in 1868, and the two will forever be linked.

The pursuit of happiness: The Slaughterhouse Cases

The first Supreme Court case to interpret the Fourteenth Amendment is also the one that marks the *invention* of substantive due process. The three cases grouped together as the *Slaughterhouse Cases* (1872) grew out of a labor dispute between the state of Louisiana and a butchers' union. After Louisiana incorporated the Crescent City Live-Stock Landing and Slaughtering Company, the state required that all butchering in New Orleans take place at Crescent City's facilities. The Butchers' Benevolent Association sued, claiming that the state of Louisiana's grant of a monopoly violated its members' right to work freely, one of the "privileges and immunities" protected by the Fourteenth Amendment. The union appealed its losing case all the way to the U.S. Supreme Court, where they lost again.

This decision was not the end of the story, however. Although five of the nine justices agreed that the Privileges and Immunities Clause did not protect the right to work as a fundamental right, Justice Stephen J. Field did not think the case was this simple. In his dissent, he argued that "the right to pursue a lawful employment in a lawful manner, without other restraint than such as equally affects all persons" is surely one of the "distinguishing privilege[s] of citizens of the United States."

Justice Field had always been a renegade (see Chapter 7), and he did not buy into the received notion that the Fourteenth Amendment had been adopted after the Civil War as a means of assuring the civil rights of former slaves. He accurately pointed out that the Fourteenth Amendment protected black and white Americans alike. And he picked up on a suggestion made by counsel for the butchers' union that certain inalienable rights — *substantive* rights — are protected from state interference by the Due Process Clause of the Fourteenth Amendment.

Four years later, in yet another dissent in *Munn v. Illinois* (1877), Field refined his theory of substantive due process. *Munn* concerned a state regulation governing prices charged by grain elevator operators. The *Munn* majority, citing the decision in the *Slaughterhouse Cases,* voted to uphold the regulation. But Field, now actually citing the Due Process Clause of the Fourteenth Amendment, declared that property rights are among the rights constitutionally protected from state interference. To permit state regulation of public businesses or private enterprise would be to "justify an intermeddling with the business of every man in the community, so soon, at least, as his business became generally useful." To Field's way of thinking, interfering with the progress of commerce was not the American way.

Field's dissents proved to be more influential than the majority opinions in the *Slaughterhouse Cases* and *Munn.* As Reconstruction gave way to the excesses of the freewheeling and free spending period that came to be known as the Gilded Age, the Court embraced Field's theory of substantive due process. Substantive due process became the centerpiece of a prolonged era of *laissez-faire* jurisprudence, which took its name — and its attitude — from the philosophy of the 18th-century Scotsman Adam Smith, the founding father of market control theory of economics. Laissez-faire constitutionalism would maintain its hold on the Court right up to the time of the New Deal (see Chapter 4).

Greed as a fundamental right: Lochner v. New York

Lochner v. New York (1905) marks the high point in the development of substantive due process — and one of the lowest points in Supreme Court history. At issue in *Lochner* was a New York state law limiting the workweek of bakeries to 60 hours. The Court voted 5-4 to strike down the law as an unconstitutional violation of the Fourteenth Amendment's guarantee of freedom of contract. Astoundingly, the conservatives on the Court — who believed in nothing so devoutly as liberal economics — had written a new fundamental *right* into the Constitution. In doing so, the justices had really overstepped their bounds, substituting their judgment for that of the legislative branch. Not only were they reading into (some would say glossing over) the language of the Fourteenth Amendment, they were overthrowing state law.

It is, of course, often the business of the U.S. Supreme Court to find state laws unconstitutional. But the decision in *Lochner* was extreme, because it invaded a realm traditionally given over to the states, public welfare. A state's power to govern this sphere is a given of federalism, but the *Lochner* majority's conception of the state's so-called *police powers* was so narrow as to be almost invisible. Reformers claimed that long bakery workdays endangered not only the workers' health but the public health by increasing the chances for contracting and spreading such contagious diseases as consumption. But Justice Rufus Peckham, writing for the Court, responded that it was a "common understanding" that baking was not an unhealthy activity.

A gilt-edged age

The Gilded Age is commonly thought to have lasted from the period after post-Civil War Reconstruction up to the Progressive Era — roughly 1870–1900. These years were named after the 1873 novel *The Gilded Age,* by Mark Twain and Charles D. Warner, which satirized the greed, materialism, and corruption that were hallmarks of the time. After the Civil War, the economy boomed, as most post-war economies do. But the Gilded Age was also born of the greed of carpetbaggers who went south to oversee Reconstruction and to rake in money on the side. The scandals and cronyism that marred the two administrations (1869–1877) overseen by the reluctant politician Ulysses S. Grant added to the mix. Speculative investments proved to be Grant's personal undoing, causing him to lose virtually all his wealth toward the end of his life. The party went on without him, ignoring his fate as well as the fates of countless others victimized by market forces.

The subjectivity of Peckham's opinion has made *Lochner* one of the Court's most discredited decisions. In 1910, the progressive President Theodore Roosevelt would cite *Lochner* as a prime example of judicial interference with much needed social reforms. But for Peckham, the opinion was itself the culmination of a progressive movement away from state paternalism. In 1889, while still a judge in the New York courts, he had dissented in a case upholding state regulation of grain elevator fees, which he called an interference "with what seems to me the most sacred rights of property and the individual liberty of contract." This was the orthodoxy of his day, later writ large in *Lochner.*

For the dissenting Oliver Wendell Holmes, however, "[A] constitution is not intended to embody a particular economic theory." In the words of his most celebrated aphorism, "The 14th Amendment does not enact Mr. Herbert Spencer's Social Statics" (a reference to the English proponent of social Darwinism, linking morality with survival). Holmes didn't hold Peckham in very high regard. Once asked what he thought of Peckham intellectually, Holmes responded quizzically, "Intellectually? I never thought of him in that connection." Instead, Holmes thought of Peckham as a man governed by "emotional predilections" when it came to "social themes." These emotional predilections had once caused Judge Peckham to call a New York grain elevator regulation "vicious in its nature, communistic in its tendency" and in *Lochner* caused him to fear state intervention in private business. It was all of a piece and, for Holmes, it was all a reactionary — even perverted — attempt to twist the Constitution into an unnatural shape. If the Fourteenth Amendment could be interpreted as a guarantee of an unnamed fundamental right, it was hard to see the *Lochner* decision as handing down law, rather than public policy.

But *Lochner was* the law for another 32 years. Numerous state laws attempting to reform wages, outlaw child labor, and regulate banking practices were overturned on the basis of *Lochner.* Finally, in 1937, in a state minimum wage law case, *West Coast Hotel Co. v. Parrish,* someone had the courage to say that the emperor had no clothes. That someone was Chief Justice Charles Evans Hughes, who wrote in his opinion for the Court, "The Constitution does not speak of freedom of contract." This decision ended the *Lochner era* and cleared the way for Franklin Roosevelt's New Deal reforms (see Chapter 4).

A spur to the civil rights movement?: Brown v. Board of Education

After 1937, substantive due process remained dormant — and discredited — for nearly two decades. Then, with *Brown v. Board of Education* (1954), the concept seemed to have been at least partially revived. Although the Warren Court was asked to determine whether the "separate but equal" doctrine violated the Equal Protection Clause of the Fourteenth Amendment, many felt that the decision reached far beyond equal protection. And they may have been right, for the ten-page decision is decidedly short on law and long on fundamental fairness — and rights.

After *Brown,* the Supreme Court began overturning numerous state laws — even those concerning economic regulation — if they were found to produce results that discriminated against groups of individuals because of race, gender, ethnic origin, and so on. Economic substantive due process may have faded from the picture, but when Congress passed the Civil Rights Act of 1964, it used economics — specifically the Commerce Clause of Article 1, section 8 of the Constitution, Congress's constitutionally mandated authority to regulate commerce between the states — as a basis for banning racial segregation. Interpreting the act in *Heart of Atlanta Motel, Inc. v. United States* (1964) and *Katzenbach v. McClung* (1964), the Court found that racial discrimination in public accommodations like motels and restaurants had a negative effect on interstate commerce and was therefore subject to Congressional legislation.

Privacy as a civil right: Roe v. Wade revisited

The social upheaval of the 1960s produced a new focus on individual expression and personal lifestyles that found its way to the Supreme Court in the form of a right to privacy. A fundamental right to personal choice and privacy was first located in the "penumbras" of the Bill of Rights in William O. Douglas's opinion for the Court in the contraception case, *Griswold v. Connecticut* (1965). This right, Douglas wrote, was made applicable to the states through the Due Process Clause of the Fourteenth Amendment.

Privacy became enshrined as a civil right in the abortion case *Roe v. Wade* (1973) eight years later. Justice Harry Blackmun's opinion for the Court based a woman's right to abortion on demand, subject to certain conditions, on a constitutional right to privacy, which he located in the Fourteenth Amendment's Due Process Clause. Critics of the opinion — and even some who agreed with *Roe*'s outcome — noted that once again the Court was using substantive due process to enforce a right not spelled out in the Constitution. In less than 100 years, *economic* substantive due process was transformed into *social* substantive due process.

The Explosion in "Rights Consciousness"

Like many aspects of the modern Supreme Court, the attention to individual rights that has come to dominate the docket had its roots in Franklin D. Roosevelt's *Court-packing* plan (see Chapter 5). The urgent need to legitimize New Deal legislation meant to bring the country out of the Great Depression impelled Roosevelt to develop a scheme for reconstituting the Court, fashioning a body that would do his bidding. The scheme failed, thankfully, but it did rouse the justices out of a long slumber that had made them unconscious of the American people's changing needs. Suddenly, they saw the need to let the elected branches of government set public policy and deal with economic issues.

The origins of incorporation

Nature — and law, too, apparently — abhors a vacuum, and when the Court lost its preoccupation with regulatory matters in the 1930s, questions of constitutional liberty took their place. The real turning point was *Palko v. Connecticut,* a 1937 case in which a state criminal defendant claimed that the Due Process Clause of the Fourteen Amendment made the Fifth Amendment's prohibition against *double jeopardy* (being tried or punished twice for the same offense) at the federal level applicable to the states. Writing for the eight-member majority, Justice Benjamin Cardozo declared that although this particular part of the Bill of Rights was not incorporated into the Fourteenth Amendment, some other parts were. Cardozo's theory of *selective incorporation* accepted the proposition that all the guarantees of the First Amendment applied to the states. The First Amendment is, after all, "the matrix, the indispensable condition" for every other freedom. But those other freedoms? Cardozo wasn't so sure about them. Only those aspects of the Second through the Eighth Amendments that were "of the very essence of a scheme of ordered liberty" should be incorporated. With this declaration, Cardozo was following Oliver Wendell Holmes's assertion in his dissent in the 1925 free speech case *Gitlow v. New York* that, unlike the majority, he believed freedom of speech and of the press are "among the personal rights and 'liberties' protected by the due process clause of the Fourteenth Amendment from impairment by the states."

Palko was followed the next year by a decision concerning interstate milk shipments that is more notable for one of its footnotes than anything in the opinion itself. Writing for the Court in *United States v. Carolene Products Co.* (1938), Harlan F. Stone declared that the Court would uphold the constitutionality of economic regulations so long as they had a "rational basis." In the famous Footnote Four, however, he added: "There may be narrower scope for operation of the presumption of constitutionality when legislation appears on its face to be within a specific prohibition of the Constitution, such as those of the first ten Amendments . . . ." The footnote goes on to announce what has since come to be known as the *preferred freedoms doctrine,* which elaborated on Cardozo's selective incorporation theory by specifying that legislation that hampers the political process or is hostile to "discrete and insular minorities" should be given less latitude. Footnote Four was a kind of announcement — however muted and tentative — of the Court's changing attitude and shift in focus from economic matters to civil rights.

Judicial activism

Hugo Black, a First Amendment absolutist (see Chapter 6) who voted with the majority in *Palko,* came to feel that selective incorporation left judges with too much discretion. The way to prevent arbitrary enforcement of unjust or unequal laws and to provide constitutional protections for all Americans, he felt, was simply to ensure that all guarantees of the Bill of Rights were enforceable at all levels of government, state and federal. In *Adamson v. California* (1947), Black dissented from the majority's view that a state criminal defendant could not invoke the Fifth Amendment's guarantee against mandatory self-incrimination. Black was not the only one dissenting; three other justices did, too, agreeing with Black's argument for *total incorporation* of all aspects of the first eight amendments.

The logic of Black's argument stretched back to *Barron v. Baltimore* (1833), in which a wharf owner sued the state for lowering the value of his property by diverting streams elsewhere. This state action, said the wharf owner, violated his rights under the Fifth Amendment, which prevents the government from *taking* private property without just compensation. Writing for a unanimous Court, the Federalist Chief Justice John Marshall recognized the increasing influence of states' rights advocates and bowed to the inevitable. The Bill of Rights, he wrote, only applied to the federal government. Those citizens looking for similar protections from state action must look to their respective state constitutions.

And there the matter stood until after the Civil War. When the Fourteenth Amendment was proposed by Congress in 1866, it made all persons born in this country citizens of the United States and provided that no state should abridge these citizens' privileges or immunities or deny them due process or equal protection of the laws. At least some of the Congressmen who framed this amendment indicated that they felt that the privileges and immunities citizens are entitled to include those protected by the Bill of Rights — and this was Justice Black's attitude. Black's total incorporation approach to the Fourteenth Amendment has never been entirely accepted, but *Adamson* would be overturned by the Court in 1965.

Judicial restraint

During the 1940s and 1950s, Black's principle opponent was Felix Frankfurter (see Chapter 6), who accepted selective incorporation but whose judicial philosophy called for deference to the legislative and executive branches. Frankfurter's judicial restraint held sway for a time, but as the Court's focus shifted from economic matters to civil liberties, his influence waned. In 1940, for example, Frankfurter wrote the opinion of the Court for the first of the so-called *flag salute cases, Minersville School District v. Gobitis,* holding that a child who was a Jehovah's Witness could be required to salute the flag in school (see Chapter 8). Religious freedom under the First Amendment was no bar to enforcement of this local regulation. Just three years later — and in the midst of World War II — the Court overturned this decision with *West Virginia State Board of Education v. Barnette* (1943). Severe public criticism of *Gobitis* — even from such quarters as the American Legion — let the justices know that a new libertarian wind was starting to blow through the country.

Frankfurter, however, continued to hold sway during the Cold War period that followed WWII. The mood of the country, guarded and introspective, matched his persistent theme of restraint. In his opinion for the Court in *Wolf v. Colorado* (1949), a criminal abortion case, Frankfurter accepted the proposition that the Fourth Amendment prohibition against illegal search and seizure did apply to the states. But he would not go so far as to permit state courts to enforce the so-called *exclusionary rule,* preventing use at trial of illegally gathered evidence.

Frankfurter's cautious approach to dispensing liberty was not confined to *incorporation* questions. His opinion for *Colegrove v. Green* (1946) held that apportionment of congressional districts was a *political question* (see Chapter 2) outside the Court's power to settle. In *Ullmann v. United States* (1956), his opinion for the Court held that the Fifth Amendment privilege against self-incrimination did not extend to a witness compelled to testify against himself before a federal grand jury investigating threats to national security. The witness was granted immunity from prosecution under the Immunity Act of 1950; any other harm — loss of employment, reputation, and so on — weren't covered by the Fifth Amendment. Similarly, in *Communist Party v. Subversive Activities Control Board* (1961), Frankfurter wrote for the 5-4 majority that the McCarran Act, requiring Communist Party members to register with the federal government, did not violate First Amendment guarantees of free association (see Chapter 8).

Many of Frankfurter's opinions would subsequently be unraveled or outright overturned — and they would be invalidated mostly on Fourteenth Amendment grounds. One by one, almost all the guarantees of the Bill of Rights were extended to the states. Judicial restraint gave way to judicial activism, with Hugo Black leading the way.

The judicial pendulum

Judicial activism reached its heyday during the years that the Court was led by Earl Warren (1953–1969). Some have argued that the Warren Court was reacting to public demand for legal guarantees for individual liberties and civil rights. Others say the Warren Court helped to create a climate that fostered *rights consciousness.* It's unquestionably true that the school desegregation case *Brown v. Board of Education* (1954), one of the Warren Court's first decisions, opened the door to an explosion of litigation over rights. *Brown* didn't create the National Association for the Advancement of Colored People, the organization that sponsored that case and many others like it. But in the decisions leading up to *Brown,* the Court had invited the NAACP to present it with an opportunity to overturn the "separate but equal" rule that had legitimized racial segregation (see Chapter 12).

And in the realm of criminal law, take a look at the landmark Fourth Amendment decision, *Mapp v. Ohio* (1961). Police raided Dolly Mapp's home in Cleveland, Ohio, without a warrant and confiscated allegedly obscene materials used to obtain a criminal conviction. In the Supreme Court, Mapp's own lawyer presented her case as an obscenity case. The Court, with some prodding from an American Civil Liberties Union's friend-of-the-court brief (see Chapter 3), turned Dolly Mapp's case into an opportunity for applying the constitutional ban on illegal searches and seizures to the states. Once again, the Warren Court was looking for an opening to overturn one of its own precedents, *Wolf v. Colorado.*

And just as surely as the Supreme Court can foster an atmosphere conducive to elaborating rights, it can rein them in. When Warren Burger took over from Earl Warren as chief justice, he did not manage to bring about the counter-revolution he was hired to produce. Rolling back the reforms of the Warren years was left to Burger successor, William Rehnquist. And Rehnquist has achieved this goal in a manner that won't surprise you one bit: He has emphasized states' rights. While still an associate justice, Rehnquist wrote the opinion for the 5-4 Court majority in *National League of Cities v. Usery* (1976), striking down a 1974 law extending the maximum hours and minimum wages provided for in the federal Fair Labor Standards Act. *Usery* marked the first time since the New Deal era that the Court had struck down a federal law because it overstepped the bounds of federalism. Citing the Tenth Amendment's reservation to the states of powers not constitutionally delegated to the central government, Rehnquist wrote that the new law violated "traditional aspects of state sovereignty."

Usery did not survive very long. It was overturned less than a decade later by *Garcia v. San Antonio Metropolitan Transit Authority* (1985), a case testing the applicability of the federal Fair Labor Standards Act to a city-owned transportation system. The very next year, however, Rehnquist took seat as chief justice and began leading (rather than steering) the Court in the opposite direction. He has been so successful that Justice John Paul Stevens, once considered a moderate, now occupies the left side of the Court's political spectrum. And once again, Rehnquist managed to turn the clock back to the time before the New Deal. In *United States v. Lopez* (1995), he again wrote the opinion for a 5-4 majority endorsing state autonomy by declaring the Gun-Free School Zones Act of 1990 unconstitutional on Commerce Clause grounds. The federal government did not have the right, said the Court, to pursue gun control by using its power to control interstate commerce.

America grew steadily more conservative during the last quarter of the 20th century. It seems pretty clear that the Supreme Court both reflected and promoted that shift by training its focus back on local government.

The due process revolution and criminal law

The due process revolution affected both criminal and civil matters, but it was the changes in criminal law that most outraged critics of the Warren Court. The incorporation into the Fourteenth Amendment (see the earlier section "The Explosion in 'Rights Consciousness'") of the guarantees of the Fourth and Fifth Amendments, in particular, produced results these critics disliked. Previously, criminal law had been almost exclusively the province of the states. Afterward, however, state law enforcement officials had to pay attention to such niceties as properly obtaining and serving search warrants and reading criminal suspects their rights. For people like Richard Nixon, campaigning for president on a law and order platform in 1968, these sorts of measures amounted to coddling criminals. After he was elected, Nixon made sure like-minded individuals were appointed to the Court. After Warren Burger failed to fulfill his promise and Harry Blackmun and Lewis F. Powell proved to be middle-of-the-roaders, Nixon hit the jackpot with William Rehnquist.

The exclusionary rule

The *exclusionary rule* applies to evidence that, because it's obtained through an illegal search and seizure, cannot be used as evidence in a criminal proceeding. An outgrowth of the Fourth Amendment's guarantee of protection from illegal searches and seizures, the rule usually applies to physical evidence (as opposed to confessions, or line-up identifications — although they, too, may be excluded as evidence that can be presented at trial). The exclusionary rule has also been used to exclude evidence taken in violation of other constitutional rights, such as the Fifth Amendment privilege against self-incrimination and the Sixth Amendment right to counsel.

The Court first set out the exclusionary rule in *Weeks v. United States,* a 1914 case in which lottery tickets seized in a warrantless search were used as evidence of Weeks's illegal use of the mails to transport them. Weeks made a pretrial motion in which he requested return of his property, and when his request was refused and the tickets were used as evidence against him, he appealed his conviction to the U.S. Supreme Court, claiming that his Fourth and Fifth Amendment rights had been trampled on. The High Court agreed, indicating that Weeks's rights to personal security and liberty and private property — all guaranteed under the Fifth Amendment — had all been violated. Nonetheless, the Court cited the Fourth Amendment ban on illegal search and seizure in overturning Weeks's conviction and ordering the return of his lottery tickets.

Weeks was one of the rare criminal cases that fell within the Supreme Court's jurisdiction because it involved the U.S. mail. Because so-called *police powers* restricting individual rights in order to promote public welfare are delegated to state and local government, most criminal matters are tried in state courts. The exclusionary rule did not really concern the Court again until it began to debate the extent of the incorporation doctrine (see "The Explosion in 'Rights Consciousness'"). In *Wolf v. Colorado* (1949), a criminal abortion case, the Court ruled that the Fourth Amendment did indeed protect individuals from state as well as federal government action, but that the states were under no obligation to enforce the exclusionary rule.

The *Wolf* ruling — which resulted in adoption of what was known as the *silver platter* doctrine — opened the door to all manner of state police abuses. The justices were shocked when *Rochin v. California* (1952) landed on their docket. In this case, a criminal suspect had had his stomach forcibly pumped so that police could recover drug capsules he had swallowed. This evidence was then used to convict Rochin, but the Court overturned the conviction. Writing for the Court, Felix Frankfurter stated that the police methods used here were "too close to the rack and the screw to permit of constitutional differentiation." Still, for almost another decade, the justices declined to enforce the exclusionary rule in criminal cases coming to them from state courts.

Then, in *Elkins v. United States* (1960), a case concerning the introduction in a federal trial of evidence illegally obtained by state officers, the Court decided to stop splitting hairs. As Potter Stewart wrote for the Court: "[S]urely no distinction can logically be drawn between evidence obtained in violation of the Fourth Amendment and that obtained in violation of the Fourteenth. The Constitution is flouted equally in either case. To the victim it matters not whether his constitutional right has been invaded by a federal agent or by a state officer." The next year, in *Mapp v. Ohio*, the Court would finally require state courts to adhere to the exclusionary rule. (See "The Explosion in 'Rights Consciousness,'" earlier in this chapter).

But the deterrence rationale that validated universal adoption of the exclusionary rule also opened the rule up to criticism. What good was the rule if it did not punish the law enforcement officials guilty of violating it? Surely other remedies — such as civil suits requiring offending officers to pay damages — were both available and more effective. In *United States v. Calandra* (1974), a federal loan sharking case, the Court went so far as to deny the exclusionary rule the status of a personal constitutional right and refused to apply it to evidence produced in a grand jury proceeding.

The Court has not abolished the exclusionary rule outright, but it has continued to whittle away at what many have come to view as an impediment to carrying out justice. In 1976, the Court held in the murder case of *Stone v. Powell* that federal courts were under no constitutional mandate to honor writs of *habeas corpus* requesting release of individuals who challenge state criminal convictions on grounds of illegally obtained evidence. In *Nix v. Williams,* a 1984 child murder case, the Court permitted use of an illegally obtained confession. The evidence subsequently obtained by police would have been "inevitably discovered," declared the majority. In another decision handed down the same year in the drug trafficking case *United States v. Leon,* the Court carved out a *good faith exception.* When evidence is obtained pursuant to an invalid warrant, that evidence obtained may still be used at trial; the fault, said the Court, lies with the magistrate who issued the warrant, not the police officers who served it. Because the purpose of the exclusionary rule is to deter police misbehavior and that purpose is not served by excluding evidence in such a situation, the exclusionary rule does not apply here.

The Court has continued to extend the *good faith exception* first developed in *Leon* to cover situations where police officers have used warrants they know to be invalid or followed a law later found to be unconstitutional. Today, the exclusionary rule first announced in *Weeks* has been diluted so that its application at both the state and federal levels is far from absolute.

"Reading you your rights"

Despite what you see on television, the requirement that police "read you your rights" before arresting you (if you're a criminal suspect, that is) may be in jeopardy. The zenith of the so-called *Miranda rights* in fact lasted only a week, although it captured the public imagination and generated a boatload of criticism.

Miranda v. Arizona, a 1966 case concerning an indigent, unschooled 23-year-old suspected of involvement with a kidnapping and rape, revolved around a coerced confession obtained without benefit of counsel. The Court had linked the Fifth Amendment privilege against self-incrimination with the Sixth Amendment right to counsel two years earlier in *Massiah v. United States* (1964). *Massiah* was a federal narcotics case in which the government had tricked the defendant into making incriminating statements by convincing one of Winston Massiah's codefendants to discuss the case with him in the *privacy* of a car that federal officers had secretly wired with a radio transmitter. The Court found Massiah's statements inadmissible as evidence. Later that same year, the Court extended the Fifth Amendment privilege to state defendants in *Malloy v. Hogan,* in which a defendant convicted of illegal gambling refused, after being released from prison, to testify about his conviction before a state committee investigating gambling. Then in *Escobedo v. Illinois,* also decided in 1964, a state murder conviction was overturned on grounds that the suspect confessed without benefit of counsel during police interrogation.

Despite this powerful series of decisions about Fifth and Sixth Amendment rights in criminal contexts, the point at which the Sixth Amendment right to counsel becomes operative was still open to question. *Miranda* settled the issue — but only for a time. Ernesto Miranda had produced a *voluntary* confession during relatively mild police questioning. But the state admitted that it had not, at any point in the proceedings, advised this Mexican-American with only an eighth-grade education that he had a right to a lawyer. To the Warren Court, this failure was decisive, and in the course of overturning Miranda's conviction, it set out the following rules:

- The Fifth Amendment applies to police interrogations.

- Unless the coercive atmosphere surrounding police interrogations is dispelled, any confession obtained at this point will be inadmissible as evidence.

- The proper procedure for dispelling the coercive atmosphere of police interrogation should involve, at a minimum, delivery of the following four warnings:

    - You have the right to remain silent.

    - Anything you say can and will be used against you.

    - You have the right to talk to a lawyer before being questioned and to have him present when you are being questioned.

    - If you cannot afford a lawyer, one will be provided for you before any questioning if you so desire.

Miranda immediately provoked a storm of controversy. A week after the decision was handed down, the Court announced that it would not apply the decision retroactively to invalidate convictions already obtained under the old rules. This announcement marked the beginning of a gradual dismantling of *Miranda*. In the drug bust case *Harris v. New York* (1971), the Court upheld its own precedent by ruling that statements made by a criminal defendant before he had been advised of his rights cannot be used as evidence against him. The kicker here was that if the defendant took the stand in his own defense, these prior statements could be used to discredit his testimony.

Three years later, writing for the majority in the rape case *Michigan v. Tucker* (1974), William Rehnquist questioned the constitutionality of the *Miranda* warnings, calling them only "prophylactic standards" laid down by the Court to "safeguard" or "provide practical reinforcement" for the privilege against self-incrimination. In 1984, the Court recognized a "public safety" exception to the *Miranda* requirements in *New York v. Quarles,* a case concerning criminal weapons possession. In 1985, in the burglary case *Oregon v. Elstad*, a confession made before *Miranda* warnings had been issued was allowed in as evidence because the defendant later waived his rights after they had been read to him.

In 2000, the Supreme Court decided *Dickerson v. United States,* a case involving a confession made to FBI agents by the driver of a getaway car before he had been given his *Miranda* warnings. The Court ruled in favor of the criminal defendant. Writing for the seven-member majority, Chief Justice Rehnquist declared that *Miranda,* "being a constitutional decision of this Court, may not be in effect overruled by an Act of Congress, and we decline to overrule *Miranda* ourselves." *Dickerson* speaks to the continuing unpopularity among politicians of *Miranda,* which Congress attempted to sidestep with the Omnibus Crime Control Act of 1968, making all voluntary confessions admissible as evidence. *Dickerson* also speaks to the reasons the Court has not yet overturned *Miranda:* "*Miranda* has become embedded in routine police practice to the point where the warnings have become part of our national culture," wrote the Chief Justice. As long as the American people stay tuned, it seems, the Court doesn't appear to be inclined to disappoint them.

The due process revolution and civil law

Unlike the new rights generated in the area of criminal law by the due process revolution (see "The due process revolution and criminal law," earlier in this chapter), new civil rights have not, for the most part, continued to expand since the middle of the 20th century. Two notable exceptions to this general rule are abortion (see Chapter 8) and affirmative action (see Chapter 10). After the landmark desegregation case *Brown v. Board of Education* (1954) (see Chapter 12), perhaps no cases have had as profound effect on American society as the political representation cases decided by the Warren Court. Although these cases owe more to the Equal Protection Clause (see Chapter 10) of the Fourteenth Amendment than they do to the Due Process Clause, the Warren Court could never have brought off the *reapportionment revolution* had it not been for the *due process revolution* that brought the Bill of Rights to where people live. After this second revolution citizens of every state, for the first time in American history, had a genuine opportunity to affect the political process on both the federal and the state level.

Article I, section 4 of the Constitution gives Congress ultimate power over the rules states create for the election of senators and representatives. In 1842, Congress decreed that members of the House of Representatives should be elected from different districts within each state. In 1872, Congress added the provision that these electoral districts were to be approximately equal in terms of population. Reapportionment laws passed by Congress in 1910 and 1911 provided that congressional districts were to be "contiguous and compact territory and containing as nearly as practicable an equal number of inhabitants."

When Congress next revisited the apportionment issue in 1929, there was no mention of the requirements put in place in 1910 and 1911. In 1932, the Supreme Court ruled that this omission was intentional, upholding a Mississippi law that failed to provide for compact, contiguous, and equally populated election districts. And there matters stood for the next three decades, a period during which American witnessed a profound population shift from the country to the city without any corresponding redrawing of electoral districts. Consequently, the power of urban dwellers to influence politics and have their views represented in Washington and in state capitals declined as the political influence of farmers rose.

How could the Court have permitted this inequality to persist? The answer is judicial restraint and a reluctance to get involved with *political questions* (see Chapter 2). In 1946, Kenneth W. Colegrove, a professor of political science at Northwestern University in Chicago challenged the inequality of Illinois voting districts, which had not been redrawn since 1901. When *Colegrove v. Green* reached the U.S. Supreme Court, the case was thrown out. Writing for the 4-3 majority, Felix Frankfurter declared:

> Nothing is clearer than that this controversy concerns matters that bring courts into immediate and active relations with party contests. From the determination of such issues this Court has traditionally held aloof. It is hostile to a democratic system to involve the judiciary in the politics of the people. . . .

> To sustain this action would cut very deep into the very being of Congress. Courts ought not to enter this political thicket. The remedy for unfairness in districting is to secure State legislatures that will apportion properly, or to invoke the ample powers of Congress.

Even nonlawyers can see the fatal flaw in Frankfurter's logic: How are people supposed to "secure State legislators that will apportion properly" if these voters' votes don't count for much? Not surprisingly, Hugo Black dissented from the majority view, stating flatly: "What is involved here is the right to vote guaranteed by the Federal Constitution. It has always been the rule that where a federally protected right has been invaded the courts will provide the remedy to rectify the wrong done." For this champion of the due process revolution, there could hardly be a more fundamental right worth protecting than the right to vote. But it would be another 16 years before the Supreme Court saw fit to overturn *Colegrove*.

"One person, one vote"

The Court's refusal to enter the "political thicket" of reapportionment remained in place until *Baker v. Carr* was decided in 1962. By this time, only three members of the *Colegrove* Court (see "The due process revolution and civil law") remained on the high bench: Felix Frankfurter, Hugo Black, and William O. Douglas — and the last two had been dissenters. The remaining members of the new Warren Court were mostly liberals who followed Chief Justice Earl Warren's lead. By this time, something else had changed. What had previously been a moderate imbalance between representation of rural and urban voters had become extreme, with rural voting districts controlling twice as many seats as they would have been entitled to if districts were redrawn on the basis of population. To make matters worse, the state of Tennessee, whose voting districts were the subject of *Baker v. Carr,* had not been redrawn for 60 years, despite a state requirement that they be redrawn every ten years following each census.

William J. Brennan was responsible for the 6-2 majority's opinion which opened federal courts to urban interests requesting reapportionment. It was left to the chief justice to declare *Baker v. Carr* the "most vital decision" handed down by the Court during his tenure and the reapportionment revolution it started the most important achievement of the Warren Court. The principle of "one person, one vote" — ensuring that each citizen's vote counted as much as the next's — was not enunciated until a year later in another challenge to a state election system, *Gray v. Sanders.* But the floodgates had been opened.

Equal representation

The principle of "one person, one vote" became reality with a set of six cases collectively known as the *Reapportionment Cases* decided on June 15, 1964. In a case decided earlier that year, *Wesberry v. Sanders,* the Warren Court had set the stage for the *Reapportionment Cases.* In *Wesberry,* the Court had declared that seats in the U.S. House of Representatives were to be filled by individuals representing districts as nearly equal in population as possible. This rule, wrote Hugo Black for the Court, was required by both Article I of the Constitution and the Fourteenth Amendment, which provides that "Representatives shall be apportioned among the several States according to their respective numbers." The Constitution's "plain objective," wrote Black, was "equal representation for equal numbers of people."

The *Reapportionment Cases* applied this objective to state legislatures, making virtually all of them unconstitutional. In *Reynolds v. Sims,* the leading case, Chief Justice Warren rejected the notion that state legislatures should be modeled along the lines of the federal Congress, with only one house based on population: "[T]he Equal Protection Clause requires that the seats in both Houses of a bicameral state legislature must be apportioned on a population basis."

The effects of this ruling were extraordinarily far-reaching, requiring nearly every state to redraw their legislative districts. Senator Everett Dirksen of Illinois was so incensed by the *Reapportionment Cases* that he proposed a constitutional amendment to override the Court's command that state legislatures must restructure both houses to represent equal population districts. He came close to getting two-thirds of the states to sign onto his proposal, as the Constitution requires, but by the early 1970, when a Constitutional convention to consider the amendment might have been called, a majority of the state legislatures had already restructured. There would be no turning back.

Chapter 10

Equal Protection: How Equal Is It?

• •

In This Chapter

▶ Retracing the career of the most important of the Civil War amendments

▶ Disentangling civil, political, and social rights

▶ Parsing state action

▶ Understanding affirmative action

• •

Equal protection under the law is one of the fundamental rights of American citizenship. Over time, though, this seemingly simple principle has assumed more forms than the shape-shifting Greek god Proteus.

A Short, Not-So-Illustrious History of the Fourteenth Amendment

Three constitutional amendments — the Thirteenth, Fourteenth, and Fifteenth — were passed in the wake of the Civil War. They constituted the first substantial alterations to the Constitution in 60 years. The brainchildren of the so-called *Radical Republicans* who gained control of Congress after the war ended, the *Civil War amendments* were intended to ensure the status of African-Americans as citizens of the United States and to guarantee that the South would not rise again.

The Thirteenth Amendment, ratified in 1865, formally abolished slavery throughout the nation. In doing so, however, the amendment also handed the former Confederate states a potential windfall. Formerly, under Article I, section 2 of the Constitution, a slave had counted as 3/5ths of a person for purposes of representation in Congress. Now, with the bulk of American's black population still residing in the South, Southern states stood a chance of gaining a great many new seats in the House of Representatives. In part to head off what they viewed as a potential political catastrophe, as well as to counteract the repressive Black Codes Southern states had begun to enact as a means of controlling newly freed slaves, the Fourteenth Amendment was proposed in Congress in 1866.

As ratified in 1868, the Fourteenth Amendment consists of five sections.

✔ Section 1, which overturns the Supreme Court's 1857 *Dred Scott* ruling (see Chapter 11), makes all persons born in the United States citizens of both the nation and the state in which they reside. Section 1 also contains the crucial prohibition against state abridgement of citizens' privileges and immunities or depravation of due process of law and guarantees equal protection of the laws.

✔ Section 2 attempts to protect African-American voting rights by reducing representation in the federal government of states that prevent male citizens from voting.

✔ Section 3 bars any state or federal official who once swore allegiance to the Constitution, and then engaged in rebellion, from holding federal office.

✔ Section 4 prohibits payment of the Confederate debt, while upholding the validity of the federal war debt.

✔ Section 5 gives Congress the power "to enforce, by appropriate legislation," Sections 1–4.

Actually, the Fourteenth Amendment was adopted to prevent *repeal* of a piece of legislation. Two years earlier, Congress had passed the Civil Rights Act of 1866 over President Andrew Johnson's veto — the first major law to override a presidential veto. Intended to counteract the Black Codes and nullify *Dred Scott,* the act declared that persons born in the United States (except tribal Indians) were U.S. citizens entitled to "full and equal benefit of laws." The act spelled out the rights to be protected, including the rights to make and enforce contracts, to sue, to give evidence, to inherit, and to purchase, lease, and convey property. Even though the act was specifically amended in the House to exclude application to state segregation statutes, it was condemned by Johnson as an invasion of states' rights. The real problem, though, was that the Civil Rights Act of 1866 was of doubtful constitutionality. Ratification of the Fourteenth Amendment put that issue to rest.

In 1868, the notion of *equality* encompassed the concepts of privileges and immunities, due process, and equal protection, all of which were lumped together in Section 2 of the amendment. The initial purpose of all three was to protect the rights of African-Americans, but as written, the Due Process and Equal Protection Clauses apply to all persons — including noncitizens. One of the supporters of the Fourteenth Amendment, Senator Jacob M. Howard, Republican of Kansas, put the matter this way: The Amendment promised to give "to the humblest, the poorest, the most despised of the race, the same rights and the same protection before the law as it gives to the most powerful, the most wealthy, or the most haughty." The lack of limitation on who was supposed to benefit from due process and equal protection — in contrast to the privileges and immunities extended to "citizens of the United

States" — could be the product of sloppy draftsmanship but more likely was a deliberate omission. Either way, this notable void would make for some peculiar Supreme Court decisions.

Another funny thing happened on the way to ratification. The congressional record of hearings on the Fourteenth Amendment makes it clear that at least the amendment's sponsors had intended it to extend the protections of the Bill of Rights to the states. The Senator responsible for ushering the amendment through his half of Congress stated that, "[T]he great object of the first section of this amendment is . . . to restrain the power of the States and compel them at all times to respect these great fundamental guarantees." And in 1871, the framer of the amendment, Senator John A. Bingham, Republican of Ohio, declared that "[T]he privileges and immunities of the citizens of the United States . . . are chiefly defined in the first eight amendments to the

The first President Johnson and the first presidential impeachment

Andrew Johnson was an improbable vice president and an accidental chief executive. In the period leading up to the election of 1864, Abraham Lincoln came under heavy criticism for foot-dragging on the issue of emancipation and leniency on the issue of Southern Reconstruction. To counteract these charges, the Republican Lincoln chose a Democrat as his running mate. Andrew Johnson was a native son of the border state of Tennessee, and like many residents of that state, he was far from sympathetic to the Confederacy. Johnson's hatred of the Southern aristocracy, which he blamed for the Civil War, was well known.

Shortly after he began his second term of office, Lincoln was assassinated. Not long after Johnson took the oath of office, it became clear that he intended to carry through with Lincoln's Reconstruction plan, which was to be overseen by the executive branch. Angered by what they saw as the plan's softness toward the South and usurpation of their power, moderate Republicans joined forces with the Radical Republicans in Congress. Together, they seized control of Reconstruction by drafting civil rights legislation and setting up a Freedman's Bureau to oversee aid to former slaves. Johnson vetoed the Civil Rights Act of 1866. Congress responded by overriding the veto and drafting the Fourteenth Amendment.

Attempting to defeat his opponents' control of Congress, Johnson embarked on an ill-advised campaign tour during the 1866 off-year election. He succeeded only in convincing the electorate that he was an irrational and eccentric individual. As for his Republican enemies, they gained a two-thirds majority in both houses of Congress. When Johnson violated the newly-passed Tenure of Office Act, prohibiting the president from dismissing any member of his cabinet without prior Senate consent, the House of Representatives voted to impeach him.

After a trial in the Senate presided over by Chief Justice Salmon P. Chase, the vote was 35 in favor of conviction for "high crimes and misdemeanors" and 19 opposed. This tally fell one vote short of the two-thirds majority required to remove the president from office, but Johnson had been essentially relieved of all authority. Radical Reconstruction got underway without him.

Constitution. . . . These eight articles . . . were never limitations upon the power of the States, until made so by the Fourteenth Amendment." All such sentiments, however, faded from view during the ratification process. State legislatures trained their focus instead on the later sections of the amendment, with their hot topics of legislative apportionment, the status of former Confederate officials, and the validity of the public war debt.

And the Fifteenth Amendment? By giving the vote to most black American males, this Civil War amendment, too, was ostensibly intended to benefit newly-freed slaves. But the impetus behind the Fifteenth Amendment, as in the case of the others, was political as well as philanthropic. In the election of 1868, the Republican Ulysses S. Grant won the presidency with 73 percent of the electoral vote, but only 52 percent of the popular vote. In order to prevent the Democrats from regaining power — especially since there was good reason to fear Southern Democratic intimidation of blacks inclined to vote for the party of Abraham Lincoln — Republicans granted African-American men the right to vote.

The 1883 Civil Rights Cases

During the 1860s when the Civil War Amendments were adopted, Congress differentiated between civil, political, and social rights. The Thirteenth and Fourteenth Amendments were meant to address civil rights, giving African-Americans equality in the legal workings of the public and private realms by bestowing on them the right to own property, the right to enter into contracts, the right to appear as a witness in court, and so on. The Fifteenth Amendment, in granting blacks the voting franchise, more or less took care of political rights. Social rights, however, were still unsettled, and in 1875, Congress attempted to address them with another Civil Rights Act.

The Civil Rights Act of 1875 was in essence a desegregation law. It granted African-Americans the right to sit on juries and the right to mingle with white society in public accommodations such as inns, theaters, and public transportation. Any attempt to violate these rights was subject to federal jurisdiction and ultimately to review at the U.S. Supreme Court. The act was the legacy of Senator Charles Sumner, Republican of Massachusetts, who did not live to see either the act's passage or its evisceration. The Civil Rights Act of 1875 was nearly a century ahead of its time.

In one of the earliest cases to test the Civil Rights Act of 1875, *Strauder v. Virginia* (1880), the Supreme Court held that a state law excluding blacks from juries was a violation of the Fourteenth Amendment's Equal Protection Clause. Three years later, however, the Court gutted the legislation in the *Civil Rights Cases*. The *Civil Rights Cases* grouped together five different cases, all concerning instances of discrimination aimed at African-Americans by private

Charles Sumner, arch-abolitionist

Charles Sumner was a Harvard-educated lawyer with a strong voice and an overriding commitment to abolitionism. As early as 1849, he argued for integration of public schools in Massachusetts. He was one of the moving forces behind the formation of the Free-Soil Party, which opposed the extension of slavery into new territories. Elected to the Senate as a Free-Soiler in 1851, he campaigned actively against slavery. And in 1855, when the Republican Party was reformed primarily to oppose slavery, Sumner joined up.

Sumner was known for his oratory, and in May 1858, with tensions running high over Southern efforts to make the Kansas Territory into a slave-holding state, he delivered his most famous speech. "The Crime Against Kansas" passionately attacked Southerners and their sympathizers, focusing on Sumner's Senate colleague, Andrew P. Butler of South Carolina. Shortly afterward, Butler's cousin, Congressman Preston Brooks, assaulted Sumner on the floor of the Senate, beating him savagely with a cane. Sumner's injuries were so severe that he took three and a half years to recover from them, returning to the Senate in 1859. Brooks, who resigned from the House, was returned by his constituents.

Sumner was the most radical of the Radical Republicans, who urged that the Civil War be waged to abolish slavery, not just to preserve the Union. Afterward, he pressed Lincoln to grant emancipated slaves civil rights and urged that former Confederate states be forced to meet stringent conditions before being read-mitted to the Union. He was the prime mover behind the Civil Rights Act of 1875, intended to extend the civil rights of African-Americans into the North as well as the South, and into all realms of American life.

individuals. In an 8-1 decision, the Court held, in essence, that Congress could not legislate social rights. The Thirteenth Amendment, which only abolished slavery, the Court said, did not give Congress the power to pass legislation like the 1875 Civil Rights Act. Denial of access to public accommodations did not constitute a badge or incidence of slavery. Furthermore, the Fourteenth Amendment only prohibited state actions that were racially discriminatory and did not reach private acts. An individual denied even such rights as voting, jury service, or appearing as a witness should appeal to state courts, as such acts were beyond the power of Congress to control.

The lone dissenter, the first Justice Harlan (see Chapter 6), denounced the majority's grounds for decision as "narrow and artificial." The Thirteenth Amendment, he declared, gave Congress broad powers to legislate insurance that African-Americans would not only be freed from slavery, but also from all "badges of slavery." Eighty-one years later, Congress would adopt Harlan's argument in passing a new civil rights act. In the meantime, though, the federal government abandoned enforcement of social rights, permitting Southern states to develop an elaborate new set of *Jim Crow* laws that amounted to legal apartheid.

Santa Clara County v. Southern Pacific Railroad (1886)

Santa Clara County was actually presented to the Court as a due process case. It arose out of a tax controversy, in which the state of California and several of its counties were attempting to collect taxes from both the Southern Pacific and the Central Pacific railroads. The railroads argued that the Due Process Clause of the Fourteenth Amendment barred such taxation, and a unanimous Supreme Court agreed — although not on due process grounds. Instead, the Court found in favor of the railroads on very narrow grounds, striking down the California tax statute because it failed to distinguish between different types of property.

The significance of *Santa Clara,* however, came in an extraordinary preface written by Chief Justice Morrison Waite and entered into the record before the justices even heard oral argument in the case. This preface indicated that the Court would not entertain the constitutional question raised by lawyers for the railroads:

> "[W]hether the provision in the Fourteenth Amendment to the Constitution which forbade a state to deny to any person within its jurisdiction the equal protection of the Constitution, applied to these corporations. We are all of the opinion that it does."

This odd preface settled the long-running debate about whether corporations had constitutional status as "persons." After *Santa Clara,* American corporations were able to invoke the protections of due process and equal protection with assurance. And they did (see Chapter 9).

Plessy v. Ferguson (1896)

Plessy v. Ferguson is famous for having legalized racial segregation, making *separate but equal* the law of the land. Homer Plessy was a light-skinned black man who volunteered to test the constitutionality of a Louisiana law requiring railroads to provide "separate but equal accommodations for the white and colored races." The law also prohibited blacks from occupying white cars and vice-versa. Because a previous decision of the Louisiana Supreme Court held that the statute did not apply to interstate commerce — which is governed by federal law — Plessy bought a ticket for a train trip that took place entirely within the state of Louisiana. He also made sure that the railroad and the conductor knew about his mixed racial background. Then Homer Plessy took a seat in a "whites only" section of the railroad car and settled in for the ride.

Plessy's ride was soon disturbed, and he was arrested when he refused to move to the "colored only" section of the car. When the state courts refused to accept his argument that the Louisiana statute violated the Thirteenth and Fourteenth Amendment, Plessy took his case to the U.S. Supreme Court. And by a vote of 7-1, the Supreme Court, in its turn, turned its back on equal protection, proclaiming that it could not enforce social rights:

> "If the two races are to meet upon terms of social equality, it must be the result of natural affinities, a mutual appreciation of each other's merits, and a voluntary consent of individuals. . . . Legislation is powerless to eradicate racial instincts, or to abolish distinctions based upon physical differences, and the attempt to do so can only result in accentuating the difficulties of the present situation. If the civil and political rights of both races be equal one cannot be inferior to the other civilly or politically. If one race be inferior to the other socially, the constitution of the United States cannot put them upon the same plane."

The lone dissenter, John Marshall Harlan, wasn't buying this line of argument. "Our constitution," he proclaimed, "is color-blind, and neither knows nor tolerates classes among citizens." His ringing rejection of "separate but equal" made little impression at the time, but a half century later, it would be repeatedly cited by those working to integrate American society.

Ironically, perhaps, *Plessy* pointed the way for the case that would ultimately overturn "separate but equal," *Brown v. Board of Education* (1954) (see Chapter 12). The author of the majority opinion in *Plessy*, Justice Henry Billings Brown, sought to justify racial separation on trains by linking it with America's long — and highly popular — tradition of segregated schooling. In the short run, this linkage served to expand the field in which segregation could be legally justified and to provide aid and comfort to those building upon the system of Jim Crow laws that governed racial relations in the South. In the long run, however, *Plessy* showed the National Association for the

"Jim Crow"

The name *Jim Crow* became a synonym for *Negro* after composer Thomas D. Rice published a minstrel song by that name in 1832. The term *Jim Crow laws,* however, did not become common until the 1890s, when Southern states began legislating formal codes to keep blacks and whites apart. Jim Crow laws became almost inevitable after the Radical Republicans who had instituted Reconstruction in the South lost power as a result of the unpopularity of the Civil Rights Act of 1875 (see "The 1883 *Civil Rights Cases*"). New *Redeemer* governments, under the control of the Democratic Party, gave in to white control, maintaining only the pretense of equal treatment of blacks. In the 1880s, public displays of anti-black anger — including lynchings — became more common. A coalition of former Confederates began passing state and local laws that extended segregation to new areas, such as public transportation, and later drinking fountains and telephone booths. This was the Jim Crow South, and it lasted for more than 70 years.

Advancement of Colored People exactly where they should concentrate their limited legal resources. If the NAACP could crack the tough nut of school segregation, then the whole edifice of "separate but equal" would crumble. And that's exactly what happened.

Korematsu v. United States (1944)

One of the few Supreme Court cases to uphold equal protection for racial minorities prior to the watershed *Brown v. Board of Education* decision of 1954 concerned Asians, who constituted a significant percentage of the population on the West Coast. In *Yick Wo. v. Hopkins* (1886), a Chinese immigrant who had legally operated a laundry in San Francisco for 22 years was denied a business license after a newly-passed ordinance resulted in only one Chinese laundry being licensed. Citing Fourteenth Amendment guarantees, the Court struck down the local law.

Yick Wo made little impact at the time, and during World War II, the simmering prejudice against Asians in California bubbled back up to the surface. After the Japanese bombed Pearl Harbor, the military ordered all Japanese-Americans to leave the West Coast, while at the same time preventing them from relocating. Instead, these citizens were left with no choice but to report to assembly centers, from which they were sent to inland government internment camps. Fred

Discriminating among discriminations

All laws discriminate among categories of people and things. But while some categorization may be necessary, even beneficial, not every classification is benign. Whenever a law is challenged on equal protection grounds, federal courts must determine whether its classifications are constitutionally permissible. In doing so, courts follow a fairly rigid — though still evolving — set of standards:

✔ Before civil rights began to dominate federal dockets in the middle of the 20th century, most legal classifications were considered acceptable if a state could show that they were *reasonably* related to a *legitimate* government interest.

✔ With the shift from property rights to individual rights in the 1930s, the Supreme Court

developed a so-called *active standard*, which calls for *heightened scrutiny* of *suspect classifications,* those based on race or *alienage*, or citizenship status. To pass muster under this standard, a law must be *closely* related to a *compelling* government interest.

✔ And in 1976, the Court began developing a third level of *intermediate scrutiny,* applied to classifications such as those based on gender or illegitimacy and requiring that a government action be *substantially* related to an *important* government interest.

Good thing the justices can keep all this straight.

Korematsu was an American-born descendant of Japanese immigrants who decided to disobey the military order. He moved from the San Francisco Bay area to a nearby town, where he changed his name, underwent plastic surgery, and posed as a Mexican-American. When his true identity was discovered, he was arrested and relocated to Utah.

When Korematsu challenged the military orders that landed him in an internment camp in Topaz, Utah, the Supreme Court upheld the orders as a valid exercise of the war powers granted Congress and the president in wartime. The Court — and the country — would later regret this decision, and in 1980, Congress authorized payments of $20,000 each to survivors of the internment camps. Still, something of enormous legal significance came out of *Korematsu:* For the first time, the Court said that it would consider any law restricting the civil rights of a single racial group as "immediately suspect" and would subject it to "rigid scrutiny." This was the inception of the system of standards federal courts would in use in the future to assess the constitutionality of laws challenged under the Equal Protection Clause.

Redressing Old Wrongs: The 1964 Civil Rights Act

The Civil Rights Act of 1964 was enacted primarily to restore the government's power to eliminate racial discrimination, absent since the 1883 *Civil Rights Cases.* (See the section "The 1883 *Civil Rights Cases,*" earlier in this chapter.) The legislation is divided into 11 titles, or sections, the most significant of which are Titles II, VI, and VII. Title II guarantees racial minorities open access to all public facilities connected with interstate commerce. Such "public accommodations" can include gas stations, restaurants, and recreation areas. Title VI prohibits discrimination in programs that accept federal funding. Title VII outlaws employment discrimination based on race, color, religion, sex, or national origin and is enforced through a body created by this title, the Equal Employment Opportunity Commission. The Court upheld the various sections of the Civil Rights Act in a series of landmark cases.

Heart of Atlanta Motel v. United States

Heart of Atlanta Motel v. United States (1964) was the major test of the constitutionality of Title II of the 1964 Civil Rights Act. The case arose when a motel operator in Atlanta, who catered to interstate travelers, refused to accept African-American patrons. Claiming that the recently-enacted Civil Rights Act violated the Fifth Amendment's Due Process Clause (see Chapter 9) and the Thirteenth Amendment (see "A Short, Not-So-Illustrious History of the

Fourteenth Amendment," earlier in this chapter), the motel operator also asserted that the federal government had exceeded its authority under the Commerce Clause to regulate interstate business.

Congress had based the Civil Rights Act on the Commerce Clause, because the Supreme Court had declared in the 1883 *Civil Rights Cases* (see "The 1883 Civil Rights Cases," earlier in this chapter) that the Equal Protection Clause of the Fourteenth Amendment could not be used to control private businesses. Now, in *Heart of Atlanta Motel*, the Court effectively overruled this previous decision. Not only did Congress have the power to regulate interstate commerce, the Court said, it also had constitutional authority to reach intrastate activities affecting interstate commerce. To put icing on the cake, a unanimous Court stated that Congress had a national "police power" to legislate against moral wrongs. For decades, due process and equal protection had been made to serve the interests of private business. Now interpretation of the Fourteenth Amendment had taken a 180-degree turn.

Griggs v. Duke Power

Griggs v. Duke Power (1971) not only upheld the constitutionality of Title VII of the 1964 Civil Rights Act, but it's the most significant case the Supreme Court has decided concerning employment discrimination. Before the act became law, the Duke Power facility in Draper, North Carolina, followed blatantly racist hiring policies. African-American applicants were hired to fill positions in an all-black labor classification that was paid less than the lowest-paid class of white workers. Job promotions for blacks were only available within their segregated department.

On July 2, 1965, the date the Civil Rights Act became effective, Duke Power management changed their hiring and promotion policies. Now, any person applying for a position in a traditionally all-white work category — and any employee wishing to transfer into such a category — was required to have a high school education and to achieve certain scores on two aptitude tests. Black employees challenged these new requirements in federal court, claiming that they not only bore no relationship to job performance but disqualified a substantially higher percentage of black than white applicants. In effect, the new requirements reinforced the company's long-standing racially segregated job classifications.

The federal district court found that Duke Power's past practices were beyond the reach of Title VII. The company's new policies were upheld because they were not intentionally discriminatory. A unanimous Supreme Court disagreed. Although Title VII does not require a company to hire an individual simply because he or she was discriminated against in the past, companies do have to remove any "artificial, arbitrary, and unnecessary" barriers to employment

"Constitutional" employment discrimination

Not every case of employment discrimination is based on Title VII of the 1964 Civil Rights Act. In 1976, a group of African-American police officers and unsuccessful applicants sued the District of Columbia Metropolitan Police Department. Citing the equal protection component of the Due Process Clause of the Fifth Amendment, the plaintiffs claimed that the police department's hiring and promotion policies were racially discriminatory. The unsuccessful applicants pointed in particular to a written screening exam, Test 21, which a disproportionate number of blacks failed.

The D.C. Circuit Court of Appeals, applying the *Griggs disparate impact* test, ruled that the police's department's Test 21 violated Title VII of the Civil Rights Act. The Supreme Court reversed this ruling, however, declaring that in order to make a case for a constitutional violation of the equal protection guarantee, there must be proof of discriminatory intent. Proof of such an intention, the Court said, could be inferred from a "totality of the relevant facts," including disproportionate impact.

The Court later strengthened this rather weak test in *Personnel Administrator v. Feeney* (1979), in which a female civil servant sued the state of Massachusetts over a statute granting lifetime preference to veterans, whom she claimed were predominately male. The Court disallowed her claim that the law violated the Equal Protection Clause of the Fourteenth Amendment. Not only was the statute gender-neutral, even if the state had foreseen that it would have had a discriminatory effect, they would have had to act *because* of this effect, not in spite of it.

Though often criticized, the rule developed in *Washington* and strengthened in *Feeney* stands. If you're a federal employee with a beef against your employer and obligated to sue under the Constitution, you're in a rather tight spot.

when they "operate invidiously to discriminate on the basis of racial or other impermissible classification." Even requirements that *appear* to be neutral are disallowed if they perpetuate discrimination.

Any employment practice, no matter what the intention behind it may be, will be struck down if it has a *disparate impact* on any of the groups protected by Title VII. The disparate impact test is *Griggs*'s primary legal legacy. The test remains valid, although it has been altered numerous times since 1971. The primary change came in 1989 with *Wards Cove Packing v. Atonio,* an employment discrimination case filed by at an Alaskan salmon cannery. Whereas *Griggs* required employers to prove that their challenged practices did not have a discriminatory effect, after *Wards Cove,* employees had the burden of proof. And even if they managed to carry this burden, employers could seek to defend themselves by claiming that a questionable practice is a *business necessity.* In 1991, however, Congress passed another Civil Rights Act eliminating the business justification defense and reversing *Wards Cove.* The 1991 act also outlawed post-hiring harassment of members of protected groups, allowing plaintiffs to sue for damages, as well as back pay and lost benefits.

Regents of the University of California v. Bakke

Regents of the University of California v. Bakke (1978) was the first significant case to put Title VI of the 1964 Civil Rights Act to the test. But Allan Bakke wasn't leaving anything to chance — when he sued the University of California for rejecting his med school application, he also claimed that the school had violated his Fourteenth Amendment right to equal protection.

Bakke, a 38-year-old white engineer, first applied to the UC-Davis med school in 1972, when his became one of 2,664 applications vying for 100 slots. Of these 100, 84 were filled via regular means (grade point average, test scores, and so on), but the remaining 16 spots were reserved for special admissions candidates. Special admissions criteria — including lower grade point average and test score requirements — had been set up in 1970 after the faculty expressed concern about the few minority students enrolled in the classes they were teaching.

Bakke did not make the cut either the first time he applied or the second. He sued, claiming what has come to be known as *reverse discrimination*. The state, for its part, claimed that it had a compelling interest in rectifying past racial injustices. But the California Supreme Court found the University's admissions program constituted an unconstitutional quota system based on race.

When *Bakke* reached the U.S. Supreme Court, the justices did not agree — either with the ruling below or with one another. The Court was divided equally into two camps. One side felt that the med school's policies clearly violated Title VI, which outlaws racial preferences in programs receiving federal aid. The other side argued that there was no real difference between the statute and the Equal Protection Clause, finding that some *affirmative action* or favorable treatment of members of protected groups by public colleges and universities was acceptable.

Lewis F. Powell cast the deciding vote for a compromise decision that admitted Bakke to the university while upholding race-conscious admission policies in certain circumstances.

The *Bakke* decision was, to say the least, confusing. Powell's opinion, written for a plurality that agreed on the outcome but not the reasoning behind it, hardly amounted to a clear statement about affirmative action. To make matters worse, Powell's opinion was really two separate opinions. One upheld the *principle* of state action intended to remedy the effects of past discrimination, while also declaring that the university could not set quotas and could only use race as one of the many factors considered in admissions decisions. The other endorsed the use of race in admissions criteria as an expression of the First Amendment's "diversity" value.

In addition to Powell's decision, five *other* opinions disagreed with one another at least to some extent. Affirmative action law has suffered from inherent contradictions ever since.

Because of *Bakke,* affirmative action has also become a political football. For a few years after the decision was handed down, the Court continued to expand affirmative action. In *United Steelworkers of America v. Weber* (1979), a reverse discrimination in employment case, the Court upheld racial quotas of private employers as a form of "private, voluntary, race-conscious" affirmative action that was not required by Title VII, but which was permissible. One year later, in *Fullilove v. Klutznick,* the Court was asked to consider minority *set-asides,* which reserved a percentage of federally funded projects for businesses owned by minorities. The law creating the set-asides, the Public Works Employment Act of 1977, was upheld as permissible exercise of remedial government action authorized by the Fourteenth Amendment and *Bakke.*

Throughout the 1980s, however, the administrations of Republicans Ronald Reagan and George Bush actively worked to put a halt to the growth of affirmative action. The Court resisted these efforts until 1989, when it changed course abruptly. In 1989, the Court increased the burden of proof for plaintiffs claiming disparate impact employment discrimination in *Wards Cove Packing v. Atonio* (see "*Griggs v. Duke* Power"). And in *Richmond v. J.A. Croson Co.,* the justices struck down minority set-asides similar to those it had upheld a decade earlier in *Fullilove.* For the first time the Court applied *strict scrutiny* (see "Discriminating among discriminations") to a benign racial classification arguing that state and local set-asides required a higher standard of review than those set up by the federal government. That decision left many people scratching their heads. And just when you thought you had a handle on affirmative action, the Democrat-controlled Congress passed the Civil Rights Act of 1991, intended to overturn *Wards Cove* and curtail other judicial efforts to limit the scope of federal civil rights protections. But that was before the changing of the palace guard in 1994, when for the first time since 1952, Republicans took control of both houses of Congress. The football game continues.

Part IV
High Drama on the High Court

The 5th Wave   By Rich Tennant

THE JUSTICES RULE ON PAPER vs. SCISSORS vs. STONE

©RICHTENNANT

In this part . . .

*J*ustice Oliver Wendell Holmes once said that the
Supreme Court is indeed a quiet place, but that its
quiet is like that of a storm center. Cases get to the
Supreme Court because they're important. This trait
doesn't mean they're entertaining — or even interesting.
But from time to time, a case has come along that has
captured everyone's attention — mainly because everyone
stands to be affected by its outcome. At such times,
passions run high, both inside the Court and out.

Two of the most significant decisions the Court has
handed down during its 213 years of existence concern
race. The first, which set the stage for the Civil War, is
universally regarded as the Supreme Court's very worst
decision. The second, which ignited the civil rights
movement, is thought by most to have marked one of the
Court's highest points. The stories that lie behind the
Dred Scott Case and *Brown v. Board of Education* are
among the most interesting in U.S. Supreme Court history.

Chapter 11

Dred Scott and the Civil War

• •

• •

*S*cott v. Sandford (1857), commonly known as the *Dred Scott Case,* is often cited as the case that started the War Between the States. While *Dred Scott* certainly did not light the spark that started the war, it clearly added fuel to the fire. Because the Founding Fathers were never able to settle the contest between *federalism,* the belief in a strong central government, and *states' rights,* which is the suspicion of strong central government, four score and a few years after its founding, the nation erupted into civil war. By the time the Supreme Court handed down its decision in *Dred Scott,* the difference in political philosophies had boiled down to the issue of slavery.

In deciding to decide the case, the Court took on an unmanageable problem that the politicians preferred not to resolve. In 1856, the Democrat James Buchanan was elected president with the support of every slaveholding state save Maryland. In his inaugural address, he informed the nation that the Supreme Court would soon tackle the burning issue of territorial status — that is, whether new states would be admitted to the union as slaveholding or nonslaveholding. In making this announcement, Buchanan inadvertently revealed that he had engaged in some illegitimate discussions with members of the Court about a pending case. He also revealed that *Scott v. Sandford* was as much a political decision as one based on the law.

The Truth Doesn't Always Set You Free, and Neither Does the Law

People don't talk about this issue often, but until it was abolished by the Thirteenth Amendment in 1865, the Constitution included a Fugitive Slave Clause. Most of the Founding Fathers were, in fact, slave owners. (George Washington freed his slaves, Thomas Jefferson didn't.) And although some of the newly formed states abolished slavery, none outlawed the capture within their boundaries of slaves who had escaped bondage in other states. The debate about what to do with runaway slaves cropped up late in the Constitutional Convention of 1787, when South Carolina delegate — and future Supreme Court justice — Pierce Butler proposed a clause that would "require fugitive slaves and servants to be delivered up like criminals." The following day, without much discussion or fanfare, the delegates adopted the following language as part of Article IV:

> No Person held to Service or Labour in one State, under the Laws thereof, escaping into another, shall, in Consequence of any Law or Regulation therein, be discharged from such Service or Labour, but shall be delivered up on Claim of the Party to whom such Service or Labour may be due.

In 1793, Congress spelled out the procedures for returning what slaveholders regarded as lost property in the first Fugitive Slave Law. Slavemasters or their agents — often called *slavecatchers* — were permitted to bring captured runaways before a magistrate to obtain a *certificate of removal* permitting the slave to be returned to his or her place of servitude. Anyone interfering with this process could be fined and/or sued.

Before 1830, many northern states passed laws to ensure the personal liberty of their freed black populations. As a kind of tradeoff, some of these same laws facilitated the return of fugitive slaves — but not all. In 1842, in *Prigg v. Pennsylvania,* the U.S. Supreme Court upheld the 1793 federal law while striking down a state personal liberty law as interfering with a "fundamental article" of the Constitution. But Joseph Story, writing for the Court, added that state officials could not be forced to comply with the Fugitive Slave Law. In a concurring opinion, Chief Justice Roger Brooke Taney (see Figure 11-1) mischaracterized Story's ruling, objecting that Story would release state judges from any obligation to hear cases against fugitive slaves. This misunderstanding helped fuel hostilities between North and South.

In 1850, slaveholders and nonslaveholders reached an agreement whereby territorial governments in lands formerly owned by Mexico and surrendered to the U.S. after the Mexican War of 1846–48 would be able to determine their own status upon being admitted to the union. As part of this Compromise of 1850, the Fugitive Slave Act was revised, providing harsher penalties against escaped slaves and against states that impeded their return. The 1850 law resulted in riots, rescues, and Harriet Beecher Stowe's influential bestseller, *Uncle Tom's Cabin* (1852). As abolitionists gained strength and numbers, resentment grew in the South against what many viewed as the North's reluctance to fulfill a constitutional obligation. The stage was set for war.

Figure 11-1:
Chief
Justice
Roger
Brooke
Taney.

© Bettman/CORBIS

A slave's own story

Born into slavery in Virginia in 1797, Dred Scott moved with his master, Peter Blow, to St. Louis. After Blow's death in 1832, Dred Scott (see Figure 11-2) was sold to Dr. John Emerson, an army surgeon. Emerson was stationed in a number of places, including the nonslaveholding state of Illinois and the free Wisconsin Territory. While in Wisconsin, Scott married Harriet Robinson, a slave whose ownership was transferred to Emerson in 1836.

Emerson left Wisconsin in 1838, leaving the Scotts behind. Dred and Harriet had two daughters, Eliza, who was born in 1843 in free territory, and Lizzie, who was born around the year 1850. Sometime after 1838, the Scotts returned to St. Louis, following Dr. Emerson. When Emerson died in 1843, his widow inherited his slaves. Irene Sanford Emerson followed a common practice of the time, hiring her slaves out to others who needed servants. In the mid-1840s, the widow Emerson moved to New York, leaving the Scott family behind with Henry and Taylor Blow, sons of Dred Scott's original owner.

Figure 11-2:
Dred Scott
and family.

Henry Blow was active in the antislavery Whig Party (see Chapter 7), and he agreed to finance a suit in the Missouri courts to secure Dred Scott's freedom. In 1846, a suit was filed against Emerson's estate, asserting that Scott's time in the free state of Illinois and the free Wisconsin Territory had made him a freedman. The basis for the suit was the state legal principle "once free, always free."

Scott's first trial ended in a mistrial, but a second lawsuit in 1850 resulted in a verdict in his favor. During the two years between trials, Scott was hired out by the county sheriff for $5 per month. His wages were held in escrow until his freedom could be finally secured.

In the meanwhile, the widow Emerson had married a radical antislavery Massachusetts congressman, and wanting to free herself of her slaves, she transferred Dred Scott's ownership to her brother, John Sanford, who was still in St. Louis. When Scott won his freedom in 1850, his new owner stood to lose control of the escrowed wages, so Sanford (his name was misspelled in the official reports) appealed the verdict. In 1852, the Missouri Supreme Court declared that Scott became a slave when he reentered Missouri.

The next year, Dred Scott, together with his wife and daughters, brought a suit in federal court in St. Louis, seeking their freedom as well as monetary damages totaling $16,500. One of the fundamental ironies of the whole case was that the United States Circuit Court for the District of Missouri accepted it at all. In order to get into the federal system, Scott's lawyers had to demonstrate that their client had standing to sue based on *diversity jurisdiction* (see Chapter 1) — that is, that the parties to the case were from different states. The Missouri federal trial court accepted the premise that the defendant, Sanford, was a citizen of New York and that the plaintiff, Scott — despite his status as a slave — was a citizen of Missouri. The upshot of this maneuvering, Scott's third attempt to gain his freedom through legal means, was a verdict declaring him still a slave.

By this time, the *Dred Scott Case* had been embraced by abolitionists and was known throughout the land. Sanford's lawyers responded to the national focus by injecting other issues into the case, which quickly found its way to the U.S. Supreme Court. There, the justices were eventually forced to confront the following two questions:

- ✔ Was Scott, an African-American, a citizen of the United States who had standing to sue in federal court? (see Chapter 2)
- ✔ Was the Missouri Compromise, which made Wisconsin a free territory, constitutional?

"Once free, always free" — the law doesn't mean what it says

Scott v. Sandford was argued twice before the Supreme Court. After the first argument, which took place February 11 to 14, 1856, the justices were inclined to avoid the real issues involved in the case. Instead, the Court intended simply to uphold the ruling of the Missouri Supreme Court, stating that a state's highest court had the last word about that state's own laws. The makeup of the Court, with Southern and pro-slavery justices in the majority, made this outcome almost inevitable. The only clearly antislavery justices on the Court then were John McLean from Ohio and Benjamin Curtis from Massachusetts. Samuel Nelson, a New Yorker who was only lukewarm toward the abolitionist cause and who had steadfastly upheld states' rights on the Court, was slated to write the majority opinion.

Politics intervened, however. 1856 was an election year, and the Court decided not to inflame the atmosphere further by delivering an opinion before the nation had elected a new president. Besides, the justices were split among themselves about which grounds to use in justifying their decision that Dred Scott was still a slave. Some wanted to hold that Scott was a slave who had no standing in federal court; others wanted to proclaim that Congress had no power to deprive citizens of property — their slaves — in the territories. The case was set down for reargument.

The Court listened to a second round of oral argument in *Scott v. Sanford* from December 15 to 18, 1856. The justices did not meet to discuss the case until the following February, and in the interim, Justice John Catron of Tennessee wrote to his friend, President-elect John Buchanan, for advice. This time, the justices — whose lineup had not changed since the first hearing — agreed to tackle the larger issues involved. Chief Justice Taney took on the job of writing the opinion for the seven justices who voted down Dred Scott's freedom.

Due, in part, to Taney's ill health, the decision of the Court was not announced until March 6 of the following year, just after Buchanan's inauguration. One sign of the significance of *Dred Scott* to a divided nation, and of the Court's own inner divisions, was that each of the nine justices wrote a separate opinion. Altogether, these totaled some 250 pages. Reading them aloud in open Court took two full days.

Taney's opinion for the Court declared Dred Scott to be still a slave. The reasons provided for this decision were many. First, and most devastatingly, although African-Americans could be citizens of a state, they could not be citizens of the United States and therefore did not enjoy such rights as suing in federal court. Second, Scott was still a slave because he had never been freed. Third, slaves are property protected by the Constitution. Therefore, the Missouri Compromise, which outlawed slavery in lands above the 36 degree, 30 minute northern latitude — such as the Wisconsin Territory — was invalidated. And finally, whatever status Scott may have had in a free state or territory, as soon as he set foot back in slaveholding Missouri — to which he had returned voluntarily — he was once again a slave, as the Missouri Supreme Court had decided. "Once free, always free" was meaningless.

Reaction to the decision was swift. While the Buchanan administration and its Southern supporters were jubilant about the outcome, the Supreme Court's dismissal of Dred Scott's suit convinced others that a conspiracy was afoot in the federal government. The decision that was supposed to settle the controversy over territorial status had, in effect, opened the entire nation up to slavery. Northern Democrats quarreled with Southern Democrats, splitting the party in two and creating an opening for the newly reformed Republican Party in the next election. As the historian Charles Warren would later write, "[I]t may fairly be said that Chief Justice Taney elected Abraham Lincoln to the presidency."

The newspapers, needless to say, had a field day with *Dred Scott,* whipping up not only partisanship but public hysteria. The Democrat-controlled Senate, which supported the Supreme Court majority, voted to print 20,000 copies of the decision for public circulation. And Northern churches — generally supportive of abolitionism — joined in the fray, reading John McLean's dissent (plainly with his cooperation) from the pulpit the day after it was delivered in Court. The other dissenter, Benjamin Curtis, remained so bitter about the majority's decision that he resigned from the Court in September 1857 after serving only six years. The nation itself grew more polarized as a result of the *Dred Scott* case, which in the end only settled the question of whether a political or legal solution could be found for the controversy over the true nature of the union. There had been bloodshed before the Supreme Court handed down what is now universally regarded as its most injudicious decision. What followed afterward was a bloodbath.

A word about the fates of the parties to the case. John Sanford died before the Court's decision was announced. The former Mrs. Emerson transferred ownership of Dred Scott and his family to Taylor Blow, the son of Scott's original owner. Blow emancipated the entire Scott family in May 1857. Dred Scott remained in St. Louis, where he worked as a hotel porter for the next decade. He reportedly felt that his suit had brought on a "heap o' trouble," and had he known it would go on so long, he never would have sued in the first place. When he died of tuberculosis on September 17, 1858, Taylor Blow's brother paid for the former slave's funeral.

The Downfall of a Great Jurist: The tragedy of Roger Brooke Taney

Roger Brooke Taney's name will forever be associated with the *Dred Scott Case*, one of the most infamous decisions ever rendered by the U.S. Supreme Court. The decision haunted him until the end of his days, undermining both his and the Court's credibility and effectiveness. Throughout the Civil War, Taney, a native of Maryland, remained loyal to the Union, but many in the North blamed him for hastening, if not inciting, the conflict that split the nation in two and killed at least 620,000. Taney lived on for six more years after announcing *Dred Scott*, but he died a frustrated, angry man whose tainted legacy survived him for generations.

This view of Taney is unfortunate — and short-sighted. Taney was, by most accounts, not only one of the most accomplished jurists of his time, but of all time. He is often thought of as a member of the Maryland aristocracy, but that, too, is partially mistaken. Although his descendants on both sides had settled in the Maryland tidewater in the 1650s and 1660s and his mother's family had always been prominent, on his father's side Taney was descended from an indentured servant whose rank in society was just above that of a slave. Taney's father was a tobacco planter who managed to ensure that his second son received an excellent education, but who could give him little else in the way of inheritance.

Roger Brooke Taney became a lawyer and a politician simultaneously, serving in various positions in state government until his party, the Federalists, broke up in the 1820s. Taney then became a Democrat and a loyal supporter of Andrew Jackson, whose coattails he rode into national politics. Taney served

Jackson's bank war

Andrew Jackson deeply distrusted centralized power, and the national bank came to symbolize all that he despised about the federal government. In his very first message to Congress after his election in 1828, Jackson made it clear that he not only doubted the need for a national bank, he believed that this institution was unconstitutional. The bank — and Jackson's determination to put an end to it — became an issue in the next presidential election. Nicholas Biddle, then president of the bank and a supporter of Jackson's Republican opponent, Henry Clay, asked Congress to renew the bank's charter in January 1832. Congress, which strongly supported the bank, did so, but Jackson vetoed the renewal and went on to win the election in a landslide. Armed with this mandate, Jackson set about gutting and then destroying the bank of the United States.

as Jackson's hatchet man during the president's bank war. Jackson was committed to killing the national Bank of the United States and went through two secretaries of the Treasury before settling on Taney, who served as acting secretary for a year. Jackson — and Taney — had so alienated the Senate with their strong-arm tactics that the Senators refused to confirm Taney as secretary of the Treasury. In January 1835, when Taney's name was again before the Senate as a Supreme Court appointee, the Senators demonstrated their unhappiness with Jackson and his lieutenant by simply sitting on the nomination. But when Chief Justice John Marshall died a few months later, Jackson tried again to reward Taney — this time with a bigger prize. After an executive session during which no records were kept, Taney was confirmed as the new chief justice of the Supreme Court.

Taney's reputation as a political hack did not smooth his early days on the Court. In the veto message he had drafted to accompany Jackson's death blow to the national bank, Taney had written, "The opinion of the judges has no more authority over Congress than the opinion of Congress has over the judges, and on that point the President is independent of both. The authority of the Supreme Court must not, therefore, be permitted to control the Congress or the Executive." So much for the power of judicial review (see Chapter 5). What's more, Taney had to fill the large shoes left by the great and greatly loved chief, John Marshall, the man who had practically invented judicial review. But early in his tenure, Taney staked out his own judicial territory, demonstrating his authority and signaling that a new era in Supreme Court jurisprudence had begun.

One signal that the status quo had changed on the Court was Taney's clothing. Instead of the customary stately knee breeches, Taney wore democratic trousers beneath his robes. And under Taney's leadership the Court did develop a body of law that addressed the rights of the public rather than private welfare. The three leading cases decided during Taney's first term had all been argued while Marshall was still chief justice, and all of them would have been decided differently had Marshall not died. Taney made sure that all three were reargued and decided during his first month on the high bench — and he made sure that they bore his stamp.

Taney's opinion for the Court in the most significant of these cases, *Charles River Bridge v. Warren Bridge* (1837), demonstrates a clear departure from the Marshall tradition. *Charles River Bridge* concerned state authorization of construction of a second bridge across the Charles River in Boston. The Charles River Bridge, which charged a hefty toll, had proven to be a gold mine for its owners, leading to a demand for another bridge that would be free to the public. A second bridge threatened to cut into the profits of the Charles Bridge shareholders, who filed suit to halt construction, claiming that Massachusetts had violated its contract with them. In ruling against the Charles River Bridge, Taney departed from the Marshall Court's nationalistic capital, emphasizing the significance of local authority: "[T]he object and end of all government is to promote the happiness and prosperity of the community. . . . While the rights of private property are sacredly guarded, we must not forget, that the community also have rights, and that the happiness and well-being of every citizen depends on their faithful preservation."

This emphasis on local autonomy would mark the remainder of Taney's long (he would serve on the Court for 28 ½ years) and successful tenure on the Supreme Court. Decisions like *Charles River Bridge* helped pave the way for a period of national economic expansion that would only be halted by the Civil War. Unfortunately, the same democratic impulse led Taney into the morass of *Dred Scott*. Under Taney's leadership, the Court had gained an even greater measure of prestige than it had during the Marshall years. It would all disappear — almost overnight — when Taney applied his states' rights orientation to the facts of *Scott v. Sandford*, overplaying his hand by declaring that Congress had erred by interfering with local authority and property rights by signing the Missouri Compromise into law 37 years earlier. This was judicial activism at its very worst, and Taney paid a hefty price for what many saw as his arrogance.

Taney was a touchy man who took offense easily and never forgot the many rejections he had endured on his way up. He was incapable of seeing his own faults, and he never truly understood the disgrace others tried to heap upon him for his miscalculation in thinking he could — and should — find the answer to a problem that had evaded all other attempts at resolution. It was a sad end to a great career.

The Birth of a Nation: A Hundred More Years of Segregation

Although Abraham Lincoln freed the slaves with the Emancipation Proclamation of 1863, the Constitution had to be amended to overturn the *Dred Scott* decision. As the Supreme Court saw it, *Scott v. Sandford* was at least in part a suit about the interpretation of a section of Article IV — thrown in almost as an afterthought — that guaranteed slave owners a right to hold onto their human property. The three constitutional amendments — the Thirteenth, Fourteenth, and Fifteenth — passed in the wake of the Civil War made up the first substantial alterations to the Constitution in 60 years. The Thirteenth Amendment, ratified in 1865, abolished slavery in the United States. The Fifteenth Amendment, which became law in 1870, granted African-Americans the right to vote. But it was the Fourteenth Amendment, ratified in 1868, that was meant to reverse the damage done by *Scott v. Sandford*.

The Fourteenth Amendment makes all persons born in the United States citizens of both the nation and the state in which they reside. The Amendment also prohibits states from abridging the "privileges or immunities" of citizens and from depriving citizens of due process of law or equal protection under the laws. The apparent intent of the drafters of this Amendment was to legislate racial equality. Racial equality under law did not come about for almost another century, though, and when it did, it did so because of another Supreme Court ruling, *Brown v. Board of Education*, a 1954 school desegregation case. In the meanwhile, the Fourteenth Amendment triggered an enormous amount of litigation, much of it construing — many would say misconstruing — the *Due Process Clause* (see Chapter 9) so as to protect private enterprise from state regulation.

Chapter 12

Brown v. Board of Education and the Civil Rights Movement

● ●

In This Chapter

▶ Revisiting the civil rights movement

▶ Connecting social change with legal decisions

▶ Reviewing the most significant case of the 20th century

● ●

*W*hen *Brown v. Board of Education* was decided in 1954, more than half a century had passed since the Supreme Court made "separate but equal" the law of the land with *Plessy v. Ferguson* (1896). Although African-Americans gained their freedom as a result of the Civil War, a system of legal segregation — particularly as implemented in the South — continued to rob them of their dignity and to ensure that they would be unable to improve their lives. Desegregation was a long time coming.

Changing Minds: The NAACP and the Supreme Court

The National Association for the Advancement of Colored People (NAACP), founded in 1909, sought to reverse the racial apartheid that continued to oppress black people. The organization's chosen method of combating segregation was the lawsuit. Again and again, the NAACP participated in cases that ended up before the U.S. Supreme Court, where NAACP lawyers would attempt to convince the justices that the so-called *Civil War Amendments* — the Thirteenth, Fourteenth, and Fifteenth — were intended to empower blacks.

In *Guinn v. United States* (1915), the NAACP joined in a successful fight against black voter disenfranchisement. In *Buchanan v. Warley* (1917), the organization overturned local laws permitting housing discrimination. In *Moore v. Dempsey* (1923), the NAACP convinced the Court to overturn criminal convictions of black defendants obtained in a courtroom that was under threat of mob violence. The NAACP clearly had the law — and now the Court — on its side. Progressivism was in the air, and much of the American public endorsed both the organization's cause and its methods.

In 1932, however, the NAACP stumbled. The year before, nine black youths accused of raping two white women on a freight train were sentenced to death after a one-day trial in an Alabama courtroom without effective legal representation. The case of the "Scottsboro Boys" quickly became a national cause célèbre, picked up by both the NAACP and the Communist Party's International Labor Defense (ILD) organization. A struggle ensued between the two organizations, as the defendants switched allegiances back and forth. Ultimately, the ILD took over the legal defense in the two Scottsboro cases, *Powell v. Alabama* (1932) and *Norris v. Alabama* (1935), in both of which the Supreme Court reversed the defendants' sentences.

In the end, though, the NAACP lost twice in the Scottsboro cases. The organization not only lost control of two high-profile cases that could have advanced its cause, when the cases were retried, five of the nine Scottsboro boys were again convicted and served lengthy jail sentences. Reassessing its legal strategy, in 1934 the NAACP hired Charles Hamilton Houston, the dean of Howard Law School, to act as its full-time legal counsel. Houston hired a number of prominent and promising lawyers — not all of them African-American — and in 1939 formed the NAACP Legal Defense Fund (LDF).

The LDF developed a constitutional law strategy that focused on equal opportunity by focusing on equal educational opportunity. It fought and won a number of education cases in the Supreme Court before achieving a history-making breakthrough with *Brown v. Board*.

The Search for the Perfect Plaintiff

The NAACP began its challenge to supposedly "separate but equal" public education by challenging the policies of colleges and universities in court. Although each victory brought the NAACP closer to its goal of ending racial segregation, no case before *Brown v. Board* presented a set of facts — or a plaintiff — that was "just right." And some of the individuals who agreed to endure the long course of litigation with NAACP support were not able to enjoy their victories.

The fugitive kind

In September 1935, Lloyd L. Gaines was a resident of Missouri and a recent graduate of all-black Lincoln University in Jefferson City, Missouri. He had achieved a good academic record there, and he wanted to go on to law school. His application to the all-white University of Missouri Law School was rejected, however, and the law school referred him to a state law indicating that Missouri was willing to pay the tuition of Missouri blacks who went to graduate school in any *other* state.

Gaines wrote on his own initiative to NAACP, which eagerly took up his case. After the NAACP filed its first lawsuit on behalf of Gaines, the University of Missouri passed a resolution making it clear that they were rejecting him solely on the basis of race. Although the NAACP lost the first round in state court, the university had done the organization a real favor by allowing them to point to the Fourteenth Amendment's Equal Protection Clause (see Chapter 10). It was clear that *Missouri ex rel. Gaines v. Canada* was headed for the U.S. Supreme Court.

First, though, some setbacks occurred. The Missouri Supreme Court bought the University of Missouri's argument that it had a right to reject Gaines because Lincoln University would eventually establish its own law school. More devastatingly, Gaines was getting cold feet. He had testified on his own behalf at the state trial and withstood cross examination, but now he seemed unable to withstand all the attention his case was getting from the national news media. He wrote to the NAACP saying that while he was awaiting a final decision in his case, he was going to work on as master's degree in economics at the University of Michigan. He was prepared to take money from the state of Missouri to finance his out-of-state graduate studies, a step that would undermine his whole case. The NAACP was forced to funnel money to Gaines secretly to keep him at the University of Michigan while his case worked its way through the U.S. Supreme Court.

In December 1938, the High Court, unconvinced that a new law school at Lincoln University would meet the separate but equal requirement, overturned the Missouri Supreme Court's ruling, sending the case back to the lower court for further proceedings. In the meanwhile, Lincoln University had hastily set up its own law school, which the NAACP cautioned Gaines not to enter. And then Lloyd Gaines disappeared. The last contact anyone connected with the case had with him was in April 1939. His case, although an important victory for the NAACP, was now moot.

A grad school built for one

In 1946, the University of Oklahoma, with its feet held to the fire, did its best to create separate but equal graduate schools for two students. Ada Sipuel, an honors graduate of all-black Langston University in Langston, Oklahoma, volunteered to be an NAACP guinea pig, applying to the all-white law school at Norman. The University of Oklahoma president helped matters along by signing a letter, at the NAACP's request, indicating that although Ada Sipuel was qualified for admission, state law prohibited her attendance.

After appealing this rejection all the way up through the state court system, in January 1948, Ada Sipuel finally had her day before the U.S. Supreme Court. The Oklahoma state attorney general told the justices that Oklahoma would open an all-black law school for Sipuel "promptly" if she asked for one. The Court took him at his word, ruling in *Sipuel v. Board of Regents of University of Oklahoma* (1948) that "[Ada Sipuel] is entitled to secure legal education afforded by a state institution . . . [Oklahoma] must provide it for her . . . and provide it as soon as it does for applicants of any other group."

And Oklahoma did just that. An Oklahoma City lawyer was selected to become the architect and dean of the "Langston University School of Law," located in room 428 of the state capitol building. The state hired three white professors to teach the single student of the new school. Needless to say, the law school was less than satisfactory to Sipuel and the NAACP — and, ultimately to Oklahoma. After the news media had a field day with this farce and Sipuel obtained a ruling from the Supreme Court ordering the University of Oklahoma Law School to admit her as part of the entering class of 1949, the "Langston University School of Law" quickly faded from view.

The University of Oklahoma tried a different tactic with George W. McLaurin, an African-American professor teaching at an all-black college. In 1946, McLaurin was in his late 60s and a citizen of Oklahoma who wanted to get a doctorate in education at the University of Oklahoma. The University rejected his application on grounds that it was against state law for blacks and whites to attend the same school. A federal district court ordered the university to admit McLaurin, adding that he was "entitled to secure a [doctorate] as soon as it is afforded to any other applicant."

The district court gave the University of Oklahoma an out, however, saying that its decision did "not mean . . . that the segregation laws of Oklahoma are incapable of constitutional enforcement." Separate but equal treatment was still possible. McLaurin was duly admitted, but when he attended his first class, he was forced to sit in a former broom closet, which the university now called an "anteroom." He could use the library, but he could only sit in a special section reserved for him alone. The campus snack bar was cleared of all white students at noon, so that McLaurin could eat there. Every place reserved for him was in fact marked with specially prepared signs reading "Colored."

In the meanwhile, the NAACP had filed *McLaurin v. Oklahoma State Regents for Higher Education* with the Supreme Court. On June 5, 1950, the Court handed down a decision declaring that this modified form of racial segregation must end. Once admitted, an African-American student must receive "the same treatment at the hands of the state as students of other races." The Court had taken an enormous burden off the shoulders of the president and regents of the university, who were now forced to do away with their "separate but equal" — and expensive — duplicate facilities.

A small black girl from Topeka, Kansas

Oliver Brown, the famous plaintiff in *Brown v. Board of Education,* had no history of social activism prior to 1950. He was an African-American railroad worker who lived — literally — on the wrong side of the tracks in Topeka, Kansas. Brown and his family lived near his workplace, and his neighborhood was next to a major switchyard. The proximity of the trains was more than nuisance, though: Because Topeka's school system was segregated, Oliver Brown's children had to walk through the switchyard to get to their all-black school, which was a mile from their home.

In September 1950, Brown walked his 7-year-old daughter, Linda, to the all-white Sumner Elementary School, a mere four blocks from home. He hoped to register his daughter girl in second grade at Sumner, but was turned away. Although the Browns lived in an integrated neighborhood, the school board would not permit the little black girl to enroll. Twenty-four years later, Linda Brown would recall the following:

> Both of my parents were extremely upset by the fact that I had to walk six blocks through a dangerous train yard to the bus stop — only to wait, sometimes up to half an hour in the rain or snow, for the school bus that took me and the other black children to "our school." Sometimes I was just so cold that I cried all the way to the bus stop . . . and two or three times I just couldn't stand it, so I came back home.

Oliver Brown was an assistant pastor in his local church and a man of peace. But now, in a towering rage, he went to his friend, Charles Scott, an attorney for the NAACP. They agreed to file suit against the Topeka school board. Brown's case was an excellent one for testing the constitutionality of "separate but equal." Kansas law permitted, but did not require, cities of more than 15,000 to segregate their schools. And Topeka, which segregated its elementary schools, did not do so at the higher grade levels. There was no justification for making little Linda Brown go so far out of her way to get to school. The NAACP had found its perfect plaintiff.

Try, Try Again: When the Supreme Court Can't Make Up Its Mind

Oliver Brown's case was one of five originating in different states and the District of Columbia that were consolidated before being heard by the U.S. Supreme Court. All challenged state — or in the case of the D.C. case — federal laws that permitted or required racial segregation in public schools. The goal of all the petitioners, however, was not only school integration, but ending the whole system of segregationist *Jim Crow* laws imposed by Southern and border states on all public accommodations. This legacy of

The conciliator

Three days after the Court delivered its decision in *Brown*, Felix Frankfurter wrote in a letter to Stanley Reed: "I have no doubt that if the *Segregation* cases had reached decision last Term there would have been four dissenters — Vinson, Reed, Jackson and Clark — and certainly several opinions for the majority view. That would have been catastrophic." Warren inherited a Court divided against itself, and *Brown* could serve as Exhibit A in a case against reunification. Desegregation was too complex an issue — too fraught with policy concerns, too fraught with emotion, simply too big for the Court to handle. Most of the justices agreed that *Plessy* should be overturned, but they could not see how the superstructure of segregation could be dismantled.

Warren, with his calm demeanor, his clear-sightedness, and his political acuteness, made the case seem simple. At his first *Brown* conference, he let every justice air his views fully and freely Then, he made it plain that he intended to face the issue of segregation squarely, and he did not mince words about his own view of the matter. "Personally," he told the others, "I can't see how today we can justify segregation based solely on race." But, he added, abolishing school segregation must be done "in a tolerant way."

Warren's statements put Court supporters of *Plessy* in the uncomfortable position of appearing to be racists, but he also made it clear that he wasn't going to strong-arm them. At the second *Brown* conference, he focused on remedies, letting the other justices know that desegregation was indeed workable (he suggested that the Court leave enforcement up to the district courts) and getting them to work together on solving the problem rather than parsing the law.

Afterward, everyone was in Chief Justice's corner except Stanley Reed. Warren continued to work on Reed, in the end telling him matter-of-factly, "Stan, you're all by yourself on this now. You've got to decide whether it's really the best thing for the country." Reed capitulated, and Warren finally had what he wanted, unanimity.

slavery, written into law at the state level, had perpetuated the parallel — and inherently unequal — lives lived by blacks and whites since colonial times. As nearly everyone knew, everything — including the Court's own manner of interpreting the Constitution — was about to change. Small wonder it took the justices a while to get used to the idea.

The death of Fred Vinson

The Court first heard oral argument in *Brown v. Board* on December 9, 1952. When the judicial conference (see Chapter 3) met to discuss the case, Chief Justice Fred Vinson opened with a set of remarks indicating that he was not prepared to overrule the "separate but equal" rule of *Plessy v. Ferguson* (1896). Not only was there a "body of law back of us on separate but equal," he said, "Congress did not pass a statute deterring and ordering no segregation."

It was a bad beginning. The other justices were split more or less down the middle, and without a leader who was willing to take a firm stand on this important case, it looked as though the Court would remain divided. As Justice William O. Douglas later wrote, if *Brown* had been decided in the 1952 Court term, "there would probably have been many opinions and a wide divergence of views and a result that would have sustained, so far as the States were concerned, segregation of students." Instead, the justices punted, ordering the case to be reargued in the next term, which would open the first Monday of October 1953.

And then something happened: On September 8, 1953, Fred Vinson died suddenly of a heart attack. Justice Felix Frankfurter, who was of the opinion that a close vote on *Brown* would have been disastrous, told two former law clerks that Vinson's death was "the first indication I have ever had that there is a God."

The initiation of Earl Warren

When *Brown v. Board* was finally reargued on December 7, 8, and 9, 1953, a new chief justice was in place. Earl Warren, a career politician who had never served on any bench, had taken the oath of office barely two months before. *Brown,* a case of monumental significance, was one of the first tasks he faced, and many thought him not up to the job.

But on this Court peopled with prima donnas like Felix Frankfurter and Robert H. Jackson and profoundly divided as to *Brown,* Warren was exactly what was needed. He was able to use his political skills to allow every member to air his opinion. And he was able to use his leadership abilities to make his own views known from the outset. "[T]he more I've read and thought," he announced, "the more I've come to conclude that the basis of segregation and 'separate but equal' rests upon a concept of the inherent inferiority of the colored race. . . . Personally, I don't see how today we can justify segregation based solely on race." But he didn't push. He gave the others time. He scheduled a second conference. He knew that the manner in which the Court announced its decision was just as important as the decision itself. He wanted a unanimous vote — and he got it.

Warren drafted the opinion of the Court himself. In its directness, its plainness, and its brevity — it was only ten pages long — the opinion reflected the man himself. As one of his law clerks later said of Warren, "He had a penchant for Anglo-Saxon words over Latin words and he didn't like foreign phrases thrown in if there was a good American word that would do." And this straightforwardness was exactly what was needed. The American people needed to hear, in unadorned language endorsed by every member of the Court, that a half century of legalized discrimination had come to an end. After the decision was handed down on May 17, 1954, legal scholars criticized Warren's opinion for its lack of specificity and failure to confront *Plessy* head on. Everyone else clearly understood what Warren meant when he announced, "We conclude, unanimously [a word you won't find in the printed text of the opinion], that in the field of public education the doctrine of 'separate but equal' has no place. Separate educational facilities are inherently unequal."

Almost as contentious as the decision in *Brown* was a footnote in the opinion of the Court. The decision in the case was based on two propositions:

- ✔ Segregated schools are inherently unequal.
- ✔ Racial segregation in and of itself made African-American children feel inferior and damaged their mental and emotional well-being.

The second proposition resulted from the NAACP's strategy of introducing sociological data to support their case. In particular, their brief cited the work of the African-American psychologist Kenneth Clark, noted for his doll tests. Clark and his wife, Mamie, had developed tests using black and white dolls to gauge the attitudes of African-American children attending segregated elementary schools. When asked which doll looked most like them, the children picked the black dolls. When asked which doll they liked more, or which one was the "good" doll, the children almost always chose the white doll. To Clark, these results demonstrated both an early awareness of color and the dire effects of segregation.

Chief Justice Warren's opinion for the Court reflected Clark's findings: "To separate [African-American children] from others of similar age and qualifications solely because of their race generates a feeling of inferiority as to their status in the community that may affect their hearts and minds in a way unlikely ever to be undone. . . . Whatever may have been the extent of psychological knowledge at the time of *Plessy v. Ferguson*, this finding is amply supported by modern authority." This statement was buttressed by a number of psychological and sociological authorities cited in footnote 11, including Kenneth Clark and — more controversially — the Swedish economist Gunnar Myrdal, whose two-volume *An American Dilemma: The Negro Problem and Modern Democracy,* published in 1944, detailed the social and economic costs of segregation.

Reporting on the decision the next day for *The New York Times,* James Reston called *Brown* "A Sociological Decision, " which "relied more on social scientists than on legal precedents." Many shared this view, particularly in the South, where Myrdal's work was much hated by white bigots. Even some who supported the outcome in *Brown* criticized the Court's use of nonlegal materials in arriving at its conclusion that segregation must end. For Earl Warren, footnote 11 was "only a note, nothing more." Warren did not say as much, but his reliance on sociological data to argue for progressive social change had a long and honorable history in the Supreme Court, starting with the *Brandeis brief* used by future Justice Louis Brandeis (see Chapter 6) to win support for maximum working hours in the 1908 decision, *Muller v. Oregon.*

Changing the Course of History

It's hard to overstate the importance of *Brown v. Board of Education.* The problem of slavery — often manifested in the struggle between federalism and states' rights, between a strong central government and local authority — had haunted America from its inception. With one ten-page opinion, the Supreme Court put an end to the controversy. *Brown* also ignited a social revolution that was carried out in the streets by civil rights activists and in Congress by legislators who passed the Civil Rights Act of 1964 and the Voting Rights Act of 1965.

Another revolution in the Supreme Court itself followed on the heels of *Brown,* which paved the way for 30 years of judicial activism linked to a new way of looking at the law by looking at society. School desegregation was followed by a total dismantling of the Jim Crow laws that had governed the lives of southern blacks since the Civil War. One by one, state control of such matters as voting, criminal procedure, and personal privacy became subjects for federal scrutiny — and they did so largely because of *Brown*'s emphasis on equal protection. It's fair to say that *Brown v. Board of Education* has changed the lives of every American, regardless of skin color.

A star is born: The triumph of Thurgood Marshall

One of the lives most changed by *Brown v. Board of Education* was Thurgood Marshall's (see Figure 12-1). Marshall, lead counsel for the petitioners in *Brown,* had headed up the NAACP's Legal Defense and Education Fund since 1938. In that position, he had crafted a legal and public relations strategy that, piece by piece, dismantled racial apartheid in the United States. In 1954, he was a hero to black America; most white Americans had never heard of him. That was about to change.

The son of a club steward and a schoolteacher, Thurgood (born Thoroughgood) Marshall was named for his grandfather, a freed slave. After graduating first in his class at Howard University Law School, Marshall briefly practiced law privately before going to work for the NAACP. Marshall's gradualist approach to desegregation, convincing the federal courts case by case that separate but equal educational facilities were inherently unconstitutional, was a product not just of smarts but of experience. In 1930, this Baltimore native son had been turned down by the University of Maryland Law School because he was black. In 1935, his first major civil rights victory was a judgment ordering the law school that had rejected him five years earlier to integrate its student body. When he went to work for the NAACP the next year, Marshall transformed his sweet revenge into a legal strategy. *Missouri ex rel. Gaines v. Canada* (1938)

was the first of 29 Supreme Court victories for Marshall and the NAACP, a progression that culminated in *Brown*. Afterward, Marshall remarked, "We struck the jackpot."

The fruits of *Brown* would not be realized immediately, for the nation or for Marshall. But in 1961, President John F. Kennedy nominated Marshall to serve on the Second Circuit Court of Appeals. The confirmation battle was prolonged, and Marshall had already been on the bench for 11 months before he was officially confirmed. During the four years he served as a federal appellate judge, he accumulated a stellar record, with none of the 98 opinions he delivered for the court majority subsequently overturned by the Supreme Court. In 1965, Marshall was named as the first African-American solicitor general, and in the position, he won 14 of the 19 cases he argued for the government before the Supreme Court.

Finally, in 1967, President Lyndon B. Johnson decided that it was time to name an African-American to sit on the nation's highest court, and Marshall was the obvious choice. Despite his fabled career, Marshall was once again subjected to racially motivated attacks, but after a nearly four-month confirmation battle, on October 2, 1967, he finally joined the Court headed by Chief Justice Earl Warren.

Marshall immediately joined the liberal voting bloc headed by the chief justice, but Warren would lead the Court for only two more years. As Earl Warren was succeeded by Warren Burger, and Burger by William Rehnquist, the Supreme Court became increasingly conservative. No longer in the majority, Marshall sided most often with another holdover from the Warren years, Justice William J. Brennan — particularly in death penalty cases, in which the two invariably voted against the imposition of capital punishment. Marshall joked that by this time he was in the majority only on one issue, "breaking for lunch."

Marshall hoped to remain on the Court long enough to have his successor appointed by a Democratic (and presumably more liberal) president. Failing health, however, forced him to retire in June 1991, while President George Bush was still in office. In announcing his departure, Marshall expressed the hope that Bush would not replace him with "the wrong Negro." (Clarence Thomas, who "inherited" Marshall's African-American seat, is a conservative Republican — clearly not the type of replacement Marshall favored.) Afterward, Marshall continued to serve occasionally on federal appellate courts until his death in January 1993.

Although the Reverend Martin Luther King, Jr. was the moving spirit behind the nonviolent struggle for civil rights in the 1960s, Marshall's contribution to the liberation of African-Americans cannot be overstated. As the architect of the winning strategy that culminated in *Brown v. Board of Education*, Marshall was the individual most responsible for enlisting the crucial support of the federal courts in enforcing the dictates of a nation founded in the belief that all persons are created equal.

Figure 12-1:
Justice
Thurgood
Marshall.

© Bettman/CORBIS

It's not over 'til it's over (part II): Brown v. Board redux

After the Court heard oral argument in *Brown v. Board of Education* for a second time in December 1953, the justices were most divided over the issue of how school desegregation could be implemented. One of the ways that Chief Justice Earl Warren managed to bring the other members of the Court over to his view of the case was to save that issue for another day. When he announced the opinion of the Court in *Brown I* on May 17, 1954, Warren also announced that "[i]n order that we may have the full assistance of the parties in formulating decrees," the case was being put on the docket for yet another argument.

The Court handed down its 9-0 decision about relief, *Brown v. Board of Education II*, as it's known, on May 31, 1955. In oral argument, the NAACP had urged the Court to order school desegregation to begin immediately. States with segregated school systems countered that such a plan was impractical. The Court's decision that desegregation should proceed with "all deliberate speed" proved an unhappy compromise. Essentially, the burden of enforcement was thrown back on the very courts where the cases leading up to *Brown* had begun. Southern states, it seemed, were back in the driver's seat.

It would be three years before the Court agreed to hear another school desegregation case. In the meanwhile, a series of unsigned *per curiam* decisions issued from the high bench ordered desegregation of state parks, beaches and bath houses, golf courses, and public transportation. Like *Brown II,* none of these decisions spelled out just how desegregation was to be implemented, and this lack of guidance produced both criticism and chaos.

The violence that followed in the wake of *Brown II* produced the Court's next school desegregation case, *Cooper v. Aaron* (1958). In September 1957, Arkansas governor Orval Faubis had called in the state national guard to prevent the entrance of nine African-American students into Little Rock Central High School. Faubis himself backed off, but a crowd of angry whites prevented the black students from starting school. The next day, President Dwight Eisenhower sent federal troops to enforce the Supreme Court's desegregation order. Eisenhower's gambit helped those nine black students, but because of the turmoil at Central High, the federal district court granted the Little Rock school board a 30-month extension of the Court's deadline for integration. When the NAACP appealed this ruling, the Court met in special session during the summer of 1958.

Although *Cooper* held that state executives and legislators are bound by decisions of the U.S. Supreme Court, the case proved to be more about the Court's own power than about equal protection. It would take an act of Congress, the Civil Rights Act of 1964, to give the federal government a mechanism for enforcing desegregation. Even then, states continued to drag their feet. In *Green v. County School Board of New Kent County* (1968), the Court ruled that *Brown* required not only abolition of state policies promoting segregation, but active *desegregation*. In *Swann v. Charlotte-Mecklenburg Board of Education* (1971), the Court upheld school busing as the best means of achieving racial balance in state education systems.

Brown v. Board of Education certainly didn't settle everything. School busing continues to be a contentious issue. Inner city schools remain segregated, for all intents and purposes. The federal government continues to debate how best to make education both integrated and equal. And racial tensions of all sorts have certainly not disappeared from the American scene. And yet, despite all of its shortcomings, *Brown* is unquestionably one of the most significant decisions the Court ever has handed down — or ever will. As Justice Arthur Goldberg once observed, America is committed to equality. *Brown v. Board of Education* helped the nation begin to live up to its promise.

Part V

Understanding Supreme Court Decisions

The 5th Wave   By Rich Tennant

"Have one of my clerks annotate these notes on a draft to a revision of one of my briefs and then issue it as a memo in the form of a madrigal."

In this part . . .

The law can seem like a foreign country. For one thing, it's written in a language that's only partially understandable. For another, simply trying to find the law can be an exercise in futility, since legal research is nothing like any other kind of research. But in this day and age, it doesn't require a law degree or even a library card to discover how the Supreme Court has treated a certain issue in the past or to decipher the meaning of a Supreme Court opinion. Welcome to the information superhighway, where masses of information about the Court are only a click away!

But how do you wade through all this stuff? Here's help. In these chapters, I offer you tips about the best sites to visit and how to locate what you need there. For those of you who don't have access to the Internet or who are both law- and computer-phobic, I also offer a guided tour through some print sources, including a couple of old-fashioned books. And for those diehards who want to discover how to do legal research the *right* way, I offer a Cook's Tour through some of the traditional resources.

Chapter 13

Using the Internet: Your Best Bet

*O*h, brave new world — the Internet makes legal research less of an obscure science and more like a form of entertainment. If you want to find out about Justice Sandra O'Connor, you can simply search under her name and discover not only that she wrote the opinion of the Court in the major religious freedom case, *Lynch v. Donnelly* (1984), but also that she was recently inducted into the Cowgirl Hall of Fame.

The Internet is a wonderful tool for exploring both case minutia and the grand sweep Supreme Court history. It's the fastest, easiest way to find things related to the Supreme Court. But it's ever-changing: The details of some of what I write about in this chapter, particularly the URLs, will almost certainly change. It's also not official. If you want to know how to get the Court's final word on a subject, see Chapter 14.

The Supreme Court Web Site

The Supreme Court didn't have a photocopier until 1969. Now it has its own Web site: `www.supremecourtus.gov`. This site is as good a place as any to start your research into the Court. It has a lot to offer, and it's not subject to the kinds of errors and omissions that creep into other sites that include Court information.

Introduction

The Court's Web site provides a brief overview of Court history and lists today's players, both the justices and the Court officers who serve them. It contains capsule biographies of the current justices, as well as a chronological list of all the justices. Short essays are devoted to the Court as an institution, the Court and its traditions, Court procedures, and the building that houses the Court. The site also provides introductory information about the justices' caseload and their assignments in the federal circuits.

Recent and pending cases

The Court's site is one of the only places you can keep track of its current docket. You can access an automated system that allows you to check the status of cases for both the current term and the prior term. The site includes the Court's current schedule, its calendar for oral argument, and transcripts of oral arguments from this term. The journal of the Supreme Court, posted here, contains the official minutes of the Court. The journal includes a list of the cases argued each day and the attorneys who presented oral argument, as well as miscellaneous announcements made by the Chief Justice from the Bench. The vast majority of the petitions sent to the Court are dismissed by unsigned order. A list of such recent orders is included here, as are the brief opinions justices sometimes attach to explain summary dispositions.

The Supreme Court Web site is an excellent place to check first for recent opinions (2000 on). Not only can you find the full texts of decisions here, you can also find the latest *slip lists* for the 2001–2002 term. These slip lists give the name and citation of cases already decided but not yet in print. The slip list includes each case's docket number and date of issuance, as well as a brief summary of the case's *holding,* or legal significance. Only the bound volumes of the United States Reports contain the final, official texts of the opinions of the Supreme Court of the United States. In the case of discrepancies between the bound volume and any other version of a case — whether print or electronic, official or unofficial — the bound volume is official.

Rules and regulations

The Court's Web site — no surprise — includes lots of formal guidelines on how to get before the justices. The Rules of the Supreme Court — detailing filing formats, deadlines, and so on — are there. You can also find less formal guides about how to file a case, both for petitioners and for their attorneys. Attorneys seeking admission to the Supreme Court bar can download an application here, along with instructions on how to file it.

The site also includes a copy of the most important rules and regulations in the land: the Constitution.

Public information

Yes, the Court would be happy to have you visit its building. It even provides a map of how to get there from other points in the federal city. The site includes a visitor's guide to the Court, a visitor's guide to oral argument, as well as information about the building itself. There are, of course, building regulations — also available at this site.

If you can't actually go to the Court in person, the site includes a list of "helpful telephone numbers," as well as information about where to send your comments. If you're interested in career opportunities or internship programs, you can find out about them here.

The Web site also includes texts of the Court's recent communiqués: press releases, media advisories, the justices' public speeches, and the chief justice's year-end report on the state of the federal judiciary.

And if you haven't had enough by this point, the Court provides links to sites where you can gather additional information about it, the rest of the federal judiciary, and the other two branches of government.

Cornell University's Legal Information Institute Supreme Court Collection

Cornell's Legal Information Institute Web site (www.law.cornell.edu) is ranked as the most linked to Web resource in the field of law. More than 90,000 Web pages at other sites, among them those of the White House and the U.S. House of Representatives, link to LII. Launched in 1992, the Web site's purpose is to reach lawyers and nonlawyers alike, helping them to do legal research, not just information retrieval. The site charges no subscription fees and takes no advertising.

Searching cases

The LII's Supreme Court Collection includes up-to-the-minute information transferred by a direct feed from the Supreme Court that automatically places court decisions on the Web site in searchable format within minutes of their being handed down. Current decisions (from the current term, stretching from October to October) are searchable, as are their syllabi, or summaries (a wonderfully useful feature — see Chapter 14), as well as current orders of the Court. The Current Awareness section also includes a Court calendar, an updated list of cases granted review, of cases waiting to be argued, and of cases already argued but awaiting decision. You can search LII's archive of older decisions by author, by party, or by topic. (The last is linked to keywords in the case summaries.) A section is also devoted to highlights from the Court's last term, providing brief synopses of important cases organized by topic.

Searching everything else under the sun

The LII Web site includes biographies of all the sitting justices, linked to their recent opinions. Biographies are also available for all the other justices who have sat on the Court. Each biography is linked to any opinions written by that justice that are housed in the LII's collection of more than 300 most significant historic decisions. The LII Supreme Court Collection also contains a searchable set of U.S. Supreme Court rules, as well as an abbreviated "Glossary of legalese." The site's "Law About . . ." feature has links to every legal topic you can think of. For example, under Copyright, LII provides links to the U.S. Copyright Act, the relevant sections of the U.S. Code, and U.S. Supreme Court and federal circuit court decisions on topic. And that's just for starters. If you want to look at international or secondary material about copyright, this site is an excellent place to link up with them.

FindLaw

FindLaw (www.findlaw.com) bills itself as a "searchable directory of all things law." And it is, in fact, nearly complete — and free. FindLaw includes a long list of different directories, some of which are directly related to the Supreme Court.

Opinions

FindLaw's directory of U.S. Supreme Court opinions (www.findlaw.com/casecode/supreme.html) is a searchable database of all the Court's decisions since 1893. Browsable by year and *U.S. Reports* volume number, they are also searchable by citation, case title, and full text. The directory home page states categorically: "This is a free service that will remain free."

Supreme Court center

Located at supreme.lp.findlaw.com/supreme_court/resources.html, this directory allows you to search all Supreme Court decisions since 1893, but it is oriented toward the Court's more recent activities. You can recover the Court's monthly docket starting with the October 1999 term though the present. An index of cases granted certiorari during the current term is searchable by topic. Here's an example of what such a search turns up for one pending case listed under *Intellectual Property*, *Eldred v. Ashcroft:*

- ✔ Subject: Copyright Term Extension Act of 1998, First Amendment, Copyright Clause

- ✔ Questions presented:

    - Did the D.C. Circuit err in holding that Congress has the power under the Copyright Clause to extend retrospectively the term of existing copyrights?

    - Is a law that extends the term of existing and future copy-rights "categorically immune from challenge[] under the First Amendment"?

- ✔ Decisions (a list of decisions already recorded in the case)

- ✔ Resources:

    - Docket listing

    - Summary of the case from Northwestern University's Medill School of Journalism

- ✔ Briefs (links to briefs for petitioner, respondent, and petitioner's reply brief, as well as five amicus briefs)

FindLaw's Supreme Court Center also includes the Court's order list, dating back to the October 1998 term, an index of cases granted certiorari in which Supreme Court briefs are available, and a colorful version of the Court's month-by-month calendar for the current term. Here, you'll also find the Supreme Court's rules, as well as two filing guides issued by the office of the clerk of the Court: a "Guide for Prospective Indigent Petitioners for Writs of Certiorari" and a "Memorandum to Those Intending to Prepare a Petition for a Writ of Certiorari and Pay the $300 Docket Fee."

Supreme Court news

This directory (news.findlaw.com/legalnews/us/sc) contains news items about the Court dating back a month. These items are really more like news sound bites, boiled down version of wire service stories. This site is useful, though, because it allows you to take in all the latest about the Court practically at a glance. At this site, you can also sign up for *message boards,* which are essentially discussion groups organized by topic and devoted to cases in the news. Numerous links on this page will take you to other Court news and information sites.

Constitutional law center

This directory (`http://supreme.lp.findlaw.com/`) brings together resources including biographies of the justices, a brief history of the Court, and much of the material you can find in other FindLaw directories. One useful feature here is a series of articles by journalists, historians, and legal experts about a wide range of subjects related to constitutional law. Recent features included a roundup of last term's decisions on criminal law and procedure, a reappraisal of the World War II Japanese-American internment case *Korematsu v. United States* (1944), and a novel look at the Ten Commandments as a legal document.

Media Web Sites: Built for the Common Man or Woman

If you really don't feel prepared to take on the law yourself, you may want to skip over cases and codes and discussions of the Supreme Court by legal experts. A layperson can go to countless places on the Web to get information about the Court that is presented in a more familiar fashion. Here are two of the best, both of them Web sites connected to great national newspapers.

Washingtonpost.com: Simply the best

The *Washington Post* Web site has a section devoted to the Supreme Court on its Federal Page (`www.washingtonpost.com/wp-dyn/politics/fedpage/supremecourt`). This section contains probably all the news you'll need about the Supreme Court, plus it includes links to other sites that allow for one-stop shopping. At this truly excellent site, you can read about a recent decision and then research aspects of the case that strike your fancy.

The current docket

The first page of this section of the *Washington Post Online* leads with the most current story about the Court but has links to all *Post* stories — sometimes briefly described — dating back to the beginning to the Court's current term. *Post* coverage from as far back as 1999 is also retrievable, although these stories are not listed on this page. Links to the Supreme Court Web site (see the section "The Supreme Court Web site," earlier in this chapter) allow you to retrieve opinions, orders, and transcripts of oral argument from recent cases. Other links to FindLaw (see the section "FindLaw," earlier in this chapter) give you access to the Court's calendar, docket, case index, and the briefs filed in recent cases.

Past history

Links to *Post* articles provide an overview of the Court, notable past justices, the Court's method of choosing which cases to review, a description of oral argument, a short analysis of the Court's decision making process, descriptions of the ten historic cases the *Post* considers "most crucial," and a piece about the Court's role in the 2000 presidential election.

Links on this page to FindLaw allow you to search all Supreme Court cases dating from 1893 by legal citation, title, or full text.

Less weighty matter

Court coverage in Washingtonpost.com includes some other items you'll find elsewhere, and some you won't. A link to a legal dictionary allows you to simply type a term that you'd like clarified. Two light-hearted quizzes test your knowledge of the Supreme Court, past and present. (Here's a sample question: "Which of the following justices are expected to retire at the end of this term?: a) Rehnquist, b) O'Connor, c) a and b, d) Who knows? ") Finally, a link to "Full Court Press," the *Post*'s column on the Supreme Court, appears on the Federal Page on the first Monday of every month. Titles of columns that have appeared this year appear on this page.

NYTimes.com: Linda Greenhouse, a great Court commentator

The *New York Times* Web site may not be able to compete with that of the *Washington Post* when it comes to accessing news and other information about the Court, but the *Times* does have a matchless resource. Linda Greenhouse, who won the Pulitzer Prize for beat reporting in 1998, is generally acknowledged to be the most astute Court reporter around. With the exception of a brief stint reporting on Congress in the mid-1980s, she has covered the Supreme Court for the *Times* since 1978.

The Supreme Court in review

Linda Greenhouse's beat coverage of the Supreme Court appears regularly (sometimes in more than one article per day) on the *Times* National page (www.nytimes.com/pages/national/index.html). She also publishes a weekly Supreme Court roundup for the paper's Week in Review Desk and a yearly review for the *Times* Year in Review feature. Sometimes, Greenhouse even reviews books for the Book Review section, as she did recently after the appearance of Justice Sandra Day O'Connor's autobiography, *LAZY B: Growing Up on a Cattle Ranch in the American Southwest.*

Using the *New York Times* on the Web can sometimes be a frustrating exercise, however. The paper's searchable online archive only goes back six years and is not user-friendly. Even when you do manage to find what you're looking for, if it's recent, you'll have to pay to get the full text.

Supreme Court Q & A

The *New York Times on the Web* National section has a columns page (`www.nytimes.com/pages/national/columns/index.htm`) that includes Linda Greenhouse's "Supreme Court Q & A," which provides answers to readers' questions on Supreme Court rules and procedures. The column, which appears on no set schedule, groups together a miscellaneous assortment of questions, which Greenhouse answers thoroughly but concisely. Links to other recent "Supreme Court Q & A" columns and to a column archive reach back three years. A link to Greenhouse's biography in turn leads to a link that permits you to submit your own question to Greenhouse for review.

Oyez, Oyez, Oyez: A U.S. Supreme Court Multimedia Database

Oyez, Oyez, Oyez (`oyez.nwu.edu`) is Northwestern University's multimedia Supreme Court Web site. In addition to including the sorts of information you can expect to find on loads of other Internet sites that deal with the Supreme Court, Oyez has some unique features.

Audio or oral argument

The OYEZ Project contains hundreds of hours of audio materials delivered through the free player available from Real.com (you'll need version 6.0 or higher) on the Oyez site. The most interesting of these materials are doubtless the recordings of oral arguments from most of the major cases that have come before the Court since 1961. Approximately ten months following the term in which cases were argued in the Court, you'll be able to listen on your own computer to the oral arguments heard in them. You must admit, this is pretty exciting stuff.

Virtual tour of the Court

Through the OYEZ Project, you can take a tour of the Supreme Court without leaving home. To view the panoramic images of the Court, you'll need to download and install QuickTime, a free program available from Apple Computer on the Oyez site. To be able to hear the audio that goes along with the tour, you'll need QuickTime 5.0 or higher.

Oyez baseball

Believe it or not, Oyez baseball is a game comparing Supreme Court justices with baseball players. The point of this exercise, according to the Web site, is to "bring the work of the nation's highest court — in text, audio and images — to the widest possible audience." To play, you have to have Macromedia Flash 5.0, which you can install on the Oyez site, loaded into your computer. If you love baseball, or if you love law, or if you're simply interested in biography, you've got to try this game.

Chapter 14

The Supreme Court Reporter Is Not a Magazine: Traditional Research

● ●

● ●

*Y*ou probably already know that law has its own special language. (There's also a sublanguage, *Law French,* to master, if you're ambitious!) Similarly, lawyers have their own, unique methods of recording and then recovering information. The Internet has made legal research simpler for more people (see Chapter 13), but you may need to get your hands on something other than a virtual law book at times. This chapter is for those occasions.

Going Official: Reading Opinions the Old-Fashioned Way

Just as there are numerous judicial systems (federal, state, military, and so on) and countless jurisdictions (federal, state, county, municipal, and so on), there is a multitude of legal reporters out there recording their decisions. A *reporter* (sometimes called a court stenographer) is the name not only of the person who writes down what goes on in court as it transpires, but it is also the name of the volumes containing the texts of the various orders and decisions handed down by courts as well.

To make matters even more complicated, the decisions of most jurisdictions are recorded in more than one series of reporters. Usually, a court has at least one official reporter and one unofficial one. The U.S. Supreme Court is no exception to this general rule.

How to read case citations

When you run across Supreme Court case names, they're often accompanied by a series of identifying numbers and letters. These abbreviations are intended to tell you which version of the decision the author is quoting or citing. (A variety of *unofficial* versions of Supreme Court decisions are published.) They also indicate where you can find the complete text of the decision.

Typically, citations of Supreme Court decisions consist of five parts, in this order:

- ✔ The title of the case (usually the names of the primary parties), which is always either italicized or underlined, and customarily followed by a comma

- ✔ The volume number of the reporter (for example, the publication) being cited

- ✔ The name of the reporter series being cited (abbreviated)

- ✔ The page on which the decision begins

- ✔ The year the Supreme Court handed down the decision (in parentheses)

For example, *Brown v. Board of Education,* 347 U.S. 483 (1954) is a citation for the decision in the case of *Brown v. Board of Education,* which appears in volume 347 of *United States Reports,* starting on page 483. The decision was handed down in 1954.

Meet the reporters

United States Reports is the official reporter for U.S. Supreme Court decisions, and all but the most recent decisions generally cite just this reporter. The exception is very early cases decided before 1874, which often carry another, parallel citation, like this: *Chisholm v. Georgia,* 2 Dall. (2 U.S.) 419 (1793). Originally, reporters were named for the *reporters* who recorded them — here Alexander J. Dallas — and then published under their own surnames. These reporters were later incorporated into *United States Reports,* so that volume 2 of Dallas's reports became volume 2 of *United States Reports.*

U.S. Supreme Court cases are also recorded in a number of unofficial commercial reporters:

✔ *Supreme Court Reporter* (S. Ct.)

- Includes full texts of all U.S. Supreme Court decisions, starting in 1882 with volume 106 of *United States Reports*

- Publishes much faster than *U.S. Reports,* with *advance sheets* or pamphlets of new decisions appearing a few weeks after they're handed down

- Contains more detailed *headnotes,* or descriptions of important aspects of the decision, than appear in *U.S. Reports*

- Uses headnotes as part of the West Publishing Company's *key number* system, which helps you find other cases addressing similar issues

✔ *United States Supreme Court Reports, Lawyers' Edition* (or Second Edition) (L. Ed., or L. Ed. 2d)

- Reprints the full text of all Court decisions as found in *U.S. Reports*

- Includes a second edition, or series, beginning with volume 100

- Publishes faster than *U.S. Reports*

- Offers a summary of the case, cross references to publications on the same subject, and its own headnotes

- Stands out as the only commercial reporter to include short summaries of the lawyers' briefs in the case

- Includes annotations in each volume on the more important cases reported inside

- Arranges annotations by topic in a companion series, *U.S. Supreme Court Digest, Lawyer's Edition,* which is also published by Matthew Bender (a member of the LexisNexis Group; see "Going Online [Semi-officially]: Lexis," later in this chapter)

✔ The following are not reporters per se, but still provide access — quicker access — to Supreme Court opinions:

- *United States Law Week:* a weekly loose-leaf, ring-bound service that provides photocopies of the Court's slip opinions within a few days after they've been distributed by the Court within three days of its announcement (see Chapter 3); no headnotes or editorial commentary

- Electronic CD-ROM versions of cases offered by a host of commercial publishers (Geronimo Development Corp.: www.casefinder. com; HoweData, Inc.: www.howedata.com/; HyperLaw, Inc.:

www.hyperlaw.com/index.htm; InfoSynthesis, Inc. : www.usscplus.com/; and Loislaw: www.pita.com/). Updated frequently, often paired with online subscription services, these CD-ROMs will cost you.

- Microfilm/Microfiche versions of cases offered by LexisNexis and other commercial publishers; for these, you will need one of those bulky library microfilm readers.

Concentrate on the top matter

In almost every case, reporters — even the official *United States Reports* — preface the text of the opinions handed down in a case with a syllabus or summary. The syllabus is where you'll probably want to concentrate your attention. While the Court often sternly warns that nothing — *Nothing* — that appears above the official text of the opinions is law (or is necessarily even accurate), this summary of the case is going to be easier for you to understand than what the justices themselves have signed off on. The opinions of the justices make for tough sledding — particularly because most are now written by law clerks using turgid law review style (see Chapter 15). In addition, these opinions do not present a straightforward argument; they're punctuated throughout with citations to other cases that you probably couldn't care less about.

Unofficial case reporters (see the preceding) are more generous with the information they supply in their top matter. For that reason alone, you may want to consult these first. You can use *U.S. Reports* when you want to make sure that you're quoting absolutely accurately from an opinion.

Here's what you'll find in the top matter of a reported decision. Bear in mind that formats and the order of the elements differ from one reporter to the next:

- ✔ **Caption:** This is the name of the case, usually stated in the form *X v. Y,* with the *X* usually standing for the appealing party and the *Y* standing for the defending party. In criminal cases, one of these parties is always going to be the government, either the United States, or a state, or the *people* of a state. Where there is no second party, as in an estate matter, the caption will begin with *In re*, like this: *In re X.*

- ✔ **Docket number, date argued, date decided:** The clerk of the Court assigned this number to the case when it was initially filed. This number can help you (and the Court) keep track of the case before it's decided. And even after a case is decided, the docket number helps in finding preliminary versions of opinions. The date argued is the date oral arguments were heard by the Court, and the date decided is the date the Court's decision is announced.

- **Attorneys:** The names of the attorneys representing the parties are listed. (This section does not appear in the official reports.) Often, more than two attorneys are listed. By the time a case reaches the Supreme Court, both parties are bound to have more than one lawyer on the job. In addition, multiple cases are often decided together, and important cases can also involve briefs written by *amici curiae,* or friends of the Court who have an indirect interest in the outcome.

- **Syllabus and/or headnotes:** The summary of the case is also sometimes called a *headnote.* In this section of the top matter, you'll find a brief summary of the facts of the case, the decisions of the courts below, and issue or issues the Supreme Court is being asked to decide.

- **Holding:** The *holding* of the case is presented separately. This statement of the law essential to deciding the legal problem presented by the case is the heart of the matter. Commercial reporters customarily also provide a series of annotations — sometimes also confusingly called headnotes — that help you find specific legal points in the opinions themselves.

- **Statement of how the Court ruled:** This section indicates whether the decision of the lower court appealed from is affirmed, overruled, modified, and so on.

- **List of opinions:** A list of which justice wrote which opinions is set out separately. This is where you can find out who wrote the opinion for the majority, who wrote concurring opinions, who wrote dissents, and who joined whom in which opinions. This part of the syllabus, believe it or not, can be rather confusing. Thank goodness it's the last part.

Going Online (Semiofficially)

In addition to the kinds of resources discussed in Chapter 13, two electronic databases are recognized as acceptable methods of finding opinions and other legal materials. They even have their own codified citation forms. Both are subscription services. And both are highly competitive, so much of what I say here about one or the other will soon be out of date, as they constantly up the ante by adding to their respective offerings.

LEXIS

LEXIS was the first commercially successful electronic legal research system. LEXIS not only supplies full texts of opinions issued by the Supreme Court (and most of the other courts around the country), it supplies them quickly, with database updates every two hours. In addition, you can use LEXIS to access all manner of other court records — including briefs in cases argued before the Court — and legislative materials. LEXIS also has an ever-expanding library of secondary sources, such as legal treatises and law reviews. If you're a subscriber, LEXIS will even notify you by e-mail about developments concerning cases you may be following closely. LEXIS has the added advantage of being linked with NEXIS, a news retrieval database that can keep you current with breaking news about important cases before the Court.

WESTLAW

WESTLAW has much in common with LEXIS. The main difference between the two databases is that opinions in WESTLAW include the West Publishing Company's proprietary summaries, headnotes, and key numbers. And although WESTLAW does include news retrieval, the scope of this service is more limited that of NEXIS.

Using Cheat Sheets: Secondary Sources

If you're interested in reading about a particular case, justice, a period in Court history, or area of the law — or you just like the feel of a book between your hands — you have a lot of choices. Many of these secondary sources are geared toward lawyers or law students who already know something about legal language and legal research. Here are three that are more accessible — and usually available in your local library.

The Oxford Companion to the Supreme Court

Edited by Kermit L. Hall and published by Oxford University Press in 1992, *The Oxford Companion to the Supreme Court of the United States* is now somewhat out of date. It is still, however, one of the most useful, user-friendly sources of information on the Court. It's alphabetically organized and includes entries on all manner of things connected with the Court: judicial biographies, explanations of legal concepts, overviews of significant cases, and so on. Each of these entries is written by a recognized legal expert graced with good style and the ability to explain complex issues straightforwardly. If you're one of those people who pick up a reference work to look up one thing, only to look up and discover that several hours have passed, this book's for you.

Facts About the Supreme Court

Now here's a good book. *Facts About the Supreme Court of the United States* was published by H.W. Wilson and written by, well, me. It appeared in 1996, and like *The Oxford Companion to the Supreme Court,* it's now somewhat out of date. But *Facts About the Supreme Court* is essentially a history book, so its lack of descriptions of decisions handed down during the most recent Court terms does not detract from its focus. The book is organized chronologically and in addition to providing a historical context for each of the 16 Supreme Courts — starting with the Jay Court and going straight through to the Rehnquist Court — it includes biographies of the justices, analyses of important cases, a breakdown of voting patterns, and special features, such as expansion and contraction in the size of the Court and its quarters.

Nutshell Summaries of the Law

When I went to law school, most students found it impossible to keep up with the workload. Trying to get through the reading — much of it couched in what may as well have been a foreign language — was an overwhelming task. Many people coped by resorting to the numerous commercial outlines on the market that purport to summarize the rules of a given area of the law in simple form. Our professors never tired of warning us away from these outlines, thought to prevent us from thinking through matters on our own.

One exception to the ban on commercial summaries of law was the West Publishing Company's *in a nutshell* series. These books are, as their series title implies, compact, portable little bundles of information. Unlike *The Oxford Companion to the Supreme Court* and *Facts About the Supreme Court,* their intended audience is not laypersons, but those who have some familiarity with legal principles. But if you have a burning interest in, for example, copyright law, there are few better places to begin than the Nutshell *Intellectual Property.* Like other volumes in the series, it's written by a recognized expert in the area in clear, uncluttered prose that anyone with an interest in law can follow. West produces new editions all the time, so you'll never be very far behind developments in the field. As one pleased reviewer of the third edition of *Intellectual Property in a Nutshell* recently wrote, "If you want to understand patents, copyrights, and trademarks, this book will make you an expert in an afternoon."

Part VI
Becoming a Court Insider

The 5th Wave By Rich Tennant

THE SUPREME COURT JUSTICES ON VACATION

In this part . . .

For those of you who want to really get behind the scenes at the Supreme Court, you've come to the right place. This part is where you find out who *really* does the work at the Marble Palace. The justices get all the glory, but behind the curtain that acts as a backdrop for their pronouncements, a bevy of workers is laboring mightily to help these black-robed men and women present a calm face to the world. And the workers aren't always happy with their place in the scheme of things. Occasionally, one of these Court insiders breaks ranks. Thanks to them, you and I both have a better idea of what goes on in there.

Chapter 15

Law Clerks: The Worker Bees

• •

In This Chapter

▶ Finding out who becomes a law clerk and how

▶ Discovering who does the grunt work

▶ Taking a peek inside closed chambers

• •

Top graduates of elite law schools are chosen by individual justices to act as temporary personal assistants. Using finely honed research, analytical, and writing skills, these clerks are responsible for helping the justices decide which cases to review and for assisting with opinion writing. Their influential positions are gained — and maintained — through drudgery.

A Roadmap to the Justices' Chambers

The practice of hiring recent law school graduates to act as the justices' personal assistants started in 1882, when Justice Horace Gray hired a recent Harvard Law School graduate to help out in chambers. Gray had had good experiences with this practice in his previous job as chief justice of the Massachusetts Supreme Court. It was an informal arrangement. Justice Gray depended upon his brother, a Harvard Law School professor, to recommend students who had graduated with honors. And Gray paid his clerks out of his own pocket.

When Oliver Wendell Holmes, Jr. replaced Justice Gray at the Court in 1902, Holmes kept up his predecessor's practice of relying on Professor Gray to supply a steady stream of recent Harvard Law School graduates for one-year tenures as clerks. Other justices came to see the wisdom of hired help and joined in. In 1922, Congress finally appropriated funds for each justice to pay one clerk a salary of $3,600 per year. Two years later, Congress officially recognized the position of Supreme Court judicial clerk, making the job — although not the individuals who fill it — a permanent part of the staff.

Today, each justice is given the funds to hire four law clerks, each of whom will be paid an annual salary of $46,000 (as of September 2003). Most — but not all — of the justices take advantage of this arrangement. The justices themselves pick out their own clerks from among the hundreds of applicants each justice receives each year.

Typically, the people chosen to clerk at the Supreme Court are 25-year-old white males who have recently graduated from high-ranking law schools like Harvard's. In one sense, things haven't changed much since Horace Gray's time. Women only began entering the ranks of Supreme Court clerks on a regular basis on the mid-1970s, but neither women nor blacks have made much headway at the tradition-bound Court. In 1999, *USA Today* observed that the Court, with two female and one African-American justices, was more diverse than its own clerks. That year, no black law clerks worked at the Court, and four of the justices — William Rehnquist, Anthony Kennedy, Antonin Scalia, and David Souter — had never hired a black clerk.

The people who are hired to clerk at the Court have invariably graduated at or near the top of their law school class. And perhaps more importantly, they have refined their legal skills by working on the esteemed law reviews published by their schools. These periodicals, which are devoted to articles about national or international legal issues or recent U.S. Supreme Court decisions, carry a lot of clout. It's not uncommon to see an article from, say, the *Harvard Law Review,* cited in a U.S. Supreme Court opinion. And I'm sure you won't be surprised to hear that there is a cause and effect relationship here: Many of these opinions are actually written by the very same people who once worked on the *Harvard Law Review* (see "The 'Junior Supreme Court'").

Getting into law school — particularly a highly-ranked law school — is not easy. Once there, a student is immediately pitted against his or her classmates in an intensely competitive hothouse atmosphere. Those who rise to the top make it onto the law review, where they're required to work what amounts to a full-time job in addition to doing their course work. You've seen the TV series *The Paper Chase?* The show doesn't grossly exaggerate the demands put on these top law students. But among law students — most of them, that is — there is still nothing so prized as making law review. One of my friends, a public interest attorney, was always chagrined when lawyer friends would introduce him to others as having once been on *Harvard Law Review.* When I knew him, my friend was in his mid-60s.

And after law review, many go on to become law clerks. And among those who go on to become law clerks, there is nothing so prized as working at the U.S. Supreme Court. The odds of getting there are slim. No more than 36 people can clerk there at any one time, and often the count is lower. Among the current justices, the chief justice and John Paul Stevens both employ fewer than four clerks. Ruth Bader Ginsburg has been known to employ a law school professor as a clerk. And some clerks stay on for more than one year. You can imagine how much it means to a highly-motivated, highly-competitive individual to be chosen as a Supreme Court law clerk. It's more exhilarating than making law review.

Work, Work, Work

By the time law clerks have made it to the Supreme Court, they have developed — in addition to the fabled ability to *think like a lawyer* — an enormous capacity for work. And that's a good thing, because for the next year or so, they will be required to work seven days a week, often far into the night. Their job will be to pick up the slack — and then some — for justices who are often too busy to do the work themselves.

24/7

In earlier times, law clerks did the same type of work as their counterparts in private practice. Like associates in law firms, their primary job was to do legal research for senior members of the organization. Justice Louis D. Brandeis once asked his clerk to search every page of every volume of *United States Reports* for a certain piece of information. Others have had it easier. Hugo Black used his clerks as tennis partners, and Harlan F. Stone wanted his clerks to accompany him on recreational walks.

More than 7,000 petitions are now filed every year with the Clerk of the Supreme Court. Of these, the Court will actually review only around 100. (The number seems to decrease every year.) The process of winnowing these petitions and then addressing the questions presented by the few cases that make it onto the Court's agenda is an enormous task that falls largely on the shoulders of the law clerks. Remember, this work is performed by 30-some-odd young people who have only just shed their caps and gowns. For many, this position is their first real job.

Following is the job description:

> ✔ Law clerks do the initial screening of petitions to the Court. Today, eight of the nine justices participate in a *pool* that determines which cases the Court will review. The petitions are divided among the clerks, who write a memorandum for each case assigned to them. These memos summarize the facts and the issues involved in each case and often recommend whether the case should be accepted for review. Copies of these memos are then circulated to all the justices participating in the pool.

- • If a clerk is employed by a justice who is not a pool member (currently only John Paul Stevens is not), that clerk must do all the sifting and sorting with the help of only the three other clerks working for that justice.

- • Even if a clerk is working for a pool participant, that clerk may be required to write additional memos concerning some of the cases selected for review by the pool or cases that have simply caught the attention of his or her boss.

✔ Before oral argument, clerks are sometimes asked to write an additional *bench memo* summarizing the case and suggesting questions the justice might ask from the bench.

✔ After the justices have voted on a case, those who want to write an opinion (for the majority, concurring, dissenting, and so on) customarily have their clerks write the first draft.

✔ While the various opinions concerning a case are being circulated among the justices for comment, it is the clerks who do the majority of the negotiating among themselves regarding wording, reasoning, and so on.

✔ Final drafts, too, are often the work of clerks. This is a well-known secret, even though the opinions bear the name of the justices, not those of the clerks who have done the work.

The "Junior Supreme Court"

Once upon a time, only about 50 years ago, Justice Louis Brandeis was able to remark that "Then reason the public thinks so much of the Justices of the Supreme Court is that they are almost the only people in Washington who do their own work." This statement is no longer true, and it has not been true for some time. Justice William O. Douglas, congratulating William Rehnquist on his appointment to the Court in 1972, wrote: "I realize that you were here before as a member of the so-called Junior Supreme Court." Rehnquist had served as a clerk to Justice Robert H. Jackson from 1952 to 1953.

Douglas was an early and outspoken critic of the practice of delegating work to individuals who have generally never worked as lawyers — let alone judges — and who have not been through much more screening than a job interview with the justice who hired them. As Douglas wrote to Rehnquist, "The law clerks are fine. Most of them are sharp and able. But after all, they have never been confirmed by the Senate." Once he suggested that the justices try doing without law clerks altogether, a kind of experiment. The suggestion, Douglas recalled in his memoirs, was met with "stony silence."

After Congress made law clerks official employees of the Court in 1924, Chief Justice Charles Evans Hughes fretted that if the justices used their clerks too much, "it might be thought that they were writing our opinions." And that's just what many Court observers have come to believe. And since the institution of the cert pool in 1972, it has become clear to all that the law clerks are also responsible for the other truly significant Court function: deciding which cases the justices will review and decide. As long as some of the justices declined to participate in the pool, there were checks on the clerk's power over the selection of cases. But William J. Brennan, who retired in 1990, was the last justice to personally go over petitions to the Court for certiorari. Today, Justice John Paul Stevens is the only holdout, and even he admits he reviews only a small fraction of the petitions filed with the Court.

Because America has evolved into such a litigious society, the Court's work-load has increased exponentially. Reliance on law clerks has become almost a necessity. But an odd thing has happened: As time goes by, the number of decisions handed down by the Court continues to shrink. Today the Court decides roughly half the number of cases it decided even as recently as 20 years ago. Justice Stevens, the only member of the current Court willing to discuss the issue, blames the slowdown on law clerks. Increasing participation in the pool has meant increasing caution on the part of those making the decisions — it is simply less risky to turn down a case than to take responsibility for recommending its review. And with the pool system, each yea or nay comes from one individual who more often than not is an insecure, inexperienced 25-year-old recent law school graduate. As a result, say critics, not only are fewer cases being decided, often they are the wrong ones. Important but less than riveting commercial cases are often overlooked in favor of attention-grabbing cases involving, say, pornography on the Internet. Those cases that don't make the cut have reached the end of the line.

Former law clerks protest that the influence of clerk on the Court is overplayed. One former clerk recently compared his role to that of the characters in the Tom Stoppard play *Rosencrantz and Guildenstern are Dead*, a send-up of *Hamlet* in which two minor figures think all the action revolves around them. Another former clerk likens the role of law clerks to that of Michelangelo's students, who executed art based on their master's design. Justice Stevens supports this view: "The idea that the clerks do all the work is nutty," he declared in a 1989 interview.

And yet, law clerks' fingerprints are all over the opinions issuing from the Court these days. As a result of what Yale Law School Dean Anthony Kronman calls the clerks' "strategies of insecurity," the Court now issues twice as many separate opinions per case than it did 50 years ago. And these opinions are often written in law review style: lengthy, all-inclusive reexaminations of the arguments pro and con, presented in the passive voice. And the writing of Supreme Court opinions *matters*. Opinions not only decide the fates of the parties to a case, they determine the fates of future litigants. American law is built on precedent, where each decision is built on others that have come before. Rulings handed down by the highest court in the land are read and reread for generations, with each word subject to careful analysis.

In former times, clerks were responsible for matters like footnotes: Earl Warren left the drafting of Footnote 11 of *Brown v. Board of Education* (1954) (see Chapter 12) to his clerks, and perhaps for that reason that footnote is still hotly debated. The justices themselves used to write their own opinions in important cases — in some instances, they wrote many drafts, as Harry Blackmun did with *Roe v. Wade* (1973). Former Supreme Court clerk, now University of Virginia Law School Professor Pamela Karlan, declares, "Justice Blackmun wrote *Roe* from the heart. These little beasts [she means law clerks] don't have them [she means hearts]."

The Delicate Matter of Discretion

Law clerks often form close personal relationships with the justices they work for and with each other. This factor, as well as the confidential nature of the information they are privy to, resulted in a code of silence that prevented them from revealing much, if anything, about their jobs. The code of silence meant that no clerk, current or past, was willing to part the veil of secrecy that has lent the Court and air of mystery for so long.

But the code of silence is an honor code. Clerks are sworn to secrecy during an initiation tea hosted by the chief justice. The honor code used to be enforced by a legendary 90-second rule, dictating that any clerk seen talking to a reporter for more than 90 seconds would be fired. But the rule was largely legend and acted mostly as a deterrent. Clerks seldom broke ranks — until recently. And recent events have caused the Court to change its confidentiality rules to bind law clerks not just for the term they work at the Supreme Court but forever.

In 1974, investigative reporter Bob Woodward, together with Carl Bernstein, published their *Washington Post* Watergate (see Chapter 4) exposé as *All the President's Men*. Five years later, Woodward — this time in collaboration with Scott Armstrong, published *The Brethren: Inside the Supreme Court*. Woodward and Armstrong had interviewed a number of former — and mainly anonymous — law clerks, and the justices felt they had been betrayed until they learned, after his death in 1985, that Justice Potter Stewart had been Woodward's and Armstrong's chief informant. A decade after *The Brethren* appeared, Edward Lazarus's *Closed Chambers: The First Eyewitness Account of the Epic Struggles Inside the Supreme Court* (1998) was perhaps even more threatening to the relationship between justices and their law clerks.

Lazarus had been a clerk to Harry Blackmun during the Court's 1988–89 term, during which he observed what he recalls as a bloc of conservative law clerks wielding extraordinary power. In one of his most serious charges, Lazarus claims that Justice Anthony Kennedy, who often served as the swing vote on death penalty cases, was easy prey for this group of ideologues who "considered expediting executions a central part of their collective mission." By such means as exaggerating procedural flaws in death penalty appeals, Lazarus says, these clerks could push Kennedy to cast his vote before he realized that his would be the last word on whether an individual lived or died. Lazarus also reports that the vote in *Webster v. Reproductive Health Services* (1989), a decision that restricted access to abortion, was engineered by this same group.

Forty years before Lazarus broke his silence, similar charges about the excess of influence wielded by Supreme Court law clerks were leveled by none other than future Justice William Rehnquist. Writing in the conservative periodical *U.S. News & World Report,* Rehnquist complained that the justices of the Warren Court were delegating too much responsibility to their clerks. Most of these young people were exceedingly liberal, he said, and they "unconsciously" carried their beliefs over to their writings. These beliefs consisted of: "extreme solicitude for the claims of Communists and other criminal defendants, expansion of federal power at the expense of State power, great sympathy toward any government regulation of business — in short, the political philosophy now espoused by the Court under Chief Justice Earl Warren." Rehnquist's view was that the justices of the Warren Court, by abrogating their responsibilities, had adopted an agenda that was not really their own and was outside the American mainstream.

Rehnquist had himself served as law clerk to Justice Robert H. Jackson in the 1952–53 Court term. In 1971, Rehnquist returned to the Supreme Court as an associate justice, and in September 1986, he was confirmed as chief justice. In the winter of that year, *Harvard Law Bulletin* published a piece in which the new chief candidly stated that "only when the case-load is heavy" does he "help by doing the first draft of a case myself." Plainly, in an institution as bound by tradition as the Supreme Court, it's difficult, if not impossible, to change the status quo.

In the *Harvard Law Bulletin,* however, Rehnquist clearly states that justices control not only the outcome of cases, but also the reasoning behind their opinions. This is the argument that supports his claims about the now infamous memo on *Brown v. Board of Education,* "A Random Thought on the Segregation Cases." At both of his confirmation hearings — first as associate and then chief justice — Rehnquist stated that he was describing Justice Jackson's views and not his when he wrote: "I realize that it is an unpopular and unhumanitarian position, for which I have been excoriated by 'liberal' colleagues but I think *Plessy v. Ferguson* [establishing the doctrine of 'separate but equal'] was right and should be affirmed" (see Chapter 4). It may be true that the legal judgment was Jackson's, but the sense of being a conservative surrounded by a sea of liberals plainly reflects Rehnquist's own sentiments as a law clerk. Edward Lazarus's *betrayal* of decorum and discretion were probably provoked by much the same sentiment.

If justices could find more time to do more petition screening and opinion writing, embarrassments such as Rehnquist's memo and Lazarus's book would not be so embarrassing. As Court observer William Domnarski recently quipped: "At the confirmation hearing, the first question a senator should ask a nominee is, 'Do you do your own work?'"

Perks of the Job

Working as a law clerk for a Supreme Court justice must surely be a heady business. Not only do you get to work one-on-one with a legal powerhouse who may also be a legend, you get to know all the other justices pretty well. It's a custom for each justice to lunch at least once each term with all the other justices' clerks. (The clerks pick up the check, though.) And Justice Sandra Day O'Connor has developed a new tradition by cooking lunch for the poor overworked underlings when they come to work on Saturdays. Indeed, lunch seems to be pretty important to law clerks. They even have their own lunchroom at the Court, specially designed to prevent eavesdropping on their weighty conversations about pending matters.

Sports seem to be an important bonding experience, too. Clerks working at the Rehnquist Court have been known to play tennis with the Chief, shoot hoops with Justice Clarence Thomas, go jogging with Justice Anthony Kennedy, and sweat through aerobics with Justice O'Connor. And when their year (or two) of service is done, the law clerks get to make fun of these people! At the end of each term, the clerks caricature the justices in a series of skits. One skit remembered with particular fondness concerns Justice Kennedy's well-known penchant for changing his vote in key cases. Every time Kennedy's name was mentioned, the clerks would play the theme song from the television show "Flipper."

After it's all over, the clerks don't exactly rest on their laurels. Instead, they go on to other significant positions, many of which give them the opportunity to be powerbrokers in public. A number of clerks become Supreme Court justices themselves. For most of the past 20 years, at least three of the sitting justices have been former Supreme Court law clerks, including the current Justices Rehnquist, Stevens, and Breyer. Some former law clerks nab teaching posts at prestigious law schools. Others become media luminaries, like CBS news commentator Laura Ingraham and ABC news president David Weston. Many law clerks go on to other high-level government service. Former secretary of state Warren Christopher was once a Supreme Court law clerk, as was Whitewater investigator Kenneth Starr. When they arrived at the Court, they may have been wet behind the ears, but when they leave, they have the authority of persons who have decided matters that change lives, change nations, and change history. They are the best and the brightest.

Chapter 16

They Also Serve: Other Court Staff

The men and women wearing the black robes and sitting up on the dais get all the attention, but a small army of people also work away behind the velvet curtain that serves as a backdrop to the dramatic pronouncements of the justices. Here's an overview of who they are and what they do. They deserve some acknowledgement.

Statutory Officers: Greasing the Wheels

A permanent staff is indispensable to the continuity and smooth running of the Supreme Court. These are the low-profile, behind-the-scenes personnel who keep the work flow flowing, even when the names on the marquee change. Most of the Court's staff serve at the pleasure of the Court or the chief justice, but in reality, few ever get booted out. Prior to 1935, when the Court moved into the *Marble Palace,* the current Supreme Court building, the Court was housed in temporary quarters, and the justices worked largely out of their own homes, alone. Many of today's Court staff positions did not exist. Now the permanent staff numbers roughly 400. Most of these individuals work for one of the five court officers whose positions were created by statute.

Administrative assistant to the chief justice

The position of administrative assistant to the chief justice was created in 1972. Appointed by the chief justice, the administrative assistant serves at the chief's pleasure and is paid whatever the chief justice wishes to pay (within limits, of course). The primary job of the administrative assistant — who is in turn assisted by other assistants (a small staff and interns) — is to help the chief justice run the place. Aside from judicial responsibilities, just about every other job theoretically falls within this person's ambit.

Internal management of the Court is one of the administrative assistant's primary jobs, of course. But the administrative assistant also acts as the liaison between the judiciary and the other branches of the federal government, as well as state and private organizations having business with the Court. The administrative assistant also serves as the Court's contact with the organizations that administer the rest of the federal judicial system: the Judicial Conference of the United States, the Federal Judicial Center, and the Administrative Office of the U.S. Courts. This is a powerful position that has attracted some talented individuals. Some of the people who have served as administrative assistant to the chief justice are Mark W. Cannon, a political economist and public administrator; Noel J. Augustyn, an official of the Association of American Law Schools; Lawrence H. Averill, Jr., a law school dean; and Robb M. Jones, a litigator.

Clerk of the Court

The position of clerk of the Court was created by statute in 1790 and is one of the two court officer positions created at the inception of the Supreme Court. Appointed by the Court, the clerk of the Court is a busy soul, responsible for all the paperwork that goes in and comes out of the Court. Accordingly, the head clerk (not to be confused with the individual justices' law clerks — see Chapter 15) has the largest staff at the Court, roughly 25 to 30 deputy clerks and other assistants.

The responsibilities that go along with this job include

- Administering the Court's dockets and argument calendars
- Receiving and recording all motions, petitions, briefs, and other documents filed with the Court
- Distributing copies of the above items to the chambers of the individual justices
- Collecting filing fees and toting up Court costs
- Preparing and maintaining the Court's order list and journal, which keeps track of all formal judgments and mandates
- Preparing the judgments and mandates themselves
- Notifying lawyers and lower courts of judgments and other formal actions taken by the Court

✔ Supervising the printing of briefs and appendixes

✔ Requesting and receiving the certified record of the proceedings of each case in lower courts

✔ Overseeing admission of attorneys to the U.S. Supreme Court bar (as well as the occasional unfortunate disbarment)

✔ Dispensing endless advice on procedural matters to lawyers and litigants who seek review of cases by the Court

The clerk also participates in monthly meetings with the other statutory officers of the Court and participates in the Court's formal opening ceremonies. Despite the demands of the job, since 1790, only 19 individuals have served as clerk of the Court. Table 16-1 lists those individuals.

Table 16-1	Clerks of the Supreme Court
John Tucker	1790–1791
Samuel Bayard	1791–1800
Elias B. Caldwell	1800–1825
William Griffith	1826–1827
William T. Carroll	1827–1863
D.W. Middleton	1863–1880
J.H. McKenney	1880–1913
James D. Maher	1913–1921
William R. Stansbury	1921–1927
C. Elmore Cropley	1927–1952
Harold B. Willey	1952–1956
John T. Fey	1956–1958
James R. Browning	1958–1961
John F. Davis	1961–1970
E. Robert Seaver	1970–1972
Michael Rodak, Jr.	1972–1981
Alexander Stevas	1981–1985
Joseph F. Spaniol, Jr.	1985–1991
William K. Suter	1991–

For the first century of its existence, the clerk's office was entirely self-sufficient, with the clerk and all his staff paid out of the filing fees they collected. From 1800 to 1803, the clerk of the Court was actually paid a great deal more than any of the justices, but Congress put a halt to this imbalance. All filing fees, docket fees, and other administrative fees collected by the clerk's office go directly to the U.S. Treasury, while Congress paid the salaries of the clerk and other officers of the Court.

Reporter of Decisions

Until 1816, when Congress set the salary for the Reporter of Decisions, this position was filled by two entrepreneurial businessmen who volunteered to write down, edit, and publish the Court's opinions. The first of these, Alexander J. Dallas, was a journalist, editor, lawyer, and future secretary of the Treasury. He was already publishing the decisions of Pennsylvania courts and selling them privately when the Supreme Court moved to Philadelphia in 1791, providing him with another business opportunity. The series of reporters he named after himself were eventually incorporated into the Court's official *United States Reports,* but "1 Dallas" contains only Pennsylvania state court opinions, as the Supreme Court had yet to decide any cases. "2 Dallas" was a mixed bag of Pennsylvania and U.S. Supreme Court opinions. Dallas continued to report Supreme Court opinion (belatedly) in this fashion until the Court moved to Washington, D.C. in 1800.

In 1800, William Cranch, a judge in the District of Columbia, took over the role of Reporter of Decisions. During the 15 years he served in that position, the justices began supplementing their oral opinions with written opinions in important cases, a practice that helped speed the reporting process. Still, Cranch, who kept his day job as a judge, grew increasingly tardy in delivering a finished product. He was probably only too happy to hand the job off to Henry Wheaton, the first reporter actually appointed by the Court. In 1816, Congress made the appointment official, and the next year, with the Judiciary Act of 1817, agreed to pay the reporter's salary. One condition of this security, however, was that the reporter had to publish opinions within six months of its delivery by the Court. Although 80 copies of each volume of reports were to be sent to the secretary of state for distribution, Wheaton was still permitted to sell copies to the public for $5 each.

Wheaton was succeeded in 1827 by Richard Peters, Jr., a man with a pronounced entrepreneurial streak. In order to increase private sales of Supreme Court reports, Peters decided to revise earlier reports, which he published as *Peter's Condensed Reports* and sold for $36. This practice cut into Wheaton's profits, so he sued, charging copyright violation. The case ended up before the Supreme Court, which ruled in *Wheaton v. Peters* (1834) that the reports were in the public domain and not private property.

The reporter's job can be a thankless one. Benjamin C. Howard, a former congressman who followed Peters as reporter of the Court, incurred the wrath of Justice Peter V. Daniel, even though Howard's volumes were praised for their quality. Howard had inadvertently omitted Daniels's name at the beginning of one of the justice's dissents, and Daniel threatened not to permit more of his dissents to appear in Howard's reports. And Justices Noah H. Swayne and Nathan Clifford complained that John W. Wallace had failed to publish some of their opinions and mangled others.

In between Howard and Wallace, Jeremiah Black, a rejected Supreme Court nominee, served two years as reporter of decisions. He quit the job to become a leader of the Supreme Court bar, where his talents as a lawyer were put to better use.

Wallace was the last reporter to lend his name to his product. In 1874, Congress appropriated funds to publish the Court's opinions under government auspices. This was the advent of *United States Reports* and the end of Wallace's tenure. William T. Otto was the first *anonymous* reporter of decisions. Many of the individuals who have the position since then have also had distinguished public careers — like J.C. Bancroft Davis, who was a legislator, judge, and diplomat — but for the most part their work for the Court is little known outside the precincts of the Marble Palace. Table 16-2 lists the Reporters of Decisions.

Table 16-2	Reporters of Decisions
Alexander J. Dallas	1790–1800
William Cranch	1801–1815
Henry Wheaton	1816–1827
Richard Peters, Jr.	1828–1843
Benjamin C. Howard	1843–1861
Jeremiah B. Black	1861–1863
John W. Wallace	1863–1875
William T. Otto	1875–1883
J.C. Bancroft Davis	1883–1902
Charles Henry Butler	1902–1916
Ernest Knaebel	1916–1944
(Vacancy)	1944–1946

(continued)

Table 16-2 *(continued)*	
Walter Wyatt	1946–1963
Henry Putzel, Jr.	1964–1979
Henry C. Lund	1979–1987
Frank D. Wagner	1987–

Marshal

The office of Supreme Court Marshal was formally created in 1867, when the Court began appointing its own caretakers. From 1794 to 1867, the 12 men who served as marshal of the District of Columbia provided Court security. Today, although the marshal continues to oversee a staff of Court police, he or she also supervises maintenance workers and messengers, escorts visiting dignitaries, and handles the money (payroll, procurements, disbursements, and so on).

In earlier times, the marshal of the Court also served papers. Frank K. Green, who was marshal from 1915 to 1938, for example, was obliged to serve J. Pierpont Morgan with a subpoena for Martha Washington's will, which Morgan's father had allegedly stolen. Today, the marshal delegates process serving to U.S. marshals. The job still has its dramatic moments, though. When the Court holds public sessions, it is the marshal who gets to say those wonderful words: "Oyez, oyez, oyez. All persons having business before the honorable, the Supreme Court of the United States, are admonished to draw near and give their attention, for the Court is now sitting. God save the United States and this honorable Court." At such times, dressed in formal wear, he or she — the current marshal is a woman — also has the perk of refusing admission to people who are improperly dressed for the occasion.

ANECDOTE

Marshal's aides to the rescue

The marshal has aides, prelaw or night law school students who in 1973 replaced the corps of younger Court pages. Marshal's aides pass messages, fill water glasses, and perform other unusual services. Justice Harry Blackmun recalled how on his first day on the high bench Justice Byron White "was leaning over to me, whispering. 'Harry! Harry, where's your spittoon?' He snapped a finger — softly — for a page. *'Get the Justice his spittoon!'*" Spittoons, which have a long and honored history at the Court, are now used as wastepaper baskets.

Librarian

The post of Supreme Court librarian was created by Congress in 1887, but it remained part of the marshal's office until 1948. (The marshal still has responsibility for the library's collections, as part of the Court's physical facilities.) The librarian is appointed by the Court. Together with staff of roughly 25, he or she is responsible for acquiring and maintaining an extensive collection of legal books and periodicals, as well as a multitude of databases. Access to the collections is limited to the justices and their staff, members of the Supreme Court bar, members of Congress, and the legal offices of the executive branch. Members of the public, however, can make special arrangements to research specific topics.

The Court did not have a library of its own until 1832, when Congress authorized its own library to donate the 2,011 law books in its collection. For the next 55 years, the clerk of the Court oversaw the library. The Court's collection circulated during that period, but the clerk was strict about fines: Overdue books cost the borrower $1 a day, and if a book was lost, the person who had checked it out had to pay twice its replacement cost. Now the rules are stricter: No borrowing allowed.

Support Staff: Holding Up Their End

In addition to the Court officers created by Congress, the Supreme Court is staffed by employees of newly-created or expanded offices. These offices report to the Chief Justice.

Legal office

The Court's legal office was created in 1973. Unlike the justices' law clerks, who change every year or two, the lawyers who make up the legal office typically stay for several years. Serving as in-house counsel, they provide advice on unusual procedural questions connected with petitions for certiorari or requests for extraordinary relief. They also help the justices with their federal circuit court work and do specialized research.

Public information office

The public information office, created in 1935, grew out of the Court's growing awareness of its need for the Fourth Estate. That year, the Associated Press misreported the decision in the controversial *Gold Bond Cases,* upholding Congress's power to combat gold hoarding by requiring holders of the precious metal to surrender it to the Treasury in exchange for devalued paper currency. Discussion among the Court clerk, the chief justice, and the Washington press corps afterward resulted in the creation of a *press clerk* who would act as a liaison between the Court and the media. With the exception of the first press clerk, all the individuals who have held this post — renamed *public information officer* in 1973 — have been journalists.

The public information office responds to questions from the media and the public. The officer, who is assisted by a small staff, is the public spokesperson for all Court matters other than the interpretation of decisions. The office does, however, release slip opinions and orders of the Court immediately after they're announced in open court and makes special announcements about the Court or the justices. The Court's schedule is posted in the public information office. The office also maintains a press room and broadcast booths, which are occupied by several of the major news organizations.

Curator's office

The curator's office was created in 1974 to oversee the Court's historical papers and collections of material such as photographs — some of which you find in this book. The curator and a small staff of permanent assistants and interns also fields questions from the public concerning Court history, provides tours of the Court building, and develops exhibitions concerning Court history.

The curator's office often works closely with the Supreme Court Historical Society, a nonprofit organization begun in 1974 by Chief Justice Warren Burger. According to the Society's mission statement, its job is "conducting public and educational programs, publishing books and other materials, supporting historical research, and collecting antiques and artifacts related to the Court's history."

Data systems office

The Court created a data systems office in 1985 as part of its effort to move into the information age. Before 1969, the Court did not have so much as a photocopier. And even now, I have my doubts about how far modern technology has penetrated into the Court. When I was in touch with the curator's office about some of the illustrations for this book, I discovered that the curator does not have access to e-mail.

Still, each of the justices now has his or her own separate word-processing and printing system. And apparently these systems are connected in some sort of network, because when one of the justices wants to share a piece of work with another, he or she can do so electronically. Printing, which used to be done by Linotype in the Court basement, is now automated. Still, change comes slowly to this institution, where spittoons and quill pens still play a role, but e-mail is unavailable.

Office of Budget and Personnel

This newly created office is responsible for two important functions: hiring and firing and controlling the purse strings. Until very recently these jobs were performed by the administrative assistant to the chief justice.

Part VII
The Part of Tens

The 5th Wave — By Rich Tennant

Okay, let's finish this petition and then call it quits. I think a few of the Justices were hoping for an early recess.

In this part . . .

This part of the book is like dessert, and you may want to consume it first, before moving on to something more substantial. Here, you find my list of top ten Supreme Court hits and a corresponding catalog of its ten worst decisions. A swift summary of how the Court has changed the country gives you just a taste of how important a role the Supreme Court plays in your own life.

Chapter 17

The Court's Ten Best Decisions

In This Chapter

▶ Reviewing the Supreme Court's top ten hits

▶ Understanding what's behind those familiar case names

You may recognize many of the case names on this list. I've listed the decisions chronologically, as that's the way the law works — each new decision builds on others that have gone before. While I have picked cases which are universally regarded as historically significant, my picks are, of course, to some extent subjective.

Marbury v. Madison (1803)

This decision empowered the U.S. Supreme Court. The case arose when William Marbury, who was to have been appointed a justice of the peace by the outgoing administration of John Adams, was denied his commission by order of the newly elected president, Thomas Jefferson. The justices voted unanimously that although Marbury was owed his commission, the Court could not deliver it because the legislative act that granted it was an unconstitutional enlargement of the Court's own power. What is important about *Marbury*, however, is that in Chief Justice John Marshall's opinion for the Court, he firmly established two things:

▶ The Supreme Court's power is based primarily on the Constitution and only secondarily on legislation.

▶ The Supreme Court has the final say about whether laws are constitutional.

McCulloch v. Maryland (1819)

This decision established the Constitution as the supreme law of the land. At issue in this case was the validity of a national bank, chartered by Congress in 1816. Many states opposed the bank as an unlawful intrusion into a realm they thought was theirs alone, and they demonstrated their unhappiness by taxing branches of the First National Bank of the United States that existed within their boundaries. The justices voted unanimously that the states did not have the power to tax the national bank. In his opinion for the Court, Chief Justice John Marshall stated the *Necessary and Proper Clause* of the Constitution granted the federal government the right to charter a national bank as an exercise of the power "To make all Laws which shall be necessary and proper for carrying into Execution the . . . Powers vested by this Constitution in the Government of the United States . . . ." This language, the Court said, trumped that of the Tenth Amendment, which gave all powers not delegated to the federal government by the Constitution to the states.

Gibbons v. Ogden (1824)

This decision gave the authority to regulate commerce between states to the federal government alone. The state of New York had granted Robert Fulton, designer of the first American steamships, the exclusive right to operate his ships in New York waterways. Fulton's monopoly was challenged by others who had federal licenses to run competing ships between New York and New Jersey. Writing for a unanimous Court, Chief Justice John Marshall struck down Fulton's monopoly, arguing that it was the federal government's right to regulate any sort of commerce when it affected more than one state. *Gibbons* spurred the growth of American business by clarifying the regulatory environment. More than a century later, it would be used to help racial desegregation in areas such as transportation.

Brown v. Board of Education (1954)

This decision sparked the civil rights movement. *Brown* was actually a collection of several school desegregation cases. In his opinion for a unanimous Court, Chief Justice Earl Warren held that separate schools for black and white children are inherently unequal and violate the Fourteenth Amendment's guarantee of equal protection under the laws. *Brown* overturned *Plessy v. Ferguson* (1896), a Supreme Court decision that had made "separate but equal" the law of the land for more than half a century.

Baker v. Carr (1962)

This decision opened the door to the *apportionment revolution,* which broadened the voting franchise so that previously underrepresented minorities could have more say in how they were governed. Always before, the Supreme Court had declared cases questioning the size and shape of voting districts to be *political questions* they had no power to decide. In *Baker,* with Justice William J. Brennan writing for the 6-2 majority, the Court found that the Fourteenth Amendment's guarantee of equal protection under the laws justified intervention by federal courts. The decision gave rise to other cases, which soon resulted in nationwide redrawing of federal congressional districts and state voting districts.

Gideon v. Wainwright (1963)

This decision empowered poor people, giving them more and better access to the law. Clarence Gideon, a homeless and largely illiterate man, was convicted of a crime by the state of Florida, which also denied him a lawyer. Part of what makes *Gideon* so compelling is the fact that Gideon handwrote a petition to the Supreme Court from his prison cell, asking the Court to look into the circumstances of his conviction. The Court granted his petition and unanimously held that the Fourteenth Amendment requires states to provide counsel to criminal defendants who cannot afford to pay for their own lawyers. Gideon was granted a new trial, and he was acquitted.

Miranda v. Arizona (1966)

This decision is the high water mark of the *due process revolution* of the mid-20th century, in which states were forced to observe Fourteenth Amendment guarantees that life, liberty, and property could not be taken away "without due process of law." Ernesto Miranda was a drifter with an eighth grade education when he was detained and questioned by police who suspected him of committing a rape-kidnapping. Initially, Miranda denied any involvement, but after two hours of interrogation, he confessed. His confession was later used to convict him. A closely divided Supreme Court ruled the confession inadmissible as evidence because it had been obtained without due process. Since then, police have been required to read criminal suspects their *Miranda rights* before detaining them. The object of this exercise — which is based on the premise that criminal defendants are presumed innocent until proven guilty — is to treat even the lowliest citizen with respect and dignity.

New York Times v. United States (1971)

This decision, in what is also known as the *Pentagon Papers case,* greatly increased the media's power as government watchdogs. Daniel Ellsberg, a former State Department official and antiwar activist, got hold of a set of classified documents concerning the government's prosecution of the Vietnam War and leaked it to the press. *The New York Times* and other newspapers began printing excerpts, and the administration of Richard Nixon tried to halt publication. The justices voted 6-3 not to grant the government an order permanently banning further publication, stating that the there was a "heavy presumption against the constitutional validity" of prior *restraint,* an attempt to stop publication of information not yet released. This crucial press freedom case also served to undermine the authority of the Nixon administration.

Roe v. Wade (1973)

This decision gave a woman's right to choose whether to abort her child or carry it full term protection under the Constitution. Norma McCovey, a pregnant, unmarried Texan, was the "Jane Roe" who challenged her state's abortion ban. The case was highly controversial and required rehearing before the Court. Justice Harry Blackmun, who wrote the opinion of the Court for the 7-2 majority, had to write it twice. After first hearing the case, Blackmun's opinion declared the Texas law invalid because of its vagueness. When this argument failed to convince a majority of the justices, the case was reargued. Blackmun's second try upheld a woman's right to choose based on a constitutionally protected right to privacy. *Roe* has proven to be the most divisive decision in recent Court history, setting off a running battle between liberals and conservatives, between those who support the *right to choose* and those who support a *right to life.* The decision has been substantially curtailed by subsequent Supreme Court decisions, but not overturned. Largely because of *Roe,* confirmations of Supreme Court justices since 1973 have become royal battles.

United States v. Nixon (1974)

This decision led to the resignation under threat of impeachment of President Richard Nixon. After the 1972 discovery of a break-in at Democratic Party headquarters in the Watergate Hotel in Washington, D.C., Nixon appointed Archibald Cox as special prosecutor to investigate the case. When congressional hearings into the burglary revealed that Nixon had secretly tape recorded conversations in the Oval Office, Cox asked him to turn the tapes over. Nixon refused and ordered the attorney general to fire Cox. When both he and his deputy refused to obey the President's order, Nixon turned to the solicitor general, Robert Bork, and Bork did the deed. But a second special prosecutor, Leon Jaworski, was appointed, and he obtained a federal court order demanding that the President surrender the tapes. Nixon refused again, claiming executive privilege and citing the doctrine of *separation of powers,* which he claimed gave the federal judiciary no authority to intervene in his dispute with the special prosecutor, another member of the executive branch. The Supreme Court unanimously rejected Nixon's argument, citing the conditional nature of executive privilege. Once again, the Court's power of *judicial review* gave it the power to say what the law is — in this case, to determine the boundaries of executive privilege. When Nixon turned over the tapes, they were found to contain evidence that he at least knew of the attempt to cover up the Watergate break-in and was, at a minimum, guilty of obstruction of justice. Less than three weeks later, Nixon resigned, becoming the first president ever to do so. The imperial presidency was dead.

Chapter 18

The Court's Ten Worst Decisions

· ·

In This Chapter

▶ Reviewing some of the Supreme Court's biggest miscalculations

▶ Understanding that even the smartest people can make really dumb mistakes

· ·

Some of the cases listed in this chapter are universally regarded as major misjudgments. Others reflect my own opinions about bad decisions the Court has made. In fact, some of the cases I have put in the category of hits (see Chapter 17) — like *Roe v. Wade* (1973) — would almost certainly end up on other peoples' list of misses. It's hard to choose which of these decisions is worst, so I've opted for chronological order.

Scott v. Sandford (The Dred Scott Case) (1857)

Many legal commentators, historians, and ordinary folks agree that *Scott v. Sandford* started the Civil War. To be sure, the war had been simmering on the back burner almost from the inception of the republic. The Supreme Court's declaration that African-Americans are not citizens — that they are, in fact, property — certainly deepened the divisions between North and South and between abolitionists and slaveholders, hastening hostilities along. If pressed to choose the Supreme Court's darkest hour, most would agree this decision is it.

Bradwell v. Illinois (1873)

Myra Bradwell was a smart and ambitious woman who had studied law in her husband's law office before going on to found *Chicago Legal News,* the Midwest's leading legal publication. And yet, when she applied to the state for bar admission, she was rejected for the simple reason that she was a woman. Bradwell's treatment in the U.S. Supreme Court was no better. Bradwell claimed that her right to practice law was one of the privileges guaranteed by the Fourteenth Amendment. Not so, said the Court, and to add insult to injury, Justice Joseph P. Bradley wrote in concurrence, "The paramount destiny and mission of woman are to fulfill the noble and benign offices of wife and mother. This is the law of the Creator." It would be another century before the Court would begin to address gender discrimination.

Minor v. Happersett (1875)

In this case, the U.S. Supreme Court declared that although American women may be citizens of the nation, they are not full citizens. When Virginia Louise Minor, "a native born, free, white citizen of the United States, and of the State of Missouri, over the age of twenty-one years," tried to register to vote in the 1872 presidential election, she was turned back. Writing for a unanimous Court, Chief Justice Morrison Waite stated flatly, "Certainly, if the courts can consider any question settled, it is this one. . . . the Constitution, when it conferred citizenship, did not necessarily confer the right of suffrage." Women would not gain the vote until the Nineteenth Amendment was ratified in 1920, and *Minor* was not overruled until 1964 when the Court made "one person, one vote" a reality with the voting district reapportionment decision *Reynolds v. Sims.*

Plessy v. Ferguson (1896)

This case made *separate but equal* the law of the land. Homer Plessy, an African-American man who appeared to be white, was a volunteer plaintiff for the Citizens' Committee to Test the Constitutionality of the Separate Car Act, a Louisiana statute requiring racially segregated train compartments. Plessy was able to buy a ticket for the *whites only* car, but he made sure that the conductor knew that he was of mixed race. When asked to move to the *colored only* car, Plessy refused and was arrested. In upholding the state law Plessy violated, the Supreme Court ensured that racial segregation persisted. *Plessy* was not overturned for more than half a century, when the landmark case of *Brown v. Board of Education* (1954) set the civil rights movement on fire.

Lochner v. New York (1905)

If any case decided by the Supreme Court is a perversion of justice, *Lochner v. New York* is it. At issue in *Lochner* was a state law limiting bakery workers' work hours to 60 per week. The Supreme Court struck the law down as a violation of the Fourteenth Amendment's guarantee of freedom of contract. There was, in fact, no such guarantee in the Fourteenth Amendment, which was passed in the wake of the Civil War to overturn the 1857 *Dred Scott* decision and ensure racial equality.

Before *Lochner,* the Court had already twisted the Fourteenth Amendment's Due Process Clause into a concept known as *substantive due process,* turning a human rights guarantee into a protection for commercial interests. But because it created a nonexistent fundamental right, *Lochner* is remembered as the high water (or low water) mark of the Court's dedication to a *laissez faire* form of justice, which let the market decide who wins and who loses. The case is also remembered for Oliver Wendell Holmes's blistering dissenting opinion, perhaps the most celebrated one of all time. Insisting that the kind of social Darwinism popular at the time was not to be found in the Constitution, Holmes thundered, "The Fourteenth Amendment does not enact Mr. Herbert Spencer's Social Statics."

Hammer v. Dagenhart (1918)

Hammer should have been an easy case. Instead the Court split 5–4, striking down a federal child labor law. The 1916 Keating-Owen Child Labor Act was a product of the Progressive Era, when government started to rein in some of the excesses of commerce. Dagenhart, who worked at a cotton mill alongside his two sons, sued the mill as well as Hammer, the attorney general for his region, who was trying to prevent the act from being enforced. He won both in the district court and at the Supreme Court. This outcome pushed the clock back to a time before labor unions had any power and business interests controlled the nation. In a passionate dissent, Oliver Wendell Holmes wrote, "I should have thought that if we were to introduce our own moral conceptions where, in my opinion, they do not belong, this was preeminently a case for upholding the exercise of all its powers by the United States." Holmes's plea for what was manifestly the right thing to do was not heeded for another 23 years.

Adkins v. Children's Hospital (1923)

At issue in *Adkins* was a federal minimum wage and maximum hour law governing women working in the District of Columbia. A hospital in the District sued the board created by the law to oversee its enforcement. Congressional intent in passing the law in 1918 was to protect the health and morals of women who had been forced into unsanitary and dangerous living conditions and prostitution because they could not make a living wage. As in *Lochner v.*

New York (1905), the Court cited the fundamental *right* to freedom of contract as a reason for striking down the law. *Adkins* marked another low point in the Court's history, combining the distorted logic of *substantive due process* with the power of *judicial review* to invalidate a federal law designed to promote public welfare.

Buck v. Bell (1927)

Most legal critics agree that the eminent Justice Oliver Wendell Holmes stumbled badly in *Buck v. Bell*. A Virginia law mandating sterilization of mentally impaired individuals was an unfortunate byproduct of the Progressive Era's push for thoroughgoing social improvement through government intervention. The Virginia law was actually a thinly veiled attempt to promote eugenics, or racial purity, through selective reproduction. The brainchild of Albert Priddy, superintendent at the State Colony of Epileptics and Feeble-Minded in Lynchburg, Virginia, the law legalized what had been standard practice during Priddy's tenure.

Carrie Buck, an 18-year-old with the mental age of 9, was committed to Priddy's Colony when she became pregnant as the result of rape. Her mother, who was also mentally retarded, was confined to the institution as well. After the birth of Carrie's daughter (who was apparently also mentally impaired), Priddy recommended she be sterilized because she was both feebleminded and a "moral delinquent." He made hers a test case, telling the trial court that the whole Buck family was part of a "shiftless, ignorant, and worthless class of anti-social whites" that inhabited the South. When Carrie Buck's case reached the U.S. Supreme Court, the Court accepted the eugenics arguments used against her. Writing for the 8-1 majority, Holmes endorsed these popular ideas, stating that if the country could afford to send its "best citizens" off to fight in a world war, it could demand a "lesser" sacrifice from those "who sap the strength" of society. Slamming shut the window, Holmes flatly declared, "Three generations of imbeciles are enough." The eugenics practiced by Nazi Germany just a couple of decades later demonstrated just how blinded even the great Justice Holmes could be by prejudice.

Korematsu v. United States (1944)

After the Japanese bombed Pearl Harbor, the military forced Japanese Americans to move away from the West Coast. In essence, they were given no choice but to report to assembly centers, from which they were shipped off to inland internment camps for the duration of World War II. Fred Korematsu, an American descended from Japanese immigrants, disobeyed orders by moving from the San Francisco Bay area to a nearby town, changing his name and undergoing plastic surgery in order to pose as a Mexican-American. He was found out, arrested, convicted, and sent to a relocation camp in Utah.

A majority of the justices who heard Fred Korematsu's case never stopped to question whether Japanese-Americans actually posed a security threat to America's prosecution of the war. Despite Hugo Black's assertion that "all legal restrictions which curtail the civil rights of a single racial group are immediately suspect," this champion of individual liberties wrote the opinion of the Court upholding Korematsu's conviction. In 1980, Congress finally authorized payments of $20,000 each to survivors of the internment camps.

Bowers v. Hardwick (1986)

This decision cast serious doubt on the constitutional right to privacy by ruling that consensual homosexual acts between adults in the privacy of home could be outlawed by state government. Michael Hardwick, a gay Atlanta bartender, was arrested for performing oral sex with another man in his own bedroom. Although Georgia's antisodomy laws could have resulted in a felony conviction, the district attorney did not press charges against Hardwick. But the D.A. also did not drop the charge, and Hardwick challenged the law's constitutionality in federal court.

In his opinion for the one-vote majority, Justice Byron White distinguished *Bowers* from the Court's earlier privacy decisions, saying that cases such as *Griswold v. Connecticut* (1965) involved "family, marriage, or procreation" and had "no connection" with homosexual sex. He also declared that *Bowers* differed from *Stanley v. Georgia,* a 1969 case upholding the right to possess and consume obscene materials at home. While the latter was protected by the First Amendment, White said, not every sexually related activity in the home received this protection.

In 1990, Justice Lewis Powell, who had provided the crucial *swing vote* in *Bowers,* told a group of law students that he had "probably made a mistake" in voting the way he did. He still maintained, however, that *Bowers* was "a frivolous case" because no one had been prosecuted. Gay men and women across the country concerned about their civil rights undoubtedly agree with the first assertion — but not the second.

Chapter 19

Ten Ways the Court Has Changed the Course of History

• •

In This Chapter

▶ Putting the Court's influence in perspective

▶ Highlighting some low points in constitutional interpretation

▶ Connecting national strength with judicial rulings

▶ Understanding how the Supreme Court has dealt with death and taxes

• •

*I*t's a truism that the decisions of the Supreme Court change individual fates. What people sometimes fail to appreciate is the Court's ability to change the entire nation. Not all these cases involved life-or-death matters, but many of them did. One even helped ignite a war. And while you may think that politics is strictly the business of politicians, some of these cases prove otherwise. And, oh yes, where would the nation be without the IRS? America has the Supreme Court to thank for that, too.

The Balance of Powers

In one of the cases decided in the early years of the Supreme Court, *Marbury v. Madison* (1803), the Supreme Court breathed life into the concept of *judicial review*. Judicial review is a power peculiar to the Court that does not appear in the Constitution. Article I and II, which set out the powers and precincts of, respectively, the legislative and executive branches, are quite detailed and specific. Although the Founding Fathers clearly intended the federal government to consist of three branches, Article III, the section of the Constitution devoted to the judicial branch, is pretty sketchy.

In *Marbury v. Madison*, the "great chief justice," John Marshall, empowered the Court by giving it the last word: "It is emphatically the province and duty of the judicial department to say what the law is." Congress and the president may set the national agenda, but the country does not move forward until the Supreme Court gives its okay. For more about *Marbury,* see Chapters 1 and 5.

Presidential Elections

Twice in the history of the United States a presidential election has in essence
been decided by the Supreme Court. The first time the Court got tangled up
in such a mess was in 1876, when the Democrat Samuel Tilden won the
popular vote, but was one electoral vote shy of the minimum for election. A
number of electoral votes were still contested. Ordinarily, Congress would be
able to sort out election disputes by themselves, but in 1876, Congress was
itself divided between Democrats and Republicans. The legislators decided
to set up a commission consisting of five senators, five congressmen, and
five Supreme Court justices. The Republican controlled Senate picked
three Republicans and two Democrats to sit on the commission, while the
Democrat controlled House selected three Democrats and two Republicans.
The congressmen chose four of the justices who were to sit on the commission:
two Republicans and two Democrats who were to select a fifth, nonpartisan
justice. In essence, it came down to that one justice.

At the time, only one justice on the Court was truly neutral, but David Davis,
apparently unable to stand the pressure, quit the commission and the Court.
The balance of the justices was all Republican, so the most seemingly nonpartisan Republican on the Court became the commission's fifteenth man.
To no one's surprise, the election was handed to the Republican presidential
candidate, Rutherford B. Hayes. For more about the Hayes-Tilden contest,
see Chapter 1.

And once again, when an election proved too close to call, the Supreme Court
got to pick who would become president. The election of 2000 was so close
that everything came down to one state, Florida, where allegations of vote
fraud, voter intimidation, and ballot rigging led to a flurry of lawsuits
between the Republican George W. Bush and the Democrat Al Gore. Perhaps
inevitably, one of these cases ended up in the Supreme Court. By stopping
the vote recount in Florida in *Bush v. Gore* (2000), the Court essentially
handed the election victory to Bush on a silver platter. (See Chapter 1 for a
more in-depth analysis.) Many felt the Court never should have taken the
case. Given the conservative orientation of the Rehnquist Court, it once
again seemed almost inevitable that the election would be handed to the
Republican candidate — and it was.

Presidential Impeachments

The Court didn't have much to do with the first presidential impeachment,
that of Andrew Johnson in 1868. The Court did, however, play a decisive role
in another aborted impeachment, as well as in the only other presidential
impeachment to date. Impeachment doesn't necessarily lead to conviction;

impeachment in the House only leads to a trial in the Senate. Ironically, perhaps, it was the impeachment that never happened that resulted in the only presidential resignation in American history.

The aborted impeachment was that of Richard Nixon, who on August 9, 1974, became the only American president ever to resign while in office. He did so under a threat of impeachment that was directly related to a decision handed down by the Court three weeks earlier. In *United States v. Nixon,* the Supreme Court ruled that the president could not cite executive privilege to shield himself from demands for evidence in a criminal proceeding. Nixon was forced by the Court to turn over tapes he had made in the Oval Office, which clearly demonstrated his involvement with at least the coverup of the Watergate fiasco, a bungled burglary linked to political shenanigans. For more about Watergate, see Chapter 1.

The second presidential impeachment occurred in 1997, when Democrat Bill Clinton was impeached by the Republican-controlled Senate. Most felt it was a political setup. Many felt Clinton deserved what he got. What he got was the result of the Supreme Court's decision, in *Clinton v. Jones,* decided May 27, 1997, that no executive immunity prevented Paula Jones from proceeding with her sexual harassment suit against Clinton while he was still in office. Although Clinton's Senate impeachment trial did not occur until February 2, 1999, in allowing Jones's suit against him to go forward, the Court created an opening for Kenneth Starr. Starr, the independent counsel supposedly investigating a lousy real estate deal known as Whitewater, used Clinton's videotaped January 1998 deposition in the Jones case to include allegations of perjury in a damning report he made to Congress that September. The deposition also gave Starr a legitimate reason to investigate Clinton's sex life. Once Monica Lewinsky's intimate involvement with the President became public knowledge, Clinton had lost his battle.

Civil War

When the Supreme Court decided *Scott v. Sandford* (also called the *Dred Scott Case;* see Chapter 11 for more information) in 1857, passions over states' rights and slavery were already running high. The slaveholding status of new states was such a hot topic that a proxy war had already been fought in what became known as *Bleeding Kansas* between abolitionists and those favoring slavery. Another preliminary battle was waged on the floor of the U.S. Senate, where the abolitionist Senator Charles Sumner was savagely beaten by Congressman Preston S. Brooks over alleged insults to Brooks's South Carolina kinsman, Senator Andrew P. Butler.

Dred Scott was a Missouri slave who had accompanied his master into the free territory of Wisconsin, where he spent several years. The Missouri

Compromise of 1820 had banished slavery from Wisconsin, and when Scott returned to Missouri, where the law was "once free, always free," he sued for his own freedom. After the Missouri courts found him still a slave, Scott took his case to the U.S. Supreme Court. In a tortured decision delivered in nine separate opinions, the justices made three inflammatory rulings:

- Scott was not free.
- Slaves are property, not citizens.
- The Missouri Compromise was unconstitutional.

Before *Dred Scott* the Civil War was probably inevitable; afterward, it was unavoidable. In 1861, the nation split in two.

Segregation and Integration

In *Plessy v. Ferguson,* decided in 1896, the Supreme Court put its stamp on the Jim Crow laws that had created what amounted to apartheid in Southern states. By declaring that "separate but equal" was the law of the land, the Court legitimized African-Americans' second class status in American society.

"Separate but equal" was a fraud, an impossibility, as the Court recognized more than a half century later in overturning *Plessy* in *Brown v. Board of Education* (1954). (See Chapter 12 for more information.) *Brown* was a school desegregation case, but the effects of the decision radiated outward, so that for the first time in its history America became — legally, at any rate — a fully racially integrated society. *Brown II*, handed down the following year, ordered school desegregation to proceed "with all deliberate speed." The fact that school busing remains a contentious issue today is one indication of how long it takes to undo two centuries of segregation.

Voting Rights

The Fifteenth Amendment, passed in the wake of the Civil War, gave African-American males the right to vote. Through a variety of means — poll taxes, literacy tests, and so on — bigoted whites nonetheless prevented black citizens from exercising their voting franchise. In a series of cases that ended with *Terry v. Adams* in 1953, the Supreme Court put an end to practices that robbed blacks of their right to cast a ballot. Even then, however, their votes often counted for little. State legislatures had drawn election district boundaries so that areas with large concentrations of black voters had fewer congressional representatives than those with sparse, often largely white populations. With its decision in *Baker v. Carr* (1962), the Supreme Court embraced the principle of "one person, one vote" — that is, equal representation of equal numbers of people. The so-called *Reapportionment Revolution* had begun, requiring the nation's political map to be redrawn. For more about the Reapportionment Revolution, see Chapter 9.

The Death Penalty

Throughout most of America's history, capital punishment has been legal. Most students of the Constitution believe that the Eighth Amendment's ban on "cruel and unusual punishment" referred to punishment such as physical torture, where the punishment is disproportionate to the crime. Furthermore, they point to the Fifth and Fourteenth Amendments' Due Process Clauses, which declare that the state cannot "be deprived of life . . . without due process of law," as authorization for the death penalty.

Nevertheless, in *Furman v. Georgia* (1972), the Supreme Court declared a moratorium on capital punishment. At the time, the death penalty was legal in 39 states. The Court majority did not find the death penalty cruel and unusual punishment per se, but because state execution procedures were ambiguous and arbitrary, the Court nullified all the state laws authorizing capital punishment.

Four years later, in *Gregg v. Georgia,* the Court reversed itself. By this time, Georgia and other death penalty states had in place safeguards such as mandatory review by their own supreme courts of all death sentences. And by this time, the U.S. Supreme Court had experienced some personnel changes, so that what had once been a 5-4 vote against the death penalty had become a 7-2 vote in its favor. Two of the justices who sat on both the *Furman* and the *Gregg* Courts, William J. Brennan and Thurgood Marshall, remained unalterably opposed to the death penalty for the remainder of their time on the high bench. One other, Harry Blackmun, announced after his retirement that while he previously had thought the death penalty was constitutional, he had changed his mind.

Recently, a few more of the sitting justices have vaguely indicated that they shared these sentiments. With the public debate about capital punishment heating up again owing to refinements in the reliability of DNA evidence it was perhaps inevitable that the Court would revisit the issue of capital punishment. At the end of its 2001 term, the Rehnquist Court issued two opinions that curtailed states' latitude in imposing the death penalty. In *Atkins v. Virginia* (2002), the Court voted 6-3 to ban execution of mentally retarded criminals as unconstitutional cruel and unusual punishment. Then, in *Ring v. Arizona* (2002), the Court declared that juries, not judges, must determine sentencing in death penalty cases. This ruling will almost certainly impact death row inmates previously sentenced by judges.

Abortion

Hands down, abortion was the most contentious issue of the late 20th century. When the Supreme Court legalized abortion in *Roe v. Wade* in 1973, it did so on the basis of a right that is not spelled out in the Constitution: privacy. (For more about Roe, see Chapter 8.) Some thought the majority's reasoning was all wet; others thought its decision was long overdue. As the Court's — and the country's — political orientation had shifted farther and farther to the right, the justices have whittled away at abortion to the point that a woman's right to choose is hanging by a thread. All it will take to reverse *Roe,* it often seems, is the appointment of just one more conservative justice — one like, say, Antonin Scalia or Clarence Thomas.

During the 2000 presidential election campaign, George W. Bush pointed to these men as the embodiment of the types of justices he would appoint to the Court. Thanks largely to the Supreme Court, Bush won the election. (See the section "Presidential Elections," earlier in this chapter.) In the next few years, at least a few members of the Court will doubtless retire. John Paul Stevens, now the most liberal justice on the Court, is also at 82 its oldest member. But Chief Justice William Rehnquist, the person who has arguably done the most to shape today's conservative Court, has been struggling with serious health problems for some time. And then there are the two female members of the Court: Sandra Day O'Connor, who has frequently been a swing vote in abortion cases, and Ruth Bader Ginsburg, who was known before her judicial appointment as "the Thurgood Marshall of gender-equality law" — that is, a crusader for women's rights. Since taking seats on the high bench, both O'Connor and Ginsburg have fought off cancer, but their public battles against their mortality have inevitably led to speculation about both women's retirement. For a host of reasons, abortion remains on the front burner at the Court.

Corporations

Where would America be without free enterprise? Most would agree that the United States would not be the last superpower left standing after the Cold War were it not for the nation's long mastery of the capitalist system. America owes this mastery, in large measure, to a decision handed down by the Supreme Court in 1837, *Charles River Bridge v. Warren Bridge*. In *Dartmouth College v. Woodward* (1819), the Marshall Court had protected the rights of investors by extending constitutional protection to private, profit-making corporations. But in his masterful opinion in the *Charles River Bridge* case, Chief Justice Roger Brooke Taney fashioned a compromise between government business regulation and private industry that served the public interest by preventing business monopolies from stifling new ventures. It was a visionary opinion, which foresaw that new technologies demand adoption. *Charles River Bridge* made it possible for old technology to make way for new without destroying incentives for private investment. This man was, in his own way, a genius.

Income Tax

The debate about the constitutionality of an income tax began during the early days of the republic and reached a crescendo in the 1890s. The issue of income tax raised two questions:

- Is it a *direct tax* or an *indirect tax?*
- If it's an indirect tax, can it be applied *uniformly?*

The problems associated with answering these questions arise from a vague constitutional ban on "Capitation, or other direct, Tax . . . unless in Proportion to the Census." The government first asked the Court to define a *direct tax* in the 1796 case *Hylton v. United States.* At issue in *Hylton* was a national tax on carriages, which the Court found to be an indirect excise tax that did not require apportionment by population. Only so-called *head taxes* and taxes on land had to be levied on the states in proportion to their respective populations.

And there matters uncomfortably rested until the Court handed down its decisions in the *Income Tax Cases* in 1895. The government had imposed a federal income tax in 1862 to help finance the Civil War. At first individuals with annual incomes over $600 were taxed, but the threshold rose to $2,000 in 1872. The tax, and the law authorizing it, expired in 1872. Nobody kicked up much of a fuss about what was essentially a war tax.

But in 1883, the nation entered a severe economic depression, and the need for a national income tax became pressing once more. In 1894, Congress passed the country's first peacetime income tax law, and a case testing its constitutionality was quickly manufactured. The Court generally refuses to hear cases in which the two sides are in collusion, but the issue of income tax was considered so pressing that — to its everlasting regret — the Court made an exception.

The Court handed down two separate decisions in *Pollock v. Farmers' Loan & Trust Co.,* both rendered in 1895. In the first, the Court ruled against a federal tax on state and municipal bonds. That ruling wasn't controversial and still stands. In the second case, however, the Court struck down the income tax as an unconstitutional, unapportioned direct tax.

This ill-advised decision had immediate — and apparently neverending — political consequences. The conservative wing of the Democratic Party, galvanized by the Court's assertion that a federal income tax threatened private property, took control at the 1896 Democratic convention. The Democratic candidate, William Jennings Bryan, embraced a populist platform that included introduction of a graduated income tax. Bryan lost to the Republican candidate William McKinley in 1896 and again in 1900. The Republicans would, in fact, remain in power — interrupted by a brief Democratic revival from 1912 to 1920 — until the Great Depression of the 1930s.

When McKinley was assassinated in 1901, he was succeeded by his vice president, Theodore Roosevelt. Once in the White House, Roosevelt began backing a progressive agenda — including a general income tax. In 1909, his hand-picked successor, President William Howard Taft, proposed a constitutional amendment overruling *Pollock v. Farmer's Trust*. And in 1913, the Sixteenth Amendment was ratified, instituting an unapportioned income tax that did not have to treat all taxpayers equally. Americans are all poorer — and richer — for the Court's 1895 gaff.

Part VIII
Appendixes

The 5th Wave — By Rich Tennant

ATTEMPTING TO ESTABLISH A TRULY BALANCED SUPREME COURT, RIP TAYLOR WAS NOMINATED TO A SEAT. HE WAS NEVER CONFIRMED, HOWEVER, BECAUSE OF THE COURT'S STRICT RULE PROHIBITING THE USE OF CONFETTI DURING JUDICIAL HEARINGS.

In this part . . .

There's no getting around it — the law *is* written in a
foreign language. I try to give you a leg up here by
defining some of the more common legal terms you'll run
across, in this book and other places. I also include an
annotated version of the Constitution, which you may
want to refer to from time to time — if only because I do so
throughout this book. And lastly, I include a chronological
listing of all the justices. After all, they *are* the Court.

Appendix A

Common Legal Terms

• •

*S*ome of the definitions listed here can help you use this book. Others may help you as you read about the law or legal issues elsewhere. References to other terms defined here are set in bold, italic type.

Abstention doctrine: Policy adopted by the Supreme Court whereby federal courts, at their discretion and in order to prevent unnecessary conflict, refrain from exercising *jurisdiction* over constitutional questions that can be decided by state courts.

Advisory opinion: Formal, but not legally binding court opinion issued at the request of an interested party or a governing body. Federal courts do not issue advisory opinions.

Affidavit: Any written statement sworn to before an officer of the court or a notary public.

Alien: Foreign-born individual who may be a resident of the United States, but who has not qualified as a citizen.

Appellant: Party appealing the decision of a lower court to a higher, appellate court.

Appellate jurisdiction: Power of a superior court to review the judicial actions of lower courts, particularly for legal errors, and to direct the lower court to revise the action it has taken.

Appellee: Party who prevailed in the lower court who argues on appeal against setting aside that court's judgment.

Apportionment: Determination of the number of elected representatives that a geographic area, such as a state, county, or other electoral district, can send to a legislative body.

Attainder, bill of: Legislative acts imposing criminal punishment on individuals without a judicial proceeding.

Black letter law: Generally accepted, unambiguous legal principles.

Brief: Written argument concerning the facts and law of a case submitted to the court by lawyers on both sides of a controversy, usually before *oral argument.*

Burden of proof: Duty of a party to provide evidence about facts or issues in dispute in order to convince the finder of facts and win at trial.

Capital case: A case that concerns a criminal offense punishable by death.

Certification: Procedure by which a case can be taken from a federal court of appeals to the Supreme Court for review of specific *questions of law.*

Certiorari, writ of: Primary means of filing a case with the Supreme Court, which issues a **writ** requesting the court below to forward a complete record of the litigation.

Circuit: Judicial divisions of individual states or the United States; originally both courts of *original* and *appellate jurisdiction*, in 1891 the old circuit courts became solely trial courts when appellate work was transferred to the circuit courts of appeals, renamed United States Courts of Appeals in 1948.

Circuit duty (or riding): Responsibility of Supreme Court justices, finally abolished in 1911, to help staff federal circuit court benches in their assigned judicial districts.

Citizenship: For purposes of litigation, an individual is a citizen of the state in which he or she resides, and for purposes of *diversity jurisdiction*, a corporation is a citizen of both the state in which it is incorporated and the state in which it maintains its principle place of business.

Class action: Law suit brought by representatives of a large group (the class) sharing a common interest in the issues; all persons who agree to become members of the class are bound by the court's final judgment.

Commercial speech: Speech connected with advertising and business, which until the 1970s, was not deemed to be protected by the First Amendment.

Common law: Judge-made law, as opposed to legislation, based on *precedent*, which was administered in the royal courts of England and became the basis of the American legal system; American, like English legal practice, was once based on two systems, one administering common law, the other *equity.*

Compelling state interest: Term used to uphold *state action* alleged to violate the First Amendment or a person's right to *equal protection* under the law when *strict scrutiny* is applied.

Complaint: Initial set of papers, setting out the facts on which a legal claim is based, what legal claim is made, and what remedy or damages are sought. The complaint is filed with a court in order to begin a civil case.

Consent decree: Agreement by a defendant to cease activities which the government alleges are illegal.

Contempt of court or Congress: Actions obstructing the administration of justice; contempt can be either civil, failing to do something ordered for the benefit of another, or criminal, willfully disobeying an order or obstructing or disrespecting the court or Congress.

Cruel and Unusual Punishment Clause: The Eighth Amendment prohibits the infliction of "cruel and unusual punishments" — that is, punishment out of proportion to the crime or that violates fundamental human dignity.

Declaratory judgment: Binding judgment of the court which sets out the rights of the parties without requiring any action or further relief.

Demurrer: Formal objection in litigation to the legal sufficiency of the plaintiff's written allegations; a demurrer, if upheld, can result in a judgment for the defendant. In federal court, a demurrer usually is filed as a *motion* for *summary judgment* and is called a "motion to dismiss for failure to state a claim upon which relief may be granted."

Deposition: Oral testimony of a witness taken out of court, under oath, and transcribed or videotaped.

Derivative suit: Suit on behalf of a corporation brought by its shareholders.

Dictum (plural: dicta): Statement in a judge's opinion that is not central to his or her judgment; it is not binding as *precedent.*

Disparate impact: Employment discrimination proven not by proof of intentional harm, but by a demonstration of harmful effect, often using statistics.

Diversity jurisdiction: Basis for granting federal courts the power to hear cases between citizens of different states (see *citizenship*), or between citizens and *aliens.*

Docket: List of cases on a court calendar.

Double Jeopardy Clause: Portion of the Fifth Amendment that bars double prosecution and double punishment for the same offense, but only in criminal matters and only when there is no successful appeal of a conviction.

Due Process Clause: Portions of the Fifth and Fourteenth Amendments guaranteeing that neither the federal government nor state governments can deprive a person of "life, liberty, or property" without "due process of law" — that is, a hearing before an authorized judicial body.

Enabling legislation: Laws providing authorities with the power to implement and enforce other statutes.

Enjoin: To command that a certain action be ceased or avoided, usually by court *injunction.*

Enumerated powers: Powers specifically granted to some branch of the federal government by the Constitution; Article I outlines those powers given to Congress.

Equal Protection Clause: Portion of section 1 of the Fourteenth Amendment that has been interpreted to mean that no individual or class of individuals can be denied rights enjoyed by other persons or classes in like circumstances.

Equity: Generally equivalent to justice, equity was also the name of a legal system administered in England based on principles of fairness, rather than determined by procedure, as in *common law* courts.

Error, writ of: Obsolete today, this *common law* writ was commonly used in early Supreme Court procedure as a method of reviewing state court decisions involving federal questions (see *federal question doctrine*), in which the Court would issue a command that the court below forward the record of the case, which would be examined for errors in application of the law.

Establishment Clause: Portion of the First Amendment ensuring that government will not establish or endorse any religion.

Exclusionary rule: Prohibition of use in criminal proceedings of evidence obtained in an unconstitutional manner in violation of the Fourth Amendment's prohibition against "unreasonable searches and seizures."

Executive privilege: Privilege of the executive branch under the doctrine of *separation of powers* to refuse to disclose information that would impair its proper functioning.

Executive power: Authority to execute laws invested in the executive branch by Article II of the Constitution.

Ex parte: When found in the titles of cases concerning parties who are either absent or not competent to testify, it signifies that the name that follows is that of the party on whose behalf the case was heard.

Ex post facto laws: Statutes making an act that was not a crime when it was committed punishable as a crime; these statutes are outlawed in Article I, section 9, clause 3 of the Constitution.

Ex rel.: Legal proceeding brought in the name of the state but at the instigation of an individual with a private interest in the outcome.

Extrajudicial activities (or duties): Participation of justices in activities outside the usual duties of the judicial office, sometimes thought to compromise the authority of the Court.

Federal question doctrine: Applicable to cases arising under the Constitution, acts of Congress, or treaties, as stipulated in Article III, section 2 of the Constitution, it usually confers *jurisdiction* on federal courts.

Federalism: System of government dividing power between local governments and a central — often more powerful — government.

Felony: More serious category of crimes, such as assault and robbery, which, unlike *misdemeanors*, often are punishable with heavy fines or lengthy jail terms.

First impression: Expression used to describe the first time a specific *question of law* is presented for determination by a court.

Foreign corporation (or individual): For purposes of litigation, a party that is a citizen of another state or country.

Free Exercise Clause: Portion of the First Amendment ensuring that government will not interfere with a person's chosen method of observing his or her faith.

Free Speech Clause: Portion of the First Amendment ensuring that government will not interfere with freedom of speech or freedom of the press.

Friendly suit: Litigation brought by agreement of parties who seek a binding judgment on an issue of concern to all.

Grand jury: Traditionally, 23 individuals (as opposed to a *petit jury*, consisting of 12 or fewer jurors) chosen to determine whether the facts and allegations presented by prosecutors in criminal cases warrant *indictment* and trial.

Habeas Corpus: Judicial procedure for determining the legality of custody, used in criminal law to challenge a convict's imprisonment.

Holding: Legal principle underlying a court's decision; it is the part of the court's opinion that is legally binding as *precedent* of subsequent similar cases (compare *Dictum*).

Impeachment: Criminal proceeding against a public official by a quasi-judicial body.

Implied powers: Powers not expressly granted in the Constitution that are necessary for exercise of those powers spelled out by the founding fathers.

Incorporation doctrine: Determination by the Supreme Court that most, but not all, of the guarantees of the Bill of Rights are binding on the states as well as the federal government through the *Due Process Clause* of the Fourteenth Amendment.

Indictment: A formal written accusation drawn up by a prosecutor and issued by a *grand jury* against an individual charged with a criminal offense.

Injunction: A remedy issued by a court ordering a defendant to cease or refrain from specified acts.

In re: "In the matter of," title of a nonadversarial judicial proceeding concerning a matter, such as an estate, requiring only adjudication.

Intermediate scrutiny: Standard under the *Equal Protection Clause* employed by federal courts in determining the constitutionality of government actions based on gender and illegitimacy. In recent cases, the Supreme Court has leaned toward applying *strict scrutiny* to cases involving gender.

Judicial activism: Theory of judging based not on *precedent* but on the court's more subjective determination of what is right for a party or for society.

Judicial restraint: Theory of judging based on *precedent* and deference to the legislative branch's power to change the law.

Judicial review: Power of the United States Supreme Court and the highest state courts to determine the constitutionality of legislation and executive branch actions.

Jurisdiction: Power to hear and decide cases.

Jurisprudence: Philosophy, or form of legal systems, rather than the laws themselves.

Justiciability: Capacity for a case to be determined by a court; applies to true controversies, rather than hypothetical issues.

Laissez faire: Philosophy of judging based on the economic theory of the same name, which favors individualism and market forces and is hostile to government regulation.

Legal fiction: Assumption of a fact, which may or may not be true, adopted by a court to aid in deciding a case.

Magistrate: Minor officials with limited judicial powers.

Mandamus, writ of: Uncommon court order, issued by courts when other legal remedies have failed, compelling an official to perform some necessary duty.

Misdemeanor: Any criminal offense less than a *felony*, it carries a lesser punishment.

Mistrial: Trial terminated before a verdict is returned, usually brought about by a deadlocked jury or by some incurable fundamental error in the legal proceedings that harms the defendant.

Mootness: Constitutional doctrine asserting that an action is no longer able to be decided by a court because for some reason the controversy between the parties no longer exists and the issue has become dead or academic.

Motion: Application to the court, usually regarding a pending action, requesting a judicial ruling that something be done that favors the applicant.

Oral argument: Arguments in court proceedings delivered by lawyers for the parties to persuade the court to decide a case in their respective clients' favors.

Original intent: Philosophy of constitutional interpretation that attempts to interpret the words of the Constitution according to the perceived intention of its creators, or framers.

Original jurisdiction: Authority to hear a case when it's filed and pass judgment on its laws and facts.

Per curiam: Unsigned opinion expressing the decision of the court.

Peremptory challenge: Right to challenge inclusion of a potential juror without giving reasons; most jurisdictions grant each party a set number of peremptories in both civil and criminal cases, and after this amount is exhausted, jurors may only be excluded if they are clearly predisposed to decide the case in favor of one of the parties.

Petitioner: See *Appellant.*

Petit jury: Ordinary trial jury, traditionally consisting of 12 individuals (less in some *jurisdictions*) who determine factual issues in civil and criminal proceedings.

Plurality: Opinion joined by less than a majority of the court, but conveying a judgment with which the majority agrees.

Police power: Authority granted governments, usually state and local, to restrict individual rights in order to promote public welfare.

Political question: Issue a court determines can't be decided in court because it should be answered by the executive or legislative branch.

Precedent: Previously decided case that supplies reasoning used in deciding the outcome of subsequent case.

Pre-emption: Doctrine giving federal legislation precedence over state legislation on the same subject matter.

Prima facie case: A complaint that is legally sufficient on its face, with enough evidence and no obvious defects, so that it can survive attempts by the opposing party to dismiss it from court.

Prior restraint: Prohibition on the communication or publication of information before it's communicated or published; generally prohibited under the First Amendment.

Privileges and Immunities Clause: Section 1 of the Fourteenth Amendment says that states cannot interfere with the privileges and immunities granted citizens of the United States.

Probable cause: Reasonable knowledge or belief, usually of criminal activity, a demonstration of which is necessary to obtain a warrant or uphold the validity of a warrantless search and seizure or arrest.

Pro bono: Legal services performed free of charge.

Procedural due process: Safeguards, such as the right to counsel, meant to protect individual liberty and private property from arbitrary government intrusion and provided for in the Fifth and Fourteenth Amendments.

Public forum: First Amendment doctrine that holds that government may not prohibit speech-related activities, such as demonstrating and leaf-letting, in areas traditionally provided for or used by the public for speechmaking or demonstrating.

Question of fact: In a legal proceeding, a disputed factual issue to be decided by the finder of fact, usually a jury, or if none is present, a judge.

Question of law: Disputed legal contentions reserved for judicial decision.

Rational basis: Test used under the *Equal Protection Clause* to determine whether some challenged government action is reasonably related to a legitimate government end.

Recuse: To disqualify a judge or for a judge to disqualify him or herself because of potential bias or self-interest in the outcome of a pending case.

Remand: To send back for further deliberation; often an *appellate* court will remand a case to the trial court for another hearing based on the outcome of the appeal.

Remove: To transfer a case from its original court to another court upon the defendant's petition; usually transfers a case from state to federal court.

Reserved powers: Powers not specifically given to the federal government or forbidden to the states in the Constitution and reserved to the states or the people of the United States.

Respondent: See *Appellee.*

Ripeness: Constitutional doctrine requiring federal courts not to decide cases brought before they have ripened into true controversies.

Separation of powers: Doctrine prohibiting any of the three branches of government — executive, legislative, and judicial — from infringing upon or exercising powers reserved for the others.

Seriatim: Successively; originally, each Supreme Court justice issued his own opinion in reverse order of seniority, seriatim.

Sovereignty: Supreme power of an independent state or nation which enables it to control its internal affairs without foreign intervention.

Standing: Right of an individual or entity, who has a sufficient stake in the outcome, to challenge another in a judicial proceeding.

Stare decisis: *Common law* policy of adhering in subsequent similar cases to principles set forth in *precedents.*

State action: Action taken by the state or federal government; among other things, laws are considered state actions.

States' rights: Assertion of the *sovereignty* of individual states in the face of federal government action, growing out of the Tenth Amendment.

Stay: To halt or suspend a judicial proceeding to await some other event.

Strict construction: Interpretation of laws, especially the Constitution, by adhering to the literal meaning of their words.

Strict scrutiny: Test of the constitutionality of a statute that creates a ***suspect category*** of individuals, particularly one based on race or ethnicity; in order to overcome a presumption that such a law is unconstitutional, government must show that the statute is both strictly necessary and the least intrusive means of achieving a ***compelling state interest.***

Subpoena: Written order issued by a court or under its authority, compelling the appearance of a witness to give testimony or to produce documents or things.

Substantive due process: Doctrine rooted in the ***Due Process Clause*** of the Fourteenth Amendment holding that the Constitution confers on individuals certain inalienable rights, above all the right to be free from arbitrary government intrusion; such rights are ensured by ***procedural due process.***

Summary judgment: Judgment rendered prior to delivery of a verdict when the judge grants either party's ***motion,*** which usually claims that no outstanding issue of material fact would prevent that party from prevailing under law.

Suspect category (or classification): Part of a test used to determine whether a law which creates categories of individuals based on race, alienage, national origin, or gender denies them equal protection.

Test case: Action selected from a number of similar cases pending in the same court, brought by several plaintiffs against one defendant, or by one plaintiff against several defendants, selected to test the right to recovery by all similarly situated plaintiffs; all parties agree in advance that they will be bound by the outcome.

Tort: A civil, rather than criminal, wrong or injury, other than a breach of contract, which is usually remedied with an injunction or a court award of money damages, or both.

Warrant: An official order, usually written, that authorizes a police search or an arrest.

Writ: Court order requiring performance of a specified act, or giving authority for its performance.

Appendix B

Constitution of the United States of America

• •

*T*his appendix is here to serve as a reference tool. You can use it to see the exact wording (and exact spelling) of sections of the Constitution cited in the book, you can use it to see how these sections relate to those that surround them, and you can use it to figure out just who those Founding Fathers *really* are.

Preamble

We the People of the United States, in Order to form a more perfect Union, establish Justice, insure domestic Tranquillity, provide for the common defence, promote the general Welfare, and secure the Blessings of Liberty to ourselves and our Posterity, do ordain and establish this Constitution for the United States of America.

Articles

ARTICLE 1

Section 1. All legislative Powers herein granted shall be vested in a Congress of the United States, which shall consist of a Senate and House of Representatives.

Section 2. The House of Representatives shall be composed of Members chosen every second Year by the People of the several States, and the Electors in each State shall have the Qualifications requisite for Electors of the most numerous Branch of the State Legislature.

No Person shall be a Representative who shall not have attained to the age of twenty five Years, and been seven Years a Citizen of the United States, and who shall not, when elected, be an Inhabitant of that State in which he shall be chosen.

[Representatives and direct Taxes shall be apportioned among the several States which may be included within this Union, according to their respective Numbers, which shall be determined by adding to the whole Number of free Persons, including those bound to Service for a Term of Years, and excluding Indians not taxed, three fifths of all other Persons.] *[The preceding section in square brackets was changed by section 2 of the Fourteenth Amendment.]* The actual Enumeration shall be made within three Years after the first Meeting of the Congress of the United States, and within every subsequent Term of ten Years, in such Manner as they shall by Law direct. The Number of Representatives shall not exceed one for every thirty Thousand, but each State shall have at Least one Representative; and until such enumeration shall be made, the State of New Hampshire shall be entitled to chuse three, Massachusetts eight, Rhode-Island and Providence Plantations one, Connecticut five, New-York six, New Jersey four, Pennsylvania eight, Delaware one, Maryland six, Virginia ten, North Carolina five, South Carolina five, and Georgia three.

When vacancies happen in the Representation from any State, the Executive Authority thereof shall issue Writs of Election to fill such Vacancies.

The House of Representatives shall chuse their Speaker and other Officers; and shall have the sole Power of Impeachment.

Section 3. The Senate of the United States shall be composed of two Senators from each State, [chosen by the Legislature thereof,] *[the preceding section in square brackets was changed by the first paragraph of the Seventeenth Amendment]* for six Years; and each Senator shall have one Vote.

Immediately after they shall be assembled in Consequence of the first Election, they shall be divided as equally as may be into three Classes. The Seats of the Senators of the first Class shall be vacated at the Expiration of the second Year, of the second Class at the Expiration of the fourth Year, and of the third Class at the Expiration of the sixth Year, so that one third may be chosen every second Year; [and if Vacancies happen by Resignation, or otherwise, during the Recess of the Legislature of any State, the Executive thereof may make temporary Appointments until the next Meeting of the Legislature, which shall then fill such Vacancies.] *[The preceding section in square brackets was changed by the second paragraph of the Seventeenth Amendment.]*

No Person shall be a Senator who shall not have attained to the Age of thirty Years, and been nine Years a Citizen of the United States, and who shall not, when elected, be an Inhabitant of that State for which he shall be chosen.

The Vice President of the United States shall be President of the Senate, but shall have no Vote, unless they be equally divided.

The Senate shall chuse their other Officers, and also a President pro tempore, in the Absence of the Vice President, or when he shall exercise the Office of President of the United States.

The Senate shall have the sole Power to try all Impeachments. When sitting for that Purpose, they shall be on Oath or Affirmation. When the President of the United States is tried, the Chief Justice shall preside: And no Person shall be convicted without the Concurrence of two thirds of the Members present.

Judgment in Cases of Impeachment shall not extend further than to removal from Office, and disqualification to hold and enjoy any Office of honor, Trust or Profit under the United States: but the Party convicted shall nevertheless be liable and subject to Indictment, Trial, Judgment and Punishment, according to Law.

Section 4. The Times, Places and Manner of holding Elections for Senators and Representatives, shall be prescribed in each State by the Legislature thereof; but the Congress may at any time by Law make or alter such Regulations, except as to the Places of chusing Senators.

The Congress shall assemble at least once in every Year, and such Meeting shall [be on the first Monday in December] *[the preceding section in square brackets was changed by section 2 of the Twentieth Amendment]*, unless they shall by Law appoint a different Day.

Section 5. Each House shall be the judge of the Elections, Returns and Qualifications of its own Members, and a Majority of each shall constitute a Quorum to do Business; but a smaller Number may adjourn from day to day, and may be authorized to compel the Attendance of absent Members, in such Manner, and under such Penalties as each House may provide.

Each House may determine the Rules of its Proceedings, punish its Members for disorderly Behaviour, and, with the Concurrence of two thirds, expel a Member.

Each House shall keep a journal of its Proceedings, and from time to time publish the same, excepting such Parts as may in their judgment require Secrecy; and the Yeas and Nays of the Members of either House on any question shall, at the Desire of one fifth of those Present, be entered on the Journal.

Neither House, during the Session of Congress, shall, without the Consent of the other, adjourn for more than three days, nor to any other Place than that in which the two Houses shall be sitting.

Section 6. The Senators and Representatives shall receive a Compensation for their Services, to be ascertained by Law, and paid out of the Treasury of the United States. They shall in all Cases, except Treason, Felony and Breach of the Peace, be privileged from Arrest during their Attendance at the Session of their respective Houses, and in going to and returning from the same; and for any Speech or Debate in either House, they shall not be questioned in any other Place.

No Senator or Representative shall, during the Time for which he was elected, be appointed to any civil Office under the Authority of the United States, which shall have been created, or the Emoluments whereof shall have been encreased during such time; and no Person holding any Office under the United States, shall be a Member of either House during his Continuance in Office.

Section 7. All Bills for raising Revenue shall originate in the House of Representatives; but the Senate may propose or concur with Amendments as on other Bills. Every Bill which shall have passed the House of Representatives and the Senate, shall, before it become a Law, be presented to the President of the United States; If he approve he shall sign it, but if not he shall return it, with his Objections to that House in which it shall have originated, who shall enter the Objections at large on their Journal, and proceed to reconsider it. If after such Reconsideration two thirds of that House shall agree to pass the Bill, it shall be sent, together with the Objections, to the other House, by which it shall likewise be reconsidered, and if approved by two thirds of that House, it shall become a Law. But in all such Cases the Votes of both Houses shall be determined by yeas and Nays, and the names of the Persons voting for and against the Bill shall be entered on the Journal of each House respectively. If any Bill shall not be returned by the President within ten Days (Sundays excepted) after it shall have been presented to him, the Same shall be a Law, in like Manner as if he had signed it, unless the Congress by their Adjournment prevent its Return, in which Case it shall not be a Law.

Every Order, Resolution, or Vote to which the Concurrence of the Senate and House of Representatives may be necessary (except on a question of Adjournment) shall be presented to the President of the United States; and before the Same shall take Effect, shall be approved by him, or being disapproved by him, shall be repassed by two thirds of the Senate and House of Representatives, according to the Rules and Limitations prescribed in the Case of a Bill.

Section 8. The Congress shall have Power To lay and collect Taxes, Duties, Imposts and Excises, to pay the Debts and provide for the common Defence and general Welfare of the United States; but all Duties, Imposts and Excises shall be uniform throughout the United States;

To borrow Money on the credit of the United States;

To regulate Commerce with foreign Nations, and among the several States, and with the Indian Tribes;

To establish an uniform Rule of Naturalization, and uniform Laws on the subject of Bankruptcies throughout the United States;

To coin Money, regulate the Value thereof, and of foreign Coin, and fix the Standard of Weights and Measures;

To provide for the Punishment of counterfeiting the Securities and current Coin of the United States;

To establish Post Offices and post Roads;

To promote the Progress of Science and useful Arts, by securing for limited Times to Authors and Inventors the exclusive Right to their respective Writings and Discoveries;

To constitute Tribunals inferior to the supreme Court;

To define and punish Piracies and Felonies committed on the high Seas, and Offences against the Law of Nations;

To declare War, grant Letters of Marque and Reprisal, and make Rules concerning Captures on Land and Water;

To raise and support Armies, but no Appropriation of Money to that Use shall be for a longer Term than two Years;

To provide and maintain a Navy;

To make Rules for the Government and Regulation of the land and naval Forces;

To provide for calling forth the Militia to execute the Laws of the Union, suppress Insurrections and repel Invasions;

To provide for organizing, arming, and disciplining, the Militia, and for governing such Part of them as may be employed in the Service of the United States, reserving to the States respectively, the Appointment of the Officers, and the Authority of training the Militia according to the discipline prescribed by Congress;

To exercise exclusive Legislation in all Cases whatsoever, over such District (not exceeding ten Miles square) as may, by Cession of particular States, and the Acceptance of Congress, become the Seat of the Government of the

United States, and to exercise like Authority over all Places purchased by the Consent of the Legislature of the State in which the Same shall be, for the Erection of Forts, Magazines, Arsenals, dock-Yards, and other needful Buildings;—And

To make all Laws which shall be necessary and proper for carrying into Execution the foregoing Powers, and all other Powers vested by this Constitution in the Government of the United States, or in any Department or Officer thereof.

Section 9. The Migration or Importation of such Persons as any of the States now existing shall think proper to admit, shall not be prohibited by the Congress prior to the Year one thousand eight hundred and eight, but a Tax or duty may be imposed on such Importation, not exceeding ten dollars for each Person.

The Privilege of the Writ of Habeas Corpus shall not be suspended, unless when in Cases of Rebellion or Invasion the public Safety may require it.

No Bill of Attainder or ex post facto Law shall be passed.

[No Capitation, or other direct, Tax shall be laid, unless in Proportion to the Census or Enumeration herein before directed to be taken.] *[The preceding section in square brackets was changed by the Sixteenth Amendment.]*

No Tax or Duty shall be laid on Articles exported from any State.

No Preference shall be given by any Regulation of Commerce or Revenue to the Ports of one State over those of another; nor shall Vessels bound to, or from, one State, be obliged to enter, clear, or pay Duties in another.

No Money shall be drawn from the Treasury, but in Consequence of Appropriations made by Law; and a regular Statement and Account of the Receipts and Expenditures of all public Money shall be published from time to time.

No Title of Nobility shall be granted by the United States: And no Person holding any Office of Profit or Trust under them, shall, without the Consent of the Congress, accept of any present, Emolument, Office, or Title, of any kind whatever, from any King, Prince, or foreign State.

Section 10. No State shall enter into any Treaty, Alliance, or Confederation; grant Letters of Marque and Reprisal; coin Money; emit Bills of Credit; make any Thing but gold and silver Coin a Tender in Payment of Debts; pass any Bill of Attainder, ex post facto Law, or Law impairing the Obligation of Contracts, or grant any Title of Nobility.

No State shall, without the Consent of the Congress, lay any Imposts or Duties on Imports or Exports, except what may be absolutely necessary for executing its inspection Laws: and the net Produce of all Duties and Imposts, laid by any State on Imports or Exports, shall be for the Use of the Treasury of the United States; and all such Laws shall be subject to the Revision and Controul of the Congress.

No State shall, without the Consent of Congress, lay any Duty of Tonnage, keep Troops, or Ships of War in time of Peace, enter into any Agreement or Compact with another State, or with a foreign Power, or engage in War, unless actually invaded, or in such imminent Danger as will not admit of delay.

ARTICLE II

Section 1. The executive Power shall be vested in a President of the United States of America. He shall hold his Office during the Term of four Years, and, together with the Vice President, chosen for the same Term, be elected, as follows:

Each State shall appoint, in such Manner as the Legislature thereof may direct, a Number of Electors, equal to the whole Number of Senators and Representatives to which the State may be entitled in the Congress: but no Senator or Representative, or Person holding an Office of Trust or Profit under the United States, shall be appointed an Elector.

[The Electors shall meet in their respective States, and vote by Ballot for two Persons, of whom one at least shall not be an Inhabitant of the same State with themselves. And they shall make a List of all the Persons voted for, and of the Number of Votes for each; which List they shall sign and certify, and transmit sealed to the Seat of the Government of the United States, directed to the President of the Senate. The President of the Senate shall, in the Presence of the Senate and House of Representatives, open all the Certificates, the Votes shall then be counted. The Person having the greatest Number of Votes shall be the President, if such Number be a Majority of the whole Number of Electors appointed; and if there be more than one who have such Majority, and have an equal Number of Votes, then the House of Representatives shall immediately chuse by Ballot one of them for President; and if no Person have a Majority, then from the five highest on the list the said House shall in like Manner chuse the President. But in chusing the President, the Votes shall be taken by States, the Representation from each State having one Vote; a quorum for this Purpose shall consist of a Member or Members from two thirds of the States, and a Majority of all the States shall be necessary to a Choice. In every Case, after the Choice of the President, the Person having the greatest Number of Votes of the Electors shall be the Vice President. But if there should remain two or more who have equal Votes, the Senate shall chuse from them by Ballot the Vice President.] *[The preceding section in square brackets has been changed by the Twelfth Amendment.]*

The Congress may determine the Time of choosing the Electors, and the Day on which they shall give their Votes; which Day shall be the same throughout the United States.

No Person except a natural born Citizen, or a Citizen of the United States, at the time of the Adoption of this Constitution, shall be eligible to the Office of President; neither shall any Person be eligible to that Office who shall not have attained to the Age of thirty five Years, and been fourteen Years a Resident within the United States.

In Case of the Removal of the President from Office, or of his Death, Resignation, or Inability to discharge the Powers and Duties of the said Office, the Same shall devolve on the Vice President, and the Congress may by Law provide for the Case of Removal, Death, Resignation or Inability, both of the President and Vice President, declaring what Officer shall then act as President, and such Officer shall act accordingly, until the Disability be removed, or a President shall be elected. *[The preceding provision has been affected by the Twenty-fifth Amendment.]*

The President shall, at stated Times, receive for his Services, a Compensation, which shall neither be encreased nor diminished during the Period for which he shall have been elected, and he shall not receive within that Period any other Emolument from the United States, or any of them.

Before he enter on the Execution of his Office, he shall take the following Oath or Affirmation: "I do solemnly swear (or affirm) that I will faithfully execute the Office of President of the United States, and will to the best of my Ability, preserve, protect and defend the Constitution of the United States."

Section 2. The President shall be Commander in Chief of the Army and Navy of the United States, and of the Militia of the several States, when called into the actual Service of the United States; he may require the Opinion, in writing, of the principal Officer in each of the executive Departments, upon any Subject relating to the Duties of their respective Offices, and he shall have Power to grant Reprieves and Pardons for Offences against the United States, except in Cases of Impeachment.

He shall have Power, by and with the Advice and Consent of the Senate, to make Treaties, provided two thirds of the Senators present concur; and he shall nominate, and by and with the Advice and Consent of the Senate, shall appoint Ambassadors, other public Ministers and Consuls, judges of the supreme Court, and all other Officers of the United States, whose Appointments are not herein otherwise provided for, and which shall be established by Law: but the Congress may by Law vest the Appointment of such inferior Officers, as they think proper, in the President alone, in the Courts of Law, or in the Heads of Departments.

The President shall have Power to fill up all Vacancies that may happen during the Recess of the Senate, by granting Commissions which shall expire at the End of their next Session.

Section 3. He shall from time to time give to the Congress Information of the State of the Union, and recommend to their Consideration such Measures as he shall judge necessary and expedient; he may, on extraordinary Occasions, convene both Houses, or either of them, and in Case of Disagreement between them, with Respect to the Time of Adjournment, he may adjourn them to such Time as he shall think proper; he shall receive Ambassadors and other public Ministers; he shall take Care that the Laws be faithfully executed, and shall Commission all the Officers of the United States.

Section 4. The President, Vice President and all civil Officers of the United States, shall be removed from Office on Impeachment for, and Conviction of, Treason, Bribery, or other high Crimes and Misdemeanors.

ARTICLE III

Section 1. The judicial Power of the United States shall be vested in one supreme Court, and in such inferior Courts as the Congress may from time to time ordain and establish. The judges, both of the supreme and inferior Courts, shall hold their Offices during good Behaviour, and shall, at stated Times, receive for their Services, a Compensation, which shall not be diminished during their Continuance in Office.

Section 2. The judicial Power shall extend to all Cases, in Law and Equity, arising under this Constitution, the Laws of the United States, and Treaties made, or which shall be made, under their Authority;—to all Cases affecting Ambassadors, other public Ministers and Consuls;—to all Cases of admiralty and maritime Jurisdiction;—to Controversies to which the United States shall be a Party;—to Controversies between two or more States;—between a State and Citizens of another State *[The Eleventh Amendment limited federal jurisdiction over civil litigation brought against a state.]*;—between Citizens of different States;—between Citizens of the same State claiming Lands under Grants of different States, and between a State, or the Citizens thereof, and foreign States, Citizens or Subjects

In all Cases affecting Ambassadors, other public Ministers and Consuls, and those in which a State shall be Party, the supreme Court shall have original jurisdiction. In all the other Cases before mentioned, the supreme Court shall have appellate Jurisdiction, both as to Law and Fact, with such Exceptions, and under such Regulations as the Congress shall make.

The Trial of all Crimes, except in Cases of Impeachment, shall be by Jury; and such Trial shall be held in the State where the said Crimes shall have been committed; but when not committed within any State, the Trial shall be at such Place or Places as the Congress may by Law have directed.

Section 3. Treason against the United States, shall consist only in levying War against them, or in adhering to their Enemies, giving them Aid and. Comfort. No Person shall be convicted of Treason unless on the Testimony of two Witnesses to the same overt Act, or on Confession in open Court.

The Congress shall have Power to declare the Punishment of Treason, but no Attainder of Treason shall work Corruption of Blood, or Forfeiture except during the Life of the Person attained.

ARTICLE IV

Section 1. Full Faith and Credit shall be given in each State to the public Acts, Records, and judicial Proceedings of every other State. And the Congress may by general Laws prescribe the Manner in which such Acts, Records and Proceedings shall be proved, and the Effect thereof.

Section 2. The Citizens of each State shall be entitled to all Privileges and Immunities of Citizens in the several States.

A Person charged in any State with Treason, Felony, or other Crime, who shall flee from Justice, and be found in another State, shall on Demand of the executive Authority of the State from which he fled, be delivered up, to be removed to the State having jurisdiction of the Crime.

[No Person held to Service or Labour in one State, under the Laws thereof, escaping into another, shall, in Consequence of any Law or Regulation therein, be discharged from such Service or Labour, but shall be delivered up on Claim of the Party to whom such Service or Labour may be due.] *[This paragraph refers to slavery and indentured servitude, abolished by the Thirteenth Amendment.]*

Section 3. New States may be admitted by the Congress into this Union; but no new State shall be formed or erected within the Jurisdiction of any other State; nor any State be formed by the Junction of two or more States, or Parts of States, without the Consent of the Legislatures of the States concerned as well as of the Congress.

The Congress shall have Power to dispose of and make all needful Rules and Regulations respecting the Territory or other Property belonging to the United States; and nothing in this Constitution shall be so construed as to Prejudice any Claims of the United States, or of any particular State.

Section 4. The United States shall guarantee to every State in this Union a Republican Form of Government, and shall protect each of them against Invasion; and on Application of the Legislature, or of the Executive (when the Legislature cannot be convened) against domestic Violence.

ARTICLE V

The Congress, whenever two thirds of both Houses shall deem it necessary, shall propose Amendments to this Constitution, or, on the Application of the Legislatures of two thirds of the several States, shall call a Convention for proposing Amendments, which, in either Case, shall be valid to all Intents and Purposes, as Part of this Constitution, when ratified by the Legislatures of three fourths of the several States, or by Conventions in three fourths thereof, as the one or the other Mode of Ratification may be proposed by the Congress; Provided that no Amendment which may be made prior to the Year One thousand eight hundred and eight shall in any Manner affect the first and fourth Clauses in the Ninth Section of the first Article; and that no State, without its Consent, shall be deprived of its equal Suffrage in the Senate.

ARTICLE VI

All Debts contracted and Engagements entered into, before the Adoption of this Constitution, shall be as valid against the United States under this Constitution, as under the Confederation.

This Constitution, and the Laws of the United States which shall be made in Pursuance thereof; and all Treaties made, or which shall be made. under the Authority of the United States, shall be the supreme Law of the Land; and the judges in every State shall be bound thereby, any Thing in the Constitution or Laws of any State to the Contrary notwithstanding.

The Senators and Representatives before mentioned, and the Members of the several State Legislatures, and all executive and judicial Officers, both of the United States and of the several States, shall be bound by Oath or Affirmation, to support this Constitution; but no religious Test shall ever be required as a Qualification to any Office or public Trust under the United States.

ARTICLE VII

The Ratification of the Conventions of nine States, shall be sufficient for the Establishment of this Constitution between the States so ratifying the Same.

Signatures

Done in Convention by the Unanimous Consent of the States present the seventeenth Day of September in the Year of our Lord one thousand seven hundred and Eighty seven and of the Independence of the United States of America the Twelfth. IN WITNESS whereof We have hereunto subscribed our Names,

George Washington,

> President and deputy from Virginia.

New Hampshire:

> John Langdon,
>
> Nicholas Gilman.

Massachusetts:

> Nathaniel Gorham,
>
> Rufus King.

Connecticut:

> William Samuel Johnson,
>
> Roger Sherman.

New York:

> Alexander Hamilton.

New Jersey:

> William Livingston,
>
> David Brearley,
>
> William Paterson,
>
> Jonathan Dayton.

Pennsylvania:

> Benjamin Franklin,
>
> Thomas Mifflin,
>
> Robert Morris,
>
> George Clymer,

Thomas FitzSimons,

Jared Ingersoll,

James Wilson,

Gouverneur Morris.

Delaware:

George Read,

Gunning Bedford Jr.,

John Dickinson,

Richard Bassett,

Jacob Broom.

Maryland:

James McHenry,

Daniel of St. Thomas Jenifer,

Daniel Carroll.

Virginia:

John Blair,

James Madison Jr.

North Carolina:

William Blount,

Richard Dobbs Spaight,

Hugh Williamson.

South Carolina:

John Rutledge,

Charles Cotesworth Pinckney,

Pierce Butler.

Georgia:

William Few,

Abraham Baldwin.

(Ratification of the Constitution was completed on June 21, 1788)

AMENDMENTS

The first ten amendments constitute the Bill of Rights, ratified
December 15, 1791.

AMENDMENT 1

Congress shall make no law respecting an establishment of religion, or
prohibiting the free exercise thereof; or abridging the freedom of speech, or
of the press; or the right of the people peaceably to assemble, and to petition
the Government for a redress of grievances.

AMENDMENT 11

A well regulated Militia, being necessary to the security of a free State, the
right of the people to keep and bear Arms, shall not be infringed.

AMENDMENT 111

No Soldier shall, in time of peace be quartered in any house, without the
consent of the Owner, nor in time of war, but in a manner to be prescribed
by law.

AMENDMENT 1V

The right of the people to be secure in their persons, houses, papers, and
effects, against unreasonable searches and seizures, shall not be violated,
and no Warrants shall issue, but upon probable cause, supported by Oath
or affirmation, and particularly describing the place to be searched, and the
persons or things to be seized.

AMENDMENT V

No person shall be held to answer for a capital, or otherwise infamous crime,
unless on a presentment or indictment of a Grand Jury, except in cases arising
in the land or naval forces, or in the Militia, when in actual service in time of
War or public danger; nor shall any person be subject for the same offences to

be twice put in jeopardy of life or limb; nor shall be compelled in any criminal case to be a witness against himself, nor be deprived of life, liberty, or property, without due process of law; nor shall private property be taken for public use, without just compensation.

AMENDMENT VI

In all criminal prosecutions, the accused shall enjoy the right to a speedy and public trial, by an impartial jury of the State and district wherein the crime shall have been committed, which district shall have been previously ascertained by law, and to be informed of the nature and cause of the accusation; to be confronted with the witnesses against him; to have compulsory process for obtaining witnesses in his favor, and to have the Assistance of Counsel for his defence.

AMENDMENT VII

In Suits at common law, where the value in controversy shall exceed twenty dollars, the right of trial by jury shall be preserved, and no fact tried by a jury, shall be otherwise re-examined in any Court of the United States, than according to the rules of the common law.

AMENDMENT VIII

Excessive bail shall not be required, nor excessive fines imposed, nor cruel and unusual punishments inflicted.

AMENDMENT IX

The enumeration in the Constitution, of certain rights, shall not be construed to deny or disparage others retained by the people.

AMENDMENT X

The powers not delegated to the United States by the Constitution, nor prohibited by it to the States, are reserved to the States respectively, or to the people.

AMENDMENT XI

(Ratified February 7, 1795)

The judicial power of the United States shall not be construed to extend to any suit in law or equity, commenced or prosecuted against one of the United States by Citizens of another State, or by Citizens or Subjects of any Foreign State.

AMENDMENT XII

(Ratified June 15, 1804)

The Electors shall meet in their respective states, and vote by ballot for President and Vice-President, one of whom, at least, shall not be an inhabitant of the same state with themselves; they shall name in their ballots the person voted for as President, and in distinct ballots the person voted for as Vice-President, and they shall make distinct lists of all persons voted for as President, and of all persons voted for as Vice-President, and of the number of votes for each, which lists they shall sign and certify, and transmit sealed to the seat of the government of the United States, directed to the President of the Senate;—The President of the Senate shall, in the presence of the Senate and House of Representatives, open all the certificates and the votes shall then be counted;—The person having the greatest number of votes for President, shall be the President, if such number be a majority of the whole number of Electors appointed; and if no person have such majority, then from the persons having the highest numbers not exceeding three on the list of those voted for as President, the House of Representatives shall choose immediately, by ballot, the President. But in choosing the President, the votes shall be taken by states, the representation from each state having one vote; a quorum for this purpose shall consist of a member or members from two-thirds of the states, and a majority of all the states shall be necessary to a choice. [And if the House of Representatives shall not choose a President whenever the right of choice shall devolve upon them, before the fourth day of March next following, then the Vice-President shall act as President, as in the case of the death or other constitutional disability of the President.—] *[The preceding section in square brackets was superceded by section 3 of the Twentieth Amendment.]* The person having the greatest number of votes as Vice-President, shall be the Vice-President, if such number be a majority of the whole number of Electors appointed, and if no person have a majority, then from the two highest numbers on the list, the Senate shall choose the Vice-President; a quorum for the purpose shall consist of two-thirds of the whole number of Senators, and a majority of the whole number shall be necessary to a choice. But no person constitutionally ineligible to the office of President shall be eligible to that of Vice-President of the United States.

AMENDMENT XIII

(Ratified December 6, 1865)

Section 1. Neither slavery nor involuntary servitude, except as a punishment for crime whereof the party shall have been duly convicted, shall exist within the United States, or any place subject to their jurisdiction.

Section 2. Congress shall have power to enforce this article by appropriate legislation.

AMENDMENT XIV

(Ratified July 9, 1868)

Section 1. All persons born or naturalized in the United States, and subject to the jurisdiction thereof, are citizens of the United States and of the State wherein they reside. No State shall make or enforce any law which shall abridge the privileges or immunities of citizens of the United States; nor shall any State deprive any person of life, liberty, or property, without due process of law; nor deny to any person within its jurisdiction the equal protection of the laws.

Section 2. Representatives shall be apportioned among the several States according to their respective numbers, counting the whole number of persons in each State, excluding Indians not taxed. But when the right to vote at any election for the choice of electors for President and Vice President of the United States, Representatives in Congress, the Executive and Judicial officers of a State, or the members of the Legislature thereof, is denied to any of the male inhabitants of such State, being twenty-one years of age, *[see the Nineteenth and Twenty-sixth Amendments]* and citizens of the United States, or in any way abridged, except for participation in rebellion, or other crime, the basis of representation therein shall be reduced in the proportion which the number of such male citizens shall bear to the whole number of male citizens twenty-one years of age in such State.

Section 3. No person shall be a Senator or Representative in Congress, or elector of President and Vice President, or hold any office, civil or military, under the United States, or under any State, who, having previously taken an oath, as a member of Congress, or as an officer of the United States, or as a member of any State legislature, or as an executive or judicial officer of any State, to support the Constitution of the United States, shall have engaged in insurrection or rebellion against the same, or given aid or comfort to the enemies thereof. But Congress may by a vote of two-thirds of each House, remove such disability.

Section 4. The validity of the public debt of the United States, authorized by law, including debts incurred for payment of pensions and bounties for services in suppressing insurrection or rebellion, shall not be questioned. But neither the United States nor any State shall assume or pay any debt or obligation incurred in aid of insurrection or rebellion against the United States, or any claim for the loss or emancipation of any slave; but all such debts, obligations and claims shall be held illegal and void.

Section 5. The Congress shall have power to enforce, by appropriate legislation, the provisions of this article.

AMENDMENT XV

(Ratified February 3, 1870)

Section 1. The right of citizens of the United States to vote shall not be denied or abridged by the United States or by any State on account of race, color, or previous condition of servitude.

Section 2. The Congress shall have power to enforce this article by appropriate legislation.

AMENDMENT XVI

(Ratified February 3, 1913)

The Congress shall have power to lay and collect taxes on incomes, from whatever source derived, without apportionment among the several States, and without regard to any census or enumeration.

AMENDMENT XVII

(Ratified April 8, 1913)

The Senate of the United States shall be composed of two Senators from each State, elected by the people thereof, for six years; and each Senator shall have one vote. The electors in each State shall have the qualifications requisite for electors of the most numerous branch of the State legislatures.

When vacancies happen in the representation of any State in the Senate, the executive authority of such State shall issue writs of election to fill such vacancies: Provided, That the legislature of any State may empower the executive thereof to make temporary appointments until the people fill the vacancies by election as the legislature may direct.

This amendment shall not be so construed as to affect the election or term of any Senator chosen before it becomes valid as part of the Constitution.

AMENDMENT XVIII

(Ratified January 16, 1919)

After one year from the ratification of this article the manufacture, sale, or transportation of intoxicating liquors within, the importation thereof into, or the exportation thereof from the United States and all territory subject to the jurisdiction thereof for beverage purposes is hereby prohibited.

The Congress and the several States shall have concurrent power to enforce this article by appropriate legislation.

This article shall be inoperative unless it shall have been ratified as an amendment to the Constitution by the legislatures of the several States, as provided in the Constitution, within seven years from the date of the submission hereof to the States by the Congress.

[The Eighteenth Amendment was repealed by section 1 of the Twenty-first Amendment.]

AMENDMENT XIX

(Ratified August 18, 1920)

The right of citizens of the United States to vote shall not be denied or abridged by the United States or by any State on account of sex.

Congress shall have power to enforce this article by appropriate legislation.

AMENDMENT XX

(Ratified January 23, 1933)

Section 1. The terms of the President and Vice President shall end at noon on the 20th day of January, and the terms of Senators and Representatives at noon on the 3rd day of January, of the years in which such terms would have ended if this article had not been ratified; and the terms of their successors shall then begin. Section 2. The Congress shall assemble at least once in every year, and such meeting shall begin at noon on the 3d day of January, unless they shall by law appoint a different day.

Section 2. The Congress shall assemble at least once in every year, and such meeting shall begin at noon on the 3d day of January, unless they shall by law appoint a different day.

Section 3. *[See the Twenty-fifth Amendment.]* If, at the time fixed for the beginning of the term of the President, the President elect shall have died, the Vice President elect shall become President. If a President shall not have been chosen before the time fixed for the beginning of his term, or if the President elect shall have failed to qualified, then the Vice President elect shall act as President until a President shall have qualified; and the Congress may by law provide for the case wherein neither a President elect nor a Vice President elect shall have qualified, declaring who shall then act as President, or the manner in which one who is to act shall be selected, and such person shall act accordingly until a President or Vice President shall have qualified.

Section 4. The Congress may by law provide for the case of the death of any of the persons from whom the House of Representatives may choose a President whenever the right of choice shall have devolved upon them, and for the case of the death of any of the persons from whom the Senate may choose a Vice President whenever the right of choice shall have devolved upon them.

Section 5. Sections 1 and 2 shall take effect on the 15th day of October following the ratification of this article.

Section 6. This article shall be inoperative unless it shall have been ratified as an amendment to the Constitution by the legislatures of three-fourths of the several States within seven years from the date of its submission.

AMENDMENT XXI

(Ratified December 5, 1933)

Section 1. The eighteenth article of amendment to the Constitution of the United States is hereby repealed.

Section 2. The transportation or importation into any State, Territory, or possession of the United States for delivery or use therein of intoxicating liquors, in violation of the laws thereof, is hereby prohibited.

Section 3. This article shall be inoperative unless it shall have been ratified as an amendment to the Constitution by conventions in the several States, as provided in the Constitution, within seven years from the date of the submission hereof to the States by the Congress.

AMENDMENT XXII

(Ratified February 27, 1951)

Section 1. No person shall be elected to the office of the President more than twice, and no person who has held the office of President, or acted as President, for more than two years of a term to which some other person was elected President shall be elected to the office of the President more than once. But this Article shall not apply to any person holding the office of President when this Article was proposed by the Congress, and shall not prevent any person who may be holding the office of President, or acting as President, during the term within which this Article becomes operative from holding the office of President or acting as President during the remainder of such term.

Section 2. This article shall be inoperative unless it shall have been ratified as an amendment to the Constitution by the legislatures of three-fourths of the several States within seven years from the date of its submission to the States by the Congress.

AMENDMENT XXIII

(Ratified March 29, 1961)

Section 1. The District constituting the seat of Government of the United States shall appoint in such manner as the Congress may direct:

A number of electors of President and Vice President equal to the whole number of Senators and Representatives in Congress to which the District would be entitled if it were a State, but in no event more than the least populous State; they shall be in addition to those appointed by the States, but they shall be considered, for the purposes of the election of President and Vice President, to be electors appointed by a State; and they shall meet in the District and perform such duties as provided by the twelfth article of amendment.

Section 2. The Congress shall have power to enforce this article by appropriate legislation.

AMENDMENT XXIV

(Ratified January 23, 1964)

Section 1. The right of citizens of the United States to vote in any primary or other election for President or Vice President, for electors for President or Vice President, or for Senator or Representative in Congress, shall not be denied or abridged by the United States or any State by reason of failure to pay any poll tax or other tax.

Section 2. The Congress shall have power to enforce this article by appropriate legislation.

AMENDMENT XXV

(Ratified February 10, 1967)

Section 1. In case of the removal of the President from office or of his death or resignation, the Vice President shall become President. Section 2. Whenever there is a vacancy in the office of the Vice President, the President shall nominate a Vice President who shall take office upon confirmation by a majority vote of both Houses of Congress.

Section 2. Whenever there is a vacancy in the office of the Vice President, the President shall nominate a Vice President who shall take office upon confirmation by a majority vote of both Houses of Congress.

Section 3. Whenever the President transmits to the President pro tempore of the Senate and the Speaker of the House of Representatives his written declaration that he is unable to discharge the powers and duties of his office, and until he transmits to them a written declaration to the contrary, such powers and duties shall be discharged by the Vice President as Acting President.

Section 4. Whenever the Vice President and a majority of either the principal officers of the executive departments or of such other body as Congress may by law provide, transmit to the President pro tempore of the Senate and the Speaker of the House of Representatives their written declaration that the President is unable to discharge the powers and duties of his office, the Vice President shall immediately assume the powers and duties of the office as Acting President.

Thereafter, when the President transmits to the President pro tempore of the Senate and the Speaker of the House of Representatives his written declaration that no inability exists, he shall resume the powers and duties of his office unless the Vice President and a majority of either the principal officers of the executive department or of such other body as Congress may by law provide, transmit within four days to the President pro tempore of the Senate and the Speaker of the House of Representatives their written declaration that the President is unable to discharge the powers and duties of his office. Thereupon Congress shall decide the issue, assembling within forty-eight hours for that purpose if not in session. If the Congress, within twenty-one days after receipt of the latter written declaration, or, if Congress is not in session, within twenty-one days after Congress is required to assemble, determines by two-thirds vote of both Houses that the President is unable to discharge the powers and duties of his office, the Vice President shall continue to discharge the same as Acting President; otherwise, the President shall resume the powers and duties of his office.

AMENDMENT XXVI

(Ratified July 1, 1971)

Section 1. The right of citizens of the United States, who are eighteen years of age or older, to vote shall not be denied or abridged by the United States or by any State on account of age.

Section 2. The Congress shall have power to enforce this article by appropriate legislation.

AMENDMENT XXVII

(Ratified May 7, 1992)

No law varying the compensation for the services of the Senators and Representatives shall take effect, until an election of Representatives shall have intervened.

Appendix C

Justices of the Supreme Court

● ●

*H*ere's a list of all the justices who have served on the Supreme Court since 1789. The list separates chief justices from associate justices and lists the names under both categories in chronological order.

Table C-1	Chief Justices		
Name	*Appointing President*	*Oath Taken*	*Term Ended*
John Jay	Washington	Oct. 19, 1789	June 29, 1795
John Rutledge	Washington	Aug. 12, 1795	Rejected by Senate Dec. 15, 1795
Oliver Ellsworth	Washington	March 8, 1796	Dec. 15, 1800
John Marshall	J. Adams	Feb. 4, 1801	July 6, 1835
Roger Brooke Taney	Jackson	Mar. 28, 1836	Oct. 12, 1864
Salmon P. Chase	Lincoln	Dec. 15, 1864	May 7, 1873
Morrison R. Waite	Grant	Mar. 4, 1874	Mar. 23, 1888
Melville W. Fuller	Cleveland	Oct. 8, 1888	July 4, 1910
Edward Douglass White	Taft	Dec, 19, 1910	May 19, 1921
William Howard Taft	Harding	July 11, 1921	Feb. 3, 1930
Charles Evans Hughes	Hoover	Feb. 24, 1930	June 30, 1941
Harlan F. Stone	F.D. Roosevelt	July 3, 1941	April 22, 1946
Fred M. Vinson	Truman	June 24, 1946	Sept. 8, 1953
Earl Warren	Eisenhower	Oct. 5, 1953	June 23, 1969
Warren Burger	Nixon	June 23, 1969	Sept. 26, 1986
William H. Rehnquist	Reagan	Sept. 26, 1986	

Table C-2			Associate Justices		
Name	**Justice Replaced**	**Appointing President**	**Oath Taken**	**Term Ended**	**Succeeding Justice**
John Rutledge		Washington	Feb. 15, 1790	Mar. 5, 1791	Thomas Johnson
William Cushing		Washington	Feb. 2, 1790	Sep. 13, 1810	Joseph Story
James Wilson		Washington	Oct. 5, 1789	Aug. 21, 1789	Bushrod Washington
John Blair, Jr.		Washington	Feb. 2, 1789	Oct. 25, 1795	Samuel Chase
James Iredell		Washington	May 12, 1790	Oct. 20, 1799	Alfred Moore
Thomas Johnson	John Rutledge	Washington	Aug. 6, 1792	Jan. 16, 1793	William Paterson
William Paterson	Thomas Johnson	Washington	Mar. 11, 1793	Sept. 9, 1806	Brockholst Livingston
Samuel Chase	John Blair, Jr.	Washington	Feb. 4, 1796	June 19, 1811	Gabriel Duvall
Bushrod Washington	James Wilson	J. Adams	Feb. 4, 1799	Nov. 26, 1829	Henry Baldwin
Alfred Moore	James Iredell	J. Adams	April 21, 1800	Jan. 26, 1804	William Johnson
William Johnson	Alfred Moore	Jefferson	May 8, 1804	Aug. 4, 1834	James M. Wayne
Henry Brockholst Livingston	William Paterson	Jefferson	Feb. 2, 1807	Mar. 18, 1823	Smith Thompson
Thomas Todd	(new seat)	Jefferson	May 4, 1807	Feb. 7, 1826	Robert Trimble
Gabriel Duvall	Samuel Chase	Madison	Nov. 23, 1811	Jan. 14, 1835	Philip P. Barbour
Joseph Story	William Cushing	Madison	Feb. 3, 1812	Sept. 10, 1845	Levi Woodbury
Smith Thompson	Brockholst Livingston	Monroe	Feb. 10, 1824	Dec. 18, 1843	Samuel Nelson

Name	*Justice Replaced*	*Appointing President*	*Oath Taken*	*Term Ended*	*Succeeding Justice*
Robert Trimble	Thomas Todd	J.Q. Adams	June 16, 1826	Aug. 25, 1828	John McLean
John McLean	Robert Trimble	Jackson	Jan. 11, 1830	April 4, 1861	Noah H. Swayne
Henry Baldwin	Bushrod Washington	Jackson	Jan. 18, 1830	April 21, 1844	Robert C. Grier
James M. Wayne	William Johnson	Jackson	Jan 14, 1835	July 5, 1867	None (size of Court decreased)
Philip P. Barbour	Gabriel Duvall	Jackson	Mar. 15, 1836	Feb. 25, 1841	Peter V. Daniel
John Catron	(new seat)	Jackson	May 1, 1837	May 30, 1865	None (size of Court decreased)
John McKinley	(new seat)	Van Buren	Jan. 9, 1838	July 19, 1852	John A. Campbell
Peter V. Daniel	Philip P. Barbour	Van Buren	Jan. 10, 1842	May 31, 1860	Samuel F. Miller
Samuel Nelson	Smith Thompson	Tyler	Feb. 27, 1845	Nov. 28, 1872	Ward Hunt
Levi Woodbury	Joseph Story	Polk	Sept. 23, 1845	Sept. 4. 1851	Benjamin R. Curtis
Robert C. Grier	Henry Baldwin	Polk	Aug. 10, 1846	Jan. 31, 1870	William Strong
Benjamin R. Curtis	Levi Woodbury	Fillmore	Oct. 10, 1851	Sept. 30, 1857	Nathan Clifford
John A. Campbell	John McKinley	Pierce	April 11, 1853	April 30, 1861	David Davis
Nathan Clifford	Benjamin R. Curtis	Buchanan	Jan. 21, 1858	July 25, 1881	Horace Gray
Noah H. Swayne	John McLean	Lincoln	Jan. 27, 1862	Jan. 24, 1881	Stanley Matthews

(continued)

Table C-2 *(continued)*

Name	Justice Replaced	Appointing President	Oath Taken	Term Ended	Succeeding Justice
Samuel F. Miller	Peter V. Daniel	Lincoln	July 21, 1862	Oct. 13, 1890	Henry B. Brown
David Davis	John A. Campbell	Lincoln	Dec. 10, 1862	Mar. 4, 1877	John Marshall Harlan
Stephen J. Field	(new seat)	Lincoln	May 20, 1863	Dec. 1, 1897	Joseph McKenna
William Strong	Robert C. Grier	Grant	Mar. 14, 1870	Dec. 14, 1880	William B. Woods
Joseph P. Bradley	(new seat)	Grant	Mar. 23, 1870	Jan. 22, 1892	George Shiras, Jr.
Ward Hunt	Samuel Nelson	Grant	Jan. 9, 1873	Jan. 27, 1882	Samuel Blatchford
John Marshall Harlan	David Davis	Hayes	Dec. 10, 1877	Oct. 14, 1911	Mahlon Pitney
William B. Woods	William Strong	Hayes	Jan. 5, 1881	May 14, 1887	Lucius Q.C. Lamar
Stanley Matthews	Noah H. Swayne	Garfield	May 17, 1881	Mar. 22, 1889	David J. Brewer
Horace Gray	Nathan Clifford	Arthur	Jan. 9, 1882	Sept. 15, 1902	Oliver Wendell Holmes, Jr.
Samuel Blatchford	Ward Hunt	Arthur	April 3, 1882	July 7, 1893	Edward Douglass White
Lucius Q.C. Lamar	William B. Woods	Cleveland	Jan. 18, 1888	Jan. 23, 1893	Howell E. Jackson
David J. Brewer	Stanley Matthews	Harrison	Jan. 6, 1890	Mar. 28, 1910	Charles Evans Hughes
Henry B. Brown	Samuel F. Miller	Harrison	Jan. 5, 1891	May 28, 1906	William H. Moody

Name	Justice Replaced	Appointing President	Oath Taken	Term Ended	Succeeding Justice
George B. Shiras	Joseph P. Bradley	Harrison	Oct. 10, 1892	Feb. 23, 1903	William R. Day
Howell E. Jackson	Lucius Q.C. Lamar	Harrison	Mar. 4, 1893	Aug. 8, 1895	Rufus W. Peckham
Edward Douglass White	Samuel Blatchford	Cleveland	Mar. 12, 1894	Dec. 18, 1910	Joseph R. Lamar
Rufus W. Peckham	Howell E. Jackson	Cleveland	Jan. 6, 1896	Oct. 24, 1909	Horace H. Lurton
Joseph McKenna	Stephen J. Field	McKinley	Jan. 26, 1898	Jan. 5, 1925	Harlan F. Stone
Oliver Wendell Holmes, Jr.	Horace Gray	T. Roosevelt	Dec. 8, 1902	Jan. 12, 1932	Benjamin N. Cardozo
William R. Day	George Shiras	T. Roosevelt	Mar. 2, 1903	Nov. 13, 1922	Pierce Butler
William H. Moody	Henry B. Brown	T. Roosevelt	Dec. 17, 1906	Nov. 20, 1910	Willis Van Devanter
Horace Lurton	Rufus W. Peckham	Taft	Jan. 3, 1910	July 12, 1914	James C. McReynolds
Charles Evans Hughes	David J. Brewer	Taft	Oct. 10, 1910	June 10, 1916	John H. Clarke
Willis Van Devanter	William H. Moody	Taft	Jan. 3, 1911	June 2, 1937	Hugo L. Black
Joseph R. Lamar	Edward Douglass White	Taft	Jan. 3, 1911	Jan. 2, 1916	Louis D. Brandeis
Mahlon Pitney	John Marshall Harlan	Taft	Mar. 18, 1912	Dec. 31, 1922	Edward T. Sanford
James C. McReynolds	Horace H. Lurton	Wilson	Sept. 5, 1914	Feb. 1, 1941	James F. Byrnes

(continued)

Table C-2 *(continued)*

Name	Justice Replaced	Appointing President	Oath Taken	Term Ended	Succeeding Justice
Louis D. Brandeis	Joseph R. Lamar	Wilson	June 5, 1916	Feb. 13, 1939	William O. Douglas
John H. Clarke	Charles Evans Hughes	Wilson	Aug. 1, 1916	Sept. 18, 1922	George Sutherland
George Sutherland	John H. Clarke	Harding	Oct. 2, 1922	Jan. 17, 1938	Stanley F. Reed
Pierce Butler	William R. Day	Harding	Jan. 2, 1923	Nov. 16, 1939	Frank Murphy
Edward T. Sanford	Mahlon Pitney	Harding	Feb. 5, 1923	Mar. 8, 1930	Owen J. Roberts
Harlan F. Stone	Joseph McKenna	Coolidge	Mar. 2, 1925	July 2, 1941	Robert H. Jackson
Owen J. Roberts	Edward T. Sanford	Hoover	June 2, 1930	July 31, 1945	Harold H. Burton
Benjamin N. Cardozo	Oliver Wendell Holmes, Jr.	Hoover	Mar. 14, 1932	July 9, 1938	Felix Frankfurter
Hugo L. Black	Willis Van Devanter	F.D. Roosevelt	Aug. 19, 1937	Sept. 17, 1971	Lewis F. Powell, Jr.
Stanley F. Reed	George Sutherland	F.D. Roosevelt	Jan. 31, 1938	Feb. 25, 1957	Charles E. Whittaker
Felix Frankfurter	Benjamin N. Cardozo	F.D. Roosevelt	Jan. 30, 1939	Aug. 28, 1962	Arthur J. Goldberg
William O. Douglas	Louis D. Brandeis	F.D. Roosevelt	April 17, 1939	Nov. 12, 1975	John Paul Stevens
Frank Murphy	Pierce Butler	F.D. Roosevelt	Jan. 18, 1940	July 19, 1949	Tom C. Clark
James F. Byrnes	James C. McReynolds	F.D. Roosevelt	July 8, 1941	Oct. 3, 1942	Wiley B. Rutledge, Jr.
Robert H. Jackson	Harlan F. Stone	F.D. Roosevelt	July 11, 1941	Oct. 9, 1954	John M. Harlan II

Name	Justice Replaced	Appointing President	Oath Taken	Term Ended	Succeeding Justice
Wiley B. Rutledge, Jr.	James F. Byrnes	F.D. Roosevelt	Feb. 15, 1943	Sept. 10, 1949	Sherman Minton
Harold H. Burton	Owen J. Roberts	Truman	Oct. 1, 1945	Oct. 13, 1958	Potter Stewart
Tom C. Clark	Frank Murphy	Truman	Aug. 24, 1949	June 12, 1967	Thurgood Marshall
Sherman Minton	Wiley B. Rutledge	Truman	Oct. 12, 1949	Oct. 15, 1956	William J. Brennan, Jr.
John M. Harlan II	Robert H. Jackson	Eisenhower	Mar. 28, 1955	Sept. 23, 1971	William H. Rehnquist
William J. Brennan, Jr.	Sherman Minton	Eisenhower	Mar. 22, 1957	July 20, 1990	David H. Souter
Charles E. Whittaker	Stanley F. Reed	Eisenhower	Mar. 25, 1957	April 1, 1962	Byron R. White
Potter Stewart	Harold H. Burton	Eisenhower	May 5, 1959	July 3, 1981	Sandra Day O'Connor
Byron R. White	Charles E. Whittaker	Kennedy	April 16, 1962	July 1, 1993	Ruth Bader Ginsburg
Arthur J. Goldberg	Felix Frankfurter	Kennedy	Oct. 1, 1962	July 25, 1965	Abe Fortas
Abe Fortas	Arthur J. Goldberg	Johnson	Oct. 4, 1965	May 14, 1969	Harry A. Blackmun
Thurgood Marshall	Tom C. Clark	Johnson	Oct. 2, 1967	June 27, 1991	Clarence Thomas
Harry A. Blackmun	Abe Fortas	Nixon	June 9, 1970	June 30, 1994	Stephen G. Breyer
Lewis F. Powell, Jr.	Hugo L. Black	Nixon	Jan. 7, 1972	June 26, 1987	Anthony M. Kennedy
William H. Rehnquist	John M. Harlan II	Nixon	Jan. 7, 1972	Sept. 26, 1986	
John Paul Stevens	William O. Douglas	Ford	Dec. 19, 1975		

(continued)

Table C-2 *(continued)*

Name	Justice Replaced	Appointing President	Oath Taken	Term Ended	Succeeding Justice
Sandra Day O'Connor	Potter Stewart	Reagan	Sept. 25, 1981		
Antonin Scalia	William H. Rehnquist	Reagan	Sept. 26, 1986		
Anthony M. Kennedy	Lewis F. Powell, Jr.	Reagan	Feb. 18, 1988		
David H. Souter	William J. Brennan, Jr.	G. Bush	Oct. 9, 1990		
Clarence Thomas	Thurgood Marshall	G. Bush	Oct. 15, 1991		
Ruth Bader Ginsburg	Byron R. White	Clinton	Aug. 10, 1993		
Stephen G. Breyer	Harry A. Blackmun	Clinton	Aug. 3, 1994		

Index

• C •

• G •

• Z •

FOR DUMMIES®

The easy way to get more done and have more fun

PERSONAL FINANCE & BUSINESS

Investing

0-7645-2431-3

Home Buying

0-7645-5331-3

Grant Writing

0-7645-5307-0

Also available:

Accounting For Dummies
(0-7645-5314-3)

Business Plans Kit For Dummies
(0-7645-5365-8)

Managing For Dummies
(1-5688-4858-7)

Mutual Funds For Dummies
(0-7645-5329-1)

QuickBooks All-in-One Desk Reference For Dummies
(0-7645-1963-8)

Resumes For Dummies
(0-7645-5471-9)

Small Business Kit For Dummies
(0-7645-5093-4)

Starting an eBay Business For Dummies
(0-7645-1547-0)

Taxes For Dummies 2003
(0-7645-5475-1)

HOME, GARDEN, FOOD & WINE

Feng Shui

0-7645-5295-3

Gardening

0-7645-5130-2

Cooking

0-7645-5250-3

Also available:

Bartending For Dummies
(0-7645-5051-9)

Christmas Cooking For Dummies
(0-7645-5407-7)

Cookies For Dummies
(0-7645-5390-9)

Diabetes Cookbook For Dummies
(0-7645-5230-9)

Grilling For Dummies
(0-7645-5076-4)

Home Maintenance For Dummies
(0-7645-5215-5)

Slow Cookers For Dummies
(0-7645-5240-6)

Wine For Dummies
(0-7645-5114-0)

FITNESS, SPORTS, HOBBIES & PETS

Fitness

0-7645-5167-1

Golf

0-7645-5146-9

Guitar

0-7645-5106-X

Also available:

Cats For Dummies
(0-7645-5275-9)

Chess For Dummies
(0-7645-5003-9)

Dog Training For Dummies
(0-7645-5286-4)

Labrador Retrievers For Dummies
(0-7645-5281-3)

Martial Arts For Dummies
(0-7645-5358-5)

Piano For Dummies
(0-7645-5105-1)

Pilates For Dummies
(0-7645-5397-6)

Power Yoga For Dummies
(0-7645-5342-9)

Puppies For Dummies
(0-7645-5255-4)

Quilting For Dummies
(0-7645-5118-3)

Rock Guitar For Dummies
(0-7645-5356-9)

Weight Training For Dummies
(0-7645-5168-X)

Available wherever books are sold.
Go to www.dummies.com or call 1-877-762-2974 to order direct

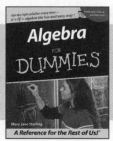